# WHO KNEW WHAT WHEN?

Who made the perilous trip to Tehran and what really happened there?

★   ★   ★

Why did Ronald Reagan sign a secret Presidential Finding authorizing the covert shipment of arms to Iran and sanctioning the sale of arms in exchange for hostages? Why and when was it changed?

★   ★   ★

Why was a Bible personally inscribed by the president given as a gift to the Iranian mediator called "The Second Channel"?

★   ★   ★

What was Israel's role? Saudi Arabia's role?

★   ★   ★

What private groups and individuals contributed funds to support the contras?

★   ★   ★

What parts did George Bush and then-CIA chief William Casey play?

★   ★   ★

You'll find the answers and much more in . . .

## UNDER FIRE

# UNDER FIRE
## AN AMERICAN STORY

# OLIVER L. NORTH

**WITH**

## William Novak

**HarperPaperbacks**

•

**Zondervan**

HarperPaperbacks  *A Division of* HarperCollins*Publishers*
10 East 53rd Street, New York, N.Y. 10022

Cover photograph by Terry Ashe

A hardcover edition of this book was copublished in 1991 by HarperCollins Publishers and Zondervan Publishing House.

First HarperPaperbacks printing: June 1992

Printed in the United States of America

HarperPaperbacks and colophon are trademarks of HarperCollins*Publishers*

❖ 10 9 8 7 6 5 4 3 2 1

*For Betsy, my best friend*

# CONTENTS

# ACKNOWLEDGMENTS

WRITING A BOOK IS NEVER EASY, AND WRITING ONE IN secret poses a special challenge. To avoid any possibility of leaks along the way, my publishers decided to treat this book as a covert operation.

To complete it, William Novak and I worked together by phone, by fax, and during a series of long meetings in a hotel room at Dulles International Airport. Just about every Monday, Bill would fly in with his laptop computer and book a ground-floor room with a back door opening onto the parking lot. Once he was settled, I would surreptitiously drive over to meet him. We always ordered lunch and dinner from room service, and when the waiter arrived with our meals, I hid in the bathroom. The poor guy must have concluded that this strange Mr. Novak, who always seemed to end up in the same room, was entertaining an imaginary friend.

The work was hard, but my sessions with Bill were both productive and fun. I appreciated his thoughtful attention to detail, his insightful questions, and perhaps most of all, his fine sense of humor. I'm also grateful to Linda Novak, who put up with our hectic schedule, offered many helpful suggestions, and even managed to produce a baby while her her husband and I were finishing this book. Who says there are no more miracles?

Special thanks must go to Nicole Seligman, one of my lawyers at the firm of Williams & Connolly, whose help was essential.

And there were many others who helped me get this

story out of the courtrooms and into the word processor.

My mother waded through old family albums and stacks of letters, and sat down with Bill and me to recall tales of my youth that I had long since forgotten—or tried to. My brothers, Jack and Tim, and our sister, Pat, pitched in with tidbits from our childhood.

Dick Bonneau, Mildred Johnson, Tom Gibbons, Bob Bowes, and Russ Robertson began contributing to this book more than thirty years ago, and helped me more than they can know.

A steadfast cadre from the Naval Academy supported me in ways too numerous to recount: Emerson Smith, Reid Olson, Bob Eisenbach, Bob Earl, and classmates Dewey Beliech, Jay Cohen, Mark Treanor, Phil Hough, and Tom Hayes.

From a long-ago war, several comrades-in-arms sought me out years later: Paul Goodwin, Bill Haskell, Richmond O'Neill, Bud Flowers, Art Vandervere, Eric Bowen, and John Rapuano. Of those who called themselves "Blue's Bastards," Wendell Thomas, Everett Whipple, Ernie Tuten, Randy Herrod, and Jim Lehnert helped me survive battles past and present.

Generals Lew Wilson, Robert Barrow, P. X. Kelley, and Tom Morgan gave new meaning to the phrase "band of brothers," as Marines like to call themselves. So, too, did Brigadier General Mike Sheridan, Lieutenant Colonel Pete Stenner, Major Gil Macklin, and Colonels Jack Holley and Larry Weeks. They were, in every sense of the phrase, *Semper Fidelis*.

When I left a quarter century of military service behind and started to hack my way into the civilian jungle, there were a handful of local guides who kept me on the path: Harry Rhoads and Bernie Swain of the Washington Speaker's Bureau; Ben Elliott, who helped me behind the scenes; Duane Ward, who got me to where I was supposed to be; and Jerry Dimenna and Dave Valinski, who kept me alive in the process.

This book could not have been finished without the

help of Lieutenant General Ed Bronars and his wife, Dot, and Major General John Grinalds and his wife, Norwood. The Reverend Brian Cox helped me examine my Christian faith with clear eyes and a better understanding of how He is glorified when we persevere in adversity. And Thad Heath showed me how to live that kind of life.

I would have liked to thank David Jacobsen, Andy Messing, Ellen Garwood, and Ken deGraffenreid from my days at the NSC, and Joe Fernandez, Dewey Clarridge, George Cave, and several others from the CIA. But if I did, they would surely suffer for it.

Rich Miller and Jeb Spencer helped find and research material that no one else could locate. And Marsha Fishbaugh, my loyal secretary, made sure it all ended up in the right place.

At Williams & Connolly, Brendan Sullivan, Barry Simon, John Cline, Nicole Seligman, and Terry O'Donnell have been my staunch advocates and have become my friends. Their able assistants, Rhonda Ritchie, Brenda Lee, Lou Ann Taylor, and Betty Donahue Vannoy, have been invaluable throughout.

From the start, Rupert Murdoch had faith that we could put this book together quickly and quietly, and the HarperCollins team of Bill Shinker, Gladys Carr, Tom Miller, Jim Fox, Tracy Devine, and Jim Hornfischer helped make it happen. At Zondervan, Jim Buick, Stan Gundry, and Scott Bolinder were enormously helpful. Vincent Virga helped me dig through mountains of photographs to find just the right ones.

Most important of all were those who encouraged me every day: Betsy, and our children Tait, Stuart, Sarah, and Dornin—who gave up a lot of bedtime stories so I could write this one. Our children had some important allies in this campaign: Isabel Schmock, Margaret Esther Powell, Opal Rhoads, Isa Saliba, and Jamey Wheeler.

For their clandestine help, my thanks to Myrtle Farmosh, Ann Keene, Steve Axelrod, and especially Taren Metson.

Larry Walsh was no help at all.

**Nir, Amiram:** Adviser on counterterrorism to Israeli Prime Minister Shimon Peres.

**O'Donnell, Terrence:** Member of Oliver North's legal defense team.

**Ortega, Daniel:** President of Nicaragua, 1980–90.

**Poindexter, John M., Vice Admiral, USN:** Deputy National Security Adviser, 1983–85; National Security Adviser to President Reagan, 1986.

**Qaddafi, Muammar al-:** Libyan dictator.

**Quintero, Raphael (Chi Chi):** Former Cuban freedom fighter; former CIA officer; employee of Richard Secord, 1984–86.

**Rafsanjani, Hashemi:** Speaker of the Iranian Parliament.

**Reagan, Ronald:**  President of the United States, 1981–88.

**Regan, Donald T.:** White House Chief of Staff, 1985–86.

**Robinette, Glenn:** Former CIA employee who installed security system at Oliver North's home.

**Secord, Richard V., Major General, USAF (Retired):** Head of contra resupply effort, 1984–86.

**Seligman, Nicole:** Member of Oliver North's legal defense team.

**Shultz, George:** Secretary of State, 1982–88

**Simon, Barry:** Member of Oliver North's legal defense team.

**Sullivan, Brendan:** Not a potted plant.

**Walsh, Lawrence:** Special Prosecutor, 1986– .

**Weinberger, Caspar:** Secretary of Defense, 1981–88.

**Weir, Rev. Benjamin:** First American hostage in Beirut released as part of the Iran initiative (September 15, 1985).

Nicaragua on October 5, 1986.

**Hussein, Saddam:** Iraqi dictator.

**Inouye, Daniel:** Democratic senator from Hawaii.

**Jacobsen, David:** American hostage in Beirut, former director of American University Hospital in Beirut. On November 2, 1986, he became the third hostage released in the Iran initiative.

**Jenco, Lawrence:** American hostage in Beirut, Catholic priest. On July 26, 1986, he became the second American released in the Iran initiative.

**Kelley, P. X., General, USMC:** Commandant, United States Marine Corps, 1982–86.

**Khamenei, Ali:** President of Iran.

**Khomeini, Ayatollah Ruhollah:** Theocratic leader of Iran, 1979–89.

**Kimche, David:** Director General of Israeli Foreign Ministry, 1985–86.

**Kirkpatrick, Jeane:** United States Ambassador to the United Nations.

**Kissinger, Henry:** Former National Security Adviser and Secretary of State; head of President Reagan's National Bipartisan Commission on Central America, 1983.

**Ledeen, Michael:** Consultant to the National Security Council.

**McFarlane, Robert C. (Bud):** National Security Adviser, October 1983 to December 1985.

**Meese, Edwin:** Counselor to President Ronald Reagan, 1981–84; Attorney General of the United States, 1985–86.

**Monster, The:** Code name for Iranian official affiliated with Second Channel.

**Moreau, Arthur, Admiral, USN:** Special Assistant to the Chairman of the Joint Chiefs of Staff, 1984–85.

**Mousavi, Mir Hussein:** Prime Minister of Iran.

**Nephew, The:** Code name for the key Iranian in the Second Channel.

**Nidal, Abu:** Terrorist, head of Al Fatah Revolutionary Council.

# CAST OF CHARACTERS

**Abrams, Elliott:** Assistant Secretary of State for Inter-American Affairs.

**Allen, Charles E.:** National Intelligence Officer for Counterterrorism, CIA.

**Australian, The:** Code name for Iranian official affiliated with Ghorbanifar.

**Bandar, bin Sultan:** Saudi prince, nephew of King Fahd and Ambassador to the United States.

**Barnes, Michael:** Democratic member, House of Representatives; Chairman of Subcommittee on Western Hemisphere Affairs.

**Bermudez, Enrique:** Military leader of the Nicaraguan resistance, Northern Front.

**Boland, Edward P.:** Democratic member, House of Representatives.

**Buchanan, Patrick J.:** Director of Communications, White House.

**Buckley, William A.:** CIA Station Chief in Lebanon. Buckley was seized in Beirut in 1984. He died, presumably under torture, in 1985.

**Bush, George:** Vice President of the United States, 1981–88.

**Calero, Adolfo:** A leader of the FDN (Nicaraguan Democratic Force), and Oliver North's primary contact among the Nicaraguan resistance.

**Casey, William J.:** Director of Central Intelligence and Director of the CIA, 1981–87.

**Cave, George:** Former CIA officer who participated in negotiations with the Iranians.

**Channell, Carl R. (Spitz):** Founder of National Endowment for the Preservation of Liberty; fund raiser on behalf of Nicaraguan resistance.

**Clark, William P.:** President Reagan's National Security Adviser, 1982–83.

**Clarridge, Duane (Dewey):** CIA Clandestine Services Officer. Chief, Latin American Division, 1981–84; Chief, European Division, 1984–85; Chief, Counterterrorism, 1986–87.

**Cline, John:** Member of Oliver North's defense team.

**Dutton, Robert C.:** Retired Air Force colonel who worked for Richard Secord.

**Fiers, Alan:** Chief, Central American Task Force, CIA.

**Furmark, Roy M.:** Associate of Adnan Khashoggi and friend of William Casey.

**Gadd, Richard:** Retired Air Force lieutenant colonel who worked for Richard Secord.

**Gates, Robert M.:** Deputy Director of CIA, 1986.

**George, Clair:** Deputy Director for Operations, CIA.

**Gesell, Gerhard A.:** U.S. district court judge who presided at the trial of Oliver North.

**Ghorbanifar, Manucher (Gorba):** Iranian-born intermediary in arms sales to Iran by Israel and the United States.

**Goode, William P.:** Oliver North's U.S. government alias.

**Grinalds, John, Major General, USMC:** Oliver North's battalion commander, 1978–79.

**Hakim, Albert:** Iranian exile, business partner of Richard Secord.

**Hall, Fawn:** Oliver North's secretary.

**Hall, Wilma:** Robert McFarlane's secretary, Fawn Hall's mother.

**Hamilton, Lee:** Democratic member, House of Representatives; Chairman, House Permanent Select Committee on Intelligence.

**Hasenfus, Eugene:** American crewman shot down over

# FOREWORD

FOR BETTER OR WORSE, MOST PEOPLE'S LIVES SEEM TO TURN
out rather differently from what they had expected.
Certainly mine has. When I first signed on with the Marine
Corps in 1961, I never dreamed that I would ever serve in
the upper echelons of government. And I surely never
imagined that I would one day find myself at the center of
a raging political controversy of historic proportions.

This book is my personal story. I will leave to others
the task of producing the definitive history of Iran-contra—assuming that's even possible. The congressional
investigators filled many volumes with reports and testimony, but I doubt that any one individual could possibly know the whole story. I was right in the middle of
these events, and there are *still* things I don't know.

Although I refer often to "Iran-contra" in these
pages, that phrase is really a misnomer. To be precise,
"Iran-contra" covers two very different secret operations
that were carried out by the Reagan administration in
the mid-1980s. One of these was an attempt to develop
an opening to the revolutionary government of Iran, an
initiative that included the sale of arms to the Iranians,

and a partially successful attempt to gain the release of the American hostages in Beirut. The other operation was a concerted effort to maintain American support for the Nicaraguan resistance after the United States Congress had forced the CIA to abandon the contras. These two projects were eventually linked by a financial connection, and also by the fact that several individuals, myself included, were involved in both operations.

In the chapters that follow, I portray certain episodes in my life that strike me as significant, and which surely affected my later activities at the National Security Council. I know, for example, that my experiences as a platoon commander in Vietnam colored my feelings about Central America in general and the contras in particular. And the way I was raised, and the values that were imparted to me over the years, certainly influenced my attitude about the American hostages in Beirut.

I don't ask the reader to endorse everything I did or failed to do. In the five years since I was fired, my detractors have often dramatized and exaggerated what really happened. But so have some of my supporters. While I certainly appreciate their endorsement, I am neither a saint nor a hero. I look back with pride on much of what we accomplished, but I also did things that I came to regret.

Although most of the events I describe took place within the past decade, the world began to change dramatically during the late 1980s. Most of Eastern Europe has now embraced the ideals of freedom and democracy, and Communism has shown itself to be the fatally flawed system that Ronald Reagan always insisted it was. I remember watching on television as the Berlin Wall came down. I had tears in my eyes, and Dornin, our youngest daughter, ran upstairs to say, "Mom, what's wrong with Daddy?"

Daddy was fine, of course; I was just overwhelmed by the moment. While I had known that these changes would come, I didn't really expect to witness them in my lifetime. I felt that way again in 1990, when, for the second time in eleven years, the people of Nicaragua rejected a brutal and corrupt regime. And yet again in August 1991, watching Boris Yeltsin stop a Soviet tank during the second Russian revolution.

During my five and a half years on the staff of the National Security Council, I spent much of my time working for the release of the American hostages held in Beirut. I have done some difficult things in my life, but nothing I've ever been involved with was as trying, or as painful, as this. Because of the obvious risks to the hostages and to certain individuals in other countries, most of this work was done in almost total secrecy. As I worked on this book and described some of these efforts, I prayed that by the time I was finished, all these men would be back with their families.

Those of us who served in the Reagan administration were privileged to be part of great changes. I fervently hope that these developments are permanent, and that the extraordinary events unfolding in Eastern Europe, Central America, and what we used to call the Soviet Union will soon be visited upon places like Cuba, Iraq, Iran—and even Lebanon

Much of this book portrays the individuals I worked with, both in and out of our government. Although I am critical of a few, most of those I am blessed to have known over the years are good and decent men and women. Like me, they were caught up in momentous events. And like me, they were sometimes less than perfect in responding to them.

Yet many of these people risked their lives and some lost them. Most can never be thanked publicly, honored for the contributions they made, or recognized for the incredible perils they faced. And though I have had to omit or change some of their names in this book, it is nonetheless a tribute to them.

O.L.N.
Narnia
September 16, 1991

# 1

## "RELIEVED OF HIS DUTIES"

BEING FIRED IS NEVER A PLEASANT EXPERIENCE, WHICH IS why it's normally done behind closed doors. My own firing was handled rather differently. The room was packed, the doors were open, and millions of Americans were watching on television.

I was one of them.

On November 25, 1986, at five minutes past noon, President Ronald Reagan and Attorney General Edwin Meese marched into the crowded White House briefing room to face the press and the TV cameras. As I watched from my office in the Old Executive Office Building, the President explained that he hadn't been told the whole story of our secret arms sales to Iran, and that he had asked the Attorney General to look into the matter. He then announced that Admiral John Poindexter, his national security adviser, had resigned, and that Lieutenant Colonel Oliver North had been "relieved of his duties on the National Security Council staff."

*What?*

Before I could catch my breath, the President turned

5

over the microphones to Attorney General Meese and left the room.

Then Ed Meese dropped the bomb: "In the course of the arms transfer, which involved the United States providing the arms to Israel and Israel, in turn, transferring the arms—in effect, selling the arms—to representatives of Iran, certain monies which were received in the transaction between representatives of Israel and representatives of Iran were taken and made available to the forces in Central America who are opposing the Sandinista government there."

In plain language, some of the profits from the arms sales to Iran had gone to the Nicaraguan resistance, also known as the contras. It took a moment before the reporters figured out what Meese had said, and the White House press corps actually fell silent for a second or two.

Then the barrage began.

Did the President know about this?

*Meese:* The President knew nothing about it until I reported it to him.

*What?*

Well, then, who did know?

*Meese:* The only person in the United States government that knew precisely about this, the only person, was Lieutenant Colonel North.

*What?!*

*Meese:* Admiral Poindexter knew that something of this nature was occurring, but he did not look into it further…. CIA Director Casey, Secretary of State Shultz, Secretary of Defense Weinberger, myself, the other members of the NSC—none of us knew.

*What?!*

"What Colonel North did," somebody asked—"is that a crime? Will he be prosecuted?"

*Meese:* We are presently looking into the legal aspects of it as to whether there's any criminality involved.

*Criminality?!*

For the past three weeks, ever since our Iran initiative had been exposed in *Al-Shiraa*, a Beirut magazine, the administration's strategy had been unspoken but unmistakable: *this must not become another Watergate*. Although Watergate had involved several violations of the law, most Americans believed that the most serious offense of all—and the one that eventually led to President Nixon's resignation—was not the burglary itself, but the cover-up.

And so in November 1986, somebody—probably Donald Regan, the White House chief of staff, and Nancy Reagan—decided that whatever had or hadn't happened in this case, there could not be even the hint of a cover-up. Before the news media could cause any damage, the White House itself would disclose the story.

It is a fundamental rule of politics that whoever gets his side of the story out first is usually able to set the agenda for the ensuing discussion. While the effort to realize the benefit of this "rule" was certainly true here, the administration did not reveal the "diversion" (as it soon came to be known) solely for strategic reasons. They disclosed it because three days earlier, when the Attorney General learned about it from a memo that was found in my office (and which I thought I had destroyed), he was terrified that if this story came out first in the press, like Watergate, it could lead to extraordinary political problems for President Reagan.

Like impeachment.[1]

The administration chose to focus almost exclusively on the "diversion," and there was certainly a lot to be gained by presenting it that way. This particular detail was so dramatic, so sexy, that it might actually—well, *divert* public attention from other, even more important aspects of the story, such as what *else* the President and his top advisers had known about and approved. And if it could be insinuated that this supposedly terrible deed was the exclusive responsibility of one mid-level staff assistant at the National Security Council (and perhaps his immediate superior, the national security adviser), and that this staffer had acted on his own (however unlikely *that* might be), and that, now that you mention it, his activities might even be *criminal*—if the public and the press focused on *that*, then maybe you didn't have another Watergate on your hands after all. Especially if you insisted that the President knew nothing about it.

I immediately called my wife, but she wasn't home. As with so many other episodes in this long ordeal, Betsy learned about my firing on the car radio. I tried to get through to my mother in Albany, but her line was busy. She had seen the press conference on television, and she was trying to call me. But by then the phone lines in my office were jammed.

This was not the way it was supposed to be. I had expected to leave, and maybe even be fired—but not quite so publicly. Still, I'd had plenty of warning that my days at the National Security Council were numbered. I was, after

---

[1] It wasn't until my trial in 1989, when he was questioned by Brendan Sullivan, my lawyer, that Attorney General Meese revealed how seriously he had taken the possibility of impeachment:

*Sullivan:* In fact, your assessment of the time was that unless something was done, a strong response, that the merging of those two factors [Iran and the contras] could very well cause the possible toppling of the President himself, correct?

*Meese:* Yes.

*Sullivan:* And there was discussion, in fact, on the days November 23rd and 24th that unless the administration, unless you and the President himself, put out to the public the facts of the use of residuals for the Freedom Fighters, unless you got it out the door first, it could possibly lead to impeachment by the Congress, correct?

Meese: Yes. That was a concern, that political opponents might try that kind of tactic.

*Judge* Gesell: And you discussed that with the President? He is asking you.

*Meese:* I believe I discussed it with the President. I certainly discussed it with others in high-ranking positions such as the chief of staff.... I don't know whether the actual word "impeachment" was referred to, but I certainly discussed the tremendous consequences for the President personally and for the administration.

all, deeply involved in two major, secret, and politically explosive projects, the Iran initiative and the contras, and both had begun to unravel a few weeks earlier. The secret Iran initiative was pretty much over after that report in *Al-Shiraa*, which was immediately picked up by the Western media. About a month before *that*, a plane full of supplies for the resistance fighters had been shot down over Nicaragua. Eugene Hasenfus, an American crew member, was captured by the Sandinista army, and documents were found that led to a safe house in El Salvador whose telephone records listed several American phone numbers—including mine. This only confirmed what many congressmen and journalists already knew: that while large segments of our government were explicitly prohibited from actively supporting the contras, several of us, including the President, were quietly involved in a host of other efforts to keep them alive.

Once both initiatives were exposed, it was only a matter of time before I would be forced to leave my job at the NSC. During those final days I worked harder than ever to limit the damage and to protect the lives of people who had risked so much to help us on both fronts. (Some are still at risk, which is why their names do not appear in this book.) We were also making a last-ditch effort to rescue the remaining American hostages in Beirut. One hostage, David Jacobsen, had been freed in early November as part of a deal with the Iranians; he was the third one to be released in this way, and we were desperately trying to extricate the others before the whole thing collapsed.

The contra initiative had ended even before David Jacobsen's release. Shortly after the Hasenfus shootdown, William Casey, the director of the CIA, had told me to "shut it down and clean it up." It was clear that somebody's head would have to roll, and I was prepared to be the victim. Offering me up as a *political* scapegoat was part of the plan, although Casey believed there would be others. "If it comes out," he had told me, "it will go above *you*, buddy." And when it did come out, he said, "It's not going to stop with you, either."

By the time of the press conference I was certainly prepared to leave the administration, and in some ways I actually looked forward to it. I had come to the National Security Council five and a half years earlier on what was supposed to be a two- or three-year assignment from the Marine Corps, and had ended up staying twice as long as I ever wanted or expected. I was eager to return to Camp Lejeune, North Carolina, the home of the Second Marine Division, where I would once again do what I really enjoyed and what I did best: commanding and leading young Marines. I hoped to take some leave, get to know my family again, and take them back to North Carolina to begin a new assignment. Betsy and I had talked this over at length. Of all my duty stations, Camp Lejeune was her favorite, and she looked forward to returning there as much as I did.

But now—not so fast, fella!

I had just been fired by the President on national television. If that was really necessary, I could live with it. But what was that the Attorney General had said? That there might be *criminality* involved?

Was he serious? I knew we were facing a political disaster, and that there would be political consequences. But never in my darkest nightmares did I imagine that anything I had done in the service of the President, my commander-in-chief, could lead to criminal charges.

I wasn't part of the President's inner circle, but one thing I knew: Ronald Reagan was in no danger of being impeached. For one thing, nobody wanted to go through *that* again; one such crisis in a generation was enough, thank you. For another, President Reagan was loved and trusted by a vast majority of the American people.

With a few exceptions, even his critics did not want to see him impeached. Although the President's approval rating underwent a sharp decline, the word "impeachment" was rarely spoken in public—not even by congressional Democrats. Lee Hamilton, chairman of the House Intelligence Committee, used the dreaded "I" word as part of a hypothetical response to a question on ABC's "This Week with David Brinkley." And on March 5, 1987, Congressman Henry Gonzalez introduced a resolution of impeachment in the House of Representatives, which went nowhere. But these were isolated exceptions.

In the fall of 1986, President Reagan was still so popular that he and Nancy could have invited Fidel Castro to a testimonial dinner at the White House for Ayatollah Khomeini without suffering overwhelming political damage. People would have shaken their heads, they would have wondered, but Ronald Reagan would have remained popular. If the Constitution had allowed him to seek a third term, I have no doubt that he would have run again in 1988. And, just as in 1984 against Mondale, he would have been reelected in a landslide. Iran-contra would have hurt him, certainly, but it wouldn't have been fatal.

By going public so quickly with the "diversion," the President's top advisers were essentially trading one risk for another. They could have decided to batten down the hatches and weather the storm while we made one final effort to get the hostages out. But when our government announced, in effect, that the Iranians had been overcharged for the arms they had purchased, and that Iran had been subsidizing the Nicaraguan resistance without even knowing it—what about *those* political damages? Who knew how the government leaders in Tehran, or the hostage-takers in Beirut, might react to this humiliation from Washington? Wasn't it possible that this announcement might lead to further recriminations against the hostages or other acts of violence against the United States?

President Reagan could have handled the whole thing very differently. He could have said, "The buck stops here. I knew about the diversion. I approved it because I would have done just about anything to get our hostages out of Iran, and to avoid abandoning the contras in the midst of their life-and-death struggle. It's the President's mandate to determine our foreign policy, and as your President, I accept responsibility for everything that happened on my watch."

If the President had said that, what would Congress have done? Sure, many Democrats would have been angry, but were they any less angry when the President said he *didn't* know?

As soon as the press conference was over, everybody's favorite Watergate question began to reverberate around the nation like a battle cry: what did the President know, and when did he know it?[2]

There were, of course, many other questions that could have been asked—especially about our foreign policy. Was it a good idea for the United States to hold secret talks with the Iranians? And if our government really was neutral in the Iran-Iraq War, as we often claimed to be, why were we secretly supplying military intelligence to Iraq? And why, for that matter, did several top administration officials, including Secretary of State George Shultz and Secretary of Defense Caspar Weinberger (who rarely agreed on *anything*) both favor the Iraqis? Not only had Iraq started the war, but the Iraqis were more deeply involved in international terrorism than the Iranians ever hoped to be. Meanwhile, Saddam Hussein was using chemical weapons—not only against Iran, but even against his own people.

The press became so focused on the "diversion" that

---

[2]The press seemed to focus on little else. "We were all children of Watergate," wrote Lou Cannon, the veteran Washington reporter, on the subject of Iran-contra. "My editors at *The Washington Post* and most of my colleagues in the press corps were from beginning to end more tantalized by the Nixon question—what did he know and when did he know it?—than by any other issue." (Lou Cannon, *President Reagan: The Role of a Lifetime* [New York, 1991], p. 706.)

they neglected to ask what President Reagan had known about other critical issues: Did the President and his advisers knowingly mislead Congress with regard to aiding the contras? Did they knowingly mislead Congress and the public with regard to selling arms to the Iranians? How was the President supposed to maintain a consistent policy in Central America when Congress kept changing its mind about whether we would help the contras? And why were so many members of Congress hostile to the Nicaraguan resistance and seemingly untroubled by an aggressive Communist government in Nicaragua?

These and other questions were there for the asking, but the one about the President and the "diversion" kept bouncing back: *what did he know and when did he know it*? It just wouldn't go away, not even when the President himself said that no, he hadn't known about it, or later, during the congressional hearings, when Admiral Poindexter backed him up.[3] When the admiral maintained that he hadn't told the President about the "diversion," that lowered the temperature. But it didn't end the speculation. "No smoking gun," said the press, extending the Watergate analogy. But the American people still found it difficult to believe that the President didn't know. According to the polls, a majority believed that President Reagan *did* know.

I thought so, too.

And now, five years later, I am even more convinced: *President Reagan knew everything*.

True, he didn't learn about the "diversion" from me—at least not directly. In all my time in Washington, I never met alone with him, and the only time we talked privately on the phone was the day I was fired. John Poindexter insisted that *he* didn't tell the President

---

[3]"On this whole issue," Poindexter said at the hearings, "the buck stops here with me." He added: "I made the decision. I felt that I had the authority to do it. I thought it was a good idea. I was convinced that the president would, in the end, think it was a good idea."

either, because Poindexter wanted him to have "plausible deniability." At the hearings, Poindexter said, "I made a very deliberate decision not to ask the President, so that I could insulate him from the decision and provide some future deniability for the President if it ever leaked out."

Even if that's true, I find it hard to believe that the President didn't know.

Here's why. The contras were not the only beneficiary of the arms sales to Iran. Part of the residuals were to be used for other projects, including several counterterrorist operations and various plans involving the release of the hostages. Because these activities were so sensitive, I made sure to get explicit permission for each one. Every time one of these projects came up, whether or not the particular plan was actually carried out in the end (and not all of them were), I wrote a memo or a computer message to Admiral Poindexter outlining how the money would be used. It was always my belief that these memos were passed up the line to the President, because documents of this type generally were. In fact, it was a copy of one of these memos, from April 1986, that made the Attorney General aware of the "diversion" three days before the press conference. For all my celebrated shredding skills, I had missed that one.

I was a little surprised when Admiral Poindexter said he hadn't told the President. But is it really possible that nobody else did? Robert McFarlane, Poindexter's predecessor, had left government, but he still had unique access to the Oval Office. He could have told the President. And is it possible that Bill Casey never once mentioned the "diversion" to Ronald Reagan, his longtime friend, in one of their many private meetings? I find that unlikely.

Casey and I had discussed the "diversion" on several occasions, and he loved the idea. He praised it effusively, and called it "the ultimate covert operation," which from him was high praise indeed. He once referred to it as the ultimate irony, because Iran had been providing arms to the Sandinista government of Nicaragua. Casey would have enjoyed sharing this story with the President, and I believe he did.

It's also quite possible that the President discussed the "diversion" with one or more other high-level officials. If any of them were not aware of how the residuals from the arms sales were being used, it's only because they went out of their way not to know. A substantial amount of money—well in excess of what the U.S. government was receiving for the arms—was generated from these transactions, and intelligence material circulated to people like Cap Weinberger and Colin Powell made that clear. Even before I became involved in the operational aspects of the Iran initiative, our government made extensive efforts to gather information on Manucher Ghorbanifar and his fellow arms dealers. These very sensitive intelligence reports were distributed to a handful of cabinet-level appointees, including the Secretary of Defense, the national security adviser, the director and deputy director of the CIA, and the director of the National Security Agency. None of them could reasonably claim ignorance of the existence of residuals, although, in the end, nearly all of them tried.

President Reagan, meanwhile, was understandably devastated when, for the first time in his political career, the public didn't believe him. Don't they trust me? he asked. Do they actually think I'm a liar?

I don't believe the President was necessarily lying. I realize, of course, that in view of what I've just written this must sound like a contradiction. If the President claimed he didn't know about the "diversion," and he actually *did* know, doesn't that mean he was lying?

Not in Reagan's case. Granted, for most people, and certainly for most presidents, these two suppositions could not both be true. For Ronald Reagan, however, they weren't necessarily in conflict. For all of his achievements, this President didn't focus much on the details. President Reagan didn't always know what he knew.

I believe he was *told* about the transfer of funds to the contras, but that doesn't mean he paid attention to it or remembered it. Early in 1987, the President made clear to his own Tower Commission that he wasn't really sure *what* he recalled about the Iran initiative, or whether he had approved a November 1985 arms shipment by the Israelis. He testified that he didn't know anything about the early TOW shipments to Iran, although by the time he wrote his memoirs he apparently remembered again.

The 1989 videotape of his testimony at the Poindexter trial showed us a terribly sad portrait of an aging and confused man who appeared to recall astonishingly little about his own administration. But even in his better years, President Reagan preferred to concentrate on broad policies and values. He was never very inquisitive or curious, and he generally left the details to his subordinates. It seemed to me that he sometimes wanted to ask a question, but then didn't do so because it would have seemed to be a "stupid question," and he didn't want to appear not to know something others would think he should have known.

Admiral Poindexter has said that, hypothetically speaking, if he had discussed the "diversion" with the President, the President would have okayed it. "I was convinced," the admiral testified at the hearings, "that I understood the President's thinking on this, and that if I had taken it to him that he would have approved it."

I agree. Ronald Reagan knew of and approved a great deal of what went on with both the Iranian initiative and the private support efforts on behalf of the contras, and he received regular, detailed briefings on both topics. He met on several occasions with private donors to the resistance, and at least once, it appears, he personally solicited a foreign leader—King Fahd of Saudi Arabia— and asked him to double his contribution.[4] Given President Reagan's policies and directives, I have no doubt that he was told about the use of residuals for the contras, and that he approved it. Enthusiastically.

\* \* \*

There is, of course, an additional possibility: that people around the President, and perhaps even President Reagan himself, were involved in an effort to protect the highest office in the land—and the man who occupied it.

In his memoirs, Ronald Reagan wrote that "we sent word to the lawyers representing Oliver North and John Poindexter, who knew what had happened, that I wanted them to tell the entire truth and do nothing to protect me." I was surprised to read that, and I asked my lawyers if they ever received such a message. They hadn't.

In fact, nobody from the administration *ever* asked me to tell the truth. The only message I heard was: exonerate the President. And I heard it from at least three different people.

At the end of January, Paul Laxalt, one of Ronald Reagan's oldest and closest political friends, called a member of my legal defense team at Williams & Connolly to say he was sending over a memo. The document, which arrived within a few days, was a legal memorandum that argued that I would not waive my Fifth Amendment rights if I chose to state publicly that the President did not know about the "diversion." My lawyers rejected this proposal out of hand.

The previous month, on December 17, I had received a visit from one of the military aides to Vice President Bush who was also a member of Bush's national security affairs staff. He and I were both military officers, and he approached me on that basis. In the presence of Brendan Sullivan, my lawyer, he suggested that I waive my Fifth Amendment rights and absolve the President of any responsibility.

Naturally, we wondered. Had this officer come on his own? Had he been sent? I still don't know.

---

[*]At the time, King Fahd was already supporting the contras. After his meeting with the President, he more than doubled his commitment. In all, the Saudi contribution came to thirty-two million dollars.

A few days before this visit, we had heard a similar message from H. Ross Perot, the celebrated Texas entrepreneur. I knew Perot and admired him. (In the early 1970s, when I was thinking of leaving the Marines to join the corporate world, Perot had talked me out of it. And in 1981, he had helped us during the kidnapping of General James Dozier by the Red Brigades in Italy.) On December 11, he came to Williams & Connolly, where he met with Brendan. "Look," he said, "why doesn't Ollie just end this thing and explain to the FBI that the President didn't know. If he goes to jail, I'll take care of his family. And I'll be happy to give him a job when he gets out."

That's just like Ross, I thought when I heard about his offer. He thinks money can buy everything.

Six days later, Perot was back. This time he met with Brendan and me together, but the message was the same: I should forfeit my Fifth Amendment rights and make a statement that "cleared" the President.

I find it hard to believe that Ross Perot was acting on his own. But if anyone sent him, they left no finger-prints.

It's also possible that these three approaches were part of a pattern that began even earlier, with President Reagan himself. A few hours after the November 25 press conference, a White House operator tracked me down in a suburban Virginia hotel, where I had gone to avoid the press. The President wanted to talk to me about the firing. During our brief conversation, he called me a "national hero," a phrase he repeated to *Time* magazine the next day. He used it again on March 25, 1988, a year and a half after I was fired, and nine days after I was indicted: "I still think Ollie North is a hero," he said.

I knew what he meant by those words, and I was grateful for his appreciation. President Reagan was well aware that in addition to my work on the Iran initiative and on behalf of the contras, I had also been involved in a variety of antiterrorist activities. On a couple of those occasions he had even sent me letters of commendation. That's why I was so surprised to read the account of that phone call which appeared years later in Reagan's memoirs. When he referred to me as a national hero, the former President wrote, "I was thinking about his service in Vietnam."

*What?!*

I found that *very* hard to believe. For one thing, during my tenure at the NSC I don't believe that anyone at the White House was even aware of my Vietnam war record. For another, I don't believe the President had ever seen me in uniform until the hearings began, which means he had no idea that there were medals on my chest or what they were for. Moreover, it wasn't until well *after* I was fired that my military record was requested by the White House and delivered to Don Regan's office.

The day after the firing, the President was interviewed by Hugh Sidey of *Time* magazine. "I have to say that there is a bitter bile in my throat these days," he said. "I've never seen the sharks circling like they are now with blood in the water." But despite his bleak mood, President Reagan went out of his way to praise me. "I do not feel betrayed," he said. "Lieutenant Colonel North was involved in all our operations: the *Achille Lauro*, Libya. He has a fine record. He is a national hero."

That made it clear, I think, that the President was not referring to my war record when he called me a hero. When I read his memoirs, I was sorry to see his transparent attempt to rewrite history. It also made me wonder about something else he had said during that phone call.

That other remark was a lot more ambiguous, and in the five years that have passed since that night I have turned it over in my mind more than once. When President Reagan came on the line, I expressed my regret for what had taken place, and the fact that the Iran initiative had blown up in our faces. "I certainly hope this doesn't hurt your presidency," I told him. "I can only tell you that I did my best to serve you and our country. I never wanted anything like this to happen."

"Ollie," said the President, "you have to understand, I just didn't know."

In the heat of the moment I took him literally.

Today, looking back, I wonder why he phrased it quite that way, and whether he was implying more than I realized at the time. There were other ways he could have said it. He could have said, "Ollie, why didn't you tell me about the diversion?" Or "Ollie, believe me, I didn't know what was going on."

Instead, it was "You have to understand, I just didn't know." I now wonder whether he was alone when he made that call. Was Don Regan standing beside him? Or Nancy? Maybe what the President was *really* trying to tell me was: Look, Ollie, you and I know better, but the line we're putting out is that I didn't know, so please go along with it.

It's possible, of course, that President Reagan meant exactly what he said. On the other hand, he was almost always scripted, and he did tend to rely on those famous file cards. I don't have to stretch very hard to imagine Donald Regan giving careful thought to the language the boss should use.


Many of my friends and supporters believe that Ronald Reagan betrayed me. "You did everything you could for him," they say. "You knocked yourself out carrying out his policies, and you even risked your life by going to Tehran. When you were wounded, he abandoned you on the battlefield. Don't you feel betrayed?"

Sometimes I do. But I'm like a yoyo on the subject of Ronald Reagan. In terms of the difference he made in the world, I'm very glad he was President for eight years. And yet I can't ignore the fact that he could have ended years of suffering for me and my family—either by granting a presidential pardon or by shutting down the office of the special prosecutor before leaving office.

Is that betrayal? Well, it sure as hell wasn't supportive.

In November 1986, responding to pressure from both sides of the aisle in Congress, President Reagan called for the appointment of a special prosecutor. This allowed the actions that I and others had taken to support the President's policy to be treated as criminal. Meanwhile, he kept changing his story. At first, he told his own Tower Commission that he hadn't even known that the NSC staff was helping the contras. Not surprisingly, almost nobody believed him.

Later, on May 15, 1987, he was considerably more candid when he addressed a group of broadcasters and newspaper editors. "As a matter of fact," he told them, "I was very definitely involved in the decisions about support to the freedom fighters. It was my idea to begin with."

# 2

## THE SECRET WITHIN A SECRET

THE "DIVERSION" DID NOT ORIGINATE WITH ME. FRANKLY, I wish it had, because I'd love to take the credit. But it wasn't my idea.

The notion of using Iranian money to support the Nicaraguan resistance first came up during a January 1986 meeting in London with Manucher Ghorbanifar and Amiram Nir, the adviser on counter-terrorism to Prime Minister Shimon Peres of Israel. Ghorbanifar, an expatriate Iranian, was a businessman and commodity trader who was based in Paris. During most of the Iran initiative, he was our only contact with government officials in Tehran. Gorba was a dark-eyed and hefty man who obviously enjoyed most of life's pleasures. In addition to being a gregarious, fast-talking self-promoter, he was also a world-class bullshooter, wheeler-dealer, and manipulator.

We were meeting to discuss an upcoming shipment of TOW missiles to Iran. Occasionally, these talks were held in Ghorbanifar's suite at the Churchill Hotel—a luxurious setting with thick Persian carpets on the floor and tapestries and paintings on the wall. At other times, we met at the Penta Hotel at Heathrow Airport.

During a break in one of the discussions, Gorba stood up and motioned for me to follow him into the bathroom. He must have suspected that these talks were being recorded (which they were), because he ran the water in both the sink and the bath to muffle the sound of our voices. "Ollie," he said softly, as if he were my oldest and closest friend in the world, "if we can make this deal work, there's a million dollars in it for you."

I had never been offered a bribe before, but I wasn't surprised by his offer. Everybody knew that Ghorbanifar operated in societies where *baksheesh* was common.

"That's out of the question," I snapped. "Don't bring it up again, or the whole thing is over."

But Gorba was a master salesman. If you didn't bite at his first proposal, he always had another one ready.

"Never mind," he said. "I understand. I know what you've been doing in your spare time. Maybe we can make some money available to your friends in Nicaragua."

Hmm, I thought, *now* you're talking. It was clear to me that the Israelis, with whom he was working at the time, kept Gorba generally well informed. He obviously knew, from them or some other connection, that I was involved in helping the Nicaraguan resistance. Now that Congress had cut off their support from the CIA, the contras were receiving funds from private sources, including foreign governments and several American philanthropists.

When I returned to Washington, I went to see John Poindexter in his office. "Admiral," I said, "I think we've found a way to support the Nicaraguan resistance." When I told him what Gorba had suggested, Poindexter agreed with me that this was a perfect way to have two of the President's policies work together. That evening, the admiral called me on the secure line and told me to "proceed along the lines of our discussion." And I did.

\* \* \*

Because the "diversion" became the central focus of the Iran-contra affair, I want to explain exactly what it was—and wasn't.

I use quotation marks around "diversion" because that word usually suggests something shifty, shady, or devious—which was one reason why the "diversion" quickly became the symbol of the entire Iran-contra episode. It was inflammatory. It implied something illegal or immoral. It suggested that money was stolen. In an enormously complicated story, it was relatively easy to understand. And perhaps most important, it provided the crucial link between separate initiatives—Iran and the contras—which had little else in common.

For all its hostility to the administration, Congress was surprisingly willing to accept the idea put forward by the White House that the "diversion" was really the key issue. The press and the public accepted it, too. But from my perspective, the transfer of funds from one project to another was not the central point. It was more like gift wrapping that fit around two separate packages: it tied everything up nicely, and made the whole parcel seem more alluring. But it wasn't nearly as significant as what was actually inside.

Despite everything that's been said or implied, the "diversion" was not illegal. You could argue that it was a bad idea—that much is certainly debatable—but despite all the allegations, the transfer of funds did not violate any laws. After five years and tens of millions of dollars spent on investigations, prosecutions, trials, and tribunals, no one involved in Iran-contra was ever tried for "diverting" anything.

Now, *if* the United States government had sold arms directly to Iran, and *if* someone in our government had decided on his own to take the money from those arms sales and send some of it to the contras instead of returning it to the Treasury, *that* would have constituted a diversion. But that's not what happened here. Our government had no direct communication with the Iranian government, and the Israelis didn't, either. The Israelis relied on third-party intermediaries to deal with Iran, and we did the same.

The "diversion" was known about and approved by American government officials who understood the need for middlemen, and who recognized that once the U.S. government had been paid, any remaining money the middlemen received belonged to them. In January 1986, President Reagan even signed a secret "Finding" that not only authorized the Iran initiative, but specifically noted this reliance on third parties in carrying out the transactions.[1]

American-made weapons reached Iran in two ways: from Israeli stockpiles, which we eventually replenished, and from U.S. military warehouses. In both cases, the weapons and the money moved through various private-sector American, Israeli, and Iranian intermediaries, including Richard Secord, Albert Hakim, Yakov Nimrodi, Al Schwimmer, and, of course, Ghorbanifar. These men purchased arms from the governments of Israel and the United States, and then, with the approval of those governments, sold them to the Iranians. Like all brokers, they were in this to make a profit. And part of that profit was to be sent to the contras to support their struggle against the Sandinistas.

That was the so-called diversion. To the extent that money was "diverted," it was diverted from the pockets of Ghorbanifar and the other middlemen.

They could certainly afford it. According to our intelligence reports, Gorba, and possibly others, were making tremendous profits on these deals. But not at the expense of the U.S. government. The Department of Defense established its own price for every item, and

---

[1] A Presidential Finding is a document signed by the President that explains and authorizes a particular covert action.

received full payment in advance. The fee for the weapons was jacked up considerably by the intermediaries who bought them, but that's another story.

Our government sells its property all the time. Take used computers, for example. A computer dealer buys a used machine at a government auction and pays the government's asking price of say, ten thousand dollars. A month later he sells that computer to a small business for thirteen thousand dollars. Does that mean there was a diversion? Does the dealer now owe the government three thousand dollars? Of course not. That's his profit, and he can do anything he likes with it.

Admittedly, a missile is very different from a computer. But the financial principle is the same.

I have already mentioned that Ghorbanifar did not exactly have the endorsement of the Better Business Bureau. Some accounts of Iran-contra have suggested that Bud McFarlane was the only one who could really see through him, and that the rest of us were naïve. Baloney. With the exception of Michael Ledeen, a consultant to the NSC, nobody trusted Gorba. Even the Israelis, who brought him to us in the first place, didn't trust him completely. As Ami Nir once told me, Gorba's loyalty had a price that had to be paid. For a long time, he was our only conduit to the Iranian government. But we also knew that he had failed three CIA polygraph exams, where he had reportedly dissembled about everything except his name and nationality.

Later, during the congressional hearings, the question came up repeatedly: how could we work with somebody like that? The answer was simple: until we could find somebody better, Gorba was our only option. Right from the start we looked for a more dependable go-between. And when we finally found one—the so-called second channel—Gorba was history.

But he did get us started, and with Gorba's help we

managed to get two hostages out of Beirut. Ghorbanifar may have been corrupt, but he didn't pretend to be anything other than what he was: a wealthy merchant who was trying to make a great deal of money. And it's not as if there were other candidates with good contacts in Iran who were lining up for the job. It would have been wonderful if Mother Teresa had volunteered to approach the Iranians on our behalf, but she wasn't available.

When I first became involved in the Iran initiative, I knew next to nothing about the specialized world of arms dealers. But I now understand that by the standards of his profession, Ghorbanifar was fairly typical. I assume that's what General Dick Secord had in mind when he recalled, during the hearings, that McFarlane had once called Ghorbanifar one of the most despicable characters he had ever met. "I found that kind of an interesting comment," Secord said, "because he was far from the most despicable character *I've* ever met."

Whatever his faults, and they were legion, nobody ever said Ghorbanifar was a fool. He couldn't have missed the fact that we didn't trust him, and that we were eager to replace him as soon as we could find someone else with equally good access.

Although Gorba was the first to suggest the "diversion," I doubt that it was his own idea. Many in our intelligence agencies believed that Gorba was in the pocket of the Israelis. That doesn't necessarily mean he was exclusively theirs; it could be that he used them, just as they used him. But it was probably no coincidence that the Israelis had recently come up with their own "diversion" plan, which was very similar to what Ghorbanifar suggested.

Shortly after this whole thing had landed in my lap, the Israelis contacted me about having our government replenish their initial shipment to Iran of five hundred TOW missiles during the summer of 1985. As they understood it, McFarlane had approved their shipment and promised we would replace the missiles quickly, and at no charge. But Bud remembered it differently. He claimed he had told the Israelis that these missiles would be replaced in the course of their normal arms purchases. The Israelis, including Prime Minister Peres and Defense Minister Yitzhak Rabin, insisted they would never have agreed to *that*.

In the long, ongoing war between Iran and Iraq, with a million or more soldiers on each side, five hundred TOWs didn't amount to much more than a fart in a hurricane. But to Israel, surrounded by enemies and with limited war reserves, even the temporary loss of these missiles had serious implications for her national security.

Early in 1986, Amiram Nir arrived in Washington to keep the initiative moving, and to ensure that Israel would receive its replacement missiles as soon as possible. One option was to have the Israelis walk into the Pentagon and buy five hundred TOWs, but there was no way to do that discreetly. Then Nir came up with an intriguing possibility—in essence, the same plan that Ghorbanifar would later suggest in London, but for a different purpose. For the February shipment to Iran, the Israeli arms dealers would charge the Iranians a high-enough price to cover not only the cost of this shipment of TOWs to be sent to Iran, but also to pay the U.S. government for the cost of five hundred additional TOWs to replenish the Israelis for the shipments they had sent to Iran in the summer of 1985.

Nir's plan, then, was the antecedent of Ghorbanifar's. Assuming the idea originated with the Israelis, Gorba's version was merely a safe, arm's-length way of introducing a more attractive variation. Gorba, of course, had his own reason to offer us an incentive: if we stopped using him, he wouldn't make any money.

To this day I don't know exactly how our contacts with Iran began, because I wasn't involved at the very beginning. But by all accounts it started with the Israelis. Later, some members of the congressional committees would attempt to gloss over the Israeli role, while others, especially in the executive branch, tried to exaggerate it, or even to blame the whole thing on Israel. Both interpretations are ridiculous.

From everything I know, the Iran initiative began when David Kimche, the director general of Israel's foreign ministry, approached Bud McFarlane in mid-1985. Like us, the Israelis had enjoyed good relations with Iran before the Ayatollah came to power, and they were eager to resume contact with the Iranians with a view toward influencing the now-hostile revolutionary government.

The Israelis also cared deeply about the outcome of the Iran-Iraq War. Although both Iran and Iraq were now sworn enemies of Israel, the Israelis recognized that Iraq was a far more dangerous threat—not only to Israel, but to the entire Middle East. Iran, by contrast, was less harmful than its rhetoric implied. For all the Ayatollah's anti-Israel talk, Iran was not part of the "Arab world" and had no recent tradition of malice toward the Israelis.

Iraq, however, was another story. Saddam Hussein had more than once sent troops to join the Arab armies allied against Israel, and the Israelis took the Iraqi threat very seriously. In 1981 Israeli planes bombed an Iraqi facility that was involved in manufacturing nuclear weapons. At the time, virtually the entire Western world condemned the Israeli raid—at least publicly.[2] But ten years later, in 1991, the critics were quietly grateful that Iraq's nuclear capability had been destroyed, or at least delayed, a decade earlier.

---

[2] Our own Defense and State Departments were furious because the Israeli planes were American-made, and had been provided to Israel for defensive purposes only. Secretary Weinberger rejected the Israeli argument of a "strategic defense," and urged an embargo on further arms shipments to Israel.

The Israelis had another motive in moving closer to Iran: they were eager to free some thirty thousand Jews who had been unable to escape from Iran when the Ayatollah came to power, and whose lives were now endangered by the militant Islamic regime. Although the Jews of Iran were not locked up and under guard like our hostages in Lebanon, they were all under the strict control of the Ministry of Internal Security, and their passports included a seal that prohibited them from traveling to "occupied Palestine." Given the level of violence against non-Islamic groups in Iran (where thousands of Baha'i adherents were imprisoned, and several hundred had been executed), the prospects for the Jews of Iran were not good. Finally, Israel was also interested in rescuing two Israeli soldiers being held in Lebanon by Shi'ite terrorists who had pledged their allegiance to the Ayatollah.

In the summer of 1985, when Kimche came to Washington, he apparently told McFarlane that the Israelis had made contact with Iranian officials whom the Israelis believed to be moderate. Kimche suggested that if the United States wanted to join Israel in developing these contacts, this might result in the release of our hostages in Beirut. But he also warned McFarlane that these particular Iranian officials would sooner or later ask for arms, which would give them credibility with both their own military and the revolutionary guards.

McFarlane signed on and discussed the Israeli overture with the President. Exactly how President Reagan responded is not clear, and McFarlane himself has given differing accounts of their meeting at Bethesda Naval Hospital, where the President was recovering from surgery. The Israelis told me later that they had asked for and received specific assurances that the President had authorized replacements for the missiles they would be sending to Iran. According to McFarlane, the President had indeed given his approval, although Bud's version differed as to exactly how the replenishment would occur.

Nothing would surprise me more than if Bud McFarlane had moved forward on this initiative without the explicit approval of President Reagan. But despite everything that's been said, I find it inconceivable that Bud McFarlane, who was educated at the U.S. Naval Academy, would ever act without the President's permission. Yes, you take initiative, but you always check with your superiors. You'd have to be an idiot not to. And whatever our flaws, none of us involved in this were idiots.

My own operational involvement began three months later, when on the afternoon of November 17, 1985, the phone rang in my office. The caller was General Yitzhak Rabin, Israel's defense minister and the military genius behind his country's dramatic victory in the 1967 Six-Day War. I had never met him, and I wondered why he wanted to speak to me.

Rabin got right to the point. "We have a problem," he said, "and McFarlane said you could help." He then started to outline the details of an Israeli shipment of American-made HAWK missiles to Iran which had been refused landing rights at the European airfield, where it was supposed to be transferred to another plane. He asked me how soon I could be in New York.

Rabin's call had come out of the blue, and we were talking on an open line, and he was a little too explicit for my comfort. Before I agreed to anything I needed to check with McFarlane.

"We can't talk about this on this phone," I told Rabin. "Give me a few minutes and I'll call you back."

I knew the Israelis were shipping weapons to Iran, and that these shipments had led to the freeing of the Rev. Benjamin Weir, one of the American hostages in Beirut. I also knew that at that point, our own government had no operational involvement in this whole process other than to recover any of our hostages who might be released. Until now, my own role had been to monitor these transactions, and at McFarlane's instructions I had initiated a major intelligence collection operation so that we could carefully track what was going on.

I was surprised that Rabin was asking us for help, and I wasn't about to provide any without McFarlane's explicit approval. Bud was in Geneva for the President's first summit with Gorbachev, and just as I reached for the phone to track him down, a call came in on my secure line. It was McFarlane, who said, "You're about to hear from the Israeli defense minister."

"I just did," I said. "What's going on?"

"Did he tell you?"

"He tried, but we were talking on an open line."

"Listen, the Israelis are trying to ship some HAWK missiles to Iran. The whole operation is being handled by a couple of private Israeli citizens. They've run into some logistical problems. Get back to Rabin and take care of it. Just fix it. Go up to New York and see Rabin."

Over the next few days, McFarlane and I had several more conversations about this new arrangement. He gave me the go-ahead for direct U.S. involvement, and assured me that the President had approved it.

This marked a major change in the U.S. government's role in the arms sales to Iran. When McFarlane first told me that the Israelis were selling arms to the Iranians with the tacit approval of our government, he had instructed me simply to monitor these transactions—to watch and to listen. Until now, it had been a hands-off operation on our side. But we had watched carefully as the Israelis shipped 504 TOW antitank missiles to Iran in 1985, which was followed by the release of the Presbyterian missionary, Benjamin Weir, after well over a year in captivity.

As soon as Weir arrived in the U.S., McFarlane and Casey had sent me in a CIA plane to a military airfield in Virginia to deliver a personal letter from President Reagan along with a request that he cooperate with us in a debriefing. It was not a pleasant experience. Weir was openly hostile to the United States and to Israel, and despite everything he had gone through, including an entire year of solitary confinement, he clearly sympathized with his captors. Banging on the table, he let me know that he emphatically refused to provide us with any information that might result in the use of military force to rescue his fellow hostages. He showed no hostility toward the hostage-takers; all his anger was directed at us.

While I was disappointed by his attitude, I wasn't altogether surprised. Weir had been through hell. He was chained up and abused for eighteen months, and it must have seemed to him that we hadn't done anything to help. But this wasn't a case of the much-discussed Stockholm Syndrome, where hostages come to identify with their captors. Weir had lived in Lebanon for thirty-one years, and he had apparently held these views well before he was taken. But he was so hostile and uncooperative after his release that some of those who had tried to debrief him started referring to him as the Reverend Weird.[3]

By the time of Weir's release it was fairly clear to us that the American hostages weren't the only point of interest in the Israeli arms shipments to Iran. About a month before Rabin called me, I had come across a hint that these transactions had another dimension. In the fall of 1985, the intelligence I had been told to collect produced a report from CIA and FAA channels that a chartered transport aircraft had run into unusual problems over Turkey. We learned later that this flight had been operated by a private network in Israel, that it had carried arms to Tehran, and that arrangements had been made to allow the plane to overfly Turkey on its way back to Israel.

---

[3]As Michael Ledeen describes it, a few days after Weir's release Ledeen asked Ghorbanifar "if it was possible for the Iranians to take Weir back, and send us a patriotic American instead." (Michael Ledeen, Perilous Statecraft [New York, 1988], p. 136.)

But apparently an air traffic controller in Iran had dropped the ball, and neglected to convey the message to his counterpart in Turkey. The Turkish air controller spotted the unregistered plane on his radar and immediately asked it for identification. When the pilot responded with his prearranged cover story, the Turks, being out of the loop, sent up interceptors to deal with a possible intruder. The pilot of the charter then took evasive measures and eventually declared a midair emergency over the Mediterranean. He was instructed to land in Tel Aviv, whereupon the Israelis rolled the plane into a hangar, closed the doors, and declared that the entire incident had never happened.

Our intelligence services had begun looking into it until McFarlane told me to have the investigation called off because the Israelis had things under control. We learned later that this chartered plane had not returned to Israel empty. Inside were sixty Iranian Jews. These exchanges had apparently been going on ever since the fall of the Shah: Israel was redeeming captives by sending arms.

With this background and little else, I flew to New York to meet with Rabin at the Waldorf-Astoria. I had met a number of prominent people since coming to the National Security Council, but I was genuinely excited to be meeting Rabin. Like most infantry officers, I had read about him and studied his tactics. In American military circles, Yitzhak Rabin is considered one of the great generals of all time. When he planned and executed Israel's bold air/armor/airborne strike against Egypt in 1967, Rabin had actually saved the life of his country. How many military men could say *that*?

Although he had a reputation for being cold and aloof, Rabin turned out to be far more personable and engaging than I expected. I've always considered a subordinate's perspective to be a pretty good measure of the man, and Rabin's small staff clearly revered him. He was low-keyed and direct with them, rather than arrogant. I could see that this was a man who had led other men in dangerous circumstances, and had earned their respect.

I spent about an hour with Rabin, who explained that Israel had run into major problems in trying to ship HAWK missiles to Tehran. Because of the incident over Turkey a few months earlier, the Israelis had concluded that direct flights were too dangerous. Instead, they had arranged to move the shipment through several other intermediate points, disguised and manifested as oil drilling equipment. But at the last minute they had run into problems with landing rights and other clearances.

"Can you find us an acceptable airline that can move this stuff?" Rabin asked.

"I don't know," I replied. "Why don't you send it by sea?"

"Too slow," he said. "This is all about credibility. We've got to get it there fast."

"It sounds like an operational nightmare," I said. "We just don't have those kinds of assets sitting around."

"Don't worry," said Rabin. "Our people will take care of the logistics. We just need an airline."

When I returned to Washington, I called McFarlane on the secure phone patch to Geneva, and suggested that we enlist General Dick Secord to help straighten out this mess. I picked Secord for several reasons. First, I knew that he could got the job done. Second, he was especially well connected in the places in Europe the Israelis wanted to use as waypoints for Iran because Dick was using the same locations as points of departure for supplies and arms being shipped to the contras. Third, he was an expert on fixing aviation problems. Finally, he had spent a good deal of time in Iran.

In a perfect world, I would have chosen somebody else. Although Secord was an excellent candidate, he was already absorbed in another covert operation—helping the contras—and his involvement in a second clandestine activity violated a cardinal rule of covert operations. I mentioned my concern to McFarlane, and later to Poindexter, but none of us could think of anyone who was better suited for the job. The message was clear: just take care of it, Ollie.

So I did. I called Dick, and although he was, as he put it, up to his ass in alligators, he agreed to meet with the Israelis to see what could be done.

I also called Dewey Clarridge, who was then the CIA division chief for Europe, to ask if he could help the Israelis get landing rights in various places, and if he could also recommend an airline they could charter. Clarridge checked with his staff of experts, who suggested a CIA proprietary airline.[4] I passed that information on to Dick, who arranged for one of the proprietary's 707s to carry what was supposed to be the first of several shipments to Tehran. Shortly after arriving at the European pick-up point chosen by the Israelis, Dick concluded that the headaches, chaos, and visibility of trying to ship through this airport just weren't worth it. He promptly flew to Israel to arrange for shipments directly out of Tel Aviv.

But even so, things went from bad to worse. Only eighteen missiles were able to fit on that first plane, and when they finally arrived, the Iranians were furious. Somebody—presumably Ghorbanifar—had assured the Iranians that these missiles were capable of shooting down high-flying Soviet reconnaissance planes and Iraqi bombers. But the HAWK is a low-altitude air defense system. Moreover, some of the missiles still carried Israeli markings, which infuriated the Iranians. Because their feelings ran so high, we would later do everything possible to make it seem as if the United States had absolutely no involvement in this particular transaction.

The Iran initiative was never a screaming success, but

---

[4]A CIA proprietary is a company owned or controlled by the Agency that, as a cover for its clandestine operation, provides services

after this unbelievably screwed-up operation, things could only improve. And they did—at least for a while.

Initially, I was brought in just to handle the logistics; the policy decisions had already been made. But while I had nothing to do with our original decision to get involved, I eventually got to the point where I had considerable input into our policy. I'm certainly willing to accept responsibility for my part in the operation, and there is no doubt that it was one of the biggest mistakes of my life.

I believe it made sense to open a dialogue with Iran. It also made sense to search for pragmatists or moderates in their government. And despite everything, I still believe there are such people in Tehran. This doesn't mean they're about to salute the American flag, but they might at least be less inclined to burn it. Moreover, the Israelis kept assuring us that some officials in Tehran had a relatively pro-Western perspective.

At the time, it seemed that selling a small amount of arms to Iran was worth the risk to try to make it all work. But to get involved in a quid pro quo arrangement of arms for hostages? This placed all of us in a moral quandary. On the one hand, human life is sacrosanct. On the other, making what people would inevitably see as concessions to terrorists was a terrible idea—especially since it violated our prohibition on arms sales to Iran. The decision to proceed was made well above my level, but I became a willing participant.

I could have resigned in protest. But I didn't do that, either, despite the fact that I had once questioned another man for a similar decision.

During 1980–81, when I spent a year at the Naval War College in Newport, Rhode Island, each of the Joint Chiefs came up to give an address. General H. Barrow was the commandant of the and during his presentation, h opposed to Desert One, President Carter's ill-fated mission to rescue our embassy people who were held hostage in Tehran toward the end of his presidency.

Later that evening, at a private reception for the Marines, I went up to him and asked, "General, if you were that strongly opposed to the plan, why didn't you resign?"

He replied: "I thought that by staying I could prevent other mistakes of that type."

In 1985, I found myself in a similar position, working to carry out a policy about which I had serious doubts. I certainly could have resigned, but I didn't. And while there have been days since then when I thought I should have, I also remember how it felt to sit and talk with the men whose freedom we bought, and who otherwise might still be hostages in Lebanon.

It was one thing to monitor the Israeli arms sales to Iran, but when McFarlane called me and said, "Fix it," I could have challenged him and said, "Wait a minute, what are we really talking about here? Does this make any sense? Doesn't direct American involvement in this operation violate two of our basic principles?"

But I already knew the answer, which is why I didn't ask the question. I was intimately familiar with the administration's tough policies regarding terrorists and the governments that supported them. I had personally written a number of the President's statements on the subject. Later, as the Iran initiative progressed, I had growing doubts as to whether it was a good idea. But I did nothing to bring it to a halt.

Although General Barrow did not resign over the decision to proceed with Desert One, another member of the Carter Administration did. There was a lot I didn't like about the policies of Cyrus Vance, President Carter's Secretary of State, but I'll always respect him for acting on his convictions. When Vance objected to what Carter and Zbigniew Brzezinski were planning, he resigned—with great dignity, citing personal reasons.

Only later was it revealed that he had quit in opposition and in protest, and by then it was too late for the President he had served to suffer any damage from the resignation.

For me, the most difficult aspect of the endeavor was accepting that we had established a price for a human life; five hundred TOW missiles. To this day, I find this part of our Iran initiative to be the most troubling.

But there were other problems as well. We did not adequately consider the consequences of a leak. Any premature disclosure of our dealings with Iran might not only harm the hostages, but would also damage American prestige abroad and the President's political effectiveness at home. When it *did* leak, it certainly did the latter.

And while the Iran initiative could have worked—and *did* work to some extent—there was also the danger that dealing with the kidnappers, even through intermediaries, would merely whet their appetites and encourage them to take more hostages.

Another problem was the hypocrisy of providing arms to Iran while we prohibited other nations from doing the same. There may have been good reasons for us to sell arms to Iran, reasons that were not necessarily related to the hostages, but it wasn't right for us to be doing so while we were telling the rest of the world not to.

Other countries, including France, Germany, and Italy, were willing to sell arms to *both* sides in the conflict, and to do so secretly, while denying it to the world. The difference was that they weren't screaming at everyone else not to do it.

Despite all these negatives, for me the moral issue here was still a very tough call. It's easy to condemn the trading of arms for hostages, but the State Department had achieved absolutely no success in trying to free our hostages through diplomatic channels. Given the alternatives, I'm not sure it was morally wrong to do everything in our power to free innocent Americans who were literally chained to the wall in Beirut.

Though I wasn't there when McFarlane and President Reagan first discussed the Israeli proposal to have us join their Iran initiative, Bud should have said something like this: "The Israelis are selling arms to the Iranians in order to build an alliance with any moderates they can find, and because they see Iraq as a threat, and because they'll do whatever they have to to rescue their own people. They're inviting us to get involved. This could yield some big benefits, both in terms of the Soviet threat and our hostages in Beirut, but it could also backfire. I'm inclined to go along with it, but it's dangerous, and we must be aware of the risks."

I don't know exactly what McFarlane told the President. I do know that he told me that the President had approved our involvement. "Fix it," McFarlane had said, and that's all I needed to hear. It was the kind of challenge I thrived on, and I jumped right in. I can do it, I thought. I'm a Marine. This whole deal is screwed up, but I can take care of it.

I could have followed the example of Cyrus Vance. When I found myself engaged in a process that so thoroughly compromised the anti-terrorist policies I had helped to put in place, I could have quit.

Instead, I jumped in with both feet. Which is why, in the spring of 1986, I found myself on an airplane with Bud McFarlane, heading toward Tehran.

# 3

## ANOTHER WORLD

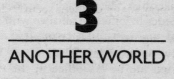

I HAD BEEN ON COVERT MISSIONS BEFORE, BUT THIS ONE was truly dangerous. As we started our descent into Tehran, I prayed that our disguised Israeli 707 wouldn't be shot down by some trigger-happy pilot who wouldn't know what to make of this unscheduled aircraft without a flight plan, and might conceivably take us for an unmarked Iraqi bomber. Iran, after all, was a country at war.

It was May 25, 1986, a Sunday morning, and several high officials were expecting us. Or so we hoped. But when we penetrated Iranian airspace, a pair of aging F-4s flew up to check us out.

This mission was so secret that Casey had urged us not to tell our wives where we were going. Bob Earl in my office had a detailed itinerary, and he was in constant contact with us on the trip. Before I left, I told Betsy that in an emergency she should call Bob, whom we had known for years. Betsy wanted to know when I would be back, because our house was on the market and she would need my signature on a sales contract. I tried to reassure her that I wouldn't be gone too long—and added a silent prayer that this would be true.

President Reagan had authorized our trip, and so had Admiral Poindexter. There were others in our government who knew we were going, although it's been fascinating to see how many of them seem to have forgotten all about it.

Even assuming we landed safely, there were still reasons to worry. Before I left Washington, William Casey had summoned me to his office in the Old Executive Office Building, where he calmly handed me a strip of six white, triangular pills sealed in a plastic wrapper. "Take these with you," he said. "You may need them if things get bad."

It was right out of a spy novel. But for Casey, I realized, this was almost routine. He must have provided this same morbid going-away gift to dozens of men and women, not only at the CIA, but decades earlier, too. During World War II, Casey had been in charge of secret intelligence operations for the Allied forces in Europe, and I had no doubt that some of Casey's capsules had been used by brave agents in Nazi Germany and Occupied France.

The head of our little delegation was Bud McFarlane, my former boss, and a man for whom I had held considerable respect and affection. Although McFarlane had resigned as the President's national security adviser almost six months earlier, he was flying to Tehran as Ronald Reagan's personal envoy. The other members of the group were George Cave, a former CIA officer who had been stationed in Tehran before the Khomeini revolution, and who spoke fluent Farsi; Howard Teicher, my colleague on the staff of the National Security Council; Amiram Nir, who was in charge of counterterrorism for the Israeli government; and a CIA communicator. A second communicator remained in Tel Aviv: he would receive our coded messages and relay them on to Washington, where they would be deciphered both at CIA headquarters and in the White House Situation Room.

No mission from the land of the Great Satan could expect to be greeted with flowers by the immigration officials at Medrabad Airport, which is why we were traveling under phony names and false passports—courtesy of the CIA, and much to the chagrin of those who issue the real passports, who were not amused when this particular detail became known. McFarlane was Sean Devlin. George Cave, traveling as Sam O'Neill, had grown a mustache and changed his hairstyle to avoid being recognized. Nir was presented as an American named Miller, while I was John Clancy. To complete the fiction, our Israeli Air Force 707 had been repainted with the marking of Aer Lingus, the Irish airline.

It was a long trip. We couldn't fly directly from Tel Aviv to Tehran, as this route would have taken us over Jordan, Iraq, or Saudi Arabia—not exactly friendly territory for a clandestine flight out of Israel. Instead, we took off west over the Mediterranean, then turned around, flew back over Israel and down to Eilat, and continued south along the Red Sea before eventually turning back north to Iran. There was an anxious moment or two when we overflew the Soviet fleet off the coast of Ethiopia, but they left us alone.

Even getting to Israel to begin our mission had been done covertly, and involved several stopovers and changes along the way. I had gone earlier, by way of Cyprus, while my fellow Americans made their way to Frankfurt, where they boarded a special charter for Tel Aviv. Don't ask me why, but this particular aircraft had apparently been used the previous day to haul a load of chickens. The plane was filled with chicken feathers, dust, and Lord knows what else, and my traveling companions arrived in Israel in—well, a foul mood.

Our flight to Tehran was the culmination of several previous meetings in Europe and elsewhere with both private individuals and Iranian government officials. But when we finally landed and walked into the terminal, nobody was there to greet us. A bored airport official showed us into a holding area, which George Cave recognized as the former VIP Reception Center. "They used to receive Americans here," he whispered. Whether it was congressional delegations or visiting firemen from Ohio, he added, Americans had always been welcome. This room had once been an ornate hall, with opulent Persian carpets on the floor, and huge color portraits of the Shah and his family.

Today, that was hard to imagine. Except for three or four hard chairs and a couple of unpainted wooden benches, the room was barren and stark. It reminded me of Nicaragua and other revolutionary regimes, where everything of value has disappeared long ago—either stolen by the government or ripped off by corrupt officials. Even the light bulbs were missing.

It was a scorching day, the white sun so hot you could see the heat shimmering off the roads and runways. George and I parked ourselves in front of the building in the hope that somebody would eventually appear to claim us. In the distance, a huge portrait of the Ayatollah glowered at us. A couple of young men with rifles walked back and forth, but they left us alone. After half an hour of waiting, George persuaded an immigration official to make a phone call on our behalf. A few minutes later, we were assured that somebody was coming to meet us.

That wait at the airport was a real anticlimax after the long, tense flight. I felt especially bad for McFarlane, who was pacing back and forth like a caged lion. He clearly saw this as a deliberate snub.

I wasn't so sure. From my previous dealings with the Iranians, I saw this delay as having more to do with incompetence than politics. Maybe Ghorbanifar had told the Iranians we were coming, and his contacts knew him well enough to say, "Yeah, sure they are." Or maybe he hadn't told them anything, figuring we'd never actually show up. In any case, there was nothing to do but wait.

Medrabad had once been a busy civilian airport, but most of the action was now on the military side. We spotted a number of American F-4 Phantoms, still flying from the days of the Shah. But many more deadlined aircraft sat on the ground, including Huey helicopters in various stages of disrepair—missing engines, doors, and blades. The Iranians were cannibalizing half their fleet to keep the other half flying, and their parking aprons had been turned into parts bins. An entire fleet of C-130 cargo planes lay idle, covered with dust.

Finally, after about an hour and a half, Ghorbanifar showed up with an Iranian official whom George and I had met before and whom we called the Australian. The Australian had absolutely no government experience before the revolution, but now he was near the top of the Iranian power structure. He was harmless enough, except for his breath—which, as George put it, could have curled the hide of a rhinoceros. He certainly wasn't one of the high-ranking officials we were hoping to meet, but by then we were glad to see anyone.

Ghorbanifar, charming as ever, was full of apologies, and he presented an elaborate excuse as to how he hadn't expected us to arrive until later. McFarlane, taciturn and formal, made a little speech about how we were bringing greetings from the President of the United States, and how we hoped these talks would be productive, and so on and so forth. But he also insisted, quite properly, that we were there to meet high government officials—the implication being, Listen, we didn't come all this way to see *you*, Ghorbanifar.

Gorba, who speaks perfect English, said, "Don't worry, the Parliament's in session," as though that made everything all right. But he was clearly nervous. He looked like a man who was bluffing and had just been caught.

Ghorbanifar had assured us that we would be meeting with Hashemi Rafsanjani, the Speaker of the Iranian Parliament, who was reported by the Israelis and other intelligence services to be a "moderate." We also expected to meet President Ali Khamenei and Prime Minister Mousavi. A meeting with the Ayatollah himself was apparently out of the question, which was probably just as well. According to our intelligence reports the old man was pretty much out of it, and there were rumors that he spent much of the day sitting in front of a VCR, watching Donald Duck cartoons.

Gorba and the Australian were accompanied by about a dozen young, bearded, and armed Revolutionary Guards who had arrived in a caravan of some of the oldest run-down cars I had ever seen. It looked as if somebody had bought out a small used-car lot in a bad section of town.

"Please, out to the cars," somebody said, and we all piled into this unlikely motorcade for the half-hour drive to the hotel. It was quite a scene—men brandishing guns were hanging out the windows, and most of the cars were belching blue or black smoke from their exhaust pipes. This was a country with almost unlimited oil, but apparently nobody knew how to refine it.

On the drive into town we could see the crumbling infrastructure of Tehran, the old bridges and the broken roads. I looked around for signs of war damage, as some of the buildings at the airport had clearly been hit by the Iraqis. But from what little I saw of the city, its problems were the result of neglect rather than bombs or missiles. Nearly everyone on the street was dressed in black, and I noticed a lot of bicycles—a common sight in countries at war, where gasoline is rationed. Nir and I had brought our cameras, and nobody seemed to mind when we took pictures. Several of the guards even posed with their guns.

We drove past what had once been the Shah's giant victory arch, which was now covered with revolutionary graffiti, and past the notorious Evin Prison, where Khomeini's prison guards were busily exceeding the worst abuses of the Shah's secret police. Finally, we pulled up to the front entrance of the Tehran Hilton, which was now known as the *Istiqlal*—the Independence. An entire outer wall was riddled with bullet holes, which didn't strike me as a particularly encouraging sign; it looked like somebody had opened up on it with a fifty-caliber machine gun. Some of the windows had been blown out, but I was surprised to see that the old Hilton sign was still up.

We were given the entire top floor, where we were something between guests and captives. Don't leave the building, we were told, because "we don't want others to know of your presence, which wouldn't be good for you or for us." Everything was phrased as though it were for our benefit; the team of Rev Guards ensconced in a suite near the elevator was ostensibly there to "protect" us. From what? I wondered. Even if we were foolish enough to leave the hotel, where did they think we might go? Into downtown Tehran to foment an American-led counterrevolution?

These were presumably the finest accommodations available in all of Iran, but the water pressure was low, the lights would often dim, and the elevators worked only sporadically. Every time a new shift of guards came on, you could hear them trudging up the stairs.

And yet our hosts did what they could to be hospitable, and it was clear that they wanted these talks to succeed. Every day they sent up baskets of fresh fruit to our rooms. The fruit itself was dreadful, and wouldn't even have made it to the shelves in an American market. But this seemed to be the best they had to offer. For meals we were entirely dependent on room service, which featured a Western-style menu. You couldn't actually *order* any of these items, but at least the meals you couldn't get were in English.

We did, however, end up with some tasty Iranian dishes. Some of them practically cried out for a cold beer, especially in that heat, but under Khomeini even that was forbidden.

At mealtimes, our little delegation would gather in McFarlane's suite, where we passed notes back and forth because the rooms were undoubtedly bugged. Somebody had placed a huge bouquet of flowers in the middle of the table, and each of us, from time to time, made a point of speaking directly into it, remarking with a smile on the great beauty of Tehran, or the outstanding generosity of our hosts.

When we wanted to talk among ourselves, we stepped out on the balcony and spoke in hushed tones, looking out at a spectacular view of the mountains on one side, and the city's smoky, dusty skyline on the other. We could also talk in the communications room, where our satellite system was installed and where we had taken steps to make eavesdropping more difficult.

But we did no bugging of our own. Normally, whenever we met with the Iranians, I arranged for concealed tape recorders or other monitoring devices to record our talks. But not here. If you were caught with something like that in Tehran, you could spend the rest of your life regretting it.

Shortly after we arrived at the hotel, Nir and I walked down the hall to see if we could get things moving. Near the elevator was a room filled with Rev Guards. Their guns were stacked in the corner, and their feet were up on the furniture.

They reminded me of the Iranian "students" I had seen on television, and I wondered if any of their older brothers had been involved in the seizure of our embassy in 1979. These guys weren't friendly, but they weren't threatening, either. Several spoke English and were very proud of it. We clearly aroused their curiosity; most had never been out of the country, and they obviously didn't get to meet many Americans. If nothing else, we represented a diversion from their normal routine—and certainly an agreeable change from life at the Iraqi front.

Looking around the room, I noticed that several of the guards were playing with the matched sets of pistols we had brought along as gifts. They must have gone through our plane and emptied it. I also noticed that they were eating the cake.

In November 1986, when the world learned of our visit, it was widely reported that our payload included not only electronic parts for HAWK missiles, but also a Bible signed by President Reagan and a cake in the shape of a key—to symbolize our desire to open a new relationship with Iran. The report about the Bible was wrong. I did bring a Bible to Tehran, but it belonged to me and I always traveled with it, and I brought it home with me. Several months later, however, I did present a different Bible, inscribed by President Reagan, to another group of Iranians.

But we did bring a cake.

Because that cake has become one of the best-known details of the entire Iran-contra story, let me set the record straight. It was not in the shape of a key. Moreover, it had no real connection with our mission. When Ghorbanifar was making what he optimistically called "the arrangements" for our trip to Tehran, he had asked Nir to pick up a chocolate cake as a gift for his aging and widowed mother, who lived in Tehran. It was a touching story, although on the flight over, George and I wondered aloud whether Gorba even had a mother. But it was true that such delicacies could no longer be found in the local stores or bakeries. Tehran had become like so many other revolutionary capitals, where almost everything other than the bare necessities was exported for hard currency.

Because the cake was one of Gorba's easier requests, Nir and I had driven to a kosher bakery in Tel Aviv, where we bought a large, rectangular chocolate layer cake. When we boarded the plane, I carefully laid the cake box on the sink in the galley. Several hours into the flight, George and I got up to make some coffee. As I opened the cabinet above the sink to look for the cups, I noticed that someone had stowed the pistols on the same shelf as the dishes. Each set of pistols was packed in an elegant, lined presentation case with a handsome brass key.

Unfortunately, I had left the cake box uncovered, and when I reached up to take out the coffee cups, one of the keys fell onto the cake, making a sizable indentation. When I saw how deeply the key had fallen, I carefully rearranged it to conceal the groove, and left it there, hoping it would look like an intentional decoration. "Well, George," I said, "we can always tell Mrs. Ghorbanifar that this is the key to our hearts."

As it turned out, Ghorbanifar's gift never reached his mother. We had arrived in Tehran during Ramadan, when Moslems eat only after sundown. Apparently the Ramadan fast does not apply to hungry Revolutionary Guards and chocolate cake.


Our trip to Tehran was a symbolic show of trust, a way of saying to the Iranians, Okay, despite everything your people did to our embassy staff in 1979, and despite your anger at us for supporting the Shah, we're willing to put our bodies on the line to show that we're sincere about developing a new and better relationship between our two countries.

Beyond that, we were there for several other reasons.

One reason was William Buckley, the CIA station chief in Beirut who had been captured more than two years earlier by radical Lebanese Shi'ites. When Casey handed me those pills before I left Washington, he may well have been thinking about Buckley. I know I was. Buckley was intimately familiar with CIA operations throughout the Middle East, and from everything we knew he had been violently tortured and eventually died in captivity—after his captors had compiled a four-hundred-page transcript of his interrogation. From the moment Buckley had disappeared into the trunk of a white Renault on March 16, 1984, Casey and the entire CIA had gone to enormous lengths to get him back alive. Now, by all accounts, he was dead. But the Agency was still working to retrieve his body and a copy of his "confession"—which Casey feared had ended up in the hands of the Soviets through their connections with Palestinian terrorist groups.

We were also hoping to retrieve the American hostages in Beirut: Father Martin Jenco, director of Catholic Relief Services in Beirut; Terry Anderson, a correspondent for the Associated Press; David Jacobsen, director of the American University Hospital; and Thomas Sutherland, director of the School of Agriculture of the American University. A fifth hostage, Peter Kilburn, the former librarian at the American University in Beirut, had recently been "bought" by agents of Muammar al-Qaddafi of Libya, who had murdered Kilburn in retaliation for the recent American raid on their country.[1] His death was a graphic reminder that the hostages could be killed at any time, and it gave additional urgency to our mission.

We knew the Iranians had some leverage over the kidnappers in Beirut, although we didn't know how much, or exactly how that influence worked. In any case, we regarded the release of the hostages as an early goal in a much broader strategic initiative.

At least that was our intention.

But it sure didn't work out that way. While we never wanted our Iran initiative to degenerate into a straight arms-for-hostages deal, the truth is that it did.

President Reagan could never accept this, even after he left office. In his memoirs, he again pointed out that we were not dealing directly with the kidnappers themselves—the Hezballah—but were selling weapons to the Iranians in return for their intervention in Beirut. Reagan wrote that he told Secretary of State Shultz and Secretary of Defense Weinberger that it was as if one of his children had been kidnapped—which is a pretty

---

[1]Edward Austin Tracy, who was released in the summer of 1991, was kidnapped after I was fired.

good indication of just how strongly he felt. "I don't believe in ransom," the President recalled telling them, "because it leads to more kidnapping. But if I find out that there's somebody who has access to the kidnapper and can get my child back without doing anything for the kidnapper, I'd sure do that. And it would be perfectly fitting for me to reward that individual if he got my child back. That's not paying ransom to kidnappers."[2]

On a literal level he was right. But George Shultz had already warned the President that this was too subtle a distinction, and that our dealings with the Iranians would invariably be *seen* as trading arms for hostages. I was often critical of George Shultz, but on this point he was certainly right.

Throughout our dealings with the Iranians, our position with respect to the hostages went something like this: "You folks want American technology and you need our trade. You'd like us to buy your oil. You're dying to get your hands on more American arms to help you in your war against Iraq, where you're getting creamed. You also know that the Soviets would like nothing better than to roll in here, which would be a disaster for both of us.

"Well, we're willing to talk. We realize who's in charge here, and we accept that the Shah is gone forever. We can move forward—just as soon as we get over this one hurdle. We know you have some influence over the hostage-takers in Beirut, so let's get the hostage problem out of the way so we can move on to the really big issues."

Even before we had begun talking directly to the Iranians a few months earlier, Benjamin Weir had been freed. By the time we left for Tehran, we expected that the release of the other hostages was imminent. We were wrong about that. But before the Iran initiative finally collapsed at the end of 1986, two additional hostages did get out: Father Martin Jenco and David Jacobsen.

---

[2] Ronald Reagan, An American Life (New York, 1991), p. 512.

While the hostages were certainly on our minds, the *real* reason, the *big* reason we had come to Iran had to do with the broader concerns of American foreign policy. Today, of course, it sounds positively old-fashioned to speak of a Soviet threat, but in the spring of 1986 that danger seemed very real—especially in the Persian Gulf.

Iran had always been vulnerable to a Soviet invasion. Even before there was a Soviet Union (or an Iran, for that matter), the Russians had gazed longingly at Persia. Iran's warm-water ports, which could be used year-round, were enormously appealing to the Russians. A second enticement, which became far more important after World War II, was oil—huge quantities of it. Iran is thought to contain 10 percent of the world's known oil reserves, plus huge quantities of natural gas.

These incentives alone might have been enough to tempt the Soviets to enter a country that was just sitting there on their twelve-hundred-mile-long southern border, and would have given them access to the entire Persian Gulf. But by the mid-1980s there were two additional factors that made the Soviet threat to Iran even more menacing. One was the Iran-Iraq War, which not only weakened Iran but also strengthened the ties between Iraq and Moscow, its chief supplier. The other threat to Iran was the Soviet invasion of Afghanistan. The Russian bear was now closer than ever, which was why the Iranians were quietly transferring some of the arms we had sold them to the Afghan rebels.[3]

In geostrategic terms, Iran was a treasure. While we no longer had any influence there now that the Shah was gone, so far, at least, the Soviets had overtly kept their distance. But with Russian troops in Afghanistan and Soviet weapons powering the Iraqi assault on Iran, they had the place surrounded.

There was another, more subtle reason that made a

---

[3] Iran also accepted more than two million Afghani refugees, and provided more support for the Afghan rebels than any other country in the region except Pakistan.

relationship with Iran especially attractive to Casey. Until the fall of the Shah, Iran had been one of our key listening posts for monitoring the Soviet space, missile, and nuclear war-fighting programs. Casey was deeply concerned about restoring these lost capabilities, and he saw the Iran initiative as a possible means of rebuilding this intelligence-gathering link.

The Soviet threat was why we wanted access to Iran, and why at least some members of Iran's government were willing to deal with us. Even before I became operationally involved in this initiative, President Reagan had quietly approved efforts to create a rapprochement with Tehran. Not everybody in the administration shared the President's goal, or even knew about it, and a parallel situation prevailed on the Iranian side. But for all their anti-American feeling, and it was considerable, most of the Iranian leadership understood that they had far more to fear from the Soviets than they did from us.

When the Shah fell in 1979, the one group in Iran that had expected to prosper was the well-established Tudeh Communist Party. But instead of being rewarded for their opposition to the Shah, the Iranian Communists were butchered. Under Khomeini, they were reduced to conducting isolated acts of terrorism that Americans rarely heard about. We all saw footage of the American embassy being taken over, and of anti-American demonstrations in the streets, because that's what the Iranian government wanted us to see. They took a special pleasure in humiliating us. But they were equally determined to root out the Communists and fend off the Soviets.

Would Iran become a second Afghanistan? There was a time when that seemed possible, and maybe even likely. Whether the Soviets tried to subvert the Islamic revolution for their own purposes or decided to wait for it to collapse, it would not have been a great surprise to our intelligence planners if the Russians had come in. For the potential spoils of victory in Iran were far, far greater than in landlocked, resource-poor Afghanistan.

In the end, however, the Soviet invasion of Afghanistan may have been precisely what saved Iran. Here was the world's largest military power getting their butts kicked by a primitive but determined guerrilla uprising. The Afghan resistance was fragmented and ill-equipped, but there's nothing like an invasion to turn the locals against you.

In February 1989, when the Soviets finally pulled out of Afghanistan and returned home, the American media reported their retreat just as Moscow presented it—as the result of Gorbachev's goodwill. But goodwill had nothing to do with it. The Soviets left because of all the coffins coming home to Mother Russia, and because Gorbachev was desperate to save the foundering Soviet economy. He needed economic support from the West, and he knew he couldn't get it as long as his occupying army remained in Afghanistan. This was the Soviets' Vietnam, but without the protests in the streets and the nightly news reports. For Gorbachev, Afghanistan was a disaster.

It would have been even worse for the Soviets if they had gone into Iran, with its mountainous terrain and much larger population. But that's not to say they wouldn't have tried.


In early 1986, when we first began talking directly to the Iranians, it was by no means clear that the Soviets would be forced to leave Afghanistan. In retrospect, a *lot* of things weren't clear to us about the Middle East— things we probably should have known. Incredible as it seems, we were completely unprepared not only for the collapse of the Shah but also for the rise of the Ayatollah's theocracy and the spread of his radical Islamic fundamentalism.

I'm not one of those who blames Jimmy Carter for *every* problem we face, but the devastation of our intelligence capabilities did take place on his watch. True, the process had begun earlier, during the Ford administration, when the 1975 Senate and House committee hearings chaired by Senator Frank Church and Representative Otis Pike weakened the Agency's ability to carry out covert activities. But President Carter never really understood the need for covert action, and he was convinced that the CIA had grown too powerful. In his zeal to cut the Agency down to size, he had Stansfield Turner fire hundreds of experienced intelligence officers. Incredibly, they were dismissed through a computerized form letter!

Morale in the CIA was so low that scores of other experienced officers resigned. Carter, Vice President Walter Mondale, and Turner didn't appreciate the importance of human operatives, and tried to substitute high technology for experience and common sense. In the process, they virtually emasculated the CIA's clandestine abilities.

Although many of the consequences were not felt until the Reagan administration, President Carter became the ironic victim of his own actions. After our embassy in Tehran was overrun by the Ayatollah's young militants, we didn't have a single CIA operative on the scene who could give us the necessary information we needed to plan a successful rescue. Had President Carter been able to end the hostage crisis earlier, he might have been reelected.[4]

Now it's true that our intelligence agencies don't rely only on case officers and spies. They also make use of some truly amazing technology, some of it available nowhere else in the world. The people involved in these

---

[4]In the spring of 1991, there were numerous reports of a 1980 deal between the Reagan presidential campaign and certain Iranian authorities whereby the release of our hostages in Iran would be delayed until after the election. I don't believe it, and I have yet to see an iota of evidence to suggest that anything like this ever happened. If it did, why didn't Casey or George Bush, both of whom were alleged to be engaged in this effort, ever tell me whom to deal with on the Iranian side? Surely they would have known of somebody more effective than Ghorbanifar or the Australian. Further, no Iranian ever mentioned this supposed 1980 initiative, or even hinted at it.

efforts used to say that they could detect a Cuban general coughing in his car outside Managua, or a Soviet pilot breaking wind forty thousand feet over Syria. They were exaggerating—but not by much.

But there are no machines that read the human heart, and no instruments that measure hope, ambition, or even ideology. Trying to compile useful information about another society without agents on the ground is like a doctor who treats a patient solely by consulting the charts. He can learn a lot, but unless he can also ask, "Tell me, how do you feel? Where does it hurt?"—and get real answers—there are limits on what he can accomplish.

It takes years to train agents and install them, which is why all through the Reagan years we found ourselves facing big problems in places that surprised the hell out of us. Iran. Panama. Nicaragua. Angola. Mozambique. Egypt. Somalia. Suriname. Grenada. Not to mention Cuban agents all over Central America.

If we'd had sufficient intelligence assets in these countries, they would have flooded Washington with warnings. And no matter who was running the CIA, this information would have been disseminated around the State Department, the Pentagon, the White House, Congress—until somebody said, "Wait a minute, what's going on here?"

Instead, we were shocked when the Shah was overthrown and our embassy was captured. We were devastated when our Marine barracks were bombed in Lebanon. We were dumbfounded when Sadat was gunned down, although his assassins had been planning to kill him for months. The Israelis had learned about the plot, and had issued a warning both to the Egyptians and to us, but Sadat's people were emotionally incapable of accepting that information from their former enemy. And we didn't have the assets to confirm it independently.

Our intelligence failure in Iran had another cause, too. Although the Shah enjoyed our complete support, he was terrified that the CIA had a secret plan to replace him, and he hadn't wanted the Agency to track the activities of the religious opposition. The CIA believed that if the Shah caught us looking too closely at his internal adversaries, he might conclude that we were actually supporting them. Meanwhile, intelligence analysis being done in Washington also underestimated the religious opposition in Iran, which, in turn, further decreased the incentive for the CIA to keep a close eye on it.

And so by 1985, when it came to taking the political temperature in Iran we were completely in the dark. It seemed reasonable to assume, as the Israelis believed, that some members of Iran's government were, by our standards, more rational than the Ayatollah, more moderate and pragmatic. We knew, for example, that certain Iranian officials were allowed to leave the country to deal with foreign intermediaries. And on mundane matters, such as international airline schedules, the Iranians were generally cooperative. Surely some people in their government could see that a relationship with the United States, or at least an open channel of communication, was in their best interest. But with nobody reporting to us from Tehran, we didn't know for certain whether a moderate faction even existed—let alone who might be part of it.

We were fairly certain that the Ayatollah's government was not monolithic, if only because dictators going back to the days of Julius Caesar have always tended to promote factions—usually to deter their underlings from uniting in opposition to the boss. In the case of Iran, there were persistent reports that Rafsanjani himself was relatively moderate. Surely not everyone in Khomeini's government was as fanatic as the old man, even if they all had to keep up the pretense.

Were our expectations valid, or were we the victims of our own fantasies? Even today, I can't say for sure. But I believed then, and still do, that there were at least some moderates in their government.

Despite what we didn't know, a couple of things were clear. First, it hadn't been all that long since America and Iran had been friendly. The United States had done a lot for the Shah—at least until the end, when Carter abandoned him—and despite all the hostile rhetoric emanating from the Khomeini regime, there was still a reservoir of goodwill toward America in some sectors of Iranian society, including the military. From defector reports and other intelligence sources, we knew that the radical changes at the highest levels were not totally reflected among the masses.

We also knew that the Ayatollah was very old. And despite what some of his supporters believed, we were prepared to go out on a limb and assume he was also mortal. And so the inevitable question arose: What happens when he dies? Doesn't it make sense for us to try to achieve some kind of alliance with pragmatists or moderates in the government so we'll have some leverage when a new regime takes over? And if no regime emerges, and the Ayatollah's death is followed by absolute chaos, wouldn't that be a powerful inducement for the Soviets to step in?

And wasn't it shortsighted of us to let past hostilities between our two countries be the sole determining factor in whether we would have anything to do with Iran? Germany and Japan had inflicted a thousand times more damage on us than the Iranians ever dreamed of, and they became our allies. By early 1986 we had begun warming up to the Soviets, and we were even kissing the Chinese on the cheek. We couldn't blame everybody in the Iranian government for what had happened six years earlier at the embassy. An approach to Iran was certainly politically risky, but didn't we have a lot to gain by at least making an effort?

Our first meeting in Tehran took place in McFarlane's suite at 5:00 P.M., a few hours after we arrived. Once again we were disappointed by the absence of any high-level officials from the other side. Instead of showing up with Rafsanjani or the prime minister, Gorba and the Australian trotted out a short, stocky man in his middle fifties with graying hair. Dr. No, as we referred to him, was their spokesman for Western affairs. He was higher in rank than the Australian, but he wasn't one of their top people.

He was, however, fluent in English, and very articulate, which we certainly appreciated. When Gorba was translating, you had the feeling he was making it up as he went along. You could practically see him thinking, Hmm, I can't put it quite *that* way, so let me soften it a little.

Dr. No welcomed us to Tehran, and apologized for the mix-up at the airport. He talked on for a while, and more or less told us to lower our expectations. Essentially, his message boiled down to "Please, we're trying to make this work, but I can't guarantee that the next guy through the door will be Rafsanjani. After all, we still remember the meeting in the spring of 1980 between Mehdi Barzagan, our first prime minister, and Zbigniew Brzezinski, President Carter's national security adviser. A few days later, because of that one meeting, Barzagan was deposed. Our people are interested in meeting with you, but we have to move very slowly and carefully."

When Dr. No was finished, McFarlane responded with an opening statement of his own. "We in the United States," he said, "recognize that Iran is a sovereign power. We have had some disagreements over the past eight years, but we should deal with each other on the basis of mutual respect."

Mutual respect? It sure didn't feel that way. Before the day was out McFarlane fired off a cable to Washington with a graphic assessment of the situation we were dealing with. Back in Washington, Bud was routinely mocked for his impenetrable prose and obfuscation, a circuitous dialect that was affectionately known as "McFarlanese," that was deemed evasive even by the standards of diplomacy. But this time his words were colorful, clear, and accurate. Imagine, he wrote, "what it would be like if, after nuclear attack, a surviving Tatar had become vice president, a recent grad student became secretary of state, and a bookie became the interlocutor for all discourse with foreign countries."

Bud was especially angry that the Iranians seemed completely unprepared for our visit. I was afraid this might happen, which is why I had repeatedly argued that before an American of McFarlane's stature came to Tehran, there ought to be an advance trip at the staff level to ensure that both sides were in agreement on exactly why we were coming, and what we all hoped to accomplish.

The ultimate goal, although we weren't sure it was possible, was to arrange a secret meeting between Rafsanjani and Vice President Bush, presumably on neutral ground—in Europe, the Orient, or even the Middle East. This would have let the Iranians know that we were serious not only about recovering the hostages but also about resuming some kind of relationship between our two countries. While such a meeting seemed unlikely, it would have been easier to set up than a similar meeting between Rafsanjani and George Shultz. Shultz loved being visible, and it was hard to imagine him going anywhere without the press. Bush, on the other hand, was the former head of the CIA, and he was comfortable with covert operations. As Vice President, he was the official American mourner at state funerals all over the world. As he wended his way from one funeral parlor to another, it might have been possible for him to meet discreetly with his Iranian counterpart.

It never happened, in part because Casey was strongly opposed to an advance trip. Sending McFarlane to Tehran was risky enough, he said, but for an American delegation to go over there without a high official in the group was simply too dangerous. We could all disappear, and the Iranians might claim that we never showed up. Even our own government might be forced to disavow any knowledge of our visit.

Casey may well have been right in assessing the dangers of an advance trip, but not going carried its own risks. Even with friendly governments, it's almost impossible to hold a productive diplomatic meeting without advance work. Whenever a senior American official traveled to a foreign country, we would always try to arrange in advance whom they would be meeting with, and when, and what was likely to be decided. This was part of the routine of diplomacy.

But in the case of Iran we knew very little, and much of what we *thought* we knew turned out to be wrong. Our intelligence services kept a close eye on Ghorbanifar, and most of the time we knew what he was up to. But whenever he traveled to Iran, the lights went out. When he was there, we had no idea what he was telling the Iranians, or what commitments he was making in our name.

Only after we arrived in Tehran did it become clear that Ghorbanifar hadn't prepared the necessary groundwork for these meetings, and that he had been telling different things to each side. We could also see that the Iranians didn't seem to have much respect for him, either. Well, I thought, at least we have *that* in common.

Looking back on it now, I don't believe the Iranians had really been expecting us. No wonder Ghorbanifar had looked so upset at the airport. When he finally showed up, he was almost speechless—which was highly unusual for him. When he saw us standing there—Bud, Nir, Howard, George, myself—his jaw dropped. Maybe he was shocked to see Nir, because an Israeli who came to Tehran was taking an enormous risk. But more likely it was the whole group of us that spooked him. Perhaps he had planned to go back to his contacts in the government and say, "See, I knew they weren't coming. Send me back with a better deal."

And all the while he had been telling *us*, "You must come to Tehran, and the hostages will be freed."

We should have realized that despite everything Gorba had told us, direct contact between us and the Iranians was probably the last thing in the world that he wanted. For once that happened, he would become irrelevant. By coming to Tehran, we had called his bluff.

We had been told that if we came to Tehran, the hostages would be released. Then, with that hurdle out of the way, we would move on to discuss the larger issues. But by the end of the first day we could see that nothing was going to happen quickly. To signify his displeasure, and his frustration at not meeting high-level officials, McFarlane spent the next day holed up in his suite.

Since the hostages are central to this story, it may be worth explaining why they were kidnapped in the first place. The question may seem obvious, and yet it was seldom discussed. Plain and simple, the truth is that American and other Western hostages were taken to get Americans and other Westerners out of the Middle East, and to discourage their fellow citizens from coming in. The only thing the kidnappers had against their victims was that Weir, Jenco, and the other Americans carried blue passports. The purpose of the kidnappings was to humiliate us and to instill fear into the hearts of any Americans who were thinking of traveling in the region.

It's terribly hard for Americans to accept the fact that some people just don't like us. Don't like us? They should *love* us. Look at how much we're doing to help them. We're the good guys, aren't we?

That's not how the radical fundamentalists in Beirut see it. They hate us, and everything we stand for. They despise our Judeo-Christian value system, our reverence for individual liberty, and the role America plays in the world.

President Reagan was obsessed by the hostages, and he repeatedly made it clear to all of us who worked on this issue that we should do everything possible to get them home. Many Americans shared his concern, but others felt that the hostages had been given sufficient warning to leave, and had made their own free choices. I understand that argument, and I certainly don't support the idea of a paternalistic government. But what about those brave people who stayed behind in Beirut to fulfill a humanitarian mission—and did so as Americans? David Jacobsen was the director of the American University hospital. He was helping to save lives, and his presence was an admirable symbol of American values.

While each of us must take responsibility for his own decisions, I believe the President was right to care so deeply about the hostages. When you get right down to it, what is the American government for if not to protect the rights and the lives of individual American citizens? The same is true of Israel, which was one reason Nir had come to Tehran: he was determined to rescue two Israeli soldiers who were being held in Beirut. Nir and I had become friends, and he once cited an old Jewish proverb: he who saves a single life is as if he has saved the entire world.

I have no doubt that Ronald Reagan felt the same way, and I find it difficult to fault him for trying so hard to get the hostages home. The Iran initiative had a chance of working, and to some degree it did work. But it wasn't the only effort our government made. During this same period, our State Department undertook a wide variety of diplomatic and other initiatives to achieve the same purpose. All of them were worth trying, but none of them succeeded.


On our second day in Tehran, with McFarlane remaining in his room to show his indignation, Cave, Teicher, Nir, and I continued the meetings. In Bud's absence, I became the interim negotiator. "We're very disappointed," I told the Iranians. "President Reagan has sent over his special emissary, and with all due respect, he hasn't met anybody on his level since we arrived. This is contrary to all our expectations. It was our understanding that Mr.

McFarlane would meet with Prime Minister Mousavi, or President Khamenei, or Speaker Rafsanjani."

Dr. No seemed genuinely surprised. "Who told you these things?"

"Ghorbanifar," I replied.

Dr. No just sighed. By now we couldn't avoid the fact that both sides had come to this meeting with completely different expectations. We assumed we would be meeting with high-level officials, and that the release of the hostages was only a phone call away. The Iranians didn't expect that either event would occur soon.

Moreover, they had expectations of their own. They evidently believed that if we showed up at all, we would be bringing along a shipment of HAWK antiaircraft missile parts that they had ordered and already paid for.[5] In fact, we had brought less than 10 percent of the total order.

The HAWK parts that the Iranians had purchased had been discreetly collected from American military warehouses by the Defense Department, and flown to Israel shortly before we arrived. The bulk of the consignment had been loaded onto a second Israeli 707 that was sitting in Tel Aviv and was prepared to take off for Tehran the moment we gave the signal.

Dr. No assured us that he was doing everything possible to get the hostages released. "We have already sent a man to Lebanon," he said. "We expect to hear from him tomorrow. Meanwhile, let us continue talking.

"But you must keep in mind," he repeated, "that not everybody in our government looks with favor on this dialogue. We must move slowly. When Brezhnev died, we sent a delegation to his funeral, and the leadership

---

[5]The HAWK antiaircraft system comprises sophisticated electronic detection, identification, target-acquisition, and guidance equipment, and the associated missiles that home in on enemy aircraft. It was originally sold to the Shah as a means of defending key locations in Iran. The electronic components of the system had deteriorated considerably since Khomeini had come to power, and the revolutionary government was desperate to rehabilitate it for its original purposes.

was attacked by the people for this act."

In other words, Iran is not a dictatorship. Sure, I thought, and I bet there's a bridge over in Brooklyn that you'd like to sell us.

But the Iranians were also disappointed. "We expected much more equipment than we found on your plane," Dr. No said.

I explained that we had specific orders from Washington not to send the second plane until the hostages were released.

In fact, even the parts we brought with us were supposed to remain on the plane until the Iranians had fulfilled their end of the bargain. Our pilots had been given strict instructions to stay with the aircraft the entire time—not only to guard the parts, but also to prevent saboteurs from installing listening devices, or possibly even explosives.

But on our first night in Tehran, the pilots showed up at the hotel. They were accompanied by a contingent of Rev Guards. "We know what you told us," they said, "and we didn't want to leave the plane. But see these guys? See their guns?"

A line had been crossed and we were furious. There was a great commotion in the hallway, with everybody yelling at once and waving their hands. I hit the roof, exaggerating my genuine anger for dramatic effect. "Our pilots *must* stay with the plane," I yelled, "or else we're all leaving right now!"

Soon the air was full of apologies. "Oh, there has been a misunder*stand*ing, we're so *sorry*, we thought they'd be more *comfortable* in the hotel." The pilots were returned to the airport, but by now the plane had been stripped. While we continued meeting with the Iranians, the pilots went through it inch by inch to check for sabotage.

Back at the Hilton, the talks ground on. Even if Ghorbanifar hadn't lied to both sides, there was still an enormous culture gap that had to be bridged. "We can begin the process," Dr. No kept saying, "but you must understand, these things take time." This wasn't just rhetoric. We come from a society where things unfold quickly, and by our standards, the pace in Iran was painfully slow. It had never been fast to begin with, and now, with Khomeini in power, it was as if the entire country had slipped back into the eleventh century.

In an attempt to salvage something from this trip, I told the Iranians that at the very least we wanted to continue the dialogue. "There are those in our government, too, who would prefer that we have nothing to do with Iran. But we think it is important for our two countries to communicate. Even if we can't reach an agreement today, we must continue talking."

But even that plan sounded ambitious to our hosts. "You did a great thing by coming here," said Dr. No. "But there has been a misunderstanding. When we accepted your visit, we did not mean that a direct dialogue between our two governments would start immediately. It will take time. There are still problems to work out, but there is an old Persian saying—that patience leads to victory. We can talk, but how can we be assured that your country can keep a secret?"

I explained that we were prepared to send them a satellite communications device, similar to the one we were using to stay in touch with Washington, and that we were willing to dispatch it along with a communications team to ensure quick and secure communications between our two governments. Casey had been especially interested in this arrangement. If the Iranians agreed to it, the American technicians sent in to operate the system could serve as well-connected sources of human intelligence.

The situation looked hopeless, but I decided to give it one more try. "As soon as your government can arrange the release of the Americans being held in Beirut," I said, "we will send the second plane full of HAWK missile parts. Then, as we have already discussed, we will also sell you two radar units, and deliver them to the port of Bandar 'Abbas. After that we can talk further about your military needs. But if we leave here without overcoming the obstacles"—by which I meant freeing the hostages—"then our visit will have created new and additional obstacles."

On the third day, McFarlane joined us again. But the talks quickly went from bad to worse when Dr. No reported that he had finally heard from his emissary in Beirut. Apparently a deal was still possible, but the hostage-takers had now come up with a new and expanded list of demands. We listened incredulously as Dr. No spelled them out: Israel had to withdraw from South Lebanon *and* the Golan Heights. And Kuwait had to release the seventeen Da'wa terrorists who had been arrested for bombing embassies and other buildings in Kuwait City in 1983. We had heard that one before, perhaps because one of the prisoners in Kuwait, who had been sentenced to death, was the brother-in-law of Imad Mughniyah, the leader of the Islamic Jihad, the umbrella organization that included the Hezballah, the group responsible for the Lebanese kidnappings.

And as if these terms weren't already laughable, there was a preposterous kicker: the hostage-takers wanted us to reimburse them for their expenses! As McFarlane put it in his message back to Poindexter, "How's that for chutzpah!!!"

It wasn't easy, but we tried to remain polite. What did these people take us for? I felt like a customer in a used-car lot, where the salesman comes back and says, "Listen, I just went back and checked with the manager, and he said I could offer you a very special price. If you're willing to pay cash, we'll let you have that '85 Ford for five hundred thousand dollars."

Later that day, Dr. No reported that the hostage-takers had reduced their demands. They were no longer asking for the Israelis to withdraw from South Lebanon *and* the Golan Heights, or even to be reimbursed for expenses. Suddenly, the only remaining condition was the prisoners in Kuwait.

In other words, "I've gone back to the manager, and he agrees that the initial price was a little high. He's now willing to let the car go for only two hundred thousand—*and he'll even throw in a new set of tires.*"

McFarlane, trying valiantly to control his anger, replied that his instructions were clear: unless all the hostages were released, with no additional conditions, we were going home. "As soon as they're free," he said, "you'll have the remaining parts within ten hours. As for the Da'wa prisoners in Kuwait, there's not much we can do about that. That's between you and the Kuwaitis. But we would be willing to make every effort to persuade the Kuwaitis to be humane."

After a few more hours of haggling, we seemed to be making some progress. We even agreed on a six-point plan, which I typed up on the word processor attached to our encryption device. Assuming Dr. No could sell this plan to his higher-ups, the Iranians would arrange for the release of the hostages and of William Buckley's body on the following day. Meanwhile, we would launch the jet from Israel with the remaining spare parts. But if the hostages were not released as promised, the second plane would be instructed to turn around and go back to Israel. There were also provisions for the delivery of two radar units, and for a satellite communications system with American operators.

When the Iranians left the hotel, I took McFarlane aside and said, "If this thing is going to end up as we hope, we've got to launch that plane tonight." (The plane, laden with extra fuel, had to be airborne before the heat of the day made takeoff impossible.)

"Okay," he replied, "but don't let it pass the turnaround point." Because the flight was so long, once the plane passed a certain point it would no longer have enough fuel to turn around, and would be forced to land in Iran. There had been hours of planning with

regard to that plane, and we had tried to anticipate anything that might possibly go wrong. What if the plane
lost an engine? What if it had to abort over another
country? What emergency radio frequency would the
pilot use? With McFarlane's permission, I sent a coded
message to Dick Secord, who was awaiting instructions
in Tel Aviv: "Launch at 0400. If you don't hear from
me again by 0800, turn it around."

Early the next morning the Iranians came back. "Give
us more time," they said. "We think we can get you two
hostages. We don't care what Ghorbanifar promised you.
We've told you before: we have some influence, but we
don't control things in Beirut. We can't just *make* things
happen. We can't get all the hostages out. This is the
best we can do."

This was exactly what McFarlane had feared: that the
Iranians would offer a partial deal. Admiral Poindexter
had foreseen this possibility several weeks earlier, and
had instructed us not to consider it.[6]

But having participated in those long, drawn-out
meetings, I no longer believed the Iranians were negotiating for a better deal. They were now making the only
offer they could. The choice had come down to half a
loaf or nothing at all.

I went to Bud and said, "For God's sake, we can save
two of them."

But he wouldn't hear of it. "The only authority I
have is all or nothing."

"Bud, I know that," I pleaded. "But at least ask."
Our communications system gave us instant access to
Washington, and I believe that if Bud had presented the
dilemma to the admiral, Poindexter would have taken it

---

[6]Poindexter note to North, April 16, 1986: "You may go ahead and
go, but I want several points made clear to them. There are not to be
any parts delivered until all the hostages are free in accordance with the
plan that you laid out for me before. None of this half shipment before
any are released crap. It is either all or nothing.... If they really want to
save their asses from the Soviets, they should get on board."

to the President. And the President, wanting above all to save lives, would have said yes.

But McFarlane wouldn't even consider it. "Forget it," he said. "I've got my instructions, and you've got yours. They've had their chance."

We had started the conversation out on the balcony of his suite, but now we were discussing it openly and loudly in the living room. To hell with the Iranian bugs.

"I don't like this kind of dealing. It's not right," he said.

With our entire trip going down the tubes, and only a short time remaining before the second plane from Tel Aviv reached the turnaround point, I was getting emotional. "That's true, Bud, it's *not* right. But this isn't the time to get holy. Let's not kid ourselves. What do you think we've been doing all this time? You started this process, and we've been dealing ever since."

At a level considerably above mine, President Reagan and Bud McFarlane had already decided to trade arms for hostages. And now, given the alternatives, I thought it was more important that we try to salvage the lives of two poor bastards who were chained to a wall than to try to preserve the purity of a policy that had already been violated.

Nir, too, went to Bud and made an impassioned appeal to consider the Iranian proposal. Bud threw him out, and he later chastised me for "sending" Nir. But I didn't send Nir; when Ami saw the whole thing collapsing, he was devastated.

Hearing nothing from us at the midpoint of its flight to Tehran, the second 707, with the parts aboard, dutifully returned to Israel.

A few minutes later, Bud stormed down the hall, threw open the doors, and said, "We're leaving. Pack up. We're out of here in five minutes."

McFarlane's rush to leave was so sudden that at first I thought he was bluffing. He wasn't. But the elevators weren't working, the cars weren't ready, and the Iranians were clearly panicked because the whole deal was about to go down the tubes. They tried to delay us, but Bud was too angry. "We're going home," he snapped, "even if we have to walk down the stairs and find taxis to take us to the airport."

I was sick at the idea of returning home empty-handed. Not only could we probably save two hostages, but we would have set the stage for even bigger gains. But I had given it my best shot, and now it was time to carry out my orders.

Would it have made any difference if we had stayed a few more hours, or even another day or two? I believe that two hostages would have been released, but who knows? Given the fact that they were totally unprepared for our visit, and unaware of our expectations, the Iranians had been jumping through hoops to make things work. In true American style, we wanted things done yesterday.

As we prepared to leave the hotel, they continued to plead with us. "Give us a few more hours and we'll get two of them released." CIA headquarters had already reported over our satellite link that Rafiq Dust, Iran's deputy foreign minister, had left Tehran for Damascus, as he had in previous cases when Western hostages were actually released. Later, when the French hostages came out, Rafiq Dust was again in Damascus, which would indicate that if anybody was controlling the kidnappers in Beirut, it was probably not the Iranians but the Syrians.[7]

Eventually the cars pulled up in front of the hotel to take us to the airport. I went in and told our communicator to send the prearranged departure message to Tel Aviv and Washington, and, once it was acknowledged, to pack up the equipment. I prayed that our precipitous

---

[7]"The most serious problem we must address," George Cave later told the Tower Commission, "is whether the Iranians can gain control of the hostages. The French don't think they can. This could be our real problem. The Iranian side may be most willing, but unable to gain control."

departure would not mean that the waiting cars would be taking us straight to Evin Prison.

Outside the hotel, the Australian begged me to go with him, and Nir and I climbed in his car. The Australian himself drove, grinding every gear as he continued pleading with us to stay just a few more hours.

At the airport, as we climbed out of the cars and walked toward the plane, Ghorbanifar was still begging us to reconsider. The Australian actually walked up the stairway to the plane to make one last, desperate appeal, with tears in his eyes, until McFarlane said, "Close the door."

I appealed to Bud one last time before we took off. There was still time; he could have asked for guidance right there, on the runway. All he had to do was tell the communicator to open his briefcase, and in less than a minute we would have been talking to Washington. But McFarlane wouldn't budge.

The flight back to Tel Aviv was very quiet. We were all completely drained and enormously disappointed. We had come to Tehran expecting real and dramatic progress on the hostages. We even had people standing by in Beirut and Cyprus to coordinate their travel home. And now we were returning empty-handed.

But we were also immensely relieved—more so than we had expected—to be out of Tehran. On the long flight back to Tel Aviv, George mentioned that earlier that morning, back at the hotel, he too had worried that the Iranians might be so frustrated with our visit that they would prevent us from leaving. We didn't know at the time how close that possibility really was. Nine months later, the Tower Commission report noted that a group of Revolutionary Guards had come to the hotel to arrest us, but that our own guards had turned them back.

We had all set aside our fears during those four days, when we were preoccupied with the meetings. It wasn't until we had cleared Iranian airspace that we admitted to ourselves that things could have ended a lot worse.

"You were lucky," Casey told me later, when I gave him back the pills. "For all you knew the radicals in that government could have decided to put you up against the wall and shoot you." Now I don't believe in luck, but I do believe in Divine Providence—and the power of prayer. I'm convinced that God answered my prayer that morning, and delivered us from a very unpleasant experience. Tom Hemingway, a Marine friend of mine, has a sign over his desk: "God doesn't promise a smooth passage—just a safe landing." We made ours in Tel Aviv later that day.

When we touched down, we immediately set up our satellite communications equipment and called Washington to tell them we were safe. Nir said goodbye, and went home to his family. The rest of us flew back to Washington in a tiny Lear jet, with everybody jammed into a plane so small that we had to stop three times to refuel. When we finally landed at Dulles Airport, Bud, Howard, and I drove straight to the White House for a meeting with the President. During the Oval Office meeting I said nothing about my disagreement with McFarlane, but later I unloaded my frustrations on the admiral. To this day, I'm angry that Bud wouldn't even *ask* for permission to accept the Iranian offer for two hostages. The admiral didn't commit himself, but I'm still confident that the President would have said yes.

Just before we reported to the President, I called Betsy from my office to tell her I was back. "And not a moment too soon," she said. "I've just sold the house and you've got to sign the papers." She had told the buyer and the agent that her husband was away on a trip, and she didn't know when he would be back. It wasn't clear whether they believed her, and she had already postponed the closing twice. "This is it," she told me on the phone. "We're closing today. If you don't show up, the deal is off."

I was wiped out after that terrible flight home, and terribly disappointed, and it would have been nice to have a shower and change my clothes. But I did make it to the closing in time.

The previous day, as McFarlane and I had stood on the tarmac at Ben Gurion Airport in Tel Aviv, we had a moment alone to digest what had happened in Tehran. We had disagreed about the process, but we were equally disappointed at the outcome. "Well, Bud," I said, trying to cheer him up, "it's not a total loss. The one bright spot in all of this is that part of the money from these transactions is going to help the Nicaraguan resistance."

McFarlane gave me one of his inscrutable looks. He didn't ask me to elaborate.

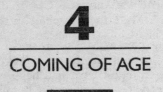

# 4

## COMING OF AGE

WHENEVER I TELL OUR KIDS ABOUT MY NEARLY IDYLLIC childhood, I get the feeling that deep down, they suspect Dad is making the whole thing up. It's not that their lives are so dramatically different from mine, or that they've experienced especially hard times. Tait, Stuart, Sarah, and Dornin have all grown up with God's abundant blessings—good health, good values, and good friends. They have all been active in our church and our family Bible study groups. But they're certainly growing up in a different world than the one I used to know.

In my entire high school there were only two or three guys who drank beer or smoked cigarettes. And while we certainly talked about girls, nobody I knew actually *did* anything. My three daughters and my son have been relatively sheltered, but they all know teenagers who have had abortions, and others who have been arrested for drugs, and still others who were victims of violence, parental abuse, and even suicide.

And this was in the suburbs of Virginia.

I was born in Texas in 1943, in the midst of the war

that America won for the world. I was named Oliver
Laurence North, and until I was eighteen everybody
called me Larry to distinguish me from my father, Oliver
Clay North—who was known as Clay to distinguish him
from *his* father. My father, a major in the Army, had
grown up in Philadelphia. My mother, Ann Clancy, was
a teacher from Oswego, New York.

When Dad returned from the war in 1945, we moved
to Philmont, New York, a small mill town about thirty-
five miles south of Albany where people didn't bother to
lock their doors at night. It sounds corny, I know, but
Philmont was the epitome of small-town America. We
had it all—a baseball diamond, empty fields, trout
streams, and plenty of woods where we could play capture the flag, cops and robbers, cowboys and Indians,
and anything else a childhood imagination allowed.
Main Street, clean and peaceful, was lined with small,
locally owned businesses like Mr. Carney's hardware
store. The local grocery store, an A & P, operated under
the company's majestic old name—the Great Atlantic
and Pacific Tea Company. We had a doctor who made
house calls, and a tiny movie house where we saw black-
and-white Buster Crabbe and Tarzan films and other
serials on rainy Saturday afternoons.

Everyone in Philmont knew everybody else, so you
couldn't get away with any savage crimes of passion—
like throwing a tomato at the kid down the block—
because your parents would invariably hear about it
within the hour. There was no anonymity. Our graduating class at Ockawamick High School consisted of thirty-six kids, and the only reason it was that big was that
the school served the entire region.

Except for my front teeth, which were blessed with a
large gap, perfect for squirting water across a swimming
pool, I wasn't a bad-looking kid. When I was in high
school, our family dentist said, "You know, Larry, we
could certainly do something about the space between
your teeth, but you probably don't want to bother with

that. It's not as if you're planning to be a movie star or on television, right?" I wonder what Dr. Link was thinking during the Iran-contra hearings in the summer of 1987, when millions of Americans decided that I reminded them of the "before" picture in a commercial for orthodontia.

I grew up as the oldest of four kids: My brother Jack was followed by our sister, Pat. Tim, our youngest brother, was born years later, when I was already at the Naval Academy. Jack and I were less than eighteen months apart; we were best friends, and virtually inseparable. With two older brothers, Pat had to endure a lot of teasing and a little jealousy, too, because she had her own room.

Like all the youngsters in Philmont, we pretty much had the run of the place. There was no such thing as a bad neighborhood, and we walked or rode our bikes everywhere. Bicycles were our oxygen, and we were continually tinkering with the gears and adjusting the handlebars. Mom didn't worry where you had gone after school—unless someone snitched and told her you had been speeding down Suicide Hill on Summit Street, where we'd go screaming onto Main Street. But Suicide Hill couldn't have been all *that* dangerous, it occurs to me now, because Main Street didn't even have a traffic light.

Mom used to hate it when the other mothers in our neighborhood would stand out on the porch at suppertime and yell at the top of their lungs, *"Billy! Peter! Time for dinner!"* The woman across the street had a better idea: a whistle that she blew twice when it was time to come in. My mother bought her own whistle, and our signal was three toots.

For real excitement, we'd ride over to the train tracks, about a mile or so from our house on Maple Avenue. When the railroad police weren't around, we'd sneak into the switching station shed (which was never locked), take out a few signal flares, and lay them across the track. That was the emergency signal for the engineer to stop the train. Then we'd climb up on the hill and wait for him to jam on the brakes, just to see how long it took that train to grind to a halt.

During a long summer afternoon we might hop a slow-moving freight train as it slowly chugged up the long slope heading north out of Philmont. We'd ride for a couple of miles and jump off near the house of a family we knew, but it was a long walk home so we didn't do it often. Our parents knew nothing about it, but in case my own kids are reading this, let me make one thing clear: don't even *think* of trying anything like that.

I suppose you could say that my childhood was like a Norman Rockwell painting. I had a paper route, and on Saturdays, after collecting from my customers, I went down to Palen's, the local ice cream shop, and spent my tips on a chocolate malt and a package of Nabs—cheese crackers filled with peanut butter. In warm weather we went fishing, using empty Campbell's Soup cans for worms. Dad taught us how to open the can without removing the lid; if you bent the lid just a little, you could hang the can on your belt loop. That was about as high-tech as things got in Philmont. Jack and I learned to shoot a .22 rifle before we could drive a car, and not a season went by when we didn't save up a few dollars for the mandatory hunting and fishing licenses.

Our family used to rent a small summer cottage on Copake Lake, and early in the morning we'd go out in the rowboat to catch breakfast, which consisted of two filleted sunfish over toast. At night I'd sit on the floor and listen to the radio exploits of the Lone Ranger, the Shadow, and Sergeant Preston of the Yukon and his dog, King. Every Sergeant Preston episode ended with the line, "Well, King, this case is closed," whereupon King would bark in agreement. I sat there transfixed, and vowed to become a Mountie when I grew up. It was easy to visualize what these radio heroes looked like. Years later, when I saw them on television, I was terribly disappointed by how ordinary they were.

Betsy has sometimes asked me whether my childhood was really as serene or as happy as I remember it. Maybe she's right; I do have a way of putting bad times out of my mind. I don't even recall fighting with my brother, and *all* brothers fight.

After I was more or less grown up, our family gained a new member. I was home on leave from the Naval Academy when Mom announced to the family that she was pregnant. She was well into her forties, and in those days pregnancy at that age was virtually unheard of. I thought it was wonderful. I don't remember Pat's response, but Jack was shocked: I guess he didn't believe our parents still did that kind of thing. Tim was born in 1962, when I was nineteen.

It wasn't until I myself became a parent that I realized just how much my mother did for us when we were young. As a father and a husband, I can see how busy Betsy is, how her life is controlled by our kids' schedules and the countless miles of driving with a howling mob of gremlins in the back seat. Maybe you can't appreciate these things until you grow up, but I sure do now.

We may have been innocent and carefree, but we weren't totally oblivious to the outside world. My parents followed the news avidly, and I remember hearing the grown-ups talk about the Army-McCarthy hearings—never imagining, of course, that thirty-three years later I would spend six days in that very same Senate hearing room as the guest of another congressional committee.

Mom is a devout Catholic, and every Sunday our whole family went to the Sacred Heart Church. I was an altar boy, and sometimes Father Dwyer would invite me to go along with him on pastoral visits. He drove a very old Buick which had a penchant for getting stuck in the mud and the snow, and I began to suspect that the real reason he asked me to come along was to help push him out.

As an altar boy, I had to memorize the liturgy and the responsorials of the Mass—in Latin, naturally. It was a good way to start the day, and I continued going almost every morning until I graduated from the Naval Academy. Later, of course, I had to learn the Mass all over again—this time in English. I still miss the Latin Mass; I liked the idea that you could attend Mass anywhere in the world and it would always be the same. These days, although I have a much more personal relationship with my Savior, I still have fond memories of that ancient liturgy.

Nearly every Sunday after church we had a big family dinner with my maternal grandmother, who lived with us, and my paternal grandfather, who came for dinner nearly every night after my Grandmother North died in 1959. As I remember it today, the Sunday menu was always the same: roast beef, mashed potatoes, homemade gravy, green beans, and Yorkshire pudding, spiced with plenty of talk about politics and world events. My parents rarely argued, but what I remember most clearly about the Chinese attack on the islands of Quemoy and Matsu in 1958 is that my mother wanted to shut off the radio while Dad insisted on listening to the news, even during dinner. They had a similar disagreement two years later, when Francis Gary Powers was shot down in a U-2 plane over the Soviet Union. These weekly dinners were the North family version of the Sunday morning TV talk shows.

My father, who owned a wool mill, was a staunch Republican. Some people have tried to portray our family as unusually patriotic, but in small-town America during the 1950s, just about everyone believed in God, country, and motherhood. My mother had been a registered Democrat, but she eventually changed parties and later ran as a Republican for the town board.

I was very close to Dad, and although he was quiet and self-possessed, we had no trouble communicating. When I moved away from home, I wrote to him often—from the

Naval Academy and from Vietnam, knowing that whatever I wanted to tell him, he'd understand.

He loved to read to us, and I grew up listening to classic children's fare: *Grimm's Fairy Tales*, *Treasure Island*, *Robin Hood*, and the collected prose and poetry of Rudyard Kipling. Our house was filled with books and newspapers. When we went off to college, Mom and Dad refused to send us any spending money unless we wrote them regularly.

Dad was far from a stereotypical military man. He had a passion for growing roses, and he loved the ballet. He'd see several performances each summer when the New York City Ballet performed in Saratoga. We weren't too far from Tanglewood, the summer home of the Boston Symphony Orchestra, and on summer afternoons we'd sit on the lawn and listen to their rehearsals. Occasionally, our parents would take us to New York. I loved the skyscrapers, but they couldn't compare to the greatest wonder of all—the Horn & Hardart Automat.

Dad was a history buff, and we must have visited every museum and battlefield on the Eastern Seaboard. His heroes were the Revolutionary War generals, and I believe we hit every revolutionary battlefield from Saratoga to Yorktown. Dad was a terrific guide, pointing out exactly where Benedict Arnold was wounded, or explaining the strategic importance of this hill or that river.

In 1969, when Jack and I were both serving in Vietnam, Dad took it upon himself to arrange a reunion for us. Without telling us, he wrote a letter to Melvin Laird, the Secretary of Defense (whom he didn't know), pointing out that both his boys were serving in Vietnam, and that it was only right that they should be able to see each other over there.

Years later, in my file, I found the Marine Corps response to his request, which simply read: "Second Lieutenant Oliver North is assigned to a Marine combat unit and is unavailable for such a visit at this time." In other words, buzz off, Dad, he's got a war to fight. But the Army was more receptive. Jack was yanked out of his unit with orders to report to Saigon, and from there to Da Nang—*and nobody told him why.* As he was being pulled out of the field, his helicopter was shot up, which is a little more excitement than you want to have on an average day, even in Vietnam. Jack wasn't hurt, but months later, when he returned home, he raised the roof with Dad.

Dad's response was classic. "Well," he said softly, "you were both over there, and you hadn't seen each other in a while, and it made your mother happy to know you'd be together."

It was hard for him to express the affection he had for his sons, but deep down, this tough guy was all heart.

Dad was always active in community affairs. He founded the local Rotary Club, and as president of the school board, he worked to centralize the schools and to provide a better education for youngsters growing up in this rural setting. These days, the phrase "community service" denotes a form of punishment, but I grew up thinking of it as a responsibility and a privilege. I didn't join the Marine Corps because my father was a military man. I signed up because he taught us all that anyone who is blessed to live in this great country ought to give something back to it. And he must have taught us well, because all three of his sons served in combat—one each in the Army, Navy, and Marines. He probably would have preferred that I join the Army, but he mentioned this only once. "I know the Marines are looking for a few good men," he said, "but remember, the Army has a whole lot more of them."

As a civilian, he wasn't one to sit on the sidelines and criticize. "If you don't like the way things are," he'd say, "don't complain about them. Work to make them better." He gave his time to a whole slew of committees, causes, and charities. He was especially generous to the

Salvation Army. He used to say that during the war, the Salvation Army volunteers were always there to give a doughnut and a cup of coffee to a soldier.

For all their civic involvement, my parents also knew how to have fun. They were active in the local theater group, where Mom acted in most of the plays and Dad worked backstage with the lights and the scenery. On weekend afternoons, they'd bring us along to the rehearsals at the D.A.R. Hall.

My parents believed in discipline, and by today's standards, at least, they were fairly strict. If one of us misbehaved, we would lose a privilege, like dessert. My parents didn't believe in sending us to our rooms, because they knew we'd have too good a time with all those books, Erector sets, model airplanes, and an enormous old RCA shortwave radio.

They insisted that we live by all of the Ten Commandments, although I seem to recall a special emphasis on number five—"Honor thy father and thy mother." Heaven help the North youngster who talked back to Mom, although my brother Jack took a little longer than I did to figure that out. I can remember only one occasion when my father actually hit me: he took off his belt and let me have it for being rude to Mom.


Dad served during World War II with the Ninety-fifth Infantry Division, part of General Patton's Third Army. In 1944, just after D-Day, his unit landed in France. Dad served as an operations officer, and later on as a logistics officer, with the Third Army. He returned home with a Silver Star and a Bronze Star, but he rarely talked about the war. Once in a while an old army buddy would drop by, and the two of them would sit out on the patio or on the porch and talk about old times. Jack and I used to sit on the steps and listen in.

He kept his decorations in the bottom drawer of his dresser, and after he died, I found the blue boxes with the medals inside, along with brittle, yellowed copies of his citations. He had been decorated for heroism during the battle for Metz, a German fortress. I also found the journals from his unit, which described the fierce fighting the men had experienced. They had even liberated a Nazi concentration camp—which my father had never mentioned.

I always knew that he had been part of something historic, but he talked about the war only in general patriotic terms: the United States did this, and our unit was part of it. There were pictures of him in uniform in our family album, and that was certainly part of his identity. But the main things I learned from my father were how to be a man, and how a husband ought to love his wife. I took that first gift early, and used it in ways that pleased him. Unfortunately, it took me far too long to open the second one.

Shortly after the war, Dad and his father had started the wool processing business where Dad worked until his retirement in 1965. Then he began a second career: teaching a course in transportation at Hudson Valley Community College in Troy. He had finally found his calling. "I will always regret making you go into the wool business," Grandfather North told my father on his deathbed, "because I can see how happy you are as a teacher."

My grandfather had come to this country from England in 1895. By the early 1920s he had become extremely successful in the textile business, with household servants and even a chauffeur to drive him around. He lost almost everything in the Depression, but he recovered. That was his lesson to me: that you can suffer a great adversity and still persevere. He didn't sit around feeling sorry for himself or waiting for some government grant. He picked himself up and started all over again.

Grandfather North was a man of great dignity, with a British accent, white hair, and a mustache. Like many English immigrants to America, he was uncomfortable with the casual nature of our society. He could never understand how Americans could be, in his terms, so "disrespectful" of their leaders as to refer to the President, for example, as "Eisenhower," rather than *President* Eisenhower. Some of that same feeling carried over to me; even today, I'm not comfortable referring to high government officials by their last names.

He was proper, punctual, and more than a little rigid. He refused to eat in a restaurant that didn't have tablecloths. Once, when my parents took him out to dinner, the waitress said, "Please keep your forks for dessert." He was horrified. "I certainly will not," he replied, and I'm sure he never entered that place again.

He and Mabel, his wife, lived on a farm in nearby Ghent. I spent many happy days there with Jack and Pat, and I still have a distinct memory of being chased by a gaggle of geese. I must have been awfully young, because the geese were as big as I was.

As we did at home, Jack and I shared a room at the farm, where we played for hours with a set of hand-painted lead toy soldiers from England which had belonged to my father when he was growing up. They were divided into British and German companies from World War I, and we used to stage mock battles on the double bed with the help of a fine set of wooden blocks. Both the soldiers and the blocks were kept in a great wooden toy chest, and although they actually belonged to my father, they weren't allowed to leave the farm. But that only made the place more special.

Because Jack and I were so close in age, and got along so well, it was almost like having a best friend living in your house. We played together constantly, and worked together, too—delivering newspapers, shoveling snow, raking leaves, or cutting the grass for families in our neighborhood.

But even though we grew up side by side, we were very different types. Jack was always more outspoken, more contentious, and more willing to argue than I was. Like a lot of younger brothers, he learned to defend himself. We had a rule in our family: if you didn't eat all your vegetables, you didn't get dessert. When that happened to Jack, he would loudly proclaim that he had spit in his dessert so that I wouldn't eat it. But that never stopped me; he was my brother.

Jack was always going to Carney's Hardware Store on Main Street to buy whoopee cushions, fake vomit, and other weapons of mischief. It was wonderful to have a brother who could always be counted on to get in trouble; I could enjoy his antics without having to pay the price.

Jack attended Niagara University, and until the day he graduated I worried that he might be the type who decided it was "fun" to go over the Falls in a barrel. Jack's willingness to seek adventure led him to the Army, where he became a paratrooper, a ranger, and a special forces officer. He served for twenty years, and now works in New England as an engineer.

In the summer of 1984, while Jack was still in the Army and I was at the NSC, Dad's emphysema took a decided turn for the worse. I was on a trip to Africa and was in Nairobi, Kenya, when the Red Cross cabled the American embassy to advise me that the end was probably near. I flew home immediately, and arrived just after Dad had come home from the hospital. He knew he was dying, and had asked to spend his final days in his own bed.

I spent the weekend at his side. He was so weak that I carried him into the bathroom and bathed him. We prayed together, and read together from the Bible: Psalms, Proverbs, Paul's Letter to the Romans, and the Gospel of John. He had been raised as an Episcopalian and had gone to church regularly, but that weekend, on his deathbed, I believe that he came to know his Savior personally. Father Robert Hart, a great old man of God from my mother's neighborhood church, came and gave Dad communion and the Last Rites.

By the next morning he had improved dramatically—so much so that I returned to Washington to file a report on my trip to Africa. The next morning, Mom called to say he had died in his sleep. The end came quickly and peacefully, and I was grateful that we'd had that last weekend together. Today, I'm glad that he didn't have to suffer through the anguish my mother has experienced during the protracted Iran-contra investigations.

I always knew that I would go to college; the only question was where I would be accepted, and what we could afford. Holy Cross and Notre Dame both said yes, but without a scholarship, so in the fall of 1961 I ended up at Brockport State near Rochester, about two hundred and fifty miles from home. The dean of students at Brockport, Dr. Harold Rakov, had gone to college with my mother. Rakov's parents were Jewish immigrants from Russia, and their son had made a success of himself through determination and hard work. When he saw that I was undecided about the future beyond a vague desire to become a teacher, he pushed me to consider either the Naval Academy or medical school. He urged me to load up on math, physics, and chemistry courses, which would be helpful at either place.

He also encouraged me to think about the Marines. Russ Robertson, our high school coach, and Bob Bowes, one of my history teachers, had already suggested the Marines when I left for college. Rakov suggested that I consider the Platoon Leader Candidate Program, which was open to college students and required two summers at the Marine Officer Candidate School in Quantico, Virginia. If you successfully completed the two summers and graduated from college, you would be commissioned as an officer and enter The Basic School as a lieutenant. There was something about men who had served in the military—Robertson, Rakov, my father—that made them seem more self-assured and a little more confident about dealing with life. I admired these men, and I wanted to follow in their footsteps. After discussing it with Russ Robertson, Dr. Rakov, and Dad, I signed up for the PLC Program during my first year at Brockport.

The moment I got to Quantico I loved the place. This was the most intense and challenging thing I had ever done, and I was surrounded by tough, hard-working, motivated men. I wasn't a bad athlete to begin with, but at Quantico I learned that I could stretch myself a lot further than I had expected. I enjoyed the discipline, but even more than that, I loved being in an environment where everybody got up in the morning headed in the same direction.

"If you don't like Quantico," Rakov had told me, "you sure won't like Annapolis. If you do like it, it will help you get in."

After that first summer, I knew I wanted to be a Marine. During my second year at Brockport, I spent the first few weeks working on my application to the Naval Academy, which was just about the biggest bureaucratic challenge I have ever encountered. I was thrilled when they accepted me.

When I arrived in Annapolis in June 1963, the first thing I did, along with about a thousand of my new classmates, was to get the shortest, fastest haircut in the history of man. How short? How fast? In about eleven seconds flat, you're practically bald. I also learned that the military's prejudice against civilians begins right there, in the barber shop. Nobody says so explicitly, but you soon come to understand that most civilians are inferior beings whom you can identify first by the length of their hair, and then by the absence of shine on their shoes, the lack of a close shave, and their generally flabby and slovenly appearance.

I have never felt comfortable with military arrogance, but I haven't been immune to it, either. "Do you want to be a *Marine*, Private Johnson," I have yelled on more than one occasion, "or would you rather be"—sneer—"a *civilian*?" It's easy to forget that your mother is a civilian, and so are your wife and your kids.

Underneath that arrogance, however, is a well-deserved pride. That swaggering, macho attitude, the confidence that comes with being part of an elite group like the Marines, that lack of patience with our civilian counterparts—these qualities were earned on battlefields all over the world.

But that pride can easily be taken too far. From the day we arrived at the Naval Academy, we were repeatedly told that we were the best, that we had been chosen from thousands of applicants, only a handful of whom were good enough to make the cut. Naturally, a lot of midshipmen believed this. Later, as a Marine instructor at Quantico, I saw hundreds of Annapolis graduates come through the rigorous Officer's Basic Course that prepares new lieutenants for command. Usually, the men from Annapolis were either among our best students or among our weakest. The worst were those who swallowed the flattery and concluded that they didn't have to work very hard.

In those days, being at Annapolis was a lot like living in a combination monastery and prison work camp. Not only were there no women around; you were insulated from the outside world and totally consumed by your day-to-day duties and the strict requirements of the Academy. This was especially true for plebes, as freshmen were known. We weren't allowed to do *anything*: watch television, listen to the radio, go out with girls, ride in a car, go into town, enjoy a beer, or even drink coffee. It was often said that the Naval Academy took away all your God-given rights and then gave them back to you, one by one, and called them privileges.

Even after you made it past your plebe year, you were still part of that insular world, where you were awakened before dawn six mornings a week by the loud clang of the bells in Bancroft Hall, the world's largest dormitory. By the time they stopped ringing, you had to be out of bed and on your feet. The entire day was controlled by bells, which marked every class, every meal, everything. You were always rushing to the next activity, because being late for anything was a reportable offense. You were constantly busy. There were many reasons why a student might choose to leave Annapolis, but boredom wasn't one of them.

One result of this busy, sheltered environment was that we didn't really know what the rest of the country was thinking. And to the extent that you're not aware of another position, it's easy to assume it doesn't count. It was at Annapolis that I came to believe that the media were exaggerating the growing antiwar sentiment among the American public as the Vietnam War heated up. The closest we ever came to witnessing such sentiments was when we marched to Memorial Stadium for athletic events. On the way to the stadium, we would pass by St. John's College. By 1967 the brigade was being treated to shouts of "Warmongers!" and the occasional egg or tomato.

We would return from Memorial Stadium informally, but we rarely encountered any problems on the way back. It was the formation itself that provoked the animosity, because it symbolized the institution. It would be several more years before antiwar protesters began to insult us as individuals.

The Academy included young men from every social and economic class, and a handful from religious and racial minorities. But even in the late 1960s there was still a fair amount of prejudice at Annapolis. Two classmates I was particularly close to at the Academy were well aware of this. Jay Martin Cohen was Jewish, and Frank Simmons was black, and both had suffered harassment, especially during their plebe years.

By June 1968, when our class graduated, most of this prejudice had melted away. You could actually see people change their attitudes and become more tolerant after a couple of years of attending the same classes and living together, elbow to elbow, twenty-four hours a day.

This was no accident. Throughout history, military organizations have been used not only for combat, but also as educational tools for the larger society. Sometimes it was blatant indoctrination. Lenin didn't create the Red Army for the sole purpose of defending

Russia. He also wanted to institutionalize the revolution by immersing young people in the philosophy of Communism. They would serve for several years, and after being thoroughly indoctrinated they would then return to the larger society to indoctrinate others.

Our own military has served a parallel purpose by teaching millions of young Americans about democratic ideals and tolerance—the need to rely on somebody regardless of his color, his religion, or his background. In 1947 President Harry Truman integrated the armed forces by Executive Order. For the first time, a white soldier from Georgia would have to use the same latrine and sleep in the same room as a black soldier from Mississippi.

In 1954, when civil rights legislation became a major issue, one reason it succeeded was that there were increasing numbers of white elected officials who had served in the military alongside blacks. It has been a long, slow struggle, but without the military it would have been a lot longer. Surprisingly, President Truman has never received much credit for one of his greatest accomplishments.

But no matter what your background, to be a plebe at Annapolis was to endure a long string of harassments by the upperclassmen. Having spent two years at Brockport and a summer at Quantico, I was a little older, a little more experienced, and perhaps a bit wiser than most of my classmates, which made my plebe experience somewhat easier. The upperclassmen at Annapolis could be petty, but at Quantico I had already been harassed by real Marines. *Their* harassment at least had a purpose, whereas at Annapolis you might be sent out in the middle of the night to polish the brass balls of Bill the Goat—a big statue of a charging goat that symbolized the Navy's fighting spirit. Or you might be ordered to "bring around everything in your room that moves," which meant you had to empty your room of everything that was portable—including your roommates.

I don't mind this kind of thing during the first sum-

mer, before the academic year really begins. It helps to
weed out some of the students who might crack under
the tough pressure of the Academy, or later on, in combat. There's probably something to be said for learning
how to endure these annoyances, because it helps you
develop a kind of protective coating that serves you well
in war—and even in civilian life. But I still resent the
guy across the hall who would walk into my room for
no reason at all and ask for fifty push-ups.

All plebes were required to memorize a set of
responses to specific questions from a little book called
*Reef Points*. If an upperclassman asked you, "How long
have you been in the Navy?" there was only one acceptable answer: "All me bloomin' life, sir! My mother was a
mermaid, my father was King Neptune. I was born on
the crest of a wave and rocked in the cradle of the deep.
Seaweed and barnacles are me clothes. Every tooth in
me head is a marlinspike; the hair on me head is hemp.
Every bone in me body is a spar, and when I spits, I
spits tar! I'se hard, I is, I am, I are!"

At any given moment, a plebe might be asked to
recite that day's menu, or the names of the movies playing in Annapolis, or the number of days before the
Army-Navy game, or the main headlines of the *New
York Times* and the *Washington Post*.

During meals you had to sit straight up on the edge
of your chair without bending over or looking down.
"Are your eyes on the boat?" you'd be asked, reminding
you to look straight ahead.

"North, is the cow heavy?"

"No, sir!" You'd be holding a half-gallon milk carton
at arm's length, and an upperclassman, wanting to know
how much milk was left, would ask, "North, how's the
cow?" And you'd answer: "Sir, she walks, she talks, she's
full of chalk. The lacteal fluid extracted from the female
of bovine species is highly prolific to the third degree!"
In other words, there were about three glasses of milk
left in the container.

The only relief from all of this was the prospect that our football team would win the annual Army-Navy game, which is always played on neutral ground (usually in Philadelphia) during the first weekend of December. Whenever Navy won—as we did during my plebe year—the hazing of plebes would come to an early end, and we were allowed to "carry on." We could actually talk during meals, and we no longer had to "double-time" everywhere we went.

But hazing was the least of my problems. In February of my plebe year my whole world almost came to an end when I was involved in a terrible car accident. It happened during Washington's Birthday weekend, when a group of us were driving to upstate New York to go skiing. It was midnight, and the snow was falling heavily as we approached the intersection of Route 11 and Route 15 in Horseheads, New York, not far from Corning. Everyone in the car had fallen asleep—including the driver. We had stopped for hamburgers a couple of hours earlier, but nobody had been drinking. I can still remember opening my eyes and seeing the headlights of a truck that was almost on top of us. That was just before impact.

Nobody wore seat belts back then, and the carnage was just awful. Bobby Wagner was killed outright. Tom Parker suffered major brain damage. Mike Cathey, in the so-called death seat, ended up with a broken pelvis, and a broken arm, and burns. Billy Mullens suffered a crippling back injury and was medically discharged. Compared to my companions, I was relatively unscathed: cranial injuries, crushed vertebrae in my lower spine, a broken nose, broken jaw, a broken leg, and a badly damaged knee.

I remember crawling out of the car into the cold, and hearing voices say, "Lie still, don't move." I was shivering, even after somebody covered me with a coat. The survivors were taken to Corning Hospital, where I was put in a body cast. When I complained that I had no feeling in my legs, and couldn't control my bladder or bowels, one of the doctors gently explained that I might never walk again.

Even then, I didn't realize how badly I was hurt until my parents showed up. I couldn't even talk to them, and it was painful just to breathe. I don't recall much about the Corning Hospital except that one of the nurses was named Lolly, and that we eventually recovered enough to sing to her from our beds, "Hey Lolly Lolly Lolly"—pause for a breath—"Hey Lolly Lolly Lo."

For the next few months, my life was a blur of pain and operations. After we were stabilized, we were flown to Bethesda Naval Hospital, and then transferred to the naval hospital at the Academy. It was located in the middle of the Academy cemetery, which created a real incentive to get better. By the summer I could be taken out in a wheelchair to sit in the sun.

My fondest memory of that period is that Bob Eisenbach, my best friend, came to see me every day. The workload at the Academy was grueling, and I don't know how he ever found the time. But he always showed up, even if it was only long enough to stick his head in and yell, "God, North, you really stink today!"

When I first got up after several months in bed, I couldn't even sit up—much less walk. They put me in a hydrotherapy tank to get me to move my arms and legs, and it was terrifying. I started sinking, and I thought I was about to drown. The physiotherapist, one of the cruelest—and kindest—men I've ever known, *made* me move, although my joints and muscles had begun to atrophy.

By summer I was well enough to take medical leave and go home. I had been surveyed, and was found to be medically unfit for further service. I was supposed to return to Annapolis in September—but only for medical treatment until I was well enough to be discharged.

My parents suggested that I sleep on the foldout couch in the living room so I wouldn't have to climb the stairs to my bedroom, but I refused. I had worked too hard to get into Annapolis, and I was determined to get back. Dad reinforced the handrail on the stairs, and I slowly made my way up and down. It was during these months that I came to understand the importance of persistence.

With Dad's help I filled out the mountain of paperwork that was necessary to appeal the decision to survey me out of the service. I still remember sitting on the patio that Jack and I had built with Dad, watching him trim his beloved roses when the letter arrived: my appeal was denied.

But I refused to give up, and Dad reinforced my determination to fight the decision and to return to Annapolis. He worked with me on my therapy and helped me graduate from crutches to a cane although my right leg was withered and thin. Russ Robertson, my old high school coach and a former Marine who had been badly wounded in the leg during World War II, stopped by periodically to encourage me.

The accident, the surgery, and the hospitalization taught me a lot about how much I could endure. They also taught me about the healing power of prayer. When I returned to the naval hospital, I made a habit of wheeling myself down to the chapel every day.

Being hospitalized certainly wasn't pleasant, but it wasn't all pain and suffering, either. There were a lot of us in one big ward, and we had some good times talking together and flirting with the nurses. One of my fellow patients was Roger Staubach, the celebrated quarterback of our football team, who had been injured in the Notre Dame game. Later, he went on to become a star for the Dallas Cowboys.

When the nurses left the ward, those of us confined to wheelchairs would occasionally hold jousting tournaments. With a crutch for a lance, and a garbage-can lid for a shield, you'd wheel yourself as fast as possible down the middle of the ward toward your opponent. Our ward was the scene of so much mayhem that it was probably just as well that we were already in the hospital.

I was eventually accepted back at the Academy on probation, but only if I was willing to repeat my plebe year. *Willing?* I was grateful to be there at all, and would have done almost anything to come back. I finally did—almost a year after the accident. I was determined to build up my strength, and every morning, while the rest of Bancroft Hall was still sleeping, I'd go out for a run along the seawall. By the time my classmates woke up, I was already in the shower.

I don't want to leave the impression that I was in love with the Naval Academy. It was a challenging place, but very restrictive. It's designed to give you more than you can hope to accomplish, which forces you to establish priorities. You could strive for perfection, but you never had enough time to achieve it.

Right from the start, I saw the Academy as the means to an end—a commission in the Marine Corps. Ever since that first summer at Quantico, I was determined to be a Marine. But after my accident, I knew I would have to fight especially hard to get there.

And I did—literally. Every midshipman at the Academy has to be involved in a sport during all three seasons of the academic year. Because of my injuries, football, soccer, lacrosse, and crew were now out of the question. That pretty much limited me to sailing in the fall and the spring, and boxing during the winter.

I especially liked boxing, because you're really on your own: if you lose the fight, there's no one to blame but yourself. I was far from a natural fighter, but I could take a punch, and I was in excellent shape from my morning runs. Coach Emerson Smith, a legend in boxing circles, used to tell us that boxing could be reduced to three basic rules: keep your hands up, your feet moving, and your ass off the deck.

I was a welterweight, and after two years of violating Smith's third commandment I eventually fought my way up to the brigade championships. That was a big deal at the Academy, and the entire brigade of midshipmen—close to four thousand men—showed up at MacDonough Hall to cheer on their favorites. My opponent that night was Jim Webb, a good fighter who went on to become Secretary of the Navy and a well-regarded novelist.

As each pair of fighters entered the ring, the band would strike up "The Look Sharp March"—better known as the famous Gillette commercial. Webb and I were about evenly matched. I had a good left, but against another lefty like Webb that wasn't much help. He was quick on his feet, so my goal was to back him into a corner to neutralize his speed advantage. It was a close fight. We both went the distance, but I beat him on points.

A year later, a medical review board had to decide whether I had recovered enough from the accident to get a commission in the Marines. I met with them and made my best case: "You people have invested thousands of dollars in training me," I said, "and I'm going to graduate with honors. I even won the brigade boxing championship. Are you seriously thinking of sending me off to be a *civilian*? I'll make a fine Marine officer if you'll only give me a chance." Emerson Smith offered to show the film of my fight against Webb as evidence of my fitness and mobility. But just in case, I also applied to the CIA.

During my final summer as a midshipman, I went off to Jump School for parachute training with the Army in Fort Benning, Georgia. When I took the physical, one of the doctors noticed that several bones in my face and nose had still not set properly from the car accident three years earlier. Not only would I have to stop boxing, but I would also require additional surgery on my nose and face if I wanted to become a Marine pilot, which was my intention at the time.

Not wanting to miss Jump School, I postponed the surgery and went off to parachute out of airplanes in Georgia. During previous summers I had gone to

Survival, Escape, Resistance and Evasion School in Nevada, and Underwater Swimmers School in California. I missed a few vacations, but these programs kept me in shape and helped prepare me for the Marines.

The final year at Annapolis is normally the best. Not only can you finally see the light at the end of the tunnel, but you get to pick the service you're going into, and the location and the date for reporting to your new command. By the spring of 1968, however, Vietnam was taking a heavy toll. Our service selection happened to coincide with the Tet offensive, and more and more names and faces of dead Marines and naval officers we had gone to school with only a year or two earlier appeared on the memorial boards at the entrance to Bancroft Hall.

First classmen (seniors) were allowed to have a car and to park it on the Yard, as the campus was known. And having a car made it a lot easier to get a date. Otherwise, your date had to drive over and pick *you* up—an awkward situation for the typical American male in that macho environment.

Having a car also made it easier to see family and friends. My uncle, John Finneran, a Navy commander, and his family lived near the Academy, and I used to spend occasional weekends at their house. His daughter Kathy, my cousin, was a college student with a part-time job at Hecht's, the department store chain. Shortly after Christmas, Kathy mentioned that she thought I should meet her boss, a very attractive young lady named Betsy Stuart. Then she showed me Betsy's picture, which was all the encouragement I needed.

The next weekend, my brother Jack, who was now a second lieutenant in the Army, met me at the Finnerans'. He and Kathy encouraged me to drive to Montgomery Mall, where Betsy worked, so that I could meet her. Jack and I jumped in my green Shelby Cobra and roared off.

As we rode up the escalator at Hecht's, Betsy was talking to one of her sales clerks. When she smiled at us, I was smitten. She was tall and slender, with wide blue eyes and very long blond hair that she wore in two braids down her back. She realized immediately that this little visit had been arranged so I could check her out, and I suddenly became embarrassed by the transparency of it all. Betsy seemed to enjoy my obvious discomfort.

"Hi," I said. "I'm Kathy Finneran's cousin. You must be Betsy Stuart."

"I am. Kathy told me you might be dropping by this afternoon to do a little shopping. But this is pretty far from Annapolis. Don't they have any stores down there?"

"Yeah, well, you see, Jack—oh, this is Jack, he's my brother—you see, Jack's going to Vietnam pretty soon and we thought we would pick up a few things he might be needing."

"Of course. So you came here, to ladies' accessories."

"Well, not exactly *here*, but well, you know, we were just kind of looking around and Kathy had told us that you might be here, and it seemed like—say, have you had lunch yet?"

"Oh, yes. About three hours ago."

"Of course, sure, it's almost time for dinner. Well, we've got a lot to do, all that shopping and all, and you seem to be busy. It's been nice to meet you. Maybe I could give you a call some time?"

"If you like. Now if you'll excuse me, I have customers to attend to."

It was awful. On the way out of the store, Jack patted me on the shoulder and said, "Well, big brother, you sure have a way with girls. Do they teach that technique at the Academy, or is it something you picked up on your own? I just hope it's not genetic! But don't feel too bad about not asking for her phone number, though, because you never even bothered to give her your name."

Kathy gave me Betsy's number, and during the next few weeks I started burning up the phone lines between Annapolis and Annandale, Virginia. But Betsy was never home, and the few times she was, she always seemed to be busy on the days I suggested—usually with another date. I ended up having countless conversations with her roommate, Dana Hanshaw, who had such a sexy voice that I was ready to date *her*. But Dana kept encouraging me to try, so I continued calling. Finally, perhaps because my sheer persistence had worn her down—or possibly because another date had canceled—I got to take Betsy to dinner.

Later, some of our friends concluded that Betsy was enchanted by my uniform. Jack swears that the only reason she ever went out with me was because he was standing there when we met. Years later, Betsy told me the truth: the uniform had nothing to do with it, and neither did Jack. She was attracted to my car.

Betsy Stuart was the youngest of three sisters. She was a farm girl from western Pennsylvania, and like me, had grown up in a clean-cut, rural, common-sense small-town environment. She had already graduated from Penn State University, where she majored in retailing. Although her father, Jeb, was a direct descendant of his namesake, General Jeb Stuart, the Confederate cavalry officer, Betsy had no experience with military types. She married into a Marine Corps career with a sense of wide-eyed innocence, and even years later she still couldn't tell the difference between a corporal and a colonel.

Our first date was at an Italian restaurant that just happened to overlook the Marine Memorial in Arlington. I must have done something right, because before long we were seeing each other almost every weekend. One beautiful spring Sunday, about a month before graduation, love triumphed over duty: I spent the day with Betsy and literally forgot what time it was. By the time I returned to the Academy I was half an hour late for the evening meal formation. In many parts of this land, being fashionably late for dinner is considered almost a virtue. But not at the Naval Academy. Showing up twenty minutes late without a valid excuse is a Major Offense for which the perpetrator is put "on report." The punishments can include demerits, restriction (being grounded), and a tour of E.D. (extra duty)—which consists of the privilege of carrying your rifle around in small circles for many hours at a time. In extreme cases, being late can even lead to expulsion.

Coming into Bancroft Hall, I was greeted by a Marine captain who had just inspected my company and found me missing. I was the company commander, so my absence was hard to ignore.

"Welcome back, Mr. North. Where were you?"

"I was with my girlfriend, sir."

"Did your car break down?"

"No, sir."

"You know what this means, don't you?"

"Yes, sir."

"You're on report, Mr. North."

My punishment consisted of being restricted from that moment all the way through graduation week. It was only due to the intervention of Major Reid Olson, my company officer, that I was allowed to keep my command. Olson also arranged for me to serve as a supervisor for various social events during graduation week, which allowed me to spend a little time with Betsy.

By then, she and I had already started discussing our future. Shortly after graduation, I would be entering the Marine Officer's Basic Course at The Basic School in Quantico, Virginia. But that wasn't a major hardship, as I would still be within an hour's drive of Betsy's apartment in Annandale.

Midway through the five-month course at Quantico, which was abbreviated on account of the war, I asked Betsy to marry me. There's a tradition at the Academy that you give your future bride a miniature version of your class ring. I liked that custom, but I wanted to do it my way. One night, before taking Betsy to dinner, I presented her with a single rose on whose stem I had carefully threaded the ring. I also had her birthstone, an aquamarine, set into my own ring.

We planned the wedding for the day I graduated from Basic School, and here, too, we were following a naval service tradition. Graduation day at Annapolis is the occasion for scores of weddings at the chapel, and back in June, at the Academy, Betsy and I had been to half a dozen ceremonies in a single day.

We were married in the chapel at Quantico on November 13, 1968. My parents were there, but just barely. There had been a nasty snowstorm the previous day, and they were turned back on the New York Thruway. They ended up flying in on a chartered plane, along with my brother Tim, who was now five. Betsy's family and mine, along with our friends, practically filled the little chapel at Quantico. One guest I was especially overjoyed to see was my friend Bob Eisenbach, who had been terribly wounded in Vietnam on July 4 the previous year. Bob had been shot in the head and given up for dead. He was still in a coma when he returned home, and had undergone several brain operations. By the time Betsy and I got married, he was in a wheelchair.

Betsy wore a beautiful white gown with a veil, and I wore my dress blues. Both our maternal grandmothers made it to the wedding. As the ceremony ended, eight of my classmates formed the traditional arch of swords for the newly married couple to pass through. The Reverend Peter John Carey, the Catholic chaplain, performed the marriage. He must have liked the idea because a few years later, he got married, too.

Those final weeks at Quantico had been a blur, with tactics, classes, and final field exercises. Within weeks, many of us would be shipping out to Flight School, Artillery School, or Armor School. But for all of us who were infantry officers, the next stop was Vietnam.

# 5

## COMBAT

With thirty days of leave before my flight to Vietnam, Betsy and I started out on a leisurely cross-country drive. We had already taken a short honeymoon trip to Puerto Rico, but now we had a chance to spend some real time together before our thirteen-month separation. One of the colonels from Quantico was moving his family to San Diego, and we volunteered to drive his car to California. We planned the trip so that by the time I was due to leave for Vietnam, I could catch a flight to San Francisco and make my way to Travis Air Force Base, while Betsy would fly back to Virginia.

After dropping off our wedding gifts with Betsy's parents in Pennsylvania, we headed north to see my folks, and then west to Michigan to visit my sister and her husband. From there we drove south, planning to drive west along the old Route 66. It was only mid-November, but we soon found ourselves racing against a series of early winter storms. To avoid the snow, we abandoned our planned route and kept driving south.

We had been gone for about a week, and were pulling in to a motel in Amarillo, Texas, when a highway patrol officer drove up behind me. "Excuse me," he said, "are you Second Lieutenant North, U.S. Marines?"

"Yes, sir."

"It's a good thing we tracked you down," he said. "Patrolmen all over the state have been watching for your car. Your father gave us your plate number in the hope that we could find you and tell you to call home. He says it's urgent."

I rushed inside to a pay phone. "Bad news," said Dad. "Your orders have been modified. You're supposed to report to Travis in three days."

Three *days*? Betsy and I had been planning on another three *weeks*!

I called Marine headquarters to check. "I'm not even near an airport," I explained.

"Then you'd better get to one," they said. "You need to be on that flight."

I didn't want Betsy to drive to California alone, so we jumped back in the car and headed straight to San Diego. It was awful: she cried and I felt terrible. I knew it wasn't my fault, but I was filled with guilt about leaving her so soon. We drove in shifts, just ahead of a blizzard that seemed to be following us, and barely stopped as we raced through Texas, New Mexico, Arizona, and into California.

We arrived in San Diego just as the sun was coming up on Thanksgiving Day. I was exhausted, having driven all night with Betsy curled up beside me in the front seat. I was due at Travis that same evening.

We stopped at a Denny's for breakfast. Because of the holiday, the place was deserted. My haircut must have given me away, because the waitress came over with coffee and asked, "Are you on your way to Vietnam?"

"Yes, ma'am," I said.

"Then I guess you won't be having any Thanksgiving dinner. Let me bring you some."

Betsy drove me to the airport, where we said a long and tearful good-bye. I flew up to San Francisco and took a cab to Travis. She delivered the car and flew back to

Washington. We had been married for less than three weeks.


The first thing I learned when I arrived at Travis was that for all the rush to get there, I wasn't going anywhere for a long time. There was a ton of paperwork to complete, but with thousands of men passing through each day, at least the place was organized. But it was also depressing to sit there and wait for hours in those pale green and red fiberglass chairs with nothing to do except listen to a steady stream of announcements. They blared out from a PA system that was so scratchy it could have been built by Thomas Edison himself, and obviously hadn't been updated since. "May I have your attention in the terminal, your attention in the terminal, please. Travis Air Force Base announces the departure of World Airways government contract flight Hotel Twenty-five for Da Nang, Vietnam. You are reminded to retain one copy of your orders on your person at all times. Please extinguish all cigarettes at this time. No photographs are permitted on the flight line. May I have your attention in the terminal, your attention in the terminal, please. Travis Air Force Base announces the departure..."

Finally our flight was called. As I climbed the stairs and entered the plane, I couldn't help but notice a steel plate next to the door, with a printed message that read something like this:

This aircraft is operated by the Far East Airway Corporation, which has leased it to the Inter-American Airway Consortium on a lien from the Greater East Asian Bank of Pakistan for the purpose of transporting sheep from Phnom Penh to Tehran. The company accepts no liability. This aircraft was last inspected on April 12, 1959.

Whatever the exact wording, this message didn't strike me as particularly reassuring. Nor did the chief stewardess, who had all the charm of a grizzly bear, with a physique to match. As soon as she picked up the microphone, we knew this was no ordinary flight. "Listen up," she began. "I've made this trip fourteen times, and I'm not going to take any crap from you guys, understand? Everybody reach down and check under your seat for your life jacket. There will be no smoking on this plane until I say so. There are call buttons above your seat. Don't even think about pressing them."

She was the flight attendant from hell.

"One more thing," she added. "Anyone gives me a hard time, I'm gonna tell the major."

"Oh, yeah?" somebody yelled. "What's he gonna do? Shave my head and send me to 'Nam?"

We were a high-spirited group, ready to take on the world. And none of us had any doubt that we would eventually be coming home alive.

It seemed like a week later when the pilot finally announced that we were landing: "Gentlemen, we'll be touching down in Da Nang, Vietnam, in about fifteen minutes. The local time is five minutes past noon, and the ground temperature is a hundred and two degrees. Please extinguish all cigarettes and fasten your seat belts. We've enjoyed having you with us on World Airways government contract flight Hotel Twenty-five, and we hope to see you again next year on your way home. Good-bye and good luck."

At Da Nang we were ushered into a huge, tin-roofed building that was covered with sandbags. Together with several other brand-new second lieutenants, I was assigned to the Third Marine Division. A few hours later, we boarded a muddy C-130 transport plane for the short flight north to Dong Ha, in Quang Tri province, the combat base in northern South Vietnam that was home to the Third Marine Division Headquarters. We took off into the afternoon sun, and when we reached Dong Ha the pilot dove right in, engines roaring, and came to a screeching halt. The plane hadn't even stopped rolling when the crew chief screamed, "Everybody off!"

As we ran off the ramp, somebody motioned for us to jump into a sandbagged trench beside the runway. A moment later the plane was airborne again as rocket fire came crashing down on the far side of the field.

Welcome to Vietnam.

Those of us who had disembarked from the C-130 filed into a sandbagged bunker to await pickup by our respective units.

After an hour or so, a Jeep came by for me. At least I think it was a Jeep. It was hard to tell, because the fenders were bent, the windshield was gone, and the back seat was missing.

I was feeling sorry for the Jeep until I got a look at the guy climbing out of it. He was tall and absolutely emaciated. His face was thick with stubble, his helmet cover was tattered, his flak jacket was ripped, and the heel was flapping on his boot. He was carrying a pistol, but the holster was rotted out in the bottom. His filthy uniform seemed to be welded to his body. His eyes were bloodshot, and he obviously hadn't been near a shower in weeks.

"Lieutenant North? Sorry I'm late, but the friggin' bridge was blown up and a convoy was ambushed." Taking a map from his jacket pocket, he pointed out Con Thien, the northernmost Marine combat base in Vietnam. "That's where we're headed," he said. "By the way, I guess I forgot to introduce myself. My name is Bob Bedingfield. I'm the chaplain."

If he's the chaplain, I thought, this must be one hell of a neighborhood.

Bedingfield took me to the headquarters of the Third Battalion, Third Marine Regiment, and to the supply building where I drew my gear, including ammunition and a holster for the .45 pistol I had brought with me. (The pistol was a prize from the Naval Academy for the greatest academic improvement over four years, which I always regarded as kind of a backhanded compliment.) I climbed into the back of the Jeep and sat on the fender, next to a box of hand grenades.

We joined up with a convoy and roared out of the base. Once we passed Cam Lo, the last major checkpoint, the road wasn't much more than a ditch. A mile or so outside of Con Thien, the entire convoy came to a screeching halt. Dusk was falling, and there was jungle on either side of us. Bedingfield checked his watch. "We have to wait here," he said. "It's almost time for the Hanoi Express."

Every evening at exactly six o'clock, the gunners north of the Hanoi River would fire rockets and artillery into Con Thien. You could count on it. It was as regular as the nightly news, and about as friendly. You definitely did not want to be driving in while *that* was going on.

Con Thien, our battalion's forward headquarters, had been built by the French back in the 1950s. It was originally constructed to house only a regiment, but had long since been expanded by the Marines and Navy Seabees (navy combat engineers). It looked like a huge bald circle on a hilltop, and was surrounded by miles of barbed wire, machine gun positions, artillery and tank revetments, and thousands of mines. The original French fort had been demolished and replaced by a warren of underground bunkers which housed troop billets, operations centers, and even an aid station. Con Thien sprouted radio antennas like whiskers, and was used as a strongpoint from which we launched operations along the northern border of South Vietnam. For the next year I thought of it as home.

Con Thien was also a vital observation post. Just north of us was a defoliated swath known as the "trace"—an open strip of land about a kilometer wide, running along the DMZ and stretching from the seacoast on the east to the base of the mountains west of us. From the wooden observation towers at Con Thien, artillery and air spotters could monitor North Vietnamese Army (NVA) units heading south. Our job was to prevent their combat and supply units from crossing the seventeenth parallel into South Vietnam.

This was Marine country, commonly known as Leatherneck Square after the old slang name for Marines. (In the old days, Marines wore a high leather collar on their tunic to protect them against enemy swords.) There were probably more Marines killed and wounded on a day-to-day basis in the area surrounding Con Thien than anywhere else in Vietnam. The officers called it Leatherneck Square. The troops called it the Meatgrinder.

It wasn't until much later that I came to realize there were actually two Vietnam wars. Those of us who fought in the northern regions of South Vietnam were part of an entirely different experience than that of the great majority of American troops, who were based farther south. Our war was more straightforward: if we set up an ambush and spotted the enemy, we could be reasonably sure it *was* the enemy. We didn't have to deal with that terrible problem of Vietnamese civilians who weren't always civilians, or with Viet Cong guerrillas who would melt off into the countryside and disappear. We were fighting against NVA regulars—well-disciplined troops with reinforcements close behind—and when you were engaged with these guys, you were really engaged. Except for occasional woodcutters and the Montagnard tribes that lived in the mountains, Leatherneck Square was virtually devoid of noncombatants.[1]

---

[1]Most of the Montagnards in Northern I Corps were Bru, an aboriginelike tribe of small and primitive mountain people. Some had served as mercenaries with the French, and many of them were helpful to us, especially as intelligence gatherers. The Bru men loved to go out on patrols with us, and after one successful ambush they prepared a victory feast where the Chef's Special featured the brains of a freshly killed monkey in its original container. I didn't want to insult our hosts, but I begged off. You have to draw the line somewhere.

Maybe this was why we didn't see many morale problems in Leatherneck Square. I never knew of anyone using drugs, for example. I'm not saying it didn't happen, especially during R & R or at the rear. But I sure didn't see any of that going on in the field, and I lived on top of those guys. Another thing I never saw was fragging, where enlisted men killed their own officers. I never even *heard* of it until I was back in the States.

The war in the north, in what was called the I Corps Tactical Zone, was fought mostly by Marines who took pride in being lean and mean. We were trained to get the job done quickly, with the lowest possible loss of life. If the Army sent out nine helicopters, we'd do the same operation with three. Because there were fewer of us, we relied extensively on air, artillery, and naval gunfire support from ships off the coast.

We were a proud bunch, with plenty of bravado. It wasn't uncommon to see a guy who had written on his flak jacket, "Yea, though I walk through the Valley of the Shadow of Death, I shall fear no Evil, because I'm the meanest mutha' in the Valley." Nobody else could criticize us, but we had no hesitation about deriding our own institution. There was a swaggering nonchalance that came up whenever a resupply was late, or some anticipated development failed to occur as planned.

Combat stimulates a special kind of profane camaraderie in the men of any unit, and my platoon was no exception. Shortly after I took command, I heard one of the squad leaders tell his men that "Blue" wanted a night ambush at a certain location. Not wanting to question the squad leader in front of his men, I asked Jim Lehnert, my radio operator, who "Blue" was.

Lehnert chuckled. "That's you, sir," he said.

"Why Blue?" I asked.

"Because that's this month's brevity code on the radio. Blue is North, Gray is South, Silver is East, Gold is West."

The name stuck, and within a few weeks the men in

my platoon were calling themselves "Blue's Bastards."

When we weren't actually in combat, we were on the move, always with enormous packs on our backs. To carry something was to "hump" it, and we built up our trapezius muscles from carrying so much for so long. After a long day of humping through the thick, sharp brush, you could barely move your arms and shoulders. When it rained, which was often, the load was even heavier. Even on days where not a shot was fired you went through hell, climbing steep hills in terrible heat, or staggering through fields of razor-sharp elephant grass that cut into your elbows and knees while you carried eighty pounds of equipment on your back. We were supposed to be "light infantry," which sounded to me like somebody's sick joke.

In addition to wearing boots, a heavy steel helmet, and a flak jacket, every man carried a web belt with ammo pouches and a large, heavy pack which carried several dozen items, including an E-tool (E for entrenching), a folding shovel used to dig a fighting hole or a latrine; a folding metal can opener; a pocket knife, to cut thread, remove splinters, cut patches for the holes in your uniform, and to slice the green stuff that came in a can and was officially known as "meat." A surefire way to get a laugh was to ask some new guy to read aloud the list of ingredients on the label of one of these cans.

We also carried a hammock, an air mattress, water-purification tablets, malaria pills and flares, and heat tabs—little foil-wrapped ovals, like solid Sterno, to heat food. Plus bug juice (military-issue mosquito repellent); it smelled like death and burned your skin, but it worked. Salt tablets, because we sweated so much. A sewing kit, because your clothes got ripped, and a first-aid kit, because your body did too. A poncho and a poncho liner, because nights were chilly, even in the summer. Fifteen M-16 magazines with rounds. Six hand grenades. Three or four full canteens. A half dozen rations. One mortar round. Half a bag of plastic explosives.

Everybody carried letters from home. Most men had pocket Bibles, courtesy of Chaplain Bedingfield. Big Dan Doan, the tallest of the forty-three men in our platoon, humped a handmade machete whose blade was made from a car spring. It was heavy, but Dan was strong enough to swing it as he hacked through the brush.

Everyone carried some small personal item: cigarettes, paperback books, a lock of your girlfriend's hair, photographs, homemade cookies, extra socks. I carried laminated photographs of Betsy, my parents, my sister, and my brothers. I wore a St. Francis medal that Grandma Clancy had given me, along with a crucifix from my father, and his Hamilton watch from World War II. The watch made it all the way through Vietnam until just before the end, when the crystal was shattered by the concussions of a mortar round hitting near my hole. I also carried a strobe light to signal helicopters and air strikes at night.

Jim Lehnert, Smitty, and the other radio operators humped PRC-25 radios with three or four extra batteries—each one the size and weight of a brick. The medical corpsmen, like Doc Conklin, carried a canvas satchel called a Unit One, filled with morphine, saline solution for treating shock, malaria tablets, battle dressings, tape, gauze pads, antibiotics, an eye kit, a breathing tube, and a large needle to poke a hole for a tracheotomy. Machine-gunners like Randy Herrod and Ernie Tuten carried a basic load plus their M-60 machine guns and ammo. M-79 grenadiers like Ev Whipple carried eighteen pounds of additional ammunition on top of the standard load.

There was no such thing as a fat Marine—not only from all that exercise, but because we didn't eat very much. We generally ate only twice a day, because if you stopped for lunch you might not be around for dinner. A guy could break out his rations on a rest break—but only if his buddy was holding his weapon at the ready.

Wendell Thomas, a typical infantryman, lost eighteen pounds in a matter of weeks. I dropped down to 140.

There were four items you carried everywhere: your weapon, ammo, grenades, and hot sauce. An experienced field Marine could take a few cans of C-ration chow and turn it into something almost edible. Food was incredibly important in Vietnam, and when time allowed, some guys would spend twenty or thirty minutes preparing a little feast. It became a ritual, a small, special moment of pleasure. You'd take an onion from a care package, dice it carefully with your pocket knife, pour the liquid out of a can of beef stew, add in some cheese and onions and hot sauce and a little black pepper, and *voilà*—the frugal gourmet.

My own favorite was turkey loaf, which was one of the few items you could eat hot or cold. My idea of heaven in Vietnam was a can of turkey loaf and a warm Black Label beer. (Cold beer was unheard of.) More often, though, you'd end up with a dish known as ham and mutha's—lima beans covered in a greenish sludge that had to be heated. I don't want to get overly graphic here, so let's just say this was not high-quality meat.

Within a few weeks, the three lieutenants in the company—Rich O'Neill, Bill Haskell, and I—became very close. Before long we had all become a little too casual, in part because our resupply situation was terrible. I was carrying a Swedish submachine gun after the one I was issued was run over by a tank. I humped an NVA-issue pack, and some of my guys were even wearing NVA trousers. By January I was also sporting a fairly impressive handlebar mustache.

That all ended one afternoon when I was out on a patrol and Haskell called me on the radio. "Blue," he said, "you better get your ass back here right away."

When we returned to the camp, an officer I had never seen before was addressing the rest of my men. He was a well-built, mean-looking guy with closely cropped reddish-blond hair who didn't look like a happy camper.

When I got a little closer, I noticed he was a captain. He was walking up and down, banging his helmet against his leg and delivering some sort of lecture. I walked up behind him and saluted. "Captain," I said, "Lieutenant North."

He turned around slowly, just like in the movies, and then glared at me. "Maybe you didn't notice, Lieutenant, but I was addressing my troops."

"I beg to differ, sir," I replied, "but I believe these are *my* troops."

"Come over here, Lieutenant," he said. We walked around behind the formation, where he leaned right into me and said, "My name is Goodwin. I'm the new company commander. You've got fifteen minutes to take a shower, cut your hair, and get a shave. Then get your butt over to my hooch."

"A shave?"

"The mustache goes, Lieutenant."

At first, O'Neill, Haskell, and I were dismayed that this tough-talking big shot had rolled in and taken over our happy band of warriors. But once we saw Goodwin in action, we quickly changed our minds. Within a day or two, the supplies we had been requesting for weeks suddenly materialized: new uniforms, boots, ammo, grenades, first-aid kits—the whole works. This quickly endeared Goodwin to all of us as a guy who really knew his stuff.

"He knows his stuff" was the greatest compliment you could give a guy in combat. It didn't just refer to his fighting abilities, but included his technical and logistical skills. A lot of men could fight, but Goodwin could also arrange a resupply when you needed it, bring in an air strike in the nick of time, or get a med-evac quickly for a wounded man. I learned a lot from him, and from the close attention he paid to details: how to place a claymore mine, how to maintain radio discipline, how to use every spare moment for training. Vietnam has been portrayed as an ad hoc war, but in the north, at least, the units that performed well worked their butts off. With Goodwin, you never just sat on your pack to wait for the next order.

A memory of Goodwin: We were on a routine patrol, slowly making our way up a steep mountain trail. The platoon paused for a moment, and I stood there, idly pulling leaves off a bush, and deep in thought about the wonderful letter I had just received from Betsy: the doctor had confirmed that she was pregnant.

By now Goodwin and I were close friends. He came up behind me and said, "How's it going?"

"Fine."

"What's new at home?"

"Lots," I whispered, not looking up. "Betsy's going to have a baby."

Goodwin leaned over my shoulder and said, "You can tell that from the *leaves*?"

If I seem to be focusing on the lighter side of my war experience, that may be because so much of what we did in Vietnam was an exercise in frustration. You'd take a hill and move on, and three days later you'd have to come back and fight again over the same piece of ground because there weren't enough troops to occupy it. It wasn't like World War II, where each battle had a distinct beginning and an end. This war had little sense of movement or progress: it began when your plane landed in Da Nang, and it ended when you left the country—preferably not in a body bag.

We were angry at the politicians back in Washington who set the rules, who made us risk our lives while putting up with enormous obstacles. One of our biggest frustrations was the DMZ—the so-called demilitarized zone on either side of the Ben Hai River, which marked the border between North and South Vietnam. Despite its name, the DMZ was probably the least demilitarized place in all of Vietnam. Although the area was crawling with soldiers of the North Vietnamese Army, we were allowed to fire into the DMZ only if fired upon. We were occasionally allowed to pursue the enemy inside, but this required written permission from God and several of the Apostles.

Shortly after I arrived in-country, and before Goodwin became our company commander, our unit was shipped south to An Hoa, a Marine base west of Da Nang. Here, too, our mission was to cut off enemy supply lines, only this time in the mountains along the Laotian border. It was the same story as the DMZ. All the enemy had to do was pull back across the border, and we weren't allowed to follow them.

This operation, known as Taylor Common, took place along the edge of the Ho Chi Minh Trail. Despite its name, the Ho Chi Minh Trail was anything *but* a trail: it was actually a large and complex looping network of roads, bicycle paths, foot trails, and even highways. Even with constant bombing attacks, we were never able to destroy more than a small part of it. And regardless of the damage our planes were able to wreak, most of the men, weapons, and supplies continued moving through to the south. The enemy made good use of Soviet-supplied radar and antiaircraft weapons, and to avoid them, our planes had to fly either very high or very low—and very fast, too—all of which made most bombing missions less than accurate. There was no such thing as a surgical air strike.

It sounded so simple: if we dropped enough bombs on the Ho Chi Minh Trail, the NVA wouldn't be able to continue the war. But one thing the American public never really understood was that the North Vietnamese, with the help of their Soviet-bloc allies, had a work force of something like three hundred thousand men and women who did nothing but repair the railroad tracks, roads, and bridges that we bombed. If a dirt road was destroyed, they'd rebuild it within hours. If we hit five trucks during the night, they'd push them off the road so fifty more could drive by.

Sometimes we could actually hear the NVA trucks at night, but it was almost impossible to stop them. Even a five-hundred- or thousand-pound-bomb, the most common ordnance dropped on the Ho Chi Minh Trail, makes a crater not much bigger than a double bed. It knocks down a few trees and blows the leaves off a few more, but that's about it. Ten minutes later, fifteen guys would show up with shovels to fill in the hole, and the trucks kept rolling.

During the Taylor Common operation, each action began with B-52 strikes on the area we were moving into. Then a reconnaissance team would go in to ensure that the hilltop in question was clear. Only then would our seventy-man unit rappel out of helicopters and snake down a rope with a sixty-five-pound pack on our backs.

We had two days to prepare a landing zone for the troops that followed. We'd start with a chain saw and demolitions, and as soon as we had cleared enough space we'd call in a CH-53 helicopter which brought in a small bulldozer. We'd flatten the hilltop and dig little revetments all around the edge for artillery pieces and a small communications trench. It was hard, fast work because another unit was on the way and was counting on us to finish by the time they arrived. As soon as we were done, the helicopters would come in to get us so we could move on and do the very same thing all over again on another hilltop, further west. We'd leave behind little signs reading NOW THAT YOU'RE HERE, THIS IS THE REAR—an irreverent dig at those with the easier jobs.

At first there was no sign of the enemy. Then the rains began, creating a fog as thick as the clouds. Now we had to operate without air cover or helicopter support, which meant that we soon ran low on food, ammunition, and medical supplies. At one point it got so bad that we went five days with nothing to eat except crackers, candy bars, and bamboo shoots.

On the fifth day, one of Bill Haskell's men ambushed and shot a wild boar. Despite the monsoon downpour, we managed to build a fire and cook it over a spit. But while the meat solved the hunger problem, the smell and the smoke gave away our position. And that wasn't all: several of the men, including Haskell, came down with trichinosis and were eventually evacuated.

We needed almost everything, including new uniforms; ours had been worn through at the knees and elbows. Our boots were in such bad shape that we had to use medical adhesive tape to hold them together. Going more than a few days without an airdrop of the basic necessities of life was a new and alarming situation, and it demoralized us all. John Rappuano, our commander at the time, tried his best, but there was nothing he or anyone else could do about the weather. Resupply was something we had always taken for granted, but suddenly we were on our own.

It was during this dismal period on the Taylor Common operation that Johnson got killed. I didn't actually see him get shot; that happened in the confused darkness as two listening posts clashed with an NVA probe of our little mountaintop perimeter. I heard the crack of Marine M-16s, the deeper, slower firing of NVA AK-47s, and then the louder bursts from our M-60 machine gun. In the midst of the shooting came the scream—like the cry of an animal—when Johnson was hit, followed by that blood-chilling call, "Corpsman! Corpsman up!"

It took only a few minutes for Doc to crawl forward, but it felt like forever. Then came the quiet fury as they peeled off Johnson's flak jacket and cut away his uniform. The bullets had struck him in the chest and the shoulder, and he was soaked with blood.

Using a poncho to hide the glare of his flashlight, Doc tried to stop the flow of blood and the gurgling from the sucking chest wound. He also started an IV for shock before pulling Johnson back for further treatment. Meanwhile, the enemy withdrew to the west, leaving the soaking jungle full of night sounds and blackness.

They pulled Johnson to the closest fighting hole inside the perimeter—mine. Doc was working furiously to save him, until he turned to me in total frustration and said, "Lieutenant, unless we get a med-evac in here fast, he won't make it."

As I got on the radio to call for help, it started to rain again—a steady downpour from the clouds hanging low over the treetops. Battalion called back and said the bird would try, although the weather made it doubtful. The airfield, twenty miles to the east, was completely socked in.

I crawled back into my hole, and with my back against the radio on Jim Lehnert's back, I sat with Johnson's head cradled in my lap. The chopper had to turn back even before we heard its rotor blades. The pilots did their best, flapping around in the soup for close to half an hour, but it was impossible. When they called on the radio with the bad news, I cursed them, along with the clouds, the rain, the enemy—everything. I prayed that God would spare Johnson's life.

It took him almost an hour to die. At one point he seemed to awaken, and looked up at me. He shuddered a few times, and I wrapped my poncho liner around him to keep him warm. I caressed his cheek and kept whispering to him, trying to encourage both of us: "We'll get you out, hang in there, this is your ticket home, God won't let you die." But He did.

When a man dies in your arms it makes you feel very small. Maybe doctors and pastors eventually get used to that feeling, but I find that hard to imagine. When Johnson was pressed up against me, with no breath, no heartbeat, no tears, nothing, I felt ashamed to be alive. I did what he could no longer do. I cried.

He died right in front of me, lying there in the rain. It was one of the very worst moments of my life. I almost got sick—with fear, with shock, and undoubtedly with gratitude that I had survived.

Johnson wasn't from my platoon. His listening post had been in the line of fire from our own machine guns. His team leader, confused in the darkness, had placed the listening post in the wrong location. When the enemy probed our position, Johnson was right in the path of the designated fire from our M-60 machine gun. The bullets that hit Johnson had been made in America; he was hit by friendly fire.

For the rest of my time in Vietnam, and in the Marine Corps, Private First Class Johnson served as a constant reminder to me. I used to tell my sergeants (and later on, my lieutenants and junior officers), "If you don't understand what you're supposed to do, *ask!* War is confusing enough. If you keep me informed as to what you're doing, where you're doing it, and how it's going, we can get the job done and prevent a lot of casualties."

We carried Johnson's body in a poncho, along with several wounded men who normally would have been flown right out of there, and whom we transported in litters made from ponchos and trees. It's awful to carry your wounded—awful for them, because they aren't getting proper treatment, and awful for the rest of the unit, because it slows you down terribly and makes you more vulnerable to the enemy. You get old very fast.

And yet the extraordinary thing about Vietnam was how quickly a wounded man could get medical attention—most of the time. Most Marines who were hurt were treated within minutes, and you'd have an IV in your arm even before the helicopter arrived. It wasn't uncommon for an injured man to find himself in surgery in less than half an hour, and because we all knew that, it helped morale tremendously. The doctors, corpsmen, and nurses did a heroic job in Vietnam, saving so many men who would have died, who *did* die in other wars.[2]

This was one area where I had enormous admiration for the North Vietnamese Army. Most of our sick or wounded were evacuated within half an hour, but their soldiers were weeks away from any serious medical treatment. Inside the DMZ they had built formidable underground bunker complexes, including hospital facilities. But they weren't equipped for major surgery, and they didn't come from a medically sophisticated society to begin with.

Still, they went through hell to get their people treated. You couldn't help but admire their bravery, bringing the battle to us while knowing their casualties would not be treated for weeks, and that many of their wounded would die. Even in the shock and violence of an ambush, the NVA always made a noble effort to drag their wounded or dead off the field.

When we captured wounded enemy soldiers, they were treated in the same hospital as our troops. There were occasional incidents of abuse, when NVA prisoners were turned over to the South Vietnamese. But these were the exception, not the rule. Captured enemy troops were given a choice: they could remain in POW camps or they could join us as scouts. Many of them decided to defect.

One of our best scouts was Phu, a former NVA corporal who had been wounded and captured near Khe San in 1967. Phu spent a lot of time with my unit, and taught me a lot about our enemy. I hadn't realized, for example, that when NVA troops came across the DMZ, or crossed the border from Laos, they weren't even told they were in South Vietnam. As far as they knew, Vietnam was all one country, and we were the aggressors.

When we captured a prisoner, Phu would often begin the interrogation. We had to keep an eye on him, though, because he had a tendency to be cruel. There

---

[2]While I was working on this book, I watched several episodes of the magnificent PBS documentary on the Civil War. I was struck by the number of soldiers on both sides who died from lack of medical attention and medical knowledge. Just about anyone who received more than a superficial wound during the Civil War was dragged off the battlefield, tossed into a wagon, and left to die.

were some critical questions that had to be asked immediately: are you alone, or are there two hundred more NVA just over the ridge? Are there any mines in the area? Is there an ambush waiting for us?

I never witnessed any brutal treatment of prisoners, although I'm sure it happened. But to a large extent the NVA themselves made it unnecessary. They had been told such ludicrous and hideous stories about what would happen if they were captured that this alone gave them a big incentive to cooperate.

When Taylor Common ended, we were ordered back north to conduct operations to push back enemy units who were moving into Leatherneck Square. We began an aggressive series of reconnaissance and combat patrols to keep the enemy off guard and to cut off their infiltration routes. We went out looking for trouble, and more often than not, we found it.

On one of these patrols, my platoon left Con Thien with two tanks and four M-111 armored personnel carriers that the Army had loaned to us. About five kilometers out, one of the tanks lost a tread, so I left two of the APCs and some of the men to guard it. With the other tank and the two remaining APCs, we proceeded east. Early in the afternoon we received an order to turn back due to heavy enemy movement ahead and increasingly bad weather. As we headed back, the tank was in the lead and I was riding on the back; behind us were two APCs and the rest of our troops.

Suddenly, a lone NVA soldier appeared out of nowhere and started hosing down the back of our tank with his AK-47. The men in the APC right behind us couldn't fire at him without the risk of hitting those of us on the back of the tank. I grabbed my shotgun and started shooting. Just then, dozens more of the enemy opened up with small-arms fire and rockets, hitting our tank and both APCs. I don't think they had intended to ambush us here, but once this guy started firing they all opened up. Almost instantly one of the APCs struck a mine and came to a halt.

From the back of the tank I directed the men to set up a defensive perimeter in the brush around the three armored vehicles. As I stood there directing traffic and dodging bullets, and trying to call in for help on the radio, the front of the tank was hit by an RPG. The two or three men who were with me quickly jumped off. I was reloading my shotgun when the turret swung around and batted me into the air like a baseball. I landed in the bushes, badly hurt, with the radio handset still in my hand. Unfortunately, the rest of the radio was back on the tank.

The pain was just terrible. Four of my ribs were cracked, and my left lung was filling with blood. The next thing I knew, Doc Conklin was on top of me, trying to rip off my flak jacket to find the bullet hole. I kept trying to get up, but Doc kept pushing me down. Every time I tried to talk, all I got was a mouthful of blood.

"It must be a fragment," he kept saying. But Doc didn't realize that I hadn't been hit, and I wasn't able to tell him. Besides, we were in danger of being overrun. We had rolled right into an NVA perimeter, and they were shooting us from all sides.

Somehow I had to get back to the tank to retrieve the radio. I eventually made it, and started calling in artillery and air strikes.

We established strong enough fire support to break the ambush, and after about forty minutes, the enemy withdrew. But we had suffered substantial losses. Out of fifteen men, two were killed and twelve were wounded. But under the circumstances, our guys had performed incredibly well. We had practiced drills on what to do if we were ambushed, and the men had handled themselves just as they were trained. The only thing we hadn't rehearsed was what to do when the lieutenant ends up as a deep line drive into right field.

I had lost a fair amount of blood, and was drifting in and out of consciousness. Conklin was beside himself with worry until an army helicopter came to pick me up. At the time I was more concerned about my men. I wasn't trying to be a hero, but there were other casualties and I didn't yet realize how badly I was hurt.

I was flown to the medical station at Dong Ha and taken immediately to triage, a large open area in a tin-roofed hut where doctors and corpsmen made life-and-death decisions as wounded men came off the helicopters. As I lay there on the stretcher, I could hear the doctors talking: "Take this guy to surgery, give that one morphine, don't bother with him." Suddenly I saw a familiar face: Father Jake Laboon, who had been our chaplain at Annapolis, and who used to visit me after the car accident. He was now the chaplain for the Third Marine Regiment.

"Listen up," he told me. "I want you to look real perky." Taking out a sweat-covered handkerchief, he wiped the blood off my face. When the doctor came to see me, Laboon piped up, "Looks pretty good, Doc, but I think he should be looked at right away."

"Okay, take him in."

Laboon used to kid me afterward that he saved me from being left out there to rot.

Instead of operating, the doctors inserted a needle between my lung and my rib cage, and hooked it up to a vacuum pump until the lung was working again. Then they wrapped me up and put me on drugs for a few days.

Soon I found myself in a hospital ward, lying in a bed with real sheets on it. Sheets! A pillow! There was even an air conditioner. This was an inflatable field hospital, which is a great idea unless the generator quits and the roof slowly collapses in on you like a gigantic balloon with a tiny leak. I got plenty of sleep in the hospital, and enjoyed hot water showers and real food. You can bounce back pretty quickly when you're young and eager, and I was back to the platoon a few days later. Normally they send injured men back to the rear, but my unit was on perimeter security duty at Con Thien, which wasn't too strenuous.

Les Shaeffer, who was killed in that same operation, was posthumously awarded a Bronze Star for taking over a machine-gun position after he was wounded on the lead APC. Doc Conklin was given a medal for saving several lives. Pete Rich, the tank platoon commander, was given a Bronze Star, and so was I.

There is a tendency in war to pray to God that you'll survive in the middle of the battle, and to blame Him afterward if one of your buddies didn't make it. After Shaeffer died, a lot of the men were terribly upset. Les had been a respected and extremely well-liked squad leader, and we all felt his loss. A few days after he was killed, one of our men was just lying there, staring off into space, while a couple of others were sitting on the ground with their packs up against ammo crates, talking softly and tossing pebbles in front of them.

I walked over and sat down. "What's wrong?" I said, although I already knew.

"Shaeffer. Man, there's no reason for that."

These guys had been in his squad. They had counted on each other day and night. Why him? they wanted to know. Why not some other jerk? Why anybody?

"He's in a better place now," I said.

"F--k, man, don't give me that. If there is a God, why does this happen? Just *look* at all this shit. He was wasted."

I believe in a merciful God, but I didn't have an answer. And although I know Him better today, I still don't. The only true response I could give at such a moment was to say, "I don't know. All I know is that God is ultimately in control, and that you can't let this make you lose your faith in Him."

Certainly the Scriptures helped. We often read the Twenty-third Psalm, which is a comfort in so many terrible situations. And a passage from Psalm Ninety-one seemed especially pertinent in Vietnam. Years later it again took on special significance:

You will not fear the terror of night,
nor the arrow that flies by day,
Nor the pestilence that stalks in darkness
nor the plague that destroys at midday.
A thousand may fall at your side,
ten thousand at your right hand;
but it will not come near you.

Occasionally one of the men would say, "Maybe God doesn't *want* us to be over here. Wasn't Jesus the Prince of Peace?"

If I had a Bible handy, I would open it to Matthew 8:5–13. Otherwise, I'd tell the story in my own words. A Roman centurion approaches Jesus. "My servant is dying," he says. "Can you help him?"

"Yes," says Jesus, "I'll come and heal him."

"No," says the soldier, "don't come to my house. I'm a military man, and I'm not worthy of your visit. Can't you say the word and heal him from here?"

Whereupon Jesus announces to His followers, "I have not seen such great faith in all of Israel." And the servant is healed.

"Notice what Jesus does *not* say," I would tell the men. "He doesn't tell the centurion, 'I'd really love to help, but I don't do soldiers.' He doesn't say, 'Before I heal your servant, I want you to lay down your sword and renounce Caesar.' Instead, Jesus says, 'This guy comes from the occupying army, and yet *he's* the one with faith. What's wrong with the rest of you characters?'"

Don Dulligan, another chaplain, had taught me this passage after a terrible incident west of Con Thien, where one of our engineers had tried to remove an unexploded white phosphorus mortar round from the edge of our perimeter. As he carefully picked it up, it detonated in his hands—burning the skin off the entire front of his body. It was by far the most gruesome thing I saw in Vietnam. As the med-evac chopper came down to get him, he turned to us and said, "Now you all pray for me, because I'm not going to make it." He showed no bitterness or rancor—only an acceptance of death, which came, as he knew it would, later that day.

The worst battle of all was the night Captain Mike Wunsch was killed. It was July, and we were on a big armored sweep west of Con Thien. The night air was chilly when Captain Goodwin sent out First Platoon to ambush the approaches to the hilltop. Third Platoon went north, while my men were ordered to establish a perimeter with the company of tanks under Captain Wunsch.

A little after 0230, one of my men awakened me to report that our listening post had detected movement. I climbed up on the tank with Mike Wunsch and we both looked through his starlight scope to see half a dozen NVA troops silently ascending on the north side of the draw. Those we could see were less than fifty yards away, and others were undoubtedly close behind. I had to alert my men immediately before the enemy launched its attack.

I never got the chance. Just as I turned away from Mike, an RPG round hit the tank's cupola and detonated. Mike was killed instantly and I was blown off the tank. Had I waited just one more second, I would have been a goner.

As it was, the blast threw me about ten feet, shredding the back of my flak jacket and peppering my legs, buttocks, and neck with fragments. Even my ears had little holes through them.

I blacked out. The next thing I knew, somebody was dragging me on my back. Randy Herrod, the machine-gun team leader, had climbed out of his hole and was risking his life to drag me to safety.

Despite the explosions around me, and the sky ablaze with orange and yellow tracer rounds, and the roar of the tank cannons and fifty-caliber machine guns, everything seemed to be happening at low volume. My eardrums, which had almost healed from a previous injury, were blown out again. Herrod threw me into his hole and stood over me, firing his machine gun as the NVA swept up the side of the hill behind a barrage of mortar fire and a hail of RPGs. I tried to push him off so I could get out and recover the radio. The only reason I succeeded is that Herrod left his hole again—this time to remount the M-60, which had been blown off its mount by an exploding grenade.

The air was thick with fire and smoke. Two of our tanks were burning, lighting up our position and silhouetting the infantry positions between them. With two tanks out of action, the west side of the perimeter was vulnerable. The only reason they hadn't broken through was Herrod's steady hand on the machine gun.

I climbed out of the hole and dashed to the back of the command tank. The radio was a shattered wreck, so I sprinted to the next tank and got on the infantry phone. The tank commander rotated his turret and adjusted his fire across our front, cutting down the first wave of the NVA attack.

There was a sudden lull as the tank's volley did its brutal job. The enemy fell back momentarily, regrouped, and fired another salvo of mortars and RPGs. An incoming round landed beside me and blew me into the air. For the second time in half an hour, Herrod left the protection of his fighting position, grabbed me by the remnants of my flak jacket, and again dragged me to safety.

The second NVA wave broke off under fire from Herrod's machine gun and the remaining tanks. I crawled out again, found Lehnert and a working radio, and started trying to adjust the air support that Goodwin had already summoned. Because I couldn't hear a thing, Lehnert passed the instructions to the aircraft and shouted to me as the pilots rained death from the heavens to break the third and final attack of the night.

It was over before dawn. Our line had held, but just barely. The carnage was awful. The tankers suffered our highest casualties; restricted to a fixed perimeter, they had been unable to maneuver. For the enemy it was far worse. Despite their strong initial assault, only a handful had survived. They had died in heaps from our tanks and machine guns. Before the sun rose over the battlefield, the survivors had melted away to die elsewhere, to be buried in unmarked graves, or to fight another day.

Shortly after first light, our choppers came in to evacuate the wounded and remove the dead. We stacked the weapons of the dead into nets: AK-47s and RPGs from the enemy, and M-16s from our side. These were flown out last. Then we buried the enemy dead and placed thermite grenades in the two most damaged tanks, abandoning them to the rust and the elements.

I put Randy Herrod in for a medal, and he was later awarded the Silver Star. During the attack, he had saved our entire position. Instead of hunkering down in the hole, he remounted the M-60 and spent the better part of the night repelling concerted attacks against us. He was a tall, scrawny kid from Oklahoma, a brave and natural leader who saved my life twice that night. I owed him a tremendous debt, and before the war was over I would have a chance to repay it.

Not all of Vietnam was chaos, carnage, and cries for help. There were some wonderful moments as well. One of mine occurred when we were out in East Boondock and a message came in over the radio: "Congratulations, Lt. North. You have just become the father of a seven-and-a-half-pound baby girl." Goodwin arranged for a helicopter so I could fly back to the rear and call Betsy on a MARS telephone.[4]

It took hours, but I finally got through. It's strange to talk to your wife in that situation, because although

---

[3]MARS (Military Affiliated Radio Station) is a network of ham operators who use their shortwave radios to broadcast messages on behalf of military personnel overseas.

you've been apart for months, there's no privacy. The operators have to listen in, and I bet those guys have heard some of the deepest emotions ever expressed— and some of the raciest lines ever spoken.

Betsy was still in the hospital, because in those days new mothers were allowed to stay more than a few hours after the delivery. The conversation was a little stilted, not only because of the operators, but also because we each had to say "over" whenever we finished talking so they'd know when to stop transmitting. And every time Betsy said "over," she started laughing.

The happiest days of my tour came near the end of my year in Vietnam, during a week of R & R with Betsy in Hawaii—which was as far east as military personnel were allowed to travel. Betsy had left our baby daughter with her sister, and we must have had the highest hotel phone bill in Honolulu as she called home every day to check on little Tait, this new member of my family whom I hadn't even met. Betsy cried a couple of nights because this was her first separation from the baby. I couldn't really understand her tears. Betsy was already a mother, but I wasn't yet a father; at the time, I only barely knew what it meant to be a husband. It didn't occur to me then that Betsy had already spent far more time with Tait than she had with me.

Looking back on that fantastic week, I remember macadamia nut pancakes. Showers. Milk. Swimming. Real bread. Milkshakes. Fresh vegetables and real salads. More milk. Fresh fruit. More milkshakes. Dry socks. Sleeping in a real bed. Newspapers! A radio. More milk. Shoes instead of boots. No uniforms. Clean clothes. More milk. No mosquitoes. More milk.

Somebody told me later that the weather in Hawaii was awful, but I didn't even notice. We walked on the beach and drove to see a volcano, but mostly we spent hours just sitting quietly together and talking, sharing memories all the way from our tearful and premature farewell in San Diego until our reunion that very week. I read through a big pile of letters from everybody in my family, and looked at stacks of pictures of Tait. It finally began to dawn on me me that I was a father. I had received a few baby pictures in the mail, but Betsy arrived with hundreds more, and she brought them to life with her stories. She also brought a picture of my pal Bob Eisenbach, still recovering from his war wounds and wearing a football helmet to protect his head. He was sitting in a wheelchair, in his bathrobe—and holding my little girl.

It was a glorious time, with no phone calls to return, no errands to run, and no plans except being together and trying to catch up on each other's lives from the past few months. But oh, what a tearful parting. It was one thing to go off to war having never seen combat. But to return to the war, having seen men die in front of you—*that* was hard.

Normally, all communication between home and Vietnam came through the mail, which was why we lived and died for letters and packages. The great occasions in the field were when a resupply mission brought in not only food and ammo, but those red and yellow mail sacks. Mail was our link to home, and we treasured it.

I used to read each letter at least five times, and that wasn't unusual. You'd break out a letter and read it again at the oddest times, trying to squeeze out an extra drop of information or affection. Even if the news wasn't all good, at least the mail gave you something to focus on aside from your wet boots. A letter might be filled with the most trivial, mundane details, and your mother, your wife, or your brother might apologize for having nothing "interesting" to say, but they couldn't imagine how wonderful it was to receive a letter, any letter, and to know that somebody back home was thinking of you and wanted you back.

Letters were so vital to the morale of the troops that

if any of our guys weren't receiving mail, I'd notify the chaplain. When a guy got hit and you went through his gear for inventory, it wasn't unusual to come across a huge wad of forty or fifty letters.

A care package was always welcome. Betsy used to send M&M candies; I don't recall having any special fondness for them before Vietnam, but I have loved them ever since. Homemade cookies were a great treat, along with birthday cakes. Occasionally, these cakes even arrived in one piece, but regardless of their condition, they disappeared instantly.

Sending letters was almost as important as receiving them. Not that we needed any encouragement, but it was a good feeling to write FREE where the stamp would normally go and know that your letter was on its way. We usually wrote home in the late afternoon, after digging in for the night. I wrote many a letter with my poncho pulled over my head, especially if the mail bird was coming early in the morning. Often the paper was so wet you had to write very lightly, so it wouldn't tear. If you didn't have paper you used the back of a C-ration carton.

Our letters home were filled with plans for after the war, which was a way of focusing beyond our immediate concerns, such as whether the resupply would arrive in time, or whether we'd be ambushed, or whether we'd stay alive until tomorrow. I wrote often to Betsy and my parents, although I didn't tell Betsy about my various injuries because I didn't want her to worry. That was a serious mistake, and I still haven't heard the end of it.

We used to refer to home as "the world," as in "He's gone back to the world." It was as if we were living on a different planet, and I suppose we were. My unit was in Vietnam during the 1969 moon landing, and while we certainly heard the news, I didn't get around to seeing the television pictures until ten years later, during a visit to the Air and Space Museum in Washington.

It's funny, the things you remember. I don't think of myself as a complainer, or as being especially susceptible to fear. And I've already noted my marvelous ability to recall the good parts of life and blot out the bad. But in writing this book, I looked through some of the letters I sent home to my parents from Vietnam in 1968 and 1969, and a few of the lines jumped out at me:

- "Last night I spent six hours just waiting for the firing to stop. Of course it was our own counter-battery fire—outgoing! Who was the new Lt. with a red face?"

- "I don't really know how much more of the John Wayne stuff I can take. This tour has just about done it."

- "Most of all, I wish the politicians would get off their fat, soft posteriors and come through with something one way or the other to clear this mess up."

- "Don't worry. I have not yet begun to write."

- "I am writing this on an ambush out west of Con Thien. Rather strange in a way, to be sitting out here in the weeds, waiting for Charlie to come along so that we can kill him, and writing to my father while I'm waiting."

- "I sent Betsy a letter explaining this whole operation. The only thing I didn't say is how much of a mess this whole thing really is. We've had two killed and five wounded to date—one guy that got it was right next to me. I never even got scratched."

- "Last night we had two killed when we went out with special forces. It's sickening because they are such good boys and there is so damned little else that can be done."

- "Believe me, I pray every day. Not just for myself, but for getting these Marines home safe."

- "We haven't had any mail for almost two weeks and I think I can understand how Betsy and you all must feel when the letters are sparse in the other direction."

- "I'm glad to be leaving. Not just because it is an escape

from the hell of war—but an escape from the particular hell of this war. An escape from the indecision of fighting an enemy that is allowed a safe harbor from the power of our storm. An escape from the haunted looks of men who have seen their friends and brothers die because they were collectively hamstrung by political gestures and spineless decision-makers. Oh, but it's been a swell war! A grand and glorious reversal of that war almost two hundred years ago when we lost all the battles but won the war, for here we've won all the battles but lost the war."

- "What's all this fuss now? They're half a world away. Let 'em help themselves. And anyway, we only gave our word and 37,000 lives."

The scariest part of combat is to be under "incoming," when you're being hit with indirect fire: artillery, rockets, or mortars. With a mortar, the first thing you hear is the distant sound of something popping in a hollow tube, which means you'd better dive for cover in a hurry. Then, *shhhh-boom!* The time between that first sound and that *shhhh-boom* feels like the longest moment of your life. All you can do is wait to see where it hits—and pray that it doesn't find you as you crouch deeper in your hole and pull the helmet tightly over your head, trying to make yourself as small as possible while you're screaming into the radio for return fire.

*That* is fear. And that's why we wore two sets of dog tags: one around our necks, the other laced into a boot. That way, if your head got separated from your body, you could be identified from your foot. If your foot was missing, well, hopefully your head was still attached. But there were plenty of times when a body could not be identified in the field, and had to wait until the lads in the morgue matched the remains with the medical and dental records.

Commanders had their own fears: you could never be

sure that you weren't inadvertently leading your men into a trap or an ambush. We were hunting the enemy, but they were also hunting us, and you never forgot that every maneuver or patrol might be the last for any number of your men. The very worst thing that could happen to a lieutenant in Vietnam was that all his men could be killed and he would be left alive.

I dealt with my fears through my faith. Trusting in God doesn't mean you take foolish risks; every time somebody shot at me, I ducked. And you've got to have a healthy respect for the consequences of being hit by a bullet, or blown up by artillery. But there's also a lot of truth to the old saying that there are no atheists in foxholes. As a group, Marines are an irreverent lot. And yet there's a real spiritual depth to many of them—and not only when the bombs are falling.

I urged my men to attend chapel services, although most of them didn't need much encouragement. And I developed a lot of respect for the chaplains who worked with us. They would give the Last Rites to a dying Marine, or provide solace for the man who had just lost his best friend and who was desperate to find some meaning amid all the tears, blood, and chaos. And they were the ones who had to answer that most difficult of all questions: if there's a God, how can He let this happen?

One of my tasks as a leader was to help the men separate the legitimate fears from the trivial ones. One night a radio call came in from a squad leader on an ambush. "I've got movement," he said.

"You know what to do," I whispered. A moment later, like clockwork, we heard the rifles, the claymore mines, the machine guns, and the illumination round. Then a long silence. Finally, from way down in the valley, a voice rang out: "Oh, *shit*! Call the lieutenant."

They had killed a bear, and the new battalion commander made them bring it back. He said he wanted proof, but the men all believed that he wanted to make a fur coat for his wife. They were so angry after lugging the animal back to base that they gutted the bear and buried its entrails next to his bunker, about an inch deep. The stench was awful.

What I'm proudest of from Vietnam are not the decorations for heroism, but the fact that I led seventy ambushes and that most of my men came home alive. "I have one goal here," I'd tell the troops, "and that's to get the job done and get you guys back home safely."

The key to good military leadership is to make the men feel like they're working *with* you rather than for you. Instead of sitting back and issuing orders, you've got to know every one of their jobs at least as well as they do. No matter how charismatic you might be, nobody in uniform will follow you unless they're convinced that you know what you're talking about. Each member of your platoon has to believe that if he does what you tell him, he will survive an otherwise unsurvivable experience.

To improve the odds, I became a stickler for detail and discipline. I made my men get frequent haircuts so they'd have a better chance of spotting leeches, slugs, ticks, and wounds. I insisted they brush their teeth, because you didn't want a guy lost for three days because of dental problems. They washed their socks once a month, whether they needed to or not. When we came to a stream, we'd set up security so everybody could bathe; the men were in enough danger without the additional risk of illness. The next best thing to heaven was to get back to Con Thien, where somebody had set up a primitive shower which consisted of a hose coming out of a fifty-five-gallon drum. After thirty seconds you'd feel like a new man.

I insisted that my men wear their helmets and flak jackets on all operations and keep them at arm's reach even back in base. Some commanders felt that the troops could move more easily without this heavy armor, and while that was certainly true, some of those men died. My own life was saved several times by my flak jacket when grenades, RPGs, and mortars exploded nearby. In my platoon you even had to sleep with your helmet and flak jacket on. It was hot, it was sweaty, and you stank. But you also lived.

Each man had to carry his gear packed exactly the same way: mortar rounds on top, canteens in the same place on the belt, grenades in the same pocket. I inspected the troops before each patrol and every ambush, and if I saw anything extraneous in a guy's pocket, out it came. A guy who stood out for any reason could end up as a target for snipers.

No chin strap? Get a new helmet. Grenades on your belt? Not in this platoon. Just came off an operation? Clean your rifle. Rest stop? One man cleans his weapon while his partner stands watch.

Training was continual. We'd go back to a fire base, and instead of resting, we'd practice combat formations or ambush drills. Americans are not a patient people, and it takes extraordinary discipline to lie perfectly still on the ground for hours while staying alert. There were times that the enemy was so close that I told the men to be sure they covered up the luminous dials on their watches. It didn't matter if they had been up all night: I was always running drills.

Sometimes I went too far. There were times when I demanded too high a standard from men who couldn't always live up to it. Sometimes I pushed my men too hard, and made them walk a little farther and dig a little deeper and carry a little more than was necessary. And there were times when I was too controlling, when I drove my men crazy by insisting there was a right and a wrong way to do *everything*. "If you took a leak," one guy complained, "North would critique the way you held yourself." He was exaggerating, but not by much.

I was blessed with the ability to motivate people, and I spent countless hours counseling, cajoling, and convincing—talking to the men in twos and threes, and sometimes one at a time—not because they were shirking, but because I was asking so much. The greatest compliment I ever received came after a firefight, when one of the Marines turned to Goodwin and said, "Captain, you should have seen my lieutenant. He was magnificent." It wasn't the word "magnificent" that meant so much. It's what he called me—not "the lieutenant," or "Blue," or "Lieutenant North," but "*my* lieutenant." That was probably the kindest thing anyone ever said about me.

I was warm and supportive when a man was hurt or in trouble, but I could also be a nasty s.o.b. if he screwed up. Jones might have worked twenty hours that day, but if he was supposed to be guarding our position at 0200, he had damn well better be awake. If I came across a man who was asleep in his hole, I'd stand right behind him, undo my chin strap, and bang my helmet against his. That usually did the trick. "You should be real glad I'm not an NVA soldier," I'd tell him when he stopped trembling, "because I would have cut your throat."

If I didn't witness it personally, I might confront the man privately the next day and say, "Smedley, I understand you fell asleep last night. If you do that again, somebody might drop a hand grenade in your hole, and I'll have to send a letter to your mother. Or somebody might drop a hand grenade in Jackson's hole, and it will be your fault, and you're the guy who's going to write that letter to Jackson's mother."

The company gunnery sergeant had a slightly different approach. If he found a man who was sleeping on the perimeter, he would pee into his foxhole.

Whereupon the guy would wake up and say, "Hey, what are you doing?"

This was what the gunny was waiting for. "You awake, Smedley?"

"Yeah."

"So tell me, Smedley, would a guy who's awake let another guy piss on him?"

"I guess not."

"That's right," the gunny would say. "So either I didn't piss on you, or else you were sleeping. If you were, I'll have you court-martialed, and you'll spend six months in the brig. Now, then, did I piss on you?"

"I guess not, Gunny."

Of all my memories of Vietnam, there was one incident that remains as vivid as anything I have ever experienced.

It was after a successful ambush, where we killed three enemy soldiers. We always searched the bodies quickly, grabbing weapons and radios, looking for documents, and collecting the enemy I.D. tags so the Red Cross could notify their families. Then we'd get the hell out of there.

This time one of my men yelled, "Hey Blue, we've got an officer." He could tell by the man's insignia, and by the fact that he'd carried a pistol. I inspected the body myself. Officers were more likely to carry documents, and I wanted to be sure we found everything.

He had been a young, dark-haired, good-looking guy, probably around my own age. The Soviet-made pistol was still in his hand. He had taken a burst of fire in the chest, which killed him instantly. In addition to documents, he was carrying a whole slew of letters wrapped in plastic, just like we did. Later that day, after I had called in a report on the ambush and everybody dug in for the night, I looked through his pack.

Among other things, I found a map and a notebook with names of men in his unit. During my final semester at Annapolis I had taken an optional course in Vietnamese, and my roommate at The Basic School was a Vietnamese Marine lieutenant. I could read the language well enough to see that the dead NVA soldier had also been a lieutenant. There were letters from his wife and his parents, along with a photo of him in his dress uniform and a big smile, posing with his wife and two little kids. He also carried a book of little drawings he had evidently been making for them. There were no scenes of combat, only pictures of mountains, birds, and trees, and little poems he had written to go with them.

It occurred to me—and how could it not?—that had things gone just a little differently a few hours ago, he would have been going through the items in my pack, looking at pictures of Betsy and our little baby. He became real to me at that moment, as it struck me that his family would never see him again, and would probably never even know the circumstances of his death.

I have thought about him a few times since, and while I don't recall crying that day, I still find it hard to tell this story without a lump in my throat. Whenever one of our men was killed, the troops would say he got "wasted." What an appropriate word. There are some deep truths embodied in the slang and jargon of war, and that's certainly one of them.

I was tempted to keep some of the materials from his pack, and then decided no, it was better to make sure it all got back to his wife. I wrote up a report on what happened, adding a few more details than usual in the hope that when it was filed with the Red Cross, his family might eventually learn that he died bravely and quickly, without pain or suffering. I slowly replaced all of his personal material in the pack, including a letter he had started writing to his family, describing how much he missed them. I could have written that letter myself.

I have always wondered about the kind of man who glorifies combat, or who could even consider going to war for money, or adventure. The bravest military men I've known have all hated war, and it was a great general who uttered that famous remark—that war is hell. War changes you forever, and I can't believe that anyone who's ever been to one is eager to go again.

# 6

## A NEW LIFE

AFTER VIETNAM I RETURNED TO QUANTICO AS A TACTICS instructor at The Basic School, where I had been a student just over a year earlier. I was now preparing young lieutenants who would soon be on their way to Vietnam to lead platoons of their own, just as I had. My specialty was patrolling and counterinsurgency tactics for small infantry units—everything from rifle squad combat formations to platoon-sized ambushes.

We would start the course with a few classroom sessions, using slides, films, and a blackboard to explain the theory and dynamics of the operations. To stress the importance of surprise in battle, we instructors would occasionally charge into a classroom without warning, firing blanks from an M-16. This was intended as a graphic reminder that in the war these men would soon be fighting, they and their troops could find themselves under fire at any moment.

After the introductory classroom work, we moved outside for field demonstrations. Some of the training areas at Quantico were remarkably similar to the terrain in Vietnam, which enabled us to replicate authentic battlefield conditions. As the students observed from the bleachers, we would organize a group of enlisted Marines into the appropriate formations for combat, reconnaissance, or ambush patrols. Then we'd take the students on demonstration exercises and walk them through these same maneuvers. We concluded with several days of field training, where we tested the men in a variety of skills. It was hard work, but this was the one place a lieutenant could screw up without getting anyone hurt or killed.

My goal was to turn every mistake into a constructive learning experience. Whenever possible, I'd begin with a positive comment: "You did a good job on that operations order. You deployed your troops well, and your use of supporting arms was excellent."

When it came time to point out the errors, I changed the focus slightly by shifting from the active voice to the passive: "Overall, Jones, you did an excellent job. But during the final objective, the first squad was deployed too far to the left. The base of fire for the machine guns should have been moved farther to the flank." The lesson I wanted the men to remember was not that Jones screwed up, but that the base of fire should have been shifted.

This technique of personalizing the praise while maintaining a certain distance around the criticism was something I had learned from my father, who spoke this way not only with the workers at his wool factory, but also with his children at the dining room table. Later on, when he became a college instructor, he continued this practice. "You took care of the first section perfectly," he would tell a student. "But this is how we should handle the ending." "We"—as if the whole class could have made that same mistake.

I loved teaching, and I enjoyed getting to know the students. There were instructors at Quantico who really knew their stuff, but never bothered to learn the names of the men in their classes. I still can't understand that. The military is full of wonderful leaders, but it also has its share of brusque, impersonal automatons. (And so, I have learned since, does business and government.) I served under some of these types, and they rarely inspired me to do my best.

There's so much that a teacher or a coach can accomplish with just a little personal effort. At the end of a long day, before I went home to my family, I'd sometimes walk through the Bachelor Officers' Quarters just to say hello. "Hi, there, Smedley, how'd it go, today?" People respond to an instructor who cares about them. If a student feels you know him personally, or is aware that you took the trouble to learn his name, he'll usually try a little harder and perform a little better. Granted, I was teaching under ideal circumstances. These guys were all highly motivated and talented volunteers, and it was a joy to work with them.

Because nearly all our students were headed for Vietnam, we kept a close eye on the latest developments in the war. If a new weapon was introduced or a new tactic was tried, we knew about it within days from reading "after action" and "incident" reports from the war. I had been back at Quantico only about three months when I read a particularly gruesome account of a Marine corporal who had been charged with murder in the deaths of sixteen Vietnamese civilians in a village near Da Nang. When I read the defendant's name I practically fainted: the alleged killer was Randy Herrod, the machine-gunner who had saved my life in Vietnam.

As if Herrod wasn't in enough trouble, this incident took place shortly after the infamous My Lai massacre was revealed, with its devastating effect on the public's perception of the U.S. military. The killing of innocent civilians was terrible, but what really infuriated the American public was that several Army officers were accused of having covered up the killings for over a year and a half until the event was exposed in the press. The facts in Randy Herrod's case were in dispute, but with My Lai still fresh in the public mind, the Marine Corps lost no time in making it public.

I couldn't believe Randy was guilty. For one thing, I had trained him better than that. For another, only a coward would murder unarmed civilians, and Randy Herrod was certainly no coward. He had proved that time and again in my platoon, and twice during a single battle he had risked his life to drag me to safety.

But even if Herrod had acted wrongly, which I doubted, I still wanted to help him. Randy Herrod had saved my life, and you don't forget something like that.

In a letter to Gene Stipe, Herrod's defense attorney, I explained that I had been Randy's platoon commander in Vietnam, and that I knew him to be a brave and responsible Marine. If Stipe and his colleagues thought it might help, I added, I would be willing to return to Vietnam to testify at Herrod's trial.

Stipe contacted me the following week to accept my offer. Some of my fellow instructors were less than delighted that I was going to abandon them in the middle of a particularly busy training period. Not only would I be going against the Marine Corps hierarchy, at least implicitly, but these guys would have to take over my teaching assignments. The commanding officer of the Basic School called me down and pointedly asked why this trip was so important. "Okay," he said when I explained the situation. "If you're convinced it's the right thing to do, I'll authorize it." (I needed his permission because military personnel could not return to Vietnam on their own.)

Betsy wasn't exactly thrilled, either. For one thing, she was now pregnant with our second child. For another, the prospect of her husband returning to the war at his own expense, and using his leave time to do it—all this did not strike her as a particularly brilliant course of action. We had been married a year and a half, and I had already spent two-thirds of that time in Vietnam.

When I returned to Vietnam in August 1970, I found that Herrod's situation was even worse than I expected. The My Lai incident had traumatized the entire military, and the word was out all over the base that there would be no cover-up in this case. (This wouldn't be the last time in my life when those around me were motivated less by the facts of the case than by the threatening memory of a previous cover-up.)

A number of the officers I met thought I was crazy. "What? You actually returned to 'Nam on permissive orders?" When I explained that I had flown over to testify at the trial of Private Herrod (he had already been demoted from corporal), the hostility was palpable. One evening I conducted an informal survey among some of the officers, and nearly every man told me the same thing—that Randy Herrod didn't stand a chance. A few days later, I was shocked when Herrod's defense counsel cited my unscientific opinion poll as evidence that a fair trial was not possible. But as I would eventually discover for myself, a good defense lawyer will do everything within the law to protect his client.

Other than what I had learned about courts-martial at The Basic School, I had no experience with legal procedures. But I spent hours in a sweltering hut overlooking Da Nang harbor, discussing Herrod's case with his lawyers. I urged them to object to anyone assigned to the court (the military equivalent of a jury) who wasn't a combat officer or NCO, because only men who had served in combat could appreciate the pressures that Herrod must have been under. In the end, every member of that court was a decorated combat Marine.

Inevitably, there were differing accounts of what had actually transpired on the night of February 19, 1970. According to Herrod, he had been leading a small ambush patrol into the village of Sonthang in the southern part of the First Corps Tactical Zone, which was known to be a Vietcong supply area. When the enemy opened fire with an M-60 machine gun, he ordered his men to shoot back. Several civilians were caught in the cross fire, and others were shot when they appeared to be reaching for weapons.

In my testimony, I explained that the charges of murder against Herrod were totally inconsistent with the qualities I had seen less than a year earlier. I also pointed out that he had been trained in a different war. We saw very few civilians in the northern part of the First Corps Tactical Zone, where the rule of thumb was: it's either us or the NVA, and if it moves in the killing zone of an ambush—*shoot!* In a night ambush, nobody asked questions. But I also recalled an incident on a daylight patrol where Herrod had ordered his machine-gun team not to fire because he wasn't 100 percent sure that what they saw was actually the enemy.

I explained how Herrod had demonstrated his courage again and again, and I described the battle for which he had been awarded the Silver Star. It takes forever for an award to be processed in the Marine Corps, and Herrod's had only just come in. It was now being held up further, pending the outcome of the trial.

When my testimony was finished, I flew back to California. When I landed in San Francisco, I learned that Randy Herrod had been acquitted.

By now a large segment of the American public had turned against the war. We could feel the hostility whenever we left the base at Quantico, and the resentment was particularly strong in and around Washington. It got to the point where the C.O. of The Basic School issued an order that officers going off base should no longer wear their uniforms. Over at Marine headquarters in Arlington, they were now wearing civilian clothes to work.

But even without uniforms, young Marines and other military men were easy to identify: their age, their build, their haircut, and their posture all made them conspicuous during an era when so many of their contemporaries wore long hair and colorful clothes. My students would occasionally tell me of being spit on in Washington, and especially in Georgetown. They used to drive there on weekends in the hope of getting a date, but the antiwar sentiment at most of the local colleges was so strong that many of these guys couldn't even get to talk to a woman. I felt bad for them. I was only a few years older than they were, and while there was plenty of antiwar sentiment when I graduated from Annapolis, it had increased exponentially between 1968 and the early 1970s.

In March 1971, the reputation of the American military took a direct hit when Lieutenant William Calley was convicted of the My Lai murders. From the reaction in some circles, you'd have thought this sort of thing was almost routine in Vietnam, rather than an aberration. At Quantico, West Point, Annapolis, and every other military school in the country, instructors spent hours discussing the proper treatment of civilians in a war zone. I can remember being asked about the Calley incident in class, and telling my students that if the stories we heard were true, Calley deserved the harshest sentence that could be meted out.

In the summer of 1971, Seymour Hersh, the reporter who first broke the My Lai story, came out with a book about the incident in which he suggested that war crimes were commonplace in Vietnam. After Hersh appeared on William F. Buckley's "Firing Line," three of us who taught at Quantico—John Bender, Don Carpenter, and I—wrote a letter to Mr. Buckley, expressing our outrage at Hersh's insinuations.

Not only did Buckley write back, but he invited us to appear on "Firing Line," to discuss the issue. We showed his letter to Col. Bill Davis, our commanding officer, who took it to the commanding general at the base, who took it to Marine headquarters, who said, "Okay, why not?"

We taped the show at American University in Washington. I was struck by Buckley's posture: he slouched so badly that I thought he was about to fall off his chair. I have never been nervous about speaking in public, and the prospect of appearing on any other television show would not have bothered me. But to be interviewed by William F.

Buckley was more than a little intimidating. Should I bring along a dictionary? Not having gone to Yale, I was not incontrovertibly certain that I would comprehend the copious elongated locutions he was inclined to approbate. In the end, I managed to understand most of Buckley's vocabulary and all of his questions.

On the air, the three of us explained that it would be a terrible injustice if everyone who served in Vietnam came home under suspicion of being a "war criminal." We were not there to defend William Calley, or to suggest that war crimes had never occurred. But all three of us had served in Vietnam, in different units and diverse areas, and none of us had even heard about anything like this until we came home. In fact, the vast majority of American units went out of their way to avoid harming civilians, even to the point of endangering their own men.

We taped the show in front of a live audience, and while their questions were tough, only a few were hostile. It was a highly satisfying experience: we had been able to present a different view of our servicemen in the war, and had helped to defend the honor of the military.

Two years later, I came very close to leaving the Marine Corps. I had originally joined up with the intention of becoming a pilot, but at Quantico in 1968 I had opted for the infantry so that I could serve in Vietnam before the war was over. (Little did I imagine how long the conflict would last.) By the time I applied again to Flight School, in 1973, the war was winding down and the maximum age for new pilots had been lowered by two years. Now that I was too old to realize this particular dream, I started looking around for other opportunities.

I applied for a job with EDS, the Texas-based company headed by Ross Perot. EDS had a wonderful reputation, and people said it was the closest you could come to a military environment within the private sector. After submitting my resignation request from the Corps, I received a call from Colonel Dick Schulze, my old battalion commander from Vietnam who was now the aide to the Secretary of the Navy. "We hate to lose you," he said, "but I understand you're interested in EDS. Ross Perot is coming in next week to have lunch with the Secretary, and I'd like you to join us."

I remember being pleased that Schulze wasn't trying to pressure me to remain in the Corps. Or so I thought.

At lunch, Dick Schulze sat with a quiet smile as Perot gave me a thirty-minute lecture on why I should remain in the Marines. He threw in everything: the value of serving your country, patriotism, mom, apple pie, the works. I found him enormously compelling. He would have made a terrific recruiter.

When he was finished, Perot turned to me and said, "Well, what are you going to do?"

By then I was feeling pretty selfish for wanting to leave. "I guess I'm staying," I said.

"Good," he said. "If that's the way you feel—" And here Perot turned to Schulze, who handed him my letter of resignation. Perot gave it to me and said, "Why don't you just tear this up?" Schulze had set up this meeting to keep me in the Marines, and it worked like a charm.

When I look back on my career in the Marines, one of the accomplishments I'm proudest of had nothing to do with combat. In the mid-1970s, when I was working at Marine headquarters, I played a major role in helping to do away with "dependent restricted" tours. This program, in which Marines used to leave their families for an entire year to serve in units in the Western Pacific, had started after World War II as a means of ensuring that Marine units overseas were always ready to deploy. Thirty years later, it was still an integral part of the Corps. Men in other services were allowed to bring their wives and families on extended overseas tours, but Marines were supposed to be tougher than anyone else, and combat-ready. We also had the highest divorce rate in the military.

Over the course of his career, a professional Marine could end up with as many as four or five of these tours, any one of which could wreck his marriage. That's why Marine wives, who had to hold the families together, deserved their own medals. But thousands of marriages *were* ruined, and many men, including some of our finest and most caring officers, left the Corps because of these tours.

My marriage to Betsy survived my dependent-restricted one-year stay in Okinawa—but just barely.

In 1971 I had been promoted to captain, and in late 1973 I was put in charge of the Northern Training Area on Okinawa. I soon had reason to be grateful to Ross Perot, because I couldn't have been happier in my work. In addition to the challenge and the responsibility that I craved, I now had the chance to do all the exciting things the Marine Corps depicts in its recruiting commercials—and without getting killed in the process. We conducted mountain-warfare training, ran jungle-warfare tactics, taught amphibious nighttime raids in rubber boats launched from ships and submarines, rappeled from helicopters, and parachuted with Army and Marine reconnaissance units. We taught survival skills to pilots and air crews, ate snakes and other jungle delights just to impress the new arrivals, and had an absolutely glorious time. It was exhausting and occasionally dangerous, but it was also the most fun I ever had as a Marine. Most of the time I was too busy to think about how much I missed home.

Our mission was to train the combat units on Okinawa in the various warfare skills they would be needing to fight in the jungles of Asia. Although American troops were being withdrawn from Vietnam, our task was to train those who might be called upon to go back in, or worse yet, to conduct evacuations.

The Northern Training Area was a sixty-square-mile

tract of rugged, mountainous terrain at the remote northern end of the island, more than thirty miles by dirt roads from any other base. My small, virtually autonomous training detachment lived at a tiny base camp of Quonset huts and primitive shelters in a clearing hacked out of the jungle. All communication was by radio. Everything about the place was sporadic—electricity, supply and mail deliveries, and even time off. Training continued around the clock, seven days a week, so the only breathing space was when there was no unit aboard. Even then, most of the day was taken up repairing rubber boats, climbing lines, and safety gear.

My staff consisted of former drill instructors. Everyone in the unit was handpicked, and all the lieutenants on Okinawa were men I had trained at The Basic School. Our austere and challenging facilities were practically inaccessible except by helicopter, and we were the toughest guys on the block. There were few complaints about the long hours or the spartan conditions because we were doing the things Marines signed up to do in the first place.

By the late summer, things were running so smoothly that I was able to take some leave. I actually had a chance to fly home and see my family, but like a jerk, I didn't even consider it. Instead, I encouraged Betsy to come to Okinawa so we could spend some time on the island followed by a few days in Tokyo.

Betsy arrived in Okinawa just ahead of a major Pacific typhoon, which meant that we had to postpone and shorten the trip to Tokyo while I returned to the NTA to supervise damage repair from the storm. She came with me, and watched from a distance as we taught the men how to rappel out of a helicopter and down the side of a mountain—a procedure that involves suspending your life on a length of nylon line seven-sixteenths of an inch thick. It was always interesting to see how a tough Marine could be reduced to a quivering mass of jelly by the mere prospect of dangling a hundred and twenty feet in the air by nothing more than that thread.

My staff included some of the most talented NCOs in the entire Marine Corps, all of whom were terribly proud of the fact that they were surviving in this remote place, braving the wild boars and the poisonous Habu snakes, scaling mountains and jumping out of helicopters and persevering in the wilderness.

Until this *woman* showed up.

Somehow, one of the lieutenants convinced Betsy to try rappeling. Without letting her see how high she was, two of the instructors helped her tie in and started her over the cliff, talking her through the procedure. As she stepped over the side, she looked down for the first time. Her voice was remarkably calm. "I don't want to be doing this," she said. It was then that Lieutenant Vince Norako explained that once you began, the only way to go was down.

To provide some encouragement, I tied on the cliff next to her and slid down beside her. This wasn't the ideal time for conversation, but Betsy wondered aloud if I could possibly understand why the mother of two small children, a woman who hadn't seen her husband in months, might not think of this as the perfect vacation. Besides, how could I be so sure that she was going to make it alive to the bottom of the cliff?

I gave Betsy the same answer I had given to so many Marines who had wondered the very same thing: "Trust in the Lord and use good equipment."

When it was over, Betsy said she had found my comment less than convincing, coming, as it did, just as she was wondering exactly how high she would bounce if she slipped off that rope and plunged to her death. I had obviously been gone too long, because I was about to ask her if she wanted to try it again. Instead, I assured her that even one such descent was a real accomplishment. But for years afterwards, Betsy continued to bring it up, saying, "I can't believe you would let me do something like that."

Fortunately, one of my fellow instructors had taken a picture of Betsy rappeling down that cliff. From then on, whenever a trainee faltered, I would pull out that photograph and show it to him, saying, "Well, if this *woman* can do it, you probably can, too."

When we finally got to Tokyo, we were the guests of a close childhood friend of Betsy's mother. I had looked forward to this trip, and had imagined it would be a lot like that marvelous week of R&R in Hawaii, just the two of us hidden from the world. We stayed at the Sanno Hotel, the former headquarters of General Douglas MacArthur during the military occupation of Japan after the war. It was now a military billeting facility, but any hope of conjugal bliss and relaxation was completely sabotaged by our hostess—a sweet and well-meaning old lady who turned out to be tougher than most of the Marines I had left behind on Okinawa. Every morning at dawn she showed up to take us sightseeing until midnight, which turned our brief vacation into an endurance contest. Betsy had traveled halfway around the world, and we hadn't done much more than say hello.

Throughout Betsy's visit I was preoccupied by the rapidly deteriorating situation in Southeast Asia. It was becoming increasingly apparent that unless the United States intervened, as we had promised to do, the Republic of Vietnam would cease to exist. Back on Okinawa we reoriented our training to focus more on evacuation operations, survival skills, escape and evasion, and the like. By this time, all Marine combat units had been pulled out of Vietnam, along with the bulk of American troops. By the fall of 1974, the Third Marine Division was making preparations in case we were sent back in.

I was given orders to select a team of men from the NTA detachment who would train with the Army's Special Forces. Although my own tour of duty was winding down, I included myself on the roster. I was eager to see my family again, but I was also obsessed with developments in Vietnam. Entire Vietnamese units were being overrun, and the Armed Forces Radio Network news was full of foreboding. American citizens and advisers were already being evacuated from Saigon.

It was against that background that a call came in from Lieutenant Colonel Chuck Hester on the other end of the island. Hester was about to take command of First Battalion, Fourth Marines—the next air-alert unit—the first to go if the Third Division sent units back to Vietnam. He was looking for additional company commanders, and he asked if I was interested.

"Sure," I said. "When do you want me?"

"Get down here as soon as you can," he said.

A couple of days later I said good-bye to my men in the Northern Training Area, and reported to Camp Hansen in the central part of Okinawa. I was now the commanding officer of Company A, First Battalion, Fourth Marines.

As soon as I arrived, I sat down and wrote a letter to Betsy. I explained that I had just taken over a rifle company, and that our battalion would soon be on air alert, ready for instant deployment to Vietnam (or Cambodia, or Laos) at any moment. Although my tour of duty was about to expire, I wrote that I didn't think it was right for these Marines to take on a new commander who would abandon them when they were facing the imminent prospect of combat.

A year earlier, I had left for Okinawa just two weeks before Christmas. And now I was telling Betsy that I wouldn't be home this Christmas, either. She was normally a faithful correspondent, but it took much longer than usual before I received an answer to my letter. When it finally came, it read something like this:

Dear Larry,

I now realize that the Marine Corps is obviously more important to you than I am—or our children. You've made that very clear over the years, and I shouldn't have taken so long to see it. Stay over there and do whatever it is you need to do, and don't forget to keep in touch with the children. But I've had enough. I want a divorce. Here's the name of my attorney.

The worst part about receiving Betsy's letter was that I more or less accepted it. I believed that what I was doing really *was* more important than my family. I was worrying about the two hundred and ten Marines whose lives I was responsible for, not to mention the fate of the free world. Betsy would just have to wait.

I kept myself so busy during those weeks that I barely thought about her. And when I did, my reaction was always the same: this will keep until I get back; I'll take care of it later.

In early December I came down with a very bad case of bronchitis. I was out in the field one night with my company, acting as the aggressor force for a major field exercise. Chuck Hester was there as an evaluator, and he turned to me and said, "What's the matter with you?"

"Me? Nothing. I'm fine."

"The hell you are. You're sick and you're exhausted. What's your rotation date?"

"I was supposed to leave next week, but I put in my extension request."

"What about your family? What do they have to say about all this?"

My eyes filled with tears. I couldn't speak.

"Go home, Ollie. It's not worth it. You care about these guys, and I appreciate that, but nobody else does. The politicians in Washington have thrown away the lives of so many young men. They don't care if your family gets ruined, or your kids grow up without you. The war is over anyway; it's only a question of when the shooting stops. Your giving your life over there won't change a thing. Go home to your family."

In my heart I knew he was right, but I still wasn't ready to admit it. I finally decided to take his advice and return to the States—after two old friends and former classmates, Pete Stenner and Bob Earl, ganged up on me one night and told me what a dope I was. They convinced me to withdraw my request to extend, and I left Okinawa a few days later.

By the time the plane landed in Los Angeles I was really sick. I was already on antibiotics, but I was still coughing up blood. There was also blood in my urine.

When I called Betsy from the airport, I could hear the chill in her voice. "I meant what I wrote in that letter," she said. "I'm sorry, but I can't live like this anymore. If you want to see the kids, call my lawyer."

I was furious. I had just returned from a year in Okinawa, training hard to save lives (or so I thought), while she was enjoying life in the safety of our nice house in Virginia. Meanwhile, the government of Vietnam and the South Vietnamese Army were collapsing. Everything I had fought for and worked for was coming apart. And now she expected me to walk away from my Marines. Okay, I had. But it didn't make any difference. I accused her of being ungrateful, unrealistic, and unilateral, but she wouldn't budge.

"If that's the way you want it, fine," I said. "It doesn't bother me."

And then I said the stupidest thing of all: "I don't care."

"I know," said Betsy. "That's the whole point. *You don't care.* That's why it's over."

I flew to Washington, still sick, and feeling very sorry for myself. Christmas was only a few days away, and I couldn't even visit my wife and kids. Tait was now five, and Stuart was four, and neither of them really knew who I was. The truth is that even before Okinawa I didn't spend much time with them. I left for work early in the morning before they got up, and came home late, when they were already asleep. I hadn't been around much on weekends, either.

I called Betsy's lawyer and ended up speaking to his secretary. "He left for the holidays," she told me. "Why don't you call back in January, and we'll try to work out some way for you to stop by and see the kids. By the way, who's *your* attorney?"

That's when it really hit me that Betsy was serious.

I moved into the BOQ (Bachelor Officers' Quarters), the only temporary officers' billeting available in the Quantico area. With Christmas approaching, the place was emptying out and becoming even more desolate than usual. There was a TV in my room, and when I turned on the evening news that first night, it was all about the impending fall of South Vietnam. Marines, *my* Marines, were being readied and deployed for evacuation operations up and down the coast of Southeast Asia. Within days, Colonel Chuck Hester and the battalion I had just left behind deployed to rescue the American crew of the *Mayaguez*, a freighter hijacked off the coast of Cambodia. Instead of being with them, I was sitting alone in Virginia with what appeared to be an unsalvageable marriage and two children whom I couldn't even see on Christmas.

The weather outside was damp and cold, and I felt the same way. When I had decided to leave Okinawa, I had convinced myself that I would be able to make everything all right with Betsy as soon as I got home. But she didn't even want to see me.

This was devastating. Until now, I had never failed at anything. Everything I had ever set out to do I had been able to accomplish by dint of hard work and persistence. At least that's what I thought. What a fool I had been to give up command of a rifle company in order to come home to—nothing.

I was hurt, angry, and confused. Physically, I was in miserable shape with a terrible cough that wouldn't go away, no desire to eat, and for the first time in my life, an inability to sleep. For years I had exercised hard every single day, but now I could barely drag myself out of bed. Today, I can look back on that period and recognize the full-blown symptoms of depression. Back then, I wouldn't have admitted it even if I had recognized it. *Real* men didn't have that kind of problem—and I knew I was a real man.

A day or two later I decided to drive to Maryland to

visit Bill Haskell, my old friend from Vietnam, who was now a CPA. Driving north on Route 95, the interstate highway right outside the base at Quantico, I was overwhelmed by the greatest sense of despair I've ever felt. Betsy and I had driven back and forth on this highway scores of times when we were dating. The day we were married we drove up this road to begin our new life together. Now I was driving alone to see an old friend and talk about old times.

As I raced up the highway, another coughing spasm struck and I nearly went off the road. I pulled off to the side and stopped the car to pull myself together. The fresh air from the open window allowed me to stop coughing long enough to catch my breath. I had to do something for this cough! I turned the car around and drove back to Quantico, where I headed straight for the dispensary.

There, sitting in the waiting room, was Colonel Dick Schulze, my old battalion commander from Vietnam and the man who had introduced me to Ross Perot. Dick had just been promoted to brigadier general, and he was there for his promotion physical. He greeted me with a bear hug, and then stepped back to look me over. "Blue? You look terrible," he said. "What's the matter?"

I was in tears. This made twice in one month, and I wasn't a guy who cried often. And certainly not about anything personal.

When the door opened to the doctor's inner office, Schulze grabbed me by the shoulders and vectored me right in. "Before you look at me," he told the doctor, "check this guy out."

After giving me a complete exam, the doctor said, "You're a wreck. You've probably got parasites, you're anemic, and you have fluid in one of your lungs. I'm putting you in the hospital today."

"Not today," I said. "I just got back, and I've got a million things to take care of."

"They'll all keep, Captain. Besides, from what you've

told me, there's nobody waiting for you, anyway."

That same afternoon, Schulze drove me up to Bethesda Naval Hospital and stayed with me while I was admitted. Dick Schulze was one of those great military leaders who can get personally involved with their men. With his deep, sad, blue eyes, he looked like Abraham Lincoln without the beard. Everybody who dealt with him came to love him. He was the kind of guy who could take a young Marine who went bad, bust him two ranks, fine him six months' pay, confine him for a month in the brig, and the kid would almost be grateful. How could such a gentle man be successful in such a violent business? I realize that this goes against the popular image of the military, but the best leaders I have known were all men of kindness and compassion.

I spent the next few days lying in bed, trying to read every book I could find. But I couldn't concentrate; I'd put the book down after five minutes, with no memory of what I had read. I have never watched much television, but I did then—even in the *daytime*, which would have been truly alarming if I had been able to pay attention. The only thing I could focus on was news from Vietnam and Cambodia, and all of it was bad. Other than the news, nothing seemed to matter except feeling sorry for myself. I tried desperately to avoid thinking about Betsy or the kids, although Christmas was growing closer by the minute.

And yet I refused to admit that I was depressed. I knew I was angry at Betsy, and I was convinced that all of this was her fault. On top of that, the war I had fought in and trained for, and trained so many others to fight, was ending all wrong. I was in trouble, but I didn't know it.

When Schulze came back to see me a few days later, we went into the solarium, a sun-filled room dotted with green vinyl couches. "I've been talking to the doctors," he said. "You don't have pneumonia, or liver disease, or anything like that. But you're still sick. You've got this terrible cough, there's blood in your urine, and you don't seem to be getting better. They tell me you're agitated and irritable. Frankly, it sounds to them like you don't care about much of anything anymore. And you certainly don't care about getting any better. They think that you'd benefit from psychiatric help."

I like to see myself as calm and in control, but when Dick Schulze said those words, I blew up at him—which was totally out of character. I must have looked ridiculous as I sat there, yelling at him, *"I'm fine. There's nothing wrong with me! I am very calm! I don't need that kind of help!"*

All I wanted was to get out of there. A decade earlier I had spent eleven months in hospitals after my car accident, which was enough to last me a lifetime. I hated hospitals, from the moment they woke you up at four in the morning to make sure you were asleep to the time they came in at night to wake you for your sleeping pill.

"Listen," he said. "In combat, I've seen you take the worst kinds of pressures that can be put on a man. But this is different. You trusted me in battle when the situation was far more dangerous than this, and you've got to trust me now. I feel strongly that you need psychiatric care, and so do the doctors. But it won't happen unless you agree to it."

This was humiliating. Me, in a psychiatrist's care? Psychiatrists were for crazy people. Maybe I had a couple of problems, but even if I did, I could solve them myself. I certainly didn't need the help of a shrink.

Schulze and I had been to hell and back together. I loved the man. How could he say this to me?

"Don't decide yet," he said. "Take a couple of hours and think it over. I'll come back later. You know I wouldn't be suggesting this unless I thought it was the right thing to do."

In the midst of my anger and frustration, I began to realize that maybe Schulze was right. Maybe the treatment I needed couldn't be found in antibiotics.

When Schulze returned, I said, "Okay, I've decided

to do it." After all, it was a place to be for Christmas.

"I figured you would," he said. "I've already made the arrangements."

He returned to visit me every one of the eleven days I was there.

Now this was something *really* new. I don't know what I expected: drugs, electroshock therapy, straitjackets, padded cells. But there was none of that. Instead, I was put on a regimen of "milieu therapy"—hours of group discussions and one-on-one sessions with a battery of doctors. I hated it. It was humiliating even to be there. I kept looking around and asking myself, *Who are these people, and why am I here?* (This was the same question I would ask myself in 1987, at the Iran-contra hearings.)

The doctors asked if I felt guilty about not being back with my unit. They asked me what seemed like thousands of probing psychiatric questions: Do you hate your father? Your mother? How do you feel about your wife? Your children? The Marine Corps? Your friends? Et cetera, et cetera, et cetera.

Looking back, I'm sure that my answers reflected my deep-seated sense that this was none of their business, and I recall being hostile and sarcastic. That was a mistake. These people were trying to help, and they *did* help.

During the group therapy sessions I was overwhelmed by some of the stories I heard. Many of the men described bouts of heavy drinking and acts of violence in their homes. I had never even seen a man strike a woman in anger, and I was shocked as some of my fellow patients recalled how their mothers had been abused or how they themselves had been violent to their own wives or children. No wonder these guys have problems, I thought. I've got nothing to match this. My father was always home for dinner. My parents loved each other. How weak I must be if I'm being bothered by something as trivial as my marriage falling apart.

And so I concluded that my own problems weren't

so serious, which I was all too inclined to believe anyway. I was too full of pride and ego to admit that anything serious was really wrong and that I needed help. I had accepted that idea on a superficial level by agreeing to stay in the hospital, but I didn't really believe it.

When one of the doctors suggested that Betsy and I might want to see a marriage counselor, I just laughed. (Just about every suggestion the psychiatrists offered was phrased in terms of "might." Coming from over ten years of a military environment, full of black and white rules and certainties, I found it hard to accept the idea that life was a series of options.) Besides, marriage counseling didn't seem to be a realistic option. Even if Betsy accepted the idea (which didn't seem likely at the time), I didn't like it. If we had a problem, we'd work it out ourselves.

What a jackass I was.

Finally, one of the younger doctors got through to me by being kind, blunt, and persistent. "You've told me so often that you don't care, but I think you do. You care very much about what happens to your wife and your kids. You don't really want this divorce, do you?"

"I already told you, I don't care. Neither does she."

"How can you be so sure? Have you ever tried counseling? Have you tried working it out?"

"She's not interested. I told you that. She told me to call her lawyer."

"Maybe she's not interested because you two are so angry at each other that you can't even discuss it. Why don't I call her?"

"No, I won't go crawling back. I refuse to beg. Besides, I don't have to stay here. I can leave at any time."

"Yes, but where would you go?"

"Back to work. I've got my orders."

"You can leave at any time, but I don't think you're ready. You've still got a lot of anger and bitterness to work out."

He was very skilled, and he badgered me without mercy. But I liked him, and that made all the difference. Eventually, when he brought up marriage counseling for the third or fourth time, I relented and agreed to his calling Betsy. I wasn't ready to accept any responsibility for what had happened, but at least I knew I was angry.

"I've got a couple of things to tell *her*," I said.

"You won't be telling her anything," he said. "Not yet. First I'm going to talk to her."

After meeting with Betsy, he came back to see me. "Let me tell you what I learned," he said. "You've always been a faithful husband. And you've been a wonderful father—when you're around. You'll do anything for the kids and for her. You've worked hard to provide for them on a Marine salary. It broke Betsy's heart that the Marine Corps was more important than she was."

When I heard this, I was too moved to speak.

"I think you're ready to leave," he said. "General Schulze knows a chaplain at Quantico who's an excellent marriage counselor. I'll put you on outpatient status, and I'd like you to call in every day and tell me how you're doing."

I was grateful for what I had learned at Bethesda, but I was even more grateful to be out of there. It had been less than two weeks, but it seemed like much longer. And I guess I showed my ambivalence by the silly things I said on the telephone when I checked in every day. "Hi. I'm calling from Mexico where I've just robbed a bank. Just kidding."

There was a lot I hadn't liked about the psychiatrists at Bethesda, including what seemed like a strong push to get the patients to blame their problems on other people—and especially our parents. To me this seemed like a way of avoiding responsibility. Another thing I didn't care for was the way some of the therapists played out a psychiatric version of good cop/bad cop. The hospitalization was helpful, but not as effective as the marriage counseling would become. But for me it was a crucial first step, and I shudder to think what would have become of my life if I hadn't been there.

During my stay at Bethesda, I had concluded that whatever problem I had stemmed from Vietnam. I felt angry and betrayed over the many lives that were wasted over there while our political leaders kept putting restraints on how we could respond. I still feel that way, but today I understand that this wasn't the singular cause of my depression. My hospitalization forced me to think about things that I had always been able to avoid—like the real nature of my relationship with Betsy. In the past I was too busy being the tough guy to see into my own heart. But now I knew what I had denied in Okinawa and in the weeks after my return— that I loved her, and that I wanted her back, and that the prospect of losing her was the basis of my depression. The doctors at Bethesda had helped me realize that I could, indeed, survive without her. But now I wanted to survive *with* her.

When I left Bethesda, it was by no means clear that Betsy and I would be able to get back together. Nor did I know what effect my hospitalization was going to have on my career as a Marine. Nobody ever stood up and announced that a Marine couldn't seek psychiatric help. But it was understood that a "successful" officer has never experienced emotional problems.

The Marine Corps was not unique in clinging to this prejudice. There is a deeply ingrained belief in our society that if you've ever suffered from depression or any other kind of emotional illness, you're never really cured. I hate to think how many people suffer from emotional ailments and don't know what to do about it, or are too afraid or embarrassed to seek help. It's not hard to get someone to a doctor for pneumonia or a broken arm, but it can be enormously difficult to get that same person to seek help for emotional distress.

Until recently, the prevailing wisdom in many institutions, and especially in the military and in government, was that anyone who has had psychiatric help, or marriage counseling, or who has overcome an addiction, is automatically suspect. It wasn't until the 1980s that a Marine could check himself into a hospital for an alcohol problem and, after treatment, return to his unit.

As a result of my own experience, I became far more attentive to signs of emotional problems in other people, and over the years I advised a number of young Marines to seek treatment or to at least talk to counselors. In the military it's often the chaplains who assume this role; a young soldier, sailor, airman, or Marine can often unload on a chaplain in a way that would be impossible with his commanding officer. And a well-trained chaplain can also offer something special to a troubled person—an awareness of God's power and love.

That certainly helped me. While I was still at Bethesda, I began to visit the small hospital chapel to ask God for His help directly, as in "Please, God, help me to get out of here, and help me save our marriage." By the time Betsy and I finished marriage counseling, I more fully understood how powerful prayer could be in healing—whether it's broken bodies, minds, or marriages.

By the time I checked out of the hospital, Betsy and I had, over the phone, set up a joint appointment with Larry Boyette, a Navy captain and one of the chaplains at Quantico. I arrived early for our first appointment, and as I sat in the waiting room, I picked up a book that was lying there called *Dare to Discipline*, by James Dobson, a professor of pediatrics at the University of Southern California School of Medicine. I didn't yet know Dobson's name, and from the title of his book I probably assumed it had something to do with the Marine Corps. It was, instead, a book of advice for parents, as I learned when I opened it to a random page and started reading: "I hope to give my daughter a small gold key on her tenth birthday," Dobson had written. "It will be attached to a chain to be worn around her neck, and will represent the key to her heart. Perhaps she'll give that key to one man only—the one man who'll share her love for the rest of her life."

Those words hit me like a bolt of lightning. I, too, had a daughter at home, although I hadn't seen her in a very long time. If this counseling didn't work out, if this *marriage* didn't work out, what kind of gift would I be able to give my own daughter, whom I barely knew, when she turned ten? What kind of example was I providing her about the kind of man she should seek as a mate? How could I ever do something as beautiful as this James Dobson had done, and had written about in that book? And for the third time in this whole ordeal, I cried.

Betsy still hadn't arrived when Chaplain Larry Boyette opened the door, and I ended up attending most of that first session without her. She had been even more reluctant to come than I was, perhaps because Boyette wore a uniform and had been recommended by General Schulze, which meant that he came from my world. When she did show up, she was on her guard. "I'll come a few times," she told Boyette, "but I hope you won't be bringing in any of this God stuff." Some chaplains might have taken offense, but Larry just leaned back and said, "You don't have to worry about that, Betsy. He's already here."

The counseling eventually helped us, but it took a long time before things got better. In one of our early sessions, Betsy blurted out that the only reason she had bothered to show up at all was because she felt sorry for me. That *really* got to me.

After several weeks of counseling, I moved back home. Betsy and I were each seeing Larry separately as well. (My appointments were on Monday evenings; heaven forbid I should miss an hour of work at Marine headquarters!) I still remember the session where I told Larry I was living with Betsy again. I expected to be congratulated, but he wasn't impressed, and I was disappointed by his reaction. But he knew how much work still lay ahead, and he wasn't especially interested in superficial changes.

On Friday afternoons, Betsy and I would see Larry together. Then we'd spend an hour or two together, sometimes doing errands, or shopping, or just going out for coffee.

I was beginning to understand that my wife was a helpmate, and that a helpmate isn't there to take orders, but to help you carry the load. We both had to learn how to talk to each other clearly but without hostility, and how to express ourselves directly, as in: "It really hurts me when I call the office and I don't get a call back." Don't tell her how *she* feels, Larry would say, tell her how *you* feel. Don't tell each other what you're doing wrong; instead, be clear about what you want and what you need. Instead of "You didn't take out the garbage," try, "I need help with the garbage," or, "I really appreciate it when you take out the garbage."

It wasn't just the long separations that led to so many divorces in the Marine Corps. It was also the striking contrast between military culture and the requirements of a marriage. As a Marine officer, I was used to giving orders and telling other people what to do. But a marriage is a partnership, not a platoon, and being a father is entirely different from being a commander.

Moreover, Betsy had changed enormously during my year in Vietnam, and again while I was in Okinawa. I returned from Vietnam saying, in effect, "I'm back, and here's how we're going to do things." But Betsy had been living without me for a year, being mother, father, and keeping house and home together while working part-time as an executive assistant at a translation service.

So many military spouses go through that same experience. In the case of the wives, while their husbands are away for long periods of time, they have to take care of everything—not only the kids, but the house, the mortgage, the car, the finances, and all the rest. When the men come back, ready to reassert themselves in their traditional roles, they discover that everything is different, and that their wives have grown stronger and more independent. In our case, all of this took place against the backdrop of enormous changes in the roles and relationships of men and women—changes so profound they permeated even the military.

Another thing I came to understand was that in addition to the two of us, there was a third entity—the relationship itself—that had to be nurtured. I started spending more time at home, and although my tendency is to fall back on old work habits, Betsy became more tolerant, and the time we spent apart was no longer as great a source of tension between us.

I began to see Betsy not only as my wife, but as my friend, too. I had never thought of a woman as a potential friend before. When I was growing up, my friends were exclusively male. Girls were people you dated, and held the door for, and occasionally even kissed.

Larry Boyette spoke often about responsibility, and how I couldn't fulfill my commitment to Betsy and my children if I wasn't around—either because I was determined to be SuperMarine or because we were divorced. He spoke of our children, Tait and Stuart, as being gifts, on loan from God. And he helped us understand that when you really need help, there is only one place you can always, always, find it—from Him who made us all.

The recovery process took time. It began the moment I turned around on Interstate 95 on that bleak December day, and it required the help of several people. There were ups and downs along the way, but by the time Saigon fell at the end of April, I was able to watch it on television with Betsy. I cried unashamedly, and Betsy had her arm around me. She understood.

With the amazing grace of God and plenty of hard work, we gradually put our marriage back together again. Now, I'm certainly not advocating that marriage repairs need to start with psychiatric treatment. But in our case, if I hadn't ended up in the hospital and gone from there to marriage counseling, I doubt that our marriage would have survived. We might have patched things up temporarily, but we wouldn't have reached a real resolution.

As I worked to repair my relationship with Betsy, there was one more relationship left to work on, although I didn't realize it at the time. And here, too, my growth was helped along by a man in uniform.

When I left Bethesda I was assigned to work in the Manpower Department of Marine headquarters in Arlington, Virginia. It was my first—and, I hoped, my last—desk job as a Marine, but for a career officer these assignments are unavoidable. There was little, however, that made a tour at the Marine headquarters attractive. The building is an old warehouse across the street from Arlington Cemetery, and old hands would point out the window and tell newcomers like me, "See those graves? They're reserved for action officers who miss their deadlines."

It was during this assignment that I worked on replacing individual dependent-restricted assignments with a new system called the unit deployment plan. Instead of sending individual Marines overseas for twelve or thirteen months (or eighteen months in the case of bachelors), we started sending entire units for six months at a time. The tours were shorter, morale was higher, unit integrity was far better, and a lot more marriages survived. A year later, I was actually awarded a medal for my work on this project; I hadn't even known you could get a medal for administrative work.

It was at Marine headquarters that I met a man who would lead me to change my life. Major John Grinalds worked at a desk across a partition from mine. Highly decorated from his two tours of duty in Vietnam, he was a graduate of West Point who went on to become a Rhodes Scholar and White House Fellow, and to earn a Harvard M.B.A. He was enormously respected in the office: whenever there was an important decision to be made, people would ask, "What does Grinalds think about this?"

He was also in terrific physical shape, which wasn't true of everyone at headquarters. There were a number of chubby Marines floating around in 1975, probably because of the commandant, who was known affectionately as "Fat Bob" Cushman. The standing joke was that the physical fitness test consisted of three laps around old Bob.

John Grinalds was on the fast track. While we were at headquarters, John was deep-selected—selected early—for lieutenant colonel. (Around the same time, I was deep-selected for major.) But this wasn't the only thing that made John Grinalds different from other officers. Instead of the training and administration manuals that most officers kept on their desks, John kept a Bible, and from time to time I would see him reading it. He was known to be a "born-again" Christian—a term I didn't really understand at the time. But he was never one to wear his faith on his sleeve. Even after we had come to know each other fairly well at headquarters, about the most he ever told me about his personal belief was to point to his Bible and say, "You might want to know a little more about this."

In 1978, when John was named to become a battalion commander in the Second Marine Division, based at Camp Lejeune, he asked if I wanted to come along as his operations officer. I was delighted with the prospect, but before Betsy and I moved the family to North Carolina, we drove down there so she could see what I hoped would be our new home. We left Virginia on a Friday afternoon, and pulled into Jacksonville, the town outside the sprawling base at Camp Lejeune, around midnight. Betsy had fallen asleep, and when she opened her eyes and looked around she almost died. "Tell me it's only a nightmare," she said, for Jacksonville in 1978 was like the towns outside most large military bases. The main street was lined with seedy bars, strip joints, pawn shops, fast-food joints and used-car lots—each with its own flashing neon sign. It looked like a poor man's

Times Square. It's better today, but back then it was a shocking, garish, and depressing sight, made all the more so by its contrast with the nearby base.

When we drove through the sentry post onto Camp Lejeune, the difference was simply amazing. The base was beautiful and immaculately maintained, with miles of forests which double as training areas for the twenty-five thousand Marines assigned there. Betsy also discovered one of the military's best-kept secrets: Camp Lejeune has a world-class recreational beach. We spent the weekend there, looked at where our new quarters would be, and returned to Virginia to sell our house, pack up our belongings, and move to North Carolina.

It was very hard to move from our house in Stafford, and not just because of all the "stuff" we had accumulated by then. (On my first military move, from Annapolis to Quantico in 1968, everything I owned fit in the back of my car. Now, ten years and three children later, we needed a forty-foot moving van.) This house was also the setting for so many memories as well. This was the first home we owned, and we had watched it being built. It was the scene of our near-divorce, and the rebuilding of our marriage. We brought our little Sarah home to this house from the Quantico base hospital where she had been born. Here, Tait and Stuart had built fast friendships with neighboring children. We had laughed, loved, and cried together in that house, and leaving it was wrenching for all of us.

As the operations officer of the Third Battalion, Eighth Marines, I was responsible for the training and the preparation of a two-thousand-man unit as it prepared to deploy to the Mediterranean—or, if necessary, the Middle East or even the Pacific. One of the great joys of this job was that I could see the early results of the new policy I had worked to implement at headquarters: because Marine units were now kept together longer, there was a speedy decline in what we called personnel turbulence, and a visible improvement in both proficiency and morale.

One morning, about two weeks before we were due to

leave for our six-month deployment to the Mediterranean, I jumped off the back of an armored amphibious vehicle and reinjured my back, exactly where I had broken it during the car accident in 1964. This had happened once before, during a parachute accident in 1973 which had landed me in the hospital for a week, followed by another week or so of bed rest, the only time since Vietnam that I missed a day of duty. Now I was lying on the ground, writhing in pain, and wondering how I was ever going to recover in time to ship out to the Mediterranean with my unit.

This was not a routine deployment: we were about to become the Landing Force for the Sixth Fleet—one of the most critical assignments in the Marine Corps. As I lay there, I didn't even want to contemplate sitting in traction while the battalion that I had trained with for months deployed without me.

Someone ran off to find the battalion commander and a corpsman. Grinalds got there first. He helped me up to a sitting position, and knelt down beside me. Placing his hands on my legs, he said, "I'm going to pray for you."

This wasn't exactly the kind of help I had in mind. I'm lying here in agony and he wants to *pray*? This guy must be nuts.

Then John Grinalds called out in prayer: "Lord Jesus Christ, You are the Great Physician. Heal this man."

Suddenly the pain disappeared. Slowly, the feeling came back in my legs. I didn't know what to say beyond a muttered "Thank you."

"Don't thank me," said Grinalds. "Thank your Lord and Savior. *He* is the Great Physician. You have to turn to *Him*."

Sometimes, if you're too thick to get the message any other way, God has to hit you over the head with a two-by-four. He'd certainly sent me the message before, but I wasn't paying attention. In the car accident in 1964, everyone I was with was either killed or terribly injured. Yet I was not only able to recover, but to win a boxing championship at Annapolis, and to graduate, and to get a commission in the Marines. When the doctors told me I might never walk again, I refused to believe them. I took a lot of pride in my recovery, and with all my persistence and hard work, I wanted to believe I had done it on my own.

Later, in Vietnam, there were times when nearly everybody around me was either killed or grievously wounded, and I escaped relatively unscathed. There were times when I was painfully hurt, but was able to recover quickly and return to duty.

After the war, when I received two early promotions in the Marine Corps, I wrote it off to being a good officer. When the Lord blessed us with our first two children, I didn't see His hand in it. When my life was coming apart, and I was sitting in the chaplain's office at Quantico, there were any number of books or magazines I could have picked up in the waiting room. *Time* and *Reader's Digest* were right there, but I started reading a book by Jim Dobson. Betsy already had a copy in our house, but I didn't even know it was there. And I had no idea that Jim Dobson, the founder of an organization called Focus on the Family, would later become an important person in my life.

What struck me so powerfully about John Grinalds's prayer and his strong admonition in the sand at Camp Lejeune that morning was that for so long I'd had it all wrong. I had been taking credit for all the things I had been able to do over the years, but I didn't deserve it, any of it. The message He had been sending was *put your faith in Me*. Not in yourself, not in others, not in the things of this earth, *but in Me*.

The profound faith of John Grinalds had a powerful effect on me. It made me realize that I was a little like the military radios I was so familiar with. They have two modes: transmit and receive, and they work on many different frequencies.

But I had been too busy transmitting to receive. I had transmitted a lot of prayers over the years, but I hadn't stopped long enough to acknowledge that my messages had been received and that *He* was answering. I came to see that He had been sending a message back: trust in *Me*. And more. "I don't do these things to glorify you," He had been telling me. "I do them that others will glorify Me. You must become an instrument by which others come to understand that. You can't take credit for healing yourself. Everything that happens to you happens because of My grace.

"If you have succeeded, give Me the credit. If you prevail in adversity, bear witness to My power. Let others see My hand in your life that they might come to know Me. And by the way, get to know Me a little better in the process. I am the God of the Universe, but I'm also your personal Savior."

I was profoundly humbled by this understanding. I now knew what others meant when they described John Grinalds as being "born again." Over the months to come, this understanding led me to a much deeper relationship with my Maker.

I had been raised to know who my Lord and Savior was. I knew *about* Him, but I didn't know Him personally. It was like reading about some important world figure, seeing him on television, reading things he had written and said, but never actually meeting him. That, to me, is the clearest way I know of explaining how that relationship has changed. Today, I've met Him and I know Him personally.

Later that month, after we'd deployed, I sat with John and our chaplain, Bruce Jayne, as they led Bible studies on Sunday evenings in the ship's wardroom. While we were at sea, I managed to read the entire Bible from cover to cover, and by the time we returned from the Mediterranean, I felt comfortable in leading a few Bible studies myself. For me, John Grinalds's extraordinary expression of faith was the first step in a long walk. By the time I was fired in November 1986, I knew that with God's help, I could withstand any pressure. In the months that followed my firing, I suffered a number of disappointments. Terrible things were said about me in public. People I had thought of as close associates, colleagues, and even friends became sources for absurd and ugly newspaper articles, media stories, and accusations.

And yet I never felt alone, and never doubted that the outcome would be positive. And while I didn't need a reminder, I got one anyway. On July 7, 1987, on the very first morning of my testimony before the Joint Congressional Committee, an elderly woman whom I had never seen before broke out from the crowd of reporters and onlookers and through the throng of security guards, and handed me a little card. During those days my lawyers wouldn't allow me to read anything except specific materials relating to the inquisition, and Brendan Sullivan, my lawyer, snatched the card from my hand even before I looked at it.

By the time we walked into the hearing room, I had forgotten all about it. But just before we sat down, Brendan put the card on the microphone stand in front of me. Every time we stood up to leave during a recess, Brendan picked it up and took it with him, and every time we returned, he put it back. The reporters who crowded around us tried to get a glimpse of what was on the card, but Sullivan wouldn't let them.

Imprinted on the card was a biblical verse:

> They that wait upon the Lord
> shall renew their strength;
> They shall mount up with wings as eagles.
> They shall run and not be weary.
> They shall walk, but not faint.
> —Isaiah 40:31

As I went through an extraordinary experience with the whole country looking on, that card was in front of me the whole time.

# 7

# BYZANTIUM ON THE POTOMAC

ALL MY LIFE I HAVE STRUGGLED TO STRIKE THE RIGHT balance between my work and my family. Mostly, I failed. But there was one year when I got it right.

In 1980, after two years in the Second Division and two six-month deployments to the Mediterranean from Camp Lejeune, I was one of about twenty Marine officers selected to spend the 1980–81 academic year in the Command and Staff course at the Naval War College in Newport, Rhode Island. This was easily the best family tour of my Marine Corps career. The classes were stimulating, the setting was idyllic, and the hours were civilized: classes ran from eight-thirty to three, and I was home for dinner every night.

I probably spent more time with my family during that one year than in the rest of the 1980s combined. We went skiing in winter, and toured Boston and a good bit of New England in the spring and fall. Betsy and I even got to see a couple of shows in New York. Whenever the weather was decent, we went sailing. I had learned to sail at Annapolis on Chesapeake Bay, where the bottom was so soft you could run aground without even knowing it. But Narragansett Bay, off Newport, is full of rocks, and I must have hit every one of them.

There were five of us when we moved to Newport, and six when we left. As I look back on the birth of our children, it's almost as if I had been acting out some broad sociological trend of the deepening involvement of fathers. I was in Vietnam when Tait was born in 1969, and I didn't even see her until months later. In 1970, when Stuart appeared, I was reading a book in the hospital waiting room. The door opened, and a nurse came out. "Congratulations," she said. "You have a healthy baby boy. You can see him through the window at the end of the hall, and you can see your wife [unspoken but implied message: *that poor woman whose terrible suffering is all your fault*] tomorrow."

In 1976, when Betsy was pregnant with Sarah, we enrolled in a Lamaze class at the clinic in Quantico. Betsy went into labor during a family dinner at McDonald's, and we rushed to the hospital just in time. When Dornin came along in the spring of 1981, Betsy and I were in a hospital room in Newport when everything seemed to happen at once. I yelled for help, and a male nurse came running in. By the time the doctor showed up, our third daughter was already in my arms.

When our year in Newport was up, I had hoped to return to the Fleet Marine Forces—preferably back at the Second Marine Division at Camp Lejeune. But the Marine Corps had other plans. One afternoon in early February I was pulled out of class and told to report to Washington for a series of interviews that might lead to my next assignment—as a staff member at the National Security Council. I didn't even know the NSC was an option, and when I learned that it was, I made clear to everybody that I wasn't interested. I didn't want another desk job, and I *certainly* didn't want one in Washington.

But in the military you go where you're sent. One of

my interviews was with General Robert Barrow, commandant of the Marine Corps. Barrow, tall and thin as a rail, stared at me from across the desk where he stood with his hands behind his back. "Majuh," he said in his long Louisiana drawl, "Ah understand that you'd prefer not to go to the National Security Council."

"Sir," I replied, "I'll go where I'm sent, of course, but I'd rather return to the fleet."

"Brotha' North," he said, "'tisn't like you to whine. Carry out yo' orders."

Although I had groused like hell about being sent to the NSC, I did appreciate the compliment. Whenever the Marine Corps picks you to go "outside the service"—whether it's to the Joint Chiefs of Staff, the CIA, the White House, embassy duty, or anywhere else where you're serving in the presence of other services, or among civilians, it's considered an honor. This is especially true in Washington, because that's where the major decisions on roles, missions, and budget are made; issues that affect the entire Marine Corps. Later, I was told that another reason I was selected was that John Lehman, Secretary of the Navy, had liked a paper I wrote at the War College in which I argued that there was still an important role for battleships in modern warfare.

Even so, I had no business being assigned to the NSC. And I ended up there for a relatively trivial reason. Ronald Reagan had been elected, in part, because he promised to shrink the size of the federal government. His advisers soon discovered that one of the easiest ways for the White House to reduce overhead was to replace political appointees on the government payroll with military officers detailed from the Army, Navy, Air Force, and Marines. Because our salaries were paid by our respective branches of the armed services, we were a source of cheap labor.

I was over my head at the NSC, and I knew it. The problem wasn't my military background, because there were military officers at the White House who certainly belonged there. But most of them had advanced degrees in foreign studies or political science, while the bulk of my experience was in military units and combat training. I was well-versed in battlefield tactics and intelligence, and I certainly believed in the goals and policies that President Reagan had articulated in the 1980 campaign—especially his promises to rebuild America's military and to restore a sense of confidence to our economy. His views matched my own: smaller government, an emphasis on entrepreneurship, and a strong America.

But none of that was especially helpful when it came to dealing with Congress, the State Department, or the other gargantuan bureaucracies in Washington. And just because in previous assignments you had worn a uniform to work didn't mean you were familiar with the inner workings of the Pentagon.

I started out as a gofer, working on the reams of paperwork that were necessary to get congressional approval for the sale of Airborne Warning and Control System planes (AWACs) to Saudi Arabia—the same planes that were used so successfully in our war with Iraq in 1991. Because I was unprepared and inexperienced, the only way to keep up, whether the subject was AWACs, terrorism, Iran, or Central America, was to read like crazy and to get my hands on every possible bit of information—books, articles, monographs, intelligence reports, and whatever else I could find. I spent just about every night and weekend studying, and talking to people from the State Department and the CIA who could teach me the things I needed to know. I was in the office by seven each morning, skimming through newspapers and poring over intelligence cables and State Department reports. I worked like a dog, right up until the day I was fired.

The National Security Council had been established in 1947, during the Truman administration, "to advise the President on all matters relating to national security." It was intended as a cabinet-level coordinating body, a bridge between the President's political goals and various implementing arms of the government, including the departments of State, Defense, Commerce, Treasury, and Justice, as well as the CIA. The NSC's mandate is to synchronize the work of the various federal bureaucracies with the President's national security objectives.

It sounds simple enough, but in practice it's enormously complicated. For unlike the larger, entrenched agencies in Washington, the staff of the National Security Council pretty much comes and goes with each new administration. For that reason, and because of its relatively small size (a few dozen staff members and a budget of four million dollars when I arrived), the NSC staff is generally close to the political sentiments and views of the President. In this respect it differs markedly from the larger agencies, like State, the Pentagon, and the CIA. These organizations are far too big and cumbersome to reflect serious political shifts within a short period of time—particularly when the shift is as dramatic as the one between a liberal Democratic President and his conservative Republican successor. The permanent bureaucracies of government tend to change slowly, and are attuned to a longer-term mentality. They don't have much respect for political appointees—a perspective I came to understand a little more clearly the day I heard a mid-level State Department official dismiss the cabinet as "the Christmas help."

This attitude is especially common at the State Department. There has always been some friction between the State Department and the NSC, but these tensions tend to be particularly pronounced during a conservative Republican administration, probably because most conservatives avoid government work in favor of the private sector. The State Department tends to attract idealistic and well-meaning liberals, and, like the other bureaucracies of Washington, is composed mostly of Democrats, with a handful of liberal Republicans. This was true even during the Reagan administration.

While that certainly wasn't the only reason Alexander Haig didn't last very long as President Reagan's first Secretary of State, it wasn't irrelevant, either. "I found no great enthusiasm in the Department of State for the Reagan administration," Haig noted in his memoirs. I noticed the same thing. But that was okay, because the feeling was mutual.

Although the State Department exists as an instrument to carry out foreign policy, it has evolved into an institution of foreign *relations*. This difference is more significant than it sounds. State Department officials who deal with a particular country often seem more concerned with that country's perception of us than with our policy toward them. Later, when I became involved in implementing the administration's counterterrorism policies, working with the State Department was often a nightmare: if we had a problem with country X or country Y, the first instinct over at State was not to convey our real views, but to avoid offending the other side.

I found a discernible corporate culture at the State Department, where many of the officials subscribed to an almost unconscious set of values, although they were never discussed or spelled out. Part of it was a tendency to assume that in just about every conflict between the United States and the Third World, the Third Worlders were right and the U.S. was wrong. The unspoken but pervasive rule was that we had been so shameful in our past treatment of these countries that we always owed them the benefit of the doubt. There was a standing joke that what we really needed at the State Department was an American embassy—to represent the views of the American people.

There was certainly a State Department perspective on Israel. Again, nobody ever said so aloud, but it seemed to me that many officials at State were automatically opposed to whatever it was the Israelis favored. There were times, of course, when the White House, too, disagreed with particular Israeli policies, and certainly the Israelis were not pleased about those AWACs going to Saudi Arabia.

But within the State Department there seemed to be a constituency that actually relished any antagonism that could be fostered between us and the Israelis. Some of this came from a long-standing and barely hidden pro-Arab tilt at State, which I'm hardly the first to notice.[1] Another large chunk, I believe, is the result of an ingrained streak of anti-Semitism in our government. Many mid-level government officials—and not only at the State Department—are the sons and grandsons of the great elite American families, where a genteel, discreet anti-Jewish prejudice was often taken for granted.

In early 1983, an adviser to a senior government official sent me a weird magazine clipping about an Israeli conspiracy to dominate the world—and suggested that I might want to look into it. When I went to see him, he showed me the publication where the article had appeared; it was put out by Lyndon LaRouche and his followers.

While this incident was certainly not typical of our government as a whole, I noticed a distinct anti-Israeli bias in some circles. This sentiment had been growing since the 1973 Arab-Israeli War, after which many Americans (including some conservatives) blamed Israel for the Arab oil embargo, and the devastation that followed in our economy. This hostility grew more pronounced in 1981, when Israeli planes destroyed Iraq's nuclear facility—which *really* infuriated the State Department. It wasn't until early 1991, when the Israelis were repeatedly attacked by Iraqi SCUD missiles during Operation Desert Storm and did not retaliate, that Israel

---

[1] In his recently published memoirs, Clark Clifford recalls "a group of Mideast experts in the State Department who were widely regarded as anti-Semitic." Clifford was referring to 1948, but things change slowly in Washington. (Clark Clifford with Richard Holbrooke, Counselor to the President [New York, 1991], p. 5.)

once again enjoyed widespread support in Washington. Unfortunately, it took a situation where Israel was once again a victim to bring about this change.

This bias did not seem to be shared by President Reagan or Vice President Bush, but Caspar Weinberger was another story. Weinberger seemed to go out of his way to oppose Israel on any issue and to blame the Israelis for every problem in the Middle East. In our planning for counterterrorist operations, he apparently feared that if we went after Palestinian terrorists, we would offend and alienate Arab governments—particularly if we acted in cooperation with the Israelis.

Weinberger's anti-Israel tilt was an underlying current in almost every Mideast issue. Some people explained it by pointing to his years with the Bechtel Corporation, the San Francisco engineering firm with contracts in many Arab countries. Others believed it was more complicated, and had to do with his sensitivity about his own Jewish ancestry.

For all our proximity to the President and his senior advisers, the NSC, too, was a bureaucracy, and much of our work was routine and tedious. Every time the United States conducted a military exercise or deployment in the vicinity of the Soviet Union or its allies, we would prepare a paper summarizing the activity which outlined how the Soviets responded to our last exercise, and what we might expect this time. If an American destroyer sailed into the Black Sea, this required a memorandum. We wrote countless letters on behalf of the President, and memoranda to the national security adviser, the secretaries of State and Defense, foreign heads of state, and the Congress on every conceivable matter affecting our national security. An average day consisted of a long stream of phone calls, two or three hundred pages of reading, a dozen or so pages of writing, and a minimum of three or four meetings—beginning with the morning staff meeting at seven-thirty.

In the summer of 1981, when I first came to work at the NSC, I was struck by how old-fashioned the place was. The Marine headquarters in Arlington was widely perceived to be light-years behind the rest of the military, but it seemed almost space-aged compared to our creaky offices in the Old Executive Office Building. The OEOB had been built just after the Civil War, and was said to be the largest solid granite structure in the world. It had been designed in the French Renaissance style, but while the outer façade is beautiful and ornate, some of the offices were downright dangerous. One of my colleagues was sitting at his desk when a two-hundred-pound block of plaster fell from the eighteen-foot ceiling and landed on his desk, just missing his chair.

Some people swore that the electrical wiring in the OEOB had been installed before the invention of electricity. The lighting was positively medieval, and the heating system was so antiquated that some staff members would bring in their own portable heaters, which often led to some blown fuses in the neighborhood.

And this was, at least technically, the White House! The State Department had the latest telecommunications equipment, but we barely had secure telephones. Initially, the NSC secretaries all left at four-thirty, and to get a secretary to work overtime you actually had to submit a memorandum—assuming, of course, that anyone was still around to type it. Half of our furniture was broken, and the drapes looked like they had been hung by Dolley Madison the year before the British burned the city in the War of 1812.

The other government agencies loved the fact that the NSC was so antiquated and therefore ineffectual. For years, the State Department, the Pentagon, and the CIA were the only ones with instant communication links to American installations and armed forces around the world. But when Judge William P. Clark came in as national security adviser in early 1982, he had Tom

Reed and Admiral Poindexter design a major upgrade of our facilities, putting the NSC on an equal footing with the larger agencies.

Unknowingly, and certainly unintentionally, I played a role in the early departure of Richard Allen, Judge Clark's predecessor. When I arrived at the NSC, I was assigned an office[2] on the third floor of the OEOB that I was to share with two army lieutenant colonels: Dick Childress and Alan Myer. We were also given a safe to keep classified documents. The first time we opened it, we were amazed to find several watches, a couple of gift-wrapped bottles of liquor, and an envelope containing ten one-hundred-dollar bills. I had heard about government perks, but this was ridiculous.

I reported our discovery to Jerry Jennings, the NSC Security Officer, who dutifully informed the FBI. The FBI determined that the contents of the safe had belonged to Richard Allen, the national security adviser. Unbeknownst to me, Allen had used this same office during the transition period between the election and the inauguration, and apparently the money and the watches were gifts from Japanese journalists who wanted to arrange an interview with Nancy Reagan. Although Allen was later cleared of any wrongdoing, the press had a field day, and he was soon replaced by Bill Clark.

Clark came in amid his own storm of controversy. The press attacked him for his lack of knowledge about foreign affairs, and made much of the fact that during his earlier confirmation hearings for Deputy Secretary of State, he had been unable to recall the names of the leaders of Zimbabwe or South Africa. Bill Clark was a man of considerable modesty who didn't pretend to be a foreign policy expert. But he was very close to Ronald Reagan, and he understood what the President wanted and how to achieve it.

---

[2]According to the local lore, this had been Henry Kissinger's old office.

Judge Clark was tall, thin, and soft-spoken; Mike Ledeen, a consultant to the NSC, once described him as the Jimmy Stewart of the Reagan administration. Maybe so, but Bill Clark was a lot smarter than people gave him credit for. He passed the California bar exam without ever graduating from law school. He eventually became a respected justice on the California Supreme Court, but when Ronald Reagan became President, Clark left a perfectly good lifetime appointment to come to Washington to serve a man he greatly admired.

With his cowboy hat and his boots, the judge cut an unusual figure in Washington. He kept a low profile, and insisted on walking to work from his apartment near Foggy Bottom. He hated any signs of pretension, but I was finally able to convince him that in light of the terrorism threat, he ought to consider a more secure form of transportation. With the help of Ed Hickey, head of the White House Military Office, I persuaded him that a driver and an armed guard were good ideas.

Back in the 1970s, when I worked at Marine headquarters, Betsy and I would occasionally drive into Washington to catch a show, or to take the kids to one of the city's magnificent memorials and museums. But my job at the NSC marked the first time I had ever worked in the District, and for a military man making his first foray into the civilian world there was a lot to get used to.

The reverse was also true, as very few White House staffers had any idea of what the military was all about. They were pretty sure that the Navy had something to do with ships, that the Air Force flew some planes, and that the Army was somewhere off in Europe, holding back the red tide at the Iron Curtain. But the Marines were a complete mystery, except that whatever it was that we actually did was thought to involve an extraordinary degree of violence.

In the military, of course, we wore our rank on our uniforms. At the White House, everybody wore business suits to work. At first I concluded that rank didn't make much difference in civilian life—which is roughly equivalent to the naïve assumption that people living under Communism have no interest in money or material objects. I soon discovered that rank and status were terribly important in government, except that in Washington such things were designated not on your uniform but through a series of perks. If you were really powerful, you had an office in the West Wing of the White House. The next level down was an office in the Old Executive Office Building, but facing the White House. If you were a drone like I was, you were lucky to have a window at all. I had one, which provided a truly breathtaking view of a dark blue dumpster.

Status was also conferred by your telephone style, and I soon learned that military officers at the NSC had created their own special rank—the telephone colonel. Nine times out of ten, Lieutenant-Colonel Smith's secretary would answer his phone by saying, "Colonel Smith's office," thereby giving her boss an instant promotion. Not wanting to lie, but also not wanting to burden my secretaries with three unnecessary syllables, I instructed them to answer the phone by saying, simply, "NSC." When I answered my own phone, I said, "Ollie North."

Now that I was part of the upper atmosphere of government, I had to learn a new form of telephone etiquette. When my secretary called someone on my behalf, she had to remember to put me on the line before he picked up. In Washington, as I soon learned, talking to a "mere" secretary is considered demeaning to the deputy assistant to the under-assistant to the deputy assistant secretary. The junior official always defers to the senior one by coming on the line first, the reason being, presumably, that the senior official's time is more valuable. So you had to know whether the Deputy Secretary of X was higher than the Under Secretary of Y, and woe unto you if you got it wrong, because people took these things *very* seriously. We were all given a protocol list which explained the various levels of appointments in the administration, and most people kept it taped to the slide shelf on their desk so they could refer to it when the phone rang.

Once you got through to the person you were trying to reach, your problems had only begun. For now you had to try to accomplish something in the peculiar language of Washington, where almost nobody communicated directly and to the point. Only on rare occasions, for example, would anyone actually admit, flat out, that he or his agency was "opposed" to a particular plan or proposal. Instead, he would say "we don't concur." If he knew he was going to get steamrolled but still wanted to register his displeasure, he would "interpose no objection." You could live with this, but the phrase you really wanted to hear, and rarely did, was "we concur." In other words, even though this wasn't our idea, we're willing to go along with it.

The OEOB was considered part of the "White House Complex," and for security reasons we were all given either a blue White House staff pass, or a red OEOB pass, which most people hung around their necks on a chain.[3] I kept my badge in my pocket, but I noticed that many of my colleagues wore theirs all over town, as if to announce: "I'm important. I work at the White House."

The White House staff badge was certainly a biggie, but the real status symbol was a parking pass for West Executive Avenue, next to the West Wing of the White House. After that, just about the only honor you could aspire to was to be appointed Secretary of State. But then, of course, you wouldn't need a parking pass at all, because you'd be driven to work.

---

[3] I was never able to figure out the criteria for who got which pass. My badge was blue, but why? Was it based on height? Weight? Astrological sign? I still wonder.

We junior dogs parked along the lower half of the Ellipse, about half a mile away, and even there you needed a special White House parking pass that you hung on your rearview mirror. But this was a mixed blessing, because you'd sometimes find that somebody had decided to express his First Amendment rights by letting the air out of your tires, or even smashing your windshield. My colleague, Alfonso Sapia-Bosch, left the office very late one night and came back half an hour later, claiming that his Volkswagen was missing. "Come on," I said, "you forgot where you parked it. How could it be stolen? That area is guarded by the Secret Service, the Metropolitan Police, and the Park Police. Look again. I'm sure you'll find it."

Al's car turned up a few days later. In Pennsylvania.

There were fewer parking spaces than passes, so you got to work early and didn't dare move your car once you arrived. This, in turn, led to another perk—the use of a White House car and driver. This one was normally above my level, but Ed Hickey, the head of the White House Military Office that ran the White House Motor Pool, was a former Marine, and he put me on the access list. I used these cars to attend meetings in other parts of the city, or to get out to Andrews Air Force Base to catch a plane.

There was a tremendous infatuation with perks. Were you invited to a state dinner? (I never was.) Did you fly with the President on Air Force One? I did twice, and that was enough, thank you. At the time, Air Force One was an old and noisy 707 that dated from the Kennedy administration. But everybody who flew on it, or on Air Force Two, received a certificate testifying that he or she had really *been there*. These souvenirs were greatly valued.

So, too, were photographs of oneself shaking hands with the President or Vice President, along with letters or notes from high-level officials. Most of the staff plastered their office walls with these *me*mentos. The walls of my office were decorated with pictures of my family, drawings done by my kids, maps of Central America and the Middle East, and several posters. One of the posters depicted a Nicaraguan freedom fighter and said, "For 53 Cents a Day You Can Feed a Contra." Another was a photograph of a female commando leader from the Nicaraguan resistance, holding a machine gun. It said, in big letters, THIS MUTHA' WEARS COMBAT BOOTS. A third poster was a fake movie advertisement for a film called *The Return of Walter Mondale*, which promised to be "more boring than ever!" There was one photograph of me with the President hanging in my office. Fawn had lifted it from the west wing of the White House.

I also displayed a handful of souvenirs that were a little unusual: a canteen cup that had been shot off my hip in Vietnam, an FLMN neckerchief with a hammer and sickle that had been found on a Communist guerrilla in El Salvador, a fur hat with a red star from the Chinese People's Liberation Army, a Cuban military helmet with a bullet hole through the side—a gift from Jonas Savimbi in Angola, and a Cuban officer's belt buckle from Grenada.

Another custom that surprised me about government life was the extent to which the entire city of Washington seemed to shut down for lunch every day. At noon the traffic was almost as bad as during the morning rush hour. I rarely ate lunch, and often used that time to go for a run, or to work out in the Secret Service gym—another of Ed Hickey's favors. When I did go out to lunch, it was usually at the McDonald's at Seventeenth and Pennsylvania.


I burned out several secretaries before I hired Fawn Hall. They were perfectly competent, but my hectic pace, late hours, and all too frequent weekends took their toll. My third secretary was so exhausted at the end of the day that I often had to drive her home, and when she left, there were several applicants for the job. My requirements were simple: I was looking for someone who could type like a banshee and didn't mind working overtime.

When Fawn came in for her job interview, she had been working in the office of the chief of naval operations. She struck me as articulate and efficient, and she was willing to work overtime. Her mother, Wilma Hall, was Bud McFarlane's secretary, but one thing that impressed me about Fawn was that she didn't try to use that connection to get the job.

And no, I didn't ask her if she knew how to operate a shredder.

And yes, I did notice that she was attractive.

It certainly wasn't Fawn's fault that she became famous around the same time as Donna Rice and Jessica Hahn. The media coverage implied that these women were all pretty much alike, which was terribly unfair to Fawn. She understood the prejudice she was up against, which was why her opening statement at the congressional hearings included a line that read, simply, "I CAN TYPE."[4]

She certainly could. "Just talk," she'd say, and about six seconds after I was finished, the memo would be completed, and in the right format. Fawn was one reason I was so productive. She was terrific at keeping my hectic schedule straight. She always knew how long a meeting would take, and even how much time it would take to get there and back. She was great on the phone, and was adept at protecting me from conversations that weren't really necessary.

Maybe these qualities are inherited, because Fawn's mother was the consummate executive assistant. Gregarious, outgoing, bright, and cheerful, Wilma Hall was Bud McFarlane's alter ego. She had first met Bud when he was a White House Fellow, and over the years she had worked for several national security advisers, including Kissinger. In every case, but especially with

---

[4] "My hours were long and arduous," she said in her testimony, "but I found my job to be most fulfilling. I was a dedicated and loyal secretary, and performed my duties in an exemplary manner." I'll vouch for

McFarlane, she helped optimize her boss's effectiveness.

Fawn Hall wasn't much older than my own daughter Tait. Like many young people, she had enormous energy, and even after a twelve-hour day she could go on to one of her occasional modeling jobs.

After Fawn started working for me, I noticed that some of the men who had previously dealt with me only by telephone were now stopping by the office. One of them was Arturo Cruz, Jr., a handsome young man and a real charmer whose father had been induced to join the leadership of the Nicaraguan resistance. Arturito, as the son was known, began showing up fairly often, and he would always stop in the outer office to chat with Fawn. I didn't realize how close they had actually become until I received a report from the CIA that Fawn had been seen with Arturito in Miami.

I called her in and said, "Listen, you've got to make a decision. This guy is a foreign national. He used to be a Sandinista adviser. We think we can trust him, but he also had a relationship with Cuban intelligence, the DGI. You have the highest security clearances in the land, and your association with him offers the potential for compromise. You'll have to make a choice between this man and your job. If you really love him, just give me two weeks notice, marry him, and have lots of kids."

Fawn was embarrassed that I had to speak to her about it, and I felt awkward for intruding in her personal life. But several weeks later, when I received another call, this time from the FBI, I had to speak to her again. Fawn eventually broke off with Arturito, whereupon I introduced her to Major Gil Macklin, a young Marine who had once worked for me. Everything seemed to be going great for them until he was sent to Okinawa—and I've already explained what *that* can do to a relationship.

In the months after I was fired, there were all kinds of stories and rumors about the "cowboy colonel" and his blond secretary, and the office they supposedly shared in the White House basement. Innuendos were even raised during the hearings. These kinds of stories, invariably based on anonymous sources, are routine in Washington, but in my case there seemed to be no limits. According to one account, I used Iran-contra money to buy Fawn Hall her red Fiero sports car, and to pay for an island in the South Pacific to which the two of us were planning to flee.

That story set me off like a rocket, and I stormed in to see Edward Bennett Williams. Ed, who had founded the law firm that represented me, was a grand old man of the law and a strong believer in "no comment" when it came to the news media.

"That does it," I said. "I know you don't like clients to respond to the press, but this thing has to be answered. My wife will see it, and so will our friends. And what about our kids?"

"Sit down, Ollie," he said. "You're getting to be like a dog chasing fleas. You're not going to get rid of the fleas until you take a flea bath, and son, you'll be taking a couple of them. You also have to understand that the people telling these stories actually believe they're true."

I was dumbfounded. "How can you say that?" I asked.

"Listen," he said, "if the people writing these stories and spreading these rumors had the chance to abuse their position, steal millions of dollars, and have an affair with a beautiful secretary, they would have done it. So they have to believe *you* did. Otherwise they couldn't face themselves in the morning."

My first major assignment at the NSC came out of the blue. One autumn afternoon, shortly after the Senate voted to supply AWACs to Saudi Arabia, several boxes of paperwork were delivered to my office along with a memo from Admiral Poindexter, asking me to look through all of this material and to brief him on it the following week. I'm still not entirely sure why it ended up on my desk, but I started reading through the various papers and documents, which turned out to be fascinating—and highly classified.

During the final year of the Carter administration, the President had been trying to conclude a major disarmament agreement with the Soviets. Zbigniew Brzezinski, his national security adviser, had convened a group of scientists and former senior government officials to consider various scenarios of war and peace, including what would happen in the event of a Soviet nuclear attack on the United States. One result would be enormous bursts of electromagnetic energy which could immediately disable our electronic communications equipment. If that happened, the scientists wanted to know, how could we ensure that the President could continue to lead the country and assert his role as Commander-in-Chief if he couldn't communicate with either the citizens or the military? We knew that the Soviet Union had made plans for its leadership to survive a nuclear war by having them whisked off to a network of secret tunnels under Moscow. But what would *our* leadership do?

I put together a summary of the papers, and was summoned to the Oval Office to brief the national security adviser and the President. (This was the first time I briefed President Reagan.) My recommendation was that the work of the "Wise Men's Group," as this outside team of advisers was known, was so important that the group ought to be reactivated. Judge Clark asked me to take charge of this effort, and for the next year and a half I did little else but work on this undertaking, which we called The Project.

As the de facto administrator of The Project, I arranged meetings of the Wise Men, wrote up the minutes, and brought back their ideas for implementation. Initially The Project was headed by Tom Reed, a former Secretary of the Air Force and a confidant of Judge Clark.

During these meetings, I sat there in awe as this incredibly brilliant collection of people discussed electromagnetic pulses and other scientific topics about which I knew next to nothing. I had taken engineering courses at Annapolis, and had completed a course in nuclear weaponry in the Marine Corps. But there were terms thrown around in that room that I'd never even heard before.

As a result of the work done by the Wise Men, a permanent government-wide working group was formed to address a number of difficult questions pertaining to a possible nuclear attack. Suppose, for example, that the President does not survive the attack, the Vice President has been killed in his helicopter, and the Speaker of the House has collapsed and died of a heart attack. Suppose further that the highest-ranking member of the cabinet who is alive and accounted for is the Secretary of the Treasury, who had gone out to Wisconsin to give a speech. The rest of our government, the American people, and particularly the military must be informed that the Secretary is now the constitutional President, but it's still too dangerous to announce his exact location. In the absence of normal channels of communication, how does the new President assert his authority? How does he stop the war, or continue it, or take whatever other actions may be necessary?

Years later, as the Iran-contra hearings began, a particularly bombastic and outrageous article appeared in the *Miami Herald* and several other newspapers, claiming that during my years at the NSC I had been involved in drawing up plans "to suspend the Constitution in the event of [a] national crisis such as nuclear war." This story was not only wrong, but offensive. The whole point of The Project was to protect our constitutional system even under the worst imaginable conditions.

During my work on The Project, I wrote several directives which President Reagan signed, authorizing further steps to be taken to ensure that our government could not be rendered impotent by enemy action or an extraordinary disaster. This was also where I came to know Vice President Bush. As the first in line to succeed the President, he took an active interest in this program. I briefed him often, and he asked detailed and penetrating questions about how things worked, and how they could be improved. It was obvious that his interest was more than a formality.

And because The Project also involved the Congress— both on matters of succession, and for funding—I also briefed two of the Reagan administration's strongest political adversaries: Speaker Tip O'Neill and Congressman Ed Boland.

Even at the NSC, only a handful of people were aware of The Project. But for me it was enormously satisfying. The Project enabled our government to safely conduct arms-reduction talks with the Soviets, secure in the knowledge that the United States would never be decapitated.

In 1983 I was given another fascinating opportunity. When the Kissinger Commission was established to study the situation in Central America, Judge Clark asked me to serve as the NSC liaison. As part of its work, the commission invited each of the three living former presidents to appear before it and present his views on the deteriorating situation in the region. It was my job to make sure they all had access to the appropriate classified information.

I soon discovered how different each of these men really was. We began with President Carter, who didn't want to be briefed and showed no interest in the documents we were prepared to send him. "Don't bother," he told me on the phone. "I have my own sources." When he appeared before the commission, he brought along close to forty pages of notes, which he delivered in a familiar monotone. Within about twenty minutes, several members of the commission appeared to be snoozing. Even the Democrats were clenching their teeth, trying to suppress a yawn.

President Carter's analysis consisted of an extended diatribe against the administration's policies in Central America. Despite his suspicions about the Sandinistas, he had obviously never envisioned that the United States would support a covert war against them. And no wonder. In his meetings at Camp David with Menachem Begin and Anwar Sadat, he had succeeded in one of the most difficult negotiations ever. It was hard to blame him for believing that Nicaragua's problems could and should be resolved in similar fashion.

President Ford, by contrast, was delighted to be briefed, and together with another staff member I flew out to Colorado to bring him back in a White House jet. We briefed him during the flight to Washington, and President Ford's presentation more or less matched the administration's view.

President Nixon was an altogether different story. About two weeks before his appearance, I began talking on the phone with him and an aide. He'd plow through the material I sent in a day or two. Then he'd call me to say, "Okay, now send me the current analysis of the economic conditions between Colombia and the Rio Grande—trade, employment, refugees, everything." I would put together a package and shoot it up to him by White House courier. Later that same day, he would call again: "Have you got anything else? That second paper you sent me wasn't deep enough."

"I'm sorry to hear that, sir." (I neglected to mention that I had written that paper myself.)

"Well, don't give me that pabulum. Send me a more detailed analysis."

President Nixon had an insatiable appetite for information, and his questions were always incisive. When he appeared before the commission, he took off his watch and set it down on the podium. "I have exactly an hour and a half," he said. "I'll talk for forty-five minutes, and then take questions for another forty-five before Major North takes me back to the airport." Then, without a single note or index card, he proceeded to review all of Central and South America from the Rio Grande down to Tierra del Fuego. He knew every head of state, every political movement, and every economic trend. Without missing a beat, he spoke for *exactly* forty-five minutes, and then answered questions. His performance was absolutely dazzling.

While President Nixon was talking, I looked over at Kissinger, who was grinning like a Cheshire cat. Maybe we have it backward, I thought. Maybe Kissinger was really Nixon's student. That day, at least, it seemed that the real mastermind behind the foreign policy of the Nixon administration was Richard Nixon himself.

I missed a lot of family dinners during my years at the NSC, but in spite of the incredible hours and far too many weekends in the office, our family managed to sneak away for a few camping trips and short vacations in North Carolina, Virginia, and Maryland. In 1986 I took the whole gang to Costa Rica, where I had planned to meet with several of the contra leaders, and with Joe Fernandez, the CIA station chief, whom I had come to know in Washington before he was posted to Costa Rica. We visited Ambassador Lew Tambs and stayed with the Fernandez family. Over a weekend, our two broods— with a combined total of eleven kids—all went to a beach house on the Pacific coast, just south of the secret airfield that Dick Secord had built at Santa Elena.

I rarely worked on Sunday mornings, and unless I was away, our family normally attended church together. But I've had an easier time loading up an entire battalion on ships than getting the six of us into one car and arriving at church on time. Stuart and I would usually end up sitting around and waiting for the girls, and he'd use the opportunity to tease me: "Way to go, Dad. Let's hear it for that ironclad military discipline."

All through my years at the NSC, our family was part of a weekly Bible-study group. This was something we had started during our year in Newport, where we normally began each session with children's Bible stories and songs. Then one of us would take all the kids over to a neighboring house while the rest of the parents studied together. We took turns leading the sessions, and we'd prepare for that evening's topic by reading various biblical commentaries, looking up the appropriate scriptural references, and integrating them with our own interpretations.

One of my favorite study sessions was on the marriage relationship as described in the fifth chapter of Ephesians, which includes the well-known verse, "Wives, submit to your husbands as to the Lord. For the husband is the head of the wife as Christ is the head of the church...."

A lot of men use that verse to justify an authoritarian, male-dominated household, but that's not what the verse says to me. It compares the husband's role to that of Jesus, and His style was to lead with love. I think the real message of this verse is directed not to the wife at all—but to her husband.[5]

Because Stuart is my only son, I've probably spent more time with him than with my daughters. We have hiked along the Appalachian Trail, paddled canoes on the Shenandoah and Potomac, and scaled a few heights in Yosemite. During that idyllic year in Newport, I even had time to coach his soccer team.

Our three girls are consumed with horses—an interest that began at the base stables when we were living at Quantico. Horses are completely foreign to my experience, and I've learned that I'm not the only father in that situation. At horse events, the dads are the ones leaning on the fence with their hearts in their throats as their offspring take thousand-pound animals over fences

---

[5]Moreover, the previous verse (5:21) reads, "Submit to one another out of reverence for Christ," which makes it clear that submission goes in both directions.

and jumps. From talking to these other dads, I've learned that their involvement, too, is limited to two specific tasks: mucking out the stables, and driving our daughters and their horses to and from these events—"but slowly, please, Daddy." It's gotten to the point where several of us show up in T-shirts that read, "They ride, I provide."

Today, when I think back on my job at the NSC, all I can see is the work. But there were some perks, too. We got to bring the kids to the Easter Egg roll on the White House lawn, and to the White House staff Christmas party, where they got to see the President and the First Lady. And occasionally, Betsy and I were given free tickets to the Kennedy Center. When foreign diplomats come to town, a member of the White House staff generally escorts them to the Kennedy Center, where the entire party sits in the President's box. Sometimes these tickets went to Bud McFarlane, and every few months, Wilma Hall, his secretary, would call and ask if Betsy and I were free to go as escorts. This invariably happened at the last moment, but we jumped at the chance whenever we could.

Now we're not talking here about Margaret Thatcher or Mikhail Gorbachev; the most socially desirable visitors were quickly snapped up by higher-ranking officials. By the time it got down to my level, these events invariably involved emissaries from countries nobody else was interested in—nations at the lower end of the alphabet, or with hyphenated names, or governments whose major industry consists of issuing colorful postage stamps.

Betsy and I would greet our guests in a little anteroom just behind the presidential box. As the host and hostess, we'd get there early enough to unlock the telephone, and to ensure that the little refrigerator was stocked with small bottles of California champagne from the White House Mess. These bottles were emblazoned with the White House seal, and most of our guests took them home as souvenirs.

I joke about it now, but Betsy and I got to see some terrific shows, and we met some fascinating people from countries we had barely heard of. (I would always do a little research on these places so as not to appear *totally* ignorant.) Before the curtain, the audience would often look up toward the box, wondering who was occupying it that night. Just before the show began, there would be an announcement: "Ladies and gentlemen, viewing from the President's box tonight is Ambassador Zlygbat and his wife, Eirwox, from the dictatorship of Epidermos."

But these intersections of work and family were all too rare. As far as my kids were concerned, I might have been working on another planet.

"How come you're never home, Dad?"

"Because I've got a lot of work to do, honey."

Poor Daddy. How smart could he be if it takes him *that* long to finish his work?

But while I couldn't talk to my kids about the details of the job, we did discuss the general issues of American policy. Tait and Stuart were both in high school, and I visited each of their classes to talk and show slides about the situation in Central America.

Betsy knew the general outline of what I was working on, but not the details. She was aware that I used to travel to Central America on NSC work and that the administration was backing the Nicaraguan resistance, but she didn't know what country I was going to, or why. During some of the busiest times she even met me at the airport with a couple of clean shirts. And while she knew in a broad sense that I was working on the hostages, she didn't know who I was meeting with, or that I had gone to Tehran. It wasn't until the congressional hearings in 1987 that Betsy learned exactly how I had been spending my time. When it was all over, she turned to me and said, "I'm glad I came. Now I know where you were all those nights."

# 8

## CLOSE-UP

DURING MY FIVE AND A HALF YEARS AT THE WHITE House, I had a fairly close-up view of several high officials in the Reagan administration.

I don't pretend to know Ronald Reagan well, and I have to admit that my negative feelings about him are the direct result of what has happened to me since I left the White House in 1986. Before I was fired, I was with him at scores of meetings during my five and a half years at the NSC, which was certainly enough to get a good sense of the man.

The first thing I noticed is that he worked a lot harder than people gave him credit for. While he undoubtedly knew how to enjoy life, it was equally clear that he plowed through a huge amount of paperwork and attended innumerable meetings. I also found him to be a far more involved President than he was portrayed in the media, and while I don't know whether that was true across the board, it was definitely the case in the areas I worked in—counterterrorism, the hostages, and the Nicaraguan resistance.

He was a great storyteller, and in my experiences the

anecdotes he told were generally relevant to the issue at hand—or to the atmosphere in the room. Sometimes he'd come up with a reminiscence to defuse tension and make the participants in the meeting feel more at ease. And sometimes he used humor to build a consensus between Democrats and Republicans.

He could also laugh at himself. Although he was the leader of the most powerful country on earth, and was reelected by an overwhelming mandate, he still had an aw, shucks attitude that endeared him to people. Part of it was an act, of course, but underneath the act he was still amiable and unassuming.

He was the same way with visiting dignitaries. In October 1983, in the midst of the Grenada operation, the President hosted a series of meetings with the leaders of the Caribbean island nations that had participated with us in the rescue mission. One of these visitors was Prime Minister Compton of Turks and Caicos, a small former British dependency, who showed up with his very attractive wife. The meeting in the Oval Office was all business—until the end, when she interrupted the good-byes to say she had brought a message from her people: "Mr. President, our people think that you are very brave to do what you have done in Grenada. They say that you have"—and here she thrust out her cupped hands, palms up, and groped for the right word—"big balls."

In this formal setting, the scene of countless historic moments, you could just about hear the strains of barely suppressed laughter as the President's senior advisers strove to choke back their natural response. As for the President, he just smiled, blushed a little, and lowered his head. "Well," he said in his inimitable manner, "well…"

I have already discussed my personal disappointment in Ronald Reagan. Politically, my regret is that instead of strengthening the office of the presidency, he actually weakened it. He just wasn't forceful enough when it came to fighting for the constitutional prerogatives of the Executive Branch. He could have opposed the appointment of a special prosecutor, and he could have challenged the War Powers Resolution when he decided to use military force in both Grenada and Libya. Instead, the President acquiesced by calling in the congressional leadership and informing them of his intentions. The War Powers Resolution, which was passed in 1973 over President Nixon's veto, greatly expanded the power of Congress at the expense of the presidency. Once you give away that authority, it's almost impossible to get it back.[1]

The same thing happened with the Boland Amendments, which severely restricted American support for the Nicaraguan resistance. When Congress started to obstruct the President's authority to carry out our foreign policy, he should have stood up to them and announced, "If you send me a bill that includes that amendment, I just won't sign it. It's unconstitutional. If necessary, the government will come to a screeching halt until you send me a bill I *can* sign."

Future presidents may well be constrained by an imperial Congress because Ronald Reagan, one of the most popular presidents in American history, did not reclaim the original powers of his office.

My attitude toward President Reagan was also affected by disclosures that have come out since we both left Washington.

As the whole world knows by now, both the President and the First Lady consulted astrologers. For the life of me, I can't understand how a man who purports to be a Christian can believe in that malarkey. I am aware that millions of

---

[1] No President has ever signed a bill restricting constitutional presidential authority to deploy military forces. But every President since Gerald Ford has complied with the provisions of the War Powers Resolution before committing American troops. Ronald Reagan was the first President popular enough to challenge the Congress on what many scholars believe is an unconstitutional restriction on the presidency. Unfortunately, he failed to do so.

Americans say they believe in the God of the Universe *and* in the stars. But the idea that a man could get up in the morning and let an interpretation of the great sidereal movement guide his day is simply beyond my understanding.

Ultimately, however, I think of Ronald Reagan in terms of my four children and their future, which is why I can't stay angry at him. I remember what the world was like in 1980. The man whom Ronald Reagan defeated in that election liked to tell us that our best days were behind us. President Carter believed that the only hope for America lay in more and bigger government, and that we had to start scaling back our expectations. He left us with a failing economy, an emasculated defense, and a sagging spirit.

Then Ronald Reagan came along and showed us another way, and the American people responded to him as a revolutionary of the right. People living under Communism saw it, too. They regarded Ronald Reagan almost as a spiritual figure who inspired them to reject the system they had known and hated all their lives.

The world we live in today is a far better place than it was in 1980. *Time* magazine gave the credit to Mikhail Gorbachev, their "man of the decade." But it was Ronald Reagan who transformed the world in the 1980s. It was he who made the changes under Gorbachev possible—and even necessary. If Karl Marx provided the stimulus for the first Russian Revolution in 1917, it was Ronald Reagan who inspired the second in 1991. And it was he who revitalized America's power and its economy, and led the whole world a few steps closer to freedom and prosperity. For the better future he offered my children, I will always be grateful.

Unfortunately, Reagan's policies were not always shared by the people around him. Some of his priorities, such as helping the contras and reducing the size of our government, could not be accomplished by one man. And several of his top advisers, like Richard Wirthlin and Mike Deaver, seemed to be more interested in Reagan's popularity than in his programs or policies.

Some people maintain that Ronald Reagan's finest

speech was his 1964 television address for Barry Goldwater. That one certainly changed Reagan's life, but as far as I'm concerned, his greatest moment as a communicator did not occur in the United States at all, but in the Soviet Union, of all places. On May 31, 1988, he stood beneath a gigantic bust of Lenin and spoke to the students at Moscow State University about the real meaning of liberty. "Freedom is the right to question and change the established way of doing things," he told them. "It is the continuing revolution of the marketplace. It is the understanding that allows us to recognize shortcomings and seek solutions. It is the right to put forth an idea, scoffed at by the experts, and watch it catch fire among the people. It is the right to dream—to follow your dream or stick to your conscience, even if you're the only one in a sea of doubters."

The greatness of Reagan wasn't just that he gave that speech, which was written for him by Josh Gilder. It was that he had made it possible for that speech to be given in the first place. As far as I'm concerned, that marked his finest moment.

The tragedy of Ronald Reagan is that he will not be remembered for that speech in Moscow. Instead, what lives on in the public mind and on the airwaves is the President's pathetic videotaped deposition at John Poindexter's trial in 1990. Ronald Reagan deserves an honored place in the history of the world, but millions of people will always think of him as a confused and muddled old man. I always assumed that Ronald Reagan had good attorneys, but I just can't understand why they allowed him to make that tape.

I had relatively little direct contact with Secretary of State Shultz and Secretary of Defense Weinberger, but

---

[2]One of the most astonishing statements in the deposition was Reagan's testimony that "to this day, I don't have any information or knowledge that . . . there was a diversion. . . . I, to this day, do not recall ever hearing that there was a diversion."

like everyone else in the national security community, I couldn't help being aware of the persistent, continual squabbling between them. Part of their rivalry was institutional: in every administration the Defense Department tends to be more suspicious of the Soviet Union, for example, while the State Department, by its very nature, is more inclined toward compromise and reconciliation. But this conflict was personal, and the hostility between Shultz and Weinberger inevitably spilled down into the bureaucracies, and undermined relations between lower-level officials at both State and Defense.

I used to see them in action during meetings of the National Security Planning Group in the White House Situation Room. Whenever Shultz spoke, Weinberger would slouch down in his chair and close his eyes. When Shultz was finished, Weinberger would usually speak up in disagreement. Sometimes—especially with regard to Central America—he'd talk as if Shultz had never spoken.

They fought constantly—in front of the President, in meetings, and through their public statements. Sometimes you had the feeling that one of them took a more extreme position just to annoy the other guy. Their quarrels were so frequent, and so out of keeping with their position, that I sometimes wondered whether Weinberger and Shultz had something to gain by creating the impression that they didn't get along.

They had apparently been at each other's throats for years—ever since 1970, when Weinberger worked for Shultz in Nixon's Office of Management and the Budget. According to the local lore, their conflict had continued at Bechtel, where Shultz was president and Weinberger was general counsel.

It was also reflected in their very different personalities. Shultz was certainly the more interesting of the two. In public, he always tried to portray himself as the cautious, behind-the-scenes conciliator, struggling hard to stay out of the limelight. But he struck me as just the opposite: a man who loved the attention of the media and wanted to be seen as being in charge of foreign policy. In private meetings he was contentious, especially with Weinberger and Casey, and he frequently contradicted them in meetings with the President.

He also struck me as the more ambitious of the two. Later, in preparing for my trial, I learned that Shultz had confided to one of his aides that he hoped to use the Iran-contra fiasco as an opportunity to become national security adviser while maintaining his position as Secretary of State. Whenever I think of him, I'm reminded of that marvelous title of John Dean's book on Watergate: *Blind Ambition*.

Weinberger, on the other hand, was clearly uneasy in front of the media, where he would often stutter and stammer his way through a press conference. He was far more effective when he held forth in the Situation Room, where his perspectives were clear and concise. He knew that in order for the United States to have credibility, we had to have military strength. Shultz, however, didn't seem to care deeply about any particular foreign policy issue—so long as he got to negotiate it.

Shultz's lack of a clear philosophy was most evident when it came to dealing with the Soviets, where he turned into Mr. Nonconfrontation Man. He didn't want to confront them over their arms deliveries to Nicaragua, and it was common knowledge that his State Department was willing to sacrifice the Strategic Defense Initiative in order to conclude a new arms treaty with the Soviets.

Just about the only thing that Shultz and Weinberger seemed to agree on was that they were both strongly opposed to our dealings with Iran. They said so loudly and often—mostly after the fact. Their opposition was real enough, but in Shultz's case, especially, I believe he made sure to cover all his bases. If the Iran initiative failed, he could credibly claim he had opposed it. After I was fired, Shultz insisted that the State Department be placed in charge of further contact with the Iranians. If they succeeded, he would be able to share in the credit.

During the firestorm of publicity on Iran-contra, the story came out that Shultz had threatened to resign in protest over the arms-for-hostages policy. I don't believe it. I'm confident that if the Secretary of State had walked into the Oval Office and said, flat out, "Either this Iran business stops or I'm leaving," the entire initiative would have been stopped dead in its tracks. As much as President Reagan cared about the hostages, after Alexander Haig left, the President simply couldn't afford to lose a second Secretary of State—especially one whose personal relationship with Foreign Minister Eduard Shevardnadze mirrored Reagan's own rapport with Gorbachev. For in the final analysis, everything else in the foreign policy arena was seen as secondary to the main issue, which was U.S.-Soviet relations.

Had Shultz and Weinberger been as strongly opposed to the Iran initiative as they later claimed, it would never have continued. Secretary Weinberger simply could have forbidden the shipment of U.S. military equipment from our stockpiles. And consider the impact if both men had gone in together to see the President and said, "Hey, boss, we finally found something to agree on. Either this thing stops or we're both out of here." Instead, as pragmatic politicians, they kept their options open.

Although his major battles were with Weinberger, Shultz was no great fan of Bill Casey either. The feeling was mutual. Casey believed that Shultz had his own private agenda, and regarded him as working for the benefit of all Shultzkind.

"Shultz thinks every problem can be negotiated," Casey once told me. "And the longer he negotiates, the more powerful he becomes. If Shultz had his way, no problem would ever be solved. All we'd do is keep negotiating."

Casey wasn't merely being sarcastic. He sincerely believed he had real solutions to problems, while Shultz was content just to talk about them.

They sparred frequently—especially over Nicaragua, where Shultz favored a multilateral negotiating process while Casey was a passionate supporter of the armed resistance. It wasn't that Casey couldn't accept a negotiated end to the conflict, or that he believed that a purely military solution was likely. But he was convinced that the pressure of the Nicaraguan resistance was essential for negotiations to succeed, and he turned out to be right. It was military pressure which eventually forced the Sandinistas to accept open elections, which led to the defeat of Daniel Ortega in 1990.

The Casey-Shultz conflict was considerably more dignified than the Shultz-Weinberger rivalry, and was more along the lines of the traditional tensions between secretaries of state and national security advisers. While Shultz's view of the world was hard to discern, Casey had already formulated what later became known as the Reagan Doctrine, which encouraged active American support for anti-Communist movements around the world. Afghanistan, Nicaragua, and Angola became its most vivid manifestations, but Casey wasn't merely anti-Communist; he was enthusiastically pro-democracy. One of his greatest frustrations was that few Americans seemed to know that many new democracies around the world had emerged (or in some cases, reemerged) during the Reagan years, including Argentina, Brazil, Ecuador, El Salvador, Grenada, Venezuela, Colombia, Honduras, Guatemala, the Philippines, and South Korea.

Casey felt strongly about the need to redress the perception around the world that the United States was an unreliable ally and a fair-weather friend. He understood why this image was so widespread, and he would cite the consequences for those who had been gullible enough to take America at its word: from the Bay of Pigs to Vietnam, Cambodia, and Laos, to the Shah, and to Latin American leaders who had believed President Carter when he assured them that the Sandinistas would be better for them than the Somoza regime. In short, he was determined to restore our credibility.

I admired Casey enormously, and I came to know him well. After his death in the spring of 1987, the nature of our association became the subject of intense speculation. According to some reports, I was like a son to him, while others swore that I barely knew the man.

Our relationship was close, and yet it wasn't especially personal. We often spoke on the secure telephone, and we met regularly at one of his offices, or occasionally at his house in Northwest Washington. He had three offices that I knew of, but knowing Casey, there may well have been others.

I admired him, and he knew it. But I was never Casey's protégé, and I don't believe he saw me as the son he never had. We were not buddies. He never picked up the phone to say, "Come on over and let's have drinks tonight." Casey had friends, but I didn't count myself among them.

And yet we were more than colleagues. He was somebody I could turn to and say, "What's going on here?" I could talk to him about wanting to return to the Marines, and I often asked him for advice. He gave it eagerly: "Here's who you should be dealing with on Nicaragua. But stay away from so-and-so; he's no good."

I knew nothing about covert operations when I came to the NSC, but Casey taught me a great deal. In 1984, when McFarlane told me that one of our allies was about to contribute significant funds to support the Nicaraguan resistance (only later did I learn it was Saudi Arabia), and instructed me to set up a procedure by which the money could be delivered, it was Casey who told me what to do. Later, people seemed to assume that a Marine infantry officer somehow just *knew* how to set up an overseas bank account to receive wire transfers, but I didn't have a clue. To me, a bank was a place where they gave you a toaster when you opened a new checking account, and where you applied for a mortgage. I had never even heard of a wire transfer, and I certainly didn't know how to arrange one. But Casey, among other things, was a financial genius. He had been chairman of the Securities and Exchange Commission during the Nixon years, and before that he had actually invented the concept of the tax shelter—and even gave it its name.

Casey's habitual mumbling obscured the fact that he was incredibly bright and knowledgeable. He was trained as a lawyer, and had apparently been a good one, as he often reminded people. He saw himself, justifiably, as an intellectual, and he gravitated toward people who were interested in big ideas and in painting a broad panorama. He had an especially good rapport with Jeane Kirkpatrick, and on two separate occasions—first, when Judge Clark left as national security adviser, and again when McFarlane resigned—he lobbied hard for Jeane to take over that job. Although both Casey and Weinberger supported her, her appointment was blocked on both occasions by George Shultz. I believe that the reason Shultz didn't want Jeane Kirkpatrick to be any closer than the U.N. was that he felt threatened both by her formidable intelligence and her strong anti-Communism.

I got to know her fairly well when I worked with the Kissinger Commission on Central America. She had been Bill Clark's first choice as a commission member, and she clearly knew more about what was going on in the region than anybody else in that group. It wasn't just book learning; she had been to the area, and she knew many of the leaders personally. Her obvious grasp of the issues and the personalities made other members of the commission—even Kissinger—uncomfortable. She was sometimes acerbic when she explained the folly of a particular proposal or idea, and those who didn't appreciate her found this grating. I thought she was terrific, and I could see why Casey admired her.

Casey's mind was always processing new data. He was relentlessly curious, and he often broke into a machine-gun burst of questions: Why? What makes you believe that? What's the proof? How do you know?

I often had the feeling that his mumbling was at least partly an act, because when he wanted to speak clearly, Casey rarely had trouble being understood. And he was actually easier to understand on the phone, which struck me as odd. In some of the high-level meetings I attended, it seemed as if Casey was mumbling to force other cabinet members to lean forward to listen to him. He didn't speak loudly, but he had a way of commanding attention. Caspar Weinberger, who often appeared to sleep during these meetings (a result, people said, of his arthritis medication), always woke up for Casey.

And Washington's most notorious mumbler certainly knew how to work a crowd. I was sometimes sent out to address new intelligence officers at CIA training centers, and I was always surprised by how many of them said they decided to apply to the CIA after hearing Casey give a speech at their college or university. Casey loved young people for their energy and enthusiasm, and it showed.

The one word he could never pronounce was the name of the country that was always on his mind. He called it Nica-wog-wa, and at meetings people would go out of their way to try to get him to say it. Some congressional Democrats joked that they would never vote to undermine the government of any country that the director of Central Intelligence couldn't pronounce. And yet Bill Casey spoke several foreign languages and paid attention to detail. Was he putting us on?

He was always reading. I was with him on a flight to Panama when I saw him start in on the paperback edition of *Modern Times*, by the British author Paul Johnson. This tome is nothing less than a history of the world from the end of World War I to the 1980s, and it runs to over eight hundred pages. I was sitting behind him, across the aisle, and as we landed he turned around and said, "Have you read this? It's really good." Then he tossed it to me.

*Modern Times* is one of the best books I've ever read, but you have to pay attention. It took me weeks to plow though it, but Casey had devoured it during a single flight.

At Mayknoll, his family home on the Long Island shore, books were stacked up from floor to ceiling. Wherever he traveled, he told his advance team to find two things: a Catholic church and a good bookstore. He was always buying more books—and giving them away. "Have you read this yet?" he'd say. "This guy knows what he's talking about."

One book that influenced him enormously was *The Terror Network*, by Claire Sterling, a free-lance American journalist living in Italy. Sterling described an international terrorist fraternity, a collection of groups who received extensive support from the Soviets and their Eastern European allies. "The KGB's role was not a matter of guesswork," she wrote, "but documented fact." And she excoriated Western governments for refusing to acknowledge this fact in the face of over-whelming evidence.

Casey was highly impressed with Sterling's work, and concluded that she had great sources. But his praise for Claire Sterling was not shared by Washington's intellectual elite. When *The Terror Network* was published, the critics dismissed it as right-wing propaganda. But only a few years later, when Communism began to crumble all over Europe, Sterling's allegations and Casey's convictions were vindicated again and again—mostly by the guilty parties themselves.[3]

Casey somehow found the time to write several books of his own, including one on Allied espionage in World War II (about which he obviously knew a great deal) and another on early American history. He carried a yellow legal tablet everywhere, and would scrawl in pencil in huge script, using up three or four lines at a time.

He had remarkable energy, and even in his seventies

he routinely put in a twelve-hour day. He realized he wouldn't live forever, and he was determined to accomplish everything in the time he had. Despite his age and a grueling schedule, I never once recall him dozing off, not even on airplanes. An assistant would always be getting him something to work on—another file to look over, another book to read. When his plane returned to Andrews Air Force Base, his exhausted aides would drive home, desperate for sleep. Casey would head right back to the office.

This hectic pace led to a certain gruffness, and with Bill Casey there were never a lot of pleases and thankyous. If, during a meal, he could finish some paperwork, read a book, or interview somebody (or ideally, all three at once), so much the better. Somebody once said that when Bill ate, he dripped. It isn't polite to disparage other people's table manners, but in Casey's case there weren't any. If he invited you to lunch, you rarely had the chance to enjoy it: he would gobble down a few mouthfuls while he gave out advice and fired questions. Throughout the meal he would be playing with his tie, and would occasionally use the back of it as a napkin.

He was always fidgeting, his hands constantly in motion. Usually he'd be playing with a paper clip—bending it or poking the straight end between his teeth. After a while he would appear to nod off, like a

---

[3]In East Germany, for example, the interior minister revealed that his government had allowed PLO operatives to use their nation as an operations base, and had knowingly given refuge to Carlos, one of the world's most notorious terrorists. The authorities in East Berlin admitted that they had not interfered when a Libyan-Palestinian terror group planned the bombing of a disco in West Berlin that killed two American servicemen and wounded over two hundred people in April 1986.

The Hungarian Interior Ministry revealed in 1990 that his country, too, had given sanctuary to Carlos and thirty-five of his men. The Czechs had provided training and explosives to terrorist groups, while Yugoslavia was a major base of operations for Abu Nidal, the master terrorist who was responsible for the massacres at the Rome and Vienna airports. In short, most of Sterling's charges turned out to be true.

crocodile sunning himself. One eye would be closed, and the other would be open just a little. Then, just when you thought the other eye was closing—*snap!* Those jaws would go into action and suddenly the air would crackle with questions. Why do you think that? How do you know? What are your sources?

He was a more sociable man than he appeared, and despite his prodigious work habits there was room in his life for golf and other enjoyments. He liked to hold forth at parties, and he got a kick out of tossing out ideas—sometimes just to see what kind of reaction he'd get.

He was usually amenable to a good laugh—even at his own expense. When a severe hurricane damaged his Florida beachfront home, I sent him a note of apology, ostensibly from something called the CIA Weather Control Office. The storm was supposed to have hit Cuba, I explained, but the weather control satellite had veered off target at the last minute.

Casey liked to joke about members of Congress, and he was well aware of their private peccadilloes. Although the world's most impressive intelligence resources were at his command, when it came to the private lives of senators and congressmen, he relied on an even more impressive network—the Washington rumor mill.

He loathed what Congress had become, and believed that the sport of preference on Capitol Hill was exposing covert operations. He hated testifying before the congressional oversight committees, where he was expected to reveal the intimate details of a covert operation merely to satisfy what he called their "prurient interests." In the belief that members of Congress couldn't be trusted to keep secrets, he told them as little as possible.

He died in the spring of 1987, at the beginning of the congressional hearings. I wanted to be at the funeral, but by then my presence would have been embarrassing for the President, who was also planning to attend. The night before the funeral, at the suggestion of Sophia, his widow, I flew up to New York with another of his close colleagues, and we had a drink at Bill Casey's wake on Long Island.⁴ While we were there, one of Bill's relatives told me that during his final days, Bill had looked up at her from his bed and said, "He'll never get away with it." I've always wondered if he meant the President.

Bud McFarlane is a mystery to me, a real enigma—and ultimately a disappointment. But it wasn't always that way. He sought me out soon after he arrived at the NSC, perhaps because he saw in me some of his own past—the young Marine who had served in Vietnam, and who later found himself as a major assigned to the White House. We grew to be close, and remained close even after he resigned. At his farewell party in December 1985, he hugged me and cried on my shoulder. There were tears in my eyes, too.

Although Bud was only six years older than I, he seemed to belong to another generation. Maybe it was his gray hair, or his long experience in Washington that gave him that older demeanor. Or perhaps it was because he had first come to the NSC back in 1973, when the Vietnam War was still going on.

There were many late nights when I would be working in the Sit Room, preparing paperwork for a meeting the next day, or for the President's morning briefing. Bud would often stop by to say good night, or to give me what Marines call a "howgoesit?"

Sometimes he would call my office at eight or nine in the evening. "You got a few minutes?"

"Sure, I'll be right over."

---

⁴The day of Casey's wake, I had been held in contempt for resisting a grand jury subpoena on the grounds that the special prosecutor had no constitutional legitimacy. The judge had ordered me jailed as soon as I returned from Long Island. While I was in New York, my attorneys successfully prevented my incarceration until the case could be heard by the Court of Appeals.

Some incident had occurred in the world that needed to be written up, or there was an intelligence report he wanted to show me.

Although nobody ever described McFarlane as the life of the party, he wasn't quite as stiff and reserved in private as he appeared to be in public. He would tell the occasional joke, and he did a terrific imitation of Henry Kissinger. We had a professional relationship, but he was a boss in whose presence I could lean back in my chair and say, "Lord, isn't this a mess!"

He was kind to me beyond the call of duty. In November 1983, when I was promoted from major to lieutenant colonel, Bud decided to turn it into an event. "Wear your uniform tomorrow," he told me. "This calls for a promotion ceremony, and we're going to have one." Without telling me, he had asked Wilma, his secretary, to arrange for Betsy and our children to be there.

"Come on, Bud," I told him. "I'm pretty busy, and besides, it's not necessary."

"Don't give me that. And I don't care what you have scheduled. Just be there."

The ceremony was held in the ornate Indian Treaty Room at the OEOB, and Bud administered the oath, reciting it from memory. Ron Hall, Wilma's husband, took pictures.

This turned out to be my fifth and final promotion. I still remember the first one, when I was commissioned as a second lieutenant upon graduation from Annapolis. And I remember this last time, when Bud presided. It was a warm and generous act, and I was moved that he thought to include my family, especially since they sacrificed so much while I was at the NSC. In keeping with a great old tradition of the Corps, Bud, after administering the oath, pinned one of his own oak leaves on my epaulet. Betsy pinned on the other, and she kissed me. Bud shook my hand.

Although Bud and I are very different types, there are some similarities in our backgrounds. Like me, Bud was a graduate of the Naval Academy, where he had taken his commission in the Marine Corps, and he, too, rose to the rank of lieutenant colonel. We had both served in Vietnam, although he had been there a few years earlier, and had participated in the earliest landings of American troops at Da Nang. And we both remembered all too well that the American military withdrawal from Vietnam was based on what turned out to be a false assumption: that the United States would continue to support the South Vietnamese even after our troops were gone.

The similarity of these events to the Nicaraguan situation was hard to ignore, and we both felt strongly that the tragedy of Vietnam should not be repeated in Central America. As Bud once put it, "The people who went through Vietnam came away with the profound sense that a government must never give its word to people who may stand to lose their lives, and then break faith."

Unlike me, Bud had come to his current job with considerable experience in both government and foreign policy. He had been a military aide to Henry Kissinger in 1973, and when Kissinger became Secretary of State, Bud remained at the NSC under Brent Scowcroft. Later, after retiring from the Marines, Bud joined the staff of the Senate Armed Services Committee under the tutelage of Senator John Tower.

After Reagan was elected, Bud's career really took off. When Al Haig became Secretary of State, he brought McFarlane to the State Department. Bud had been one of the leaders of the administration's push to get Congress to approve the sale of AWACs aircraft to Saudi Arabia, which was when I first met him. Shortly afterward, when Bill Clark replaced Richard Allen as national security adviser, Bud came over from State as Judge Clark's top deputy. In 1983, when Clark left to become Secretary of the Interior, the President named McFarlane as national security adviser.

While other candidates had been suggested, most people thought McFarlane was a good choice. Bud had earned a fine reputation as a bright and talented man who worked hard and got the job done. He was also known to have excellent relations with the Congress, a highly prized asset in the Reagan administration.

I respected and admired him. Some people came to see Bud as too ambitious, but he was so adept at covering his ego that I didn't even notice that side of him. He occasionally admitted to a desire to become Secretary of State, but I believe that his aspirations went even further. I think he wanted to be President.

And yet I never had the impression, as some observers have suggested, that McFarlane was trying to outdo Henry Kissinger, his old mentor. On the other hand, I have no doubt that Bud was influenced by Kissinger, and that he hoped to emulate some of Dr. K's accomplishments. Kissinger had been applauded around the world for making a secret trip to China and creating an historic opening to that country during the Nixon years. I believe that Bud saw our trip to Iran as his chance to accomplish something similarly impressive.

But Bud McFarlane was no Kissinger. From my contact with Kissinger, who headed the President's Commission on Central America, I could see immediately that he was a man of enormous self-confidence. When Kissinger was insulted in a meeting with the Sandinista leadership in Managua, he was strong enough not to let it bother him.

Bud McFarlane was less secure. He once stormed out of a meeting in Honduras because of a minor mistake in translation that he perceived as a slight. There was an element of this in all of Bud's trips: I'm Robert McFarlane, the emissary of the President of the United States, and I'm not going to be pushed around by any tinhorn official. This attitude surfaced several times in Tehran, when Bud perceived diplomatic insults in what was merely incompetence.

Unlike Kissinger, who was a strategic thinker, Bud was primarily a synthesizer of other people's views.

Some of us on his staff would encourage Bud to stand up to Weinberger or Shultz, but his natural inclination was to avoid confrontation. He looked for a way to work with everybody. He wanted people to like him, and most of us did.

He was reserved—almost to the point of being mysterious. He kept his own counsel, and preferred to meet with staff officers individually on issues of substance. The regular morning meetings in the Sit Room and the weekly meetings of the entire NSC staff were usually perfunctory events. Rarely did we have meetings—as I had expected when I first came to the NSC—where a group of us would sit around and discuss the wisdom of various options.

McFarlane was well aware that he was never really "one of the boys," which put him at a real disadvantage within the President's inner circle. The rest of the President's top advisers were either wealthy, self-made men or gregarious locker-room buddies; one or two, like Don Regan and Bill Casey, were both. Bud mentioned on several occasions that Ronald Reagan preferred the company of these affluent, outgoing guys over the reserved Washington types like himself. That was true, although it shouldn't have come as a surprise after Bud's many years in government. Like most politicians, Ronald Reagan disliked government bureaucrats, and McFarlane's great frustration was that he was usually perceived as just that.

And perceptions are everything in Washington. Some foreign policy officials, like Kissinger, Brzezinski, and Kirkpatrick, were valued as intellectuals or academic experts. Others, like Al Haig and John Poindexter, were respected as military officers. Then there were the self-made types, like George Shultz, Jim Baker, and Bill Casey. A fourth group of inner-circle advisers consisted of the king's own friends, like Bill Clark, Ed Meese, and Mike Deaver.

McFarlane didn't fit into any of these categories, and

it must have rankled him terribly to be relegated instead to the ranks of the despised but essential bureaucrats. He deserved better. He was both a Marine and a scholar, and had probably written a good deal of what Kissinger was credited with. Many of Ronald Reagan's positions on the big foreign policy issues of the day—arms control, Soviet-American relations, and the Middle East—had emanated from McFarlane's pen.

But while McFarlane was a good writer, in person he often came across as pretentious—assuming you could understand what he was saying. Everyone made fun of his language, which was oblique and indirect even by Washington standards. Some people thought he was putting on airs and deliberately trying to be incomprehensible. Perhaps the most famous example of McFarlanese occurred when he testified under oath before the House Foreign Affairs Committee on December 8, 1986. In response to a question about third-country support for the Nicaraguan resistance, McFarlane replied, "The concrete character of that is beyond my ken."[5]

I still don't know why Bud resigned. He said he was leaving to spend more time with his family, but nobody in Washington believed *that*, probably because almost nobody in Washington does spend much time with his family. (And I, alas, was no exception.) In addition to the constant feuding between Shultz and Weinberger, Bud had numerous run-ins with Don Regan, who generally made life miserable for him. Some people thought that Bud was leaving his job in order to run for Congress or the Senate. His father had been a Democratic congressman from Texas, and Bud had grown up in Washington and was at home inside the Beltway. But I don't think he seriously entertained that possibility.

---

[5]This statement was one reason that Bud pled guilty to a charge of withholding information from Congress.

Well after he resigned as national security adviser, Bud continued to wield considerable influence over the course of American foreign policy. Although he no longer worked at the White House, he still had a secure White House phone system and PROFS[6] terminal in his home, both of which were maintained by the White House Communications Agency and protected by a security system installed by the Secret Service. And he kept his blue White House pass, which allowed him to come and go whenever he pleased.

After he left, we stayed in touch through the PROFS and the secure telephone. He continued to be interested in what I was doing, both to assist the contras and to pursue the Iran initiative, and at the time, he clearly approved of both projects. In the spring of 1986 he even proposed that I join him in his new position at the Center for Strategic and International Studies, a conservative think tank in Washington.[7]

On February 8, 1987, just prior to his third meeting with the Tower Commission, Bud McFarlane took an overdose of Valium in an apparent suicide attempt. He was found unconscious, and was rushed by ambulance to Bethesda Naval Hospital. "I thought I had failed the country," he said later.

I heard about it on the radio, and I was shocked. By then I had learned to check with my lawyers before taking any action, and they asked me not to visit him in the

---

[6]Professional Office System, an IBM electronic mail network.

[7]PROFS message, McFarlane to North, March 11, 1986: "Frankly, I would expect the heat from the Hill to become immense on you by summer. Consequently, it strikes me as wise that you leave the White House. At the same time, there will be no one to do all (or even a small part of what) you have done. And if it isn't done, virtually all of the investment of the past five years will go down the drain. How's this for a self-serving scenario: 1. North leaves the White House in May and takes 30 days leave. 2. July 1, North is assigned as a fellow at the CSIS and (lo and behold) is assigned to McFarlane's office. 3. McFarlane/North continue to work the Iran account as well as to build other clandestine capabilities so much in demand here and there."

hospital. They did, however, permit me to write him a letter. In it, I told Bud that I, too, had once suffered despair but had come to know that God never allows us to be burdened with more than we can bear—as long as we stick with Him. Having spent most of the previous five years with Bud, I thought I could offer him some hope for the future.

He had so much to lose, and he lost it all. Iran-contra was his undoing, and his apparent suicide attempt undid him further. When I left the White House, I had expected that of all the people who might have defended me from the absurd allegation that I had been off on my own, Bud was the most likely to step forward and say, "That's ridiculous. Ollie always told me what he was doing, and I always told him to go ahead." I hoped that Admiral Poindexter, too, would say that, and he did. But from Bud I expected it.

But the Bud McFarlane who testified at the hearings, and again at my trial, was a different man from the one I thought I knew. Ironically, backup copies of thousands of computer messages that McFarlane, Poindexter, and I had written to one another were discovered just before Bud was taken to the hospital. According to one theory, this discovery precipitated his overdose of Valium. But although the PROFS notes and scores of memos taken from my office by the Iran-contra investigators provided documented evidence that he had approved of my activities, Bud continued to maintain that he knew very little about what I had been doing for the resistance.

And that's what he claimed at the hearings. But a year later, when he appeared as a prosecution witness at my trial, the full nature of his approval for my involvement with the contras was exposed during the cross-examination by Brendan Sullivan. Bud's statements were so muddled and incoherent that the judge called the lawyers up to the bench. "This man has told so many stories since he has been on direct [examination]," said the judge, "that there isn't any way to know what he believes or what he knows. He is an intensely unreliable witness in almost every respect of his testimony."[8]

Naturally, I felt betrayed by Bud's version of events. But even more than that, I felt sorry for him.

When McFarlane resigned as national security adviser, Admiral John Poindexter took over. I liked him then, and I like him now. He brings to mind a scene in a movie I once saw, where a British sergeant major and his men are attacked by a tribe of Zulu warriors. As the air is filled with spears and arrows and the defensive line begins to waver, the sergeant major calmly tucks his baton under his arm and walks along the trench line. Showing no hint of anxiety and not a trace of fear, he circulates among the troops saying, "Steady lads, steady now."

That's how I think of John Poindexter—steady. Those of us from military backgrounds tend to judge others by whether or not we would want to have that person next to us during a firefight. John Poindexter is just the man I would want at my side when the shells are coming in.

Poindexter, too, had attended the Naval Academy, and it was well known (although he never mentioned it) that he had graduated first in his class of nine hundred. He was also the midshipman brigade commander—an appointment of extraordinary honor, and a tribute to his leadership ability. (The only other man I know of who was awarded both such distinctions was Douglas MacArthur, at West Point.) Poindexter went on to earn a doctorate in nuclear physics from Cal Tech. From 1976 to 1978 he served as executive assistant to the Chief of Naval Operations, and was promoted to rear admiral in

---

[8] "I'm not at all sure that it's intentional on his part," Judge Gesell added. "I'm not at all sure he isn't a victim, a physical victim, of what he has been going through. But the fact of the matter is, he is not a reliable witness."

1980. A year later, he came to the White House as a military assistant to Richard Allen. In 1983 he became Bud McFarlane's deputy, and little more than two years later was appointed national security adviser.

When McFarlane recommended Poindexter for the job, he informed President Reagan that the admiral had already been offered the prestigious job of commander of the Sixth Fleet. The President approved Bud's memorandum recommending Poindexter's appointment as national security adviser, and added an eerily prescient notation in his own handwriting: "I hope this doesn't hurt his future career."

Contrary to popular myth, John Poindexter was more than an aloof, balding, pipe-smoking automaton. He was also capable of brief forays into anger or humor, although he didn't remain long in either place. More than any man I've ever known, the admiral kept his feelings to himself. He actually made McFarlane seem colorful.

Some people found him almost unbearably taciturn. Certainly he was reserved and formal. Even in private, he always referred to President Reagan as "the President." I was never at his home, but I knew that his wife, Linda, had been ordained an Episcopal priest, and that they had five fine boys, four of whom were in the Navy. By his standards, we were on a first-name basis: he called me Ollie, and I called him Admiral.

He would use his pipe as a way to mull over a thought before he spoke. I can see him now, measuring the competing views of his staff officers as he filled the pipe with tobacco. When it was finally lit, he'd send up a thick cloud of smoke—a signal that he was about to weigh in with his decision.

When you came to him in busy situations, he gave you only as much time as it took to clean the pipe, fill it, and light it. If you hadn't stated the gist of the problem and offered a recommendation by the time the smoke appeared, you might as well go back to your office to think things through in greater depth.

He was a tireless worker and a classic introvert—reserved, thoughtful, and careful. Later, at the hearings, he described himself as a "very low-profile person." That was an understatement. As he put it, "I don't feel that I need a lot of acknowledgment in order to get any sort of psychic income." That's true. John Poindexter was a man with no hidden agenda. He simply wanted to serve wherever he was sent.

He hated politics. Unlike McFarlane, who had excellent connections on Capitol Hill, the admiral seemed to have no friends in Congress, and certainly none in the media. He was reclusive, which was unusual in high government circles, where most people clamor to be visible. There were days when he took all three meals in his office. He was once asked why he ate breakfast and lunch at his desk, but moved over to a table in the corner for dinner. His reply was classic: "Because variety is the spice of life." He meant it, too.

Next to his family, his great love was technology. Once, during a trip to Central America, he asked me what my hobbies had been when I was a kid. I told him that I used to build and fly model airplanes, which was how I had learned the virtue of patience. Then I asked him about his hobbies—assuming he had any. The conventional wisdom around the NSC was that other than going to church and spending time with his family, John Poindexter did nothing but work.

He thought for a moment, and then distantly allowed as to how, in his "off-duty" hours, he had built several televisions and personal computers.

I was impressed. "You build them all from kits?"

"No," he replied. "I build them from scratch. It's more fun that way."

I should have known. Back in 1982, when Poindexter was a military assistant to Judge Clark, he had initiated a massive upgrade of our telecommunications capabilities. One part of this project was the installation of PROFS, which ran on a mainframe computer that was installed and maintained for the NSC by the White House Communications Agency. When you keyed into the system by typing in your password—and you had better have gotten it right the first time—a warning message would appear on the screen to remind you the system was classified. It was also protected against electronic emissions that could conceivably be read from outside the building.

The PROFS system was a godsend, for it saved us countless hours that would otherwise be taken up with meetings and phone calls. It also meant that if Fawn Hall had already left for the evening and I wanted to draft a memorandum for the State Department, I would compose the memo and transmit it directly to her terminal. The next morning, when she came in, it would be waiting for her to convert into the appropriate format and print on letterhead stationery.

But the PROFS went far beyond convenience. It also reduced the amount of paper floating around the NSC, most of which was highly sensitive and classified. Less paper, in turn, meant less risk of a security breach.

For many of us, the PROFS terminals became a free and uninhibited means of communication, just like a secure telephone. Not only was it private and easy to use, but nobody, apparently not even the admiral, suspected that the messages were permanent. We were all under the impression that once we deleted a PROFS message, it disappeared forever. It turned out, however, that the "delete" button wasn't as powerful as we believed. Our correspondence might be gone from our screens, but it was hardly forgotten. The computer kept it in its memory.

Early in 1987, during the Tower Commission's investigation, a young military technician with the White House Communications Agency suspected that copies of our PROFS messages might still be retrieved from backup tapes and the main computer. He turned out to be right. My lawyers were overjoyed at this discovery. I had described my many written exchanges with McFarlane and Poindexter, but until now the lawyers were missing what lawyers really crave—documentary evidence. The PROFS notes, along with my office files that turned up shortly before my trial, verified my claim that what I had done was known and approved by my superiors. Even so, I never imagined that the White House would allow so much of this highly classified material to be published.

Unlike McFarlane, who had extensive experience in foreign affairs, John Poindexter came to the job without much background in the upper echelons of government. And yet he made a vital contribution to our national security, although few people are aware of it. Poindexter accompanied the President to the Reykjavik summit in October 1986, where President Reagan was on the verge of capitulating on the Strategic Defense Initiative in order to achieve a breakthrough in arms-control talks with the Soviets. John Poindexter was far too modest to say so, but to my knowledge he was the only high-level American official at the summit who held firm in the face of enormous pressure from Congress, the State Department, the media, and many in the scientific community, all of whom thought that SDI should be negotiable.

The Soviets were more realistic. They understood that their technology was light-years behind ours, and that they couldn't afford even to try to catch up. Because John Poindexter convinced the President that SDI was not negotiable, the summit appeared to be a failure. But it was shortly after the Reykjavik summit that the Soviets agreed to withdraw their intermediate-range missiles from Europe, pull out of Afghanistan, and enter into serious negotiations on limiting nuclear weapons. Even if John Poindexter had accomplished nothing else in his tenure as national security adviser, he deserves America's gratitude for that alone.

He served his country loyally and well, and what was his reward? Three concurrent six-month sentences. It made me sick when I heard the verdict, and sicker still when I heard about the sentence. He never should have been charged to begin with. Breaking the law was the furthest thing from his mind.

I'm not the only one who feels that way about him. As I travel around this country, people are always coming up to ask, "How's the admiral?" They respect him, and they have a great deal of compassion for a man who served his boss, did his job, and was then punished by politicians who were out to get the President. What happened to John Poindexter was an outrage.

# 9

## "WE BAG THE BUMS"

THERE WERE ONLY TWO OCCASIONS WHEN I SAW President Reagan get really angry, and they both had to do with Beirut. The first time was on October 23, 1983, just after the terrorist bombing of our Marine barracks at the Beirut airport. The President was in Georgia on a weekend golf trip, and when the news came in he flew back immediately. He was in a white rage as he walked into the Sit Room, but he was also as alert and as purposeful as I'd ever seen him. "We'll make them pay," he said, and he clearly meant it.

The second time was in June 1985, during the hijacking of TWA flight 847 between Athens and Rome. The hijackers flew to Beirut, where they killed Robert Stethem, an American Navy diver, and dumped his body on the runway. For seventeen days there was live coverage of the hijacking, with those unforgettable pictures of the American pilot peering out of his cockpit window while a terrorist with a mad grin held a gun to his temple. The terrorists wanted us to look impotent, and they certainly succeeded.

During the crisis, the President convened several

meetings of his National Security Planning Group (NSPG) in the Situation Room. As we were leaving one such meeting, Bill Casey said to McFarlane, "I've got something to show you. Can we talk?" When we got to McFarlane's office I turned to leave, but Casey said, "If you don't mind, I think Ollie should see this." Bud nodded, and Casey handed McFarlane a sheet of paper on which he had outlined plans for a new CIA antiterrorism unit. "I've talked to Cap about this," he said. "He'll support it if you do."

McFarlane read the proposal and handed it to me saying, "Do up a new NSDD and a Finding to cover this." I ended up writing three separate National Security Decision Directives for the President to sign. One created a task force chaired by Vice President Bush to develop new ideas. The second outlined new security measures for U.S.-operated aircraft and domestic airport security. The third document formalized an improved structure for dealing with the terrorist threat, and officially sanctioned a secret entity with a mandate to coordinate our government's response to international terrorism—preemptively if possible, reactively if necessary. I became its first chairman, which made me the de facto counterterrorism coordinator.

Despite my deep involvement with the contras and on the Iran initiative, I actually spent more hours working on counterterrorism than on anything else. My appointment was never made public, but whenever a terrorist event took place—and minor incidents occurred far more often than the media reported—I was the guy who got the call.

The Task Force was established as an offshoot of the Terrorist Incident Working Group (TIWG), a government-wide committee formed in 1983. But for a variety of reasons, the TIWG just hadn't worked.

Among other things, it was simply too large to be effective. "It takes far too long to get nothing accomplished," said Admiral Art Moreau, the representative from the Joint Chiefs of Staff, before he stopped attending. The very size of the TIWG created an obstacle to confidentiality. The representatives from the CIA, the FBI, and the Pentagon often sat at these meetings like mummies, unwilling to discuss classified details about their counterterrorism capabilities for fear the information would leak.

But the biggest obstacle to an effective response was that terrorism was seen as an "international" problem, which therefore required foreign policy "expertise." For that reason, all TIWG meetings were chaired and hosted by the State Department. But a committee chaired *at* State and *by* State was inevitably regarded by the other agencies as being *for* State. And the State Department was itself so large that practically every major terrorist event touched off an internal bureaucratic battle over exactly which bureau at State would have the honor of sabotaging an effective response. After one Palestinian terrorist attack in which Americans, Europeans, and Israelis were killed, a dispute raged for hours as to which bureau—European, Middle East, or Counter-terrorism—would chair the meeting and then draft a message or prepare a press statement.

Whenever terrorists attacked an American embassy, the typical TIWG response was to build a higher wall around the complex and review the security procedures. Going after the perpetrators was rarely even considered.

The TIWG continued to exist after the Task Force came into being, but operational responses to terrorist threats or attacks were now coordinated by this small group, which met at the White House. My associates on the Task Force included Noel Koch (and later Richard Armitage) from Defense, Dewey Clarridge and Charlie Allen from the CIA, Buck Revell and Wayne Gilbert from the FBI, Bob Oakley from State, and Art Moreau (and later General Jack Moellering) from the Joint Chiefs of Staff. These were highly placed men with excellent access to the heads of their respective agencies. They were cool under pressure, and they knew how to move quickly. If a proposal was absurd, they'd say so. But if it was imaginative or bold, they wouldn't block it merely because of "NIH" syndrome—Not Invented Here, the recurring disease of Washington's bureaucracies.

The members of the Task Force were all linked by secure phone lines, fax machines, and a computer network. While the Task Force was designed to be action-oriented, much of our work was devoted to planning. One of our first projects was to start building an all-source classified data base that could be used in a crisis. This data base included information essential to resolving terrorist incidents around the world. The idea was to have this information available to those who needed it at a moment's notice.

Although the data base itself was classified, much of the information it contained was derived from open sources. But one of its more sensitive areas was a detailed description of what kinds of information could, and could not, be revealed to specific countries.

Rod McDaniel, a Navy captain who later became executive secretary of the NSC, was given the thankless task of building these data bases and coordinating the effort with the appropriate agencies of our government. His small, supersecret team worked out of a highly secure, restricted space directly below my office, and was linked to it by scores of cables drilled through the floor. McDaniel's group was still engaged in the monumental process of collecting and updating this information when I was fired in 1986.

Except for times of crisis, which had their own momentum, the Task Force normally met three or four times a month to discuss ongoing covert initiatives aimed at frustrating terrorists before they could strike. At Buck Revell's urging, we drafted, and the TIWG supported, new legislation that extended the authority of the Justice Department to apprehend international terrorists who harmed Americans or American property overseas. But operations of this kind took time. One of them, initiated in mid-1986, was aimed at capturing Fawaz Younis, a Palestinian hijacker who had come to my attention through the Drug Enforcement Agency during our hostage recovery efforts. The Task Force coordinated a remarkably effective effort among the alphabet soup of government agencies—the DEA, the CIA, and the FBI—and Younis was eventually captured. Ironically, he was tried in Washington in the same courthouse and at the same time as I was.

By no stretch of the imagination were we always successful. But on several occasions we succeeded in our ultimate goal of preventing a terrorist attack before it occurred. And sometimes we were able to engineer an effective resolution to an ongoing event.

The most famous of these, and certainly one of the most successful, followed the hijacking of an Italian cruise ship, the *Achille Lauro*.

It began on October 7, 1985, a Monday, and my forty-second birthday. The ship, which had left its home port of Genoa four days earlier, had dropped off most of its passengers that morning in the Egyptian city of Alexandria, where they began a bus tour of the Pyramids. They were to board the ship again that night in Port Said, and from there they would sail on to Israel.

The *Achille Lauro* was thirty miles from Port Said when it was taken over by four Palestinian terrorists who had come on board with false passports. It had been twenty-five years since a cruise ship was last hijacked, and like most ships, the *Achille Lauro* had no security procedures, not even a metal detector. As a result, the terrorists had been able to bring aboard all the tools they needed: weapons, ammunition, and hand grenades.

We learned later that they hadn't actually intended to hijack the ship. Originally, the terrorists had planned to carry out an attack on land when the *Achille Lauro* docked at the Israeli port of Ashdod. But when one of the ship's stewards found them cleaning their weapons in a cabin, the terrorists panicked. They rushed into the ship's dining room and rounded up about a hundred passengers. They then demanded the release of fifty Palestinian terrorists in Israeli jails.

The following day, off the coast of Syria, they murdered Leon Klinghoffer, a retired American citizen who had suffered a stroke and was confined to a wheelchair. They announced his death to the Syrians over the radio, and threatened to start killing other passengers unless their demands were met.

I had just arrived at my office that Monday morning when I was called by the Senior Watch officer in the Situation Room. He had received a "heads up" from CIA headquarters, but no hard intelligence. "Something is going on with an Italian cruise ship somewhere in the Med," he told me. "They're sending a mayday. It could be terrorists. I'll get back to you as soon as I hear more."

I immediately called Charlie Allen, the CIA's expert on terrorism. Charlie knew the name of the ship, and told me it had been seized with some Americans aboard. We both did what by now had become routine during terrorist events: we turned on CNN. The admiral called after seeing the first alert: "Why don't you get your group together and come up with some recommendations?" I quickly typed up a computer message for the Task Force members, calling them to a meeting in the Sit Room later that morning.

At the meeting, we immediately agreed that the President should authorize the dispatch of a JSOC (Joint Special Operations Command) team to the Mediterranean. In addition to a highly mobile headquarters element, JSOC also has several special ops teams. These small, highly trained military units use the latest equipment and just about every possible type of technology. They have the ability to get to the scene of action by almost any conceivable means, and are ready to deploy to a trouble spot at a moment's notice.

Recommending that the President deploy JSOC forces was not something we did lightly. It meant that the United States was about to commit American military forces to possible hostile action. But it was essential to start planning for a possible military operation in case the hijacking could not be resolved peacefully. As more and more information arrived, the group began to explore a wide range of options, including some that were right out of James Bond stories and others that were somewhat less preposterous.

The main challenge facing JSOC was how to board the ship and subdue the terrorists without hurting the hostages. After several conversations between Admiral Art Moreau and General Carl Stiner, the JSOC commander, it was agreed that we should position a special ops team near the scene so that it could quickly move to the ship. By noon on that first day, we knew the terrorists were heavily armed. And while the ship's captain had reported only four of them, he might have been saying that with a gun to his head. There could also be additional terrorists on board who hadn't yet shown themselves.

The uncertainty about the size of the terrorist force on the ship delayed the JSOC deployment. They could accomplish this mission in a number of interesting ways, but they wanted to make sure that they took with them everything they might possibly need. Once they took off, they would be ten to twelve hours from their U.S. base.

You might have thought that by this time, with all the terrorist incidents that had occurred during the 1980s, the United States would have had several counterterrorist units stationed overseas and ready to strike. Incredibly, we didn't.

In the Task Force, we had done everything we could to make that happen, but we hadn't succeeded. The State Department didn't want us to position counterterrorist units overseas covertly, because this could anger our allies when they eventually learned about it. The CIA and the Joint Chiefs didn't want us to do it openly—not only for security reasons, but also because the host governments might not approve of a particular mission.

And so nothing happened. Despite the obvious need to move quickly in an emergency, we never succeeded in getting the upper echelons at State and Defense to agree to this crucial preparation for a crisis *before* it occurred. I used to wonder: how many dead Americans will it take before we do something?

The Israelis had time and again offered to make their own bases available for such prepositioning, but Cap Weinberger wouldn't hear of it. And the State Department was totally uncooperative—although Shultz was usually the first to complain when we didn't have forces on the scene. The Air Force had hundreds of transport planes, but the Pentagon refused to leave two of them sitting on a runway unless a crisis was already in progress. But by then, of course, the whole world can see what you're up to. The press gathers at the end of the runway at Pope Air Force Base in North Carolina, just waiting for the planes to take off.

At midnight on Monday, the special ops team finally took off for the Mediterranean. Meanwhile, the job of the Task Force was to look for other solutions. Working out of the Crisis Management Center at the OEOB, we drafted a flurry of cables to our embassies in Egypt, Syria, Italy, Algeria, Greece, and even the Soviet Union. It was my job to draft cables from Robert McFarlane to his British counterpart.

The biggest challenge in drafting these messages wasn't putting the words on paper; it was coordinating those words within the U.S. government—where it seemed that practically everybody had a "need to know" and a comment. By comparison, my later dealings with the Iranians were relatively easy. The Iranians we met with didn't always tell the truth, but at least their numbers were limited.

By Tuesday afternoon, the *Achille Lauro* was

approaching Tartus, Syria, where the terrorists requested political asylum. We drafted several urgent cables for State to send on to our embassy in Syria. The U.S. ambassador was instructed to immediately ask the Syrian government, in the strongest possible terms, to deny the terrorists' requests.

It was during this Syrian standoff that Leon Klinghoffer was killed. We later learned that the terrorists shot him in the head and ordered two crew members to dump his body and his wheelchair into the ocean. But all we knew at the time was what the hijackers told the Syrians over the ship's radio. They bragged about murdering an American, and threatened to kill additional passengers unless they were granted asylum. Although we had no way of knowing for sure that the terrorists' claim was true, we were all stunned as we read the reports of the murder and the threat to kill more of their seaborne hostages. Art Moreau went into the Situation Room Watch Officers' area, picked up the handset to the satellite radio, and had a long conversation with General Stiner, who was now on the ground at an allied base in the Mediterranean. Moreau signed off by saying, "We've got to get those bastards."

The Syrians refused to give in to the hijackers' demands—not from any lack of sympathy for the terrorists, but because by now the whole world was watching. We also suspected that President Assad relished the opportunity to undermine Yasir Arafat. And we were fairly sure that despite Arafat's fervent denials, he was up to his ears in this event.

When the Syrians turned them down, the terrorists ordered the ship's captain to return to Egypt. Night had fallen, and the weather in the eastern Med was rapidly deteriorating. As the storm intensified, we lost track of the ship. Until now, our intelligence agencies had been tracking the *Achille Lauro* by satellite, Navy aircraft, and the ship's own navigation reports. For a while, the captain had continued his normal practice of announcing his exact location during his calls to the ship's home office. But when the terrorists caught on, they quickly put a stop to it.

Despite our advanced technology, it is extremely difficult to pinpoint a single vessel among many in a big ocean, especially in bad weather. If you're forced to rely on ships and aircraft for surveillance, there's a risk that the terrorists might notice, and could retaliate by killing passengers. After several anxious hours and long discussions with the CIA and other agencies, I called Major General Uri Simhoni, the military attaché at the Israeli embassy in Washington. Back in June, we had worked together on the hijacking of TWA flight 847, and we trusted each other. I gave Simhoni the last reported position we had for the *Achille Lauro*, and asked if his people could help. About a half an hour later, he called me back with the ship's exact location. From his prompt response, I surmised that the Israelis had been following the ship ever since the hijacking began. Israel's ability to gather human intelligence in the Middle East was widely respected, but even our own government often underestimated their technical abilities.

We spent a long, sleepless night in the Situation Room watching and waiting as the ship sailed back to Egypt. Early Wednesday morning we lost the ship again. Once again, Simhoni put us back on track.

Meanwhile, looking through the intelligence traffic, Charlie Allen noticed that Abul Abbas, the head of the Palestine Liberation Front and a member of the PLO executive committee, had suddenly been granted diplomatic clearance into Egypt. Charlie, who had been working nonstop in the Crisis Management Center and the Sit Room since Monday, had returned to his office for a change of clothes and a brief rest. He called us on the speakerphone and pointed out that Abbas was a key Arafat lieutenant with a history of brutal but poorly executed attacks on Israeli citizens. "Let's watch this guy," he said. "I wouldn't be surprised if he planned the whole thing."

As soon as Abbas arrived in Egypt, he began to play the role of a neutral peacemaker dispatched by Arafat to help "resolve" the hijacking. But when the *Achille Lauro* came within radio range of Alexandria, and Abbas started "negotiating" with the terrorists, they greeted him with the words, "Commander, we are happy to hear your voice." That's when we knew Charlie was right.

But what we didn't know was that Arafat and Abbas had struck a deal with Egyptian president Hosni Mubarak. Over the ship's radio, Abbas explained to the terrorists that if they surrendered to the Egyptians they would be given safe passage out of the country. Early Wednesday evening, a tugboat sailed out of the harbor to bring the terrorists ashore. When they heard about this, Art Moreau and the JSOC planners were both relieved and disappointed. Earlier that day, the President had approved the plan to put the special ops team aboard the ship that night.

Shortly after the *Achille Lauro* arrived off Alexandria, Nick Veliotes, our ambassador in Cairo, boarded the ship. With the help of the Egyptians, the terrorists had fled just prior to his arrival. Veliotes's first words on the ship-to-shore radio came just after he had learned from the traumatized passengers and crew about the brutal murder of Leon Klinghoffer: "You tell the foreign ministry that we demand that they prosecute these sons of bitches!"

Ambassadors don't normally talk this way, and to the exhausted handful of us in the Task Force, these words came as a shock. But they were also a refreshing breath of air in the diplomatic fog.

With the murder of an American citizen confirmed, we sent a series of messages to the Egyptians—both to their embassy in Washington, and through our diplomats in Cairo—asking them to turn over the hijackers. Together with Jim Stark, a Navy captain on the NSC staff, I drafted a strongly worded personal message from President Reagan to President Mubarak, asking that the Egyptians turn the terrorists over to us—or at least to the Italians.

Following the usual procedures, the document went from the NSC staff to McFarlane. Then, with clearance from State, it went to the President and on to Mubarak.

But with the hijackers safely ashore, the Egyptian government suddenly clammed up. Veliotes was unable to deliver the message to the Egyptian foreign minister, who was conferring with Mubarak and the defense minister.

By now I was thoroughly exhausted, and on Wednesday night I drove home for the first time since the hijacking began. The passengers were out of danger, and we had reason to hope that Egypt might even allow the terrorists to be extradited to the United States and put on trial for their crimes. This had never happened before, which was why Buck Revell had wanted the new anti-terrorist legislation extending the reach of the FBI. But now it was up to the diplomats. Our part was over—or so we thought.

Early Thursday morning, after a few hours' sleep, I returned to the White House. For the first time in days, the Crisis Management Center was quiet and empty. The room was littered with empty coffee cups and cigarette butts—signs of intense activity and fatigue. With a cup of coffee in my hand, I went down to the Sit Room to look through the overnight cables before the morning staff meeting. There, in the stack, was a cable that indicated the Egyptian government had let the four terrorists leave Egypt. There was also a cable reporting Mubarak's public statement about their departure. "I don't know where they went," he had said. "Possibly to Tunis. When we accepted their surrender, we hadn't known about the murder."

I was stunned to read that the terrorists had left Egypt. Mubarak might not have known for sure about the murder of Leon Klinghoffer when he cut the deal with the PLO, but he certainly knew about it by the time he let the terrorists go. And President Reagan had practically begged him to hold them.

From the Sit Room, I called Simhoni's office at the

Israeli embassy. Uri wasn't in yet, so I told one of his colleagues that the hijackers had left Egypt.

"I saw that, too," he said, "but I don't believe it, and you shouldn't either."

"What do you mean?" I asked.

"They're still there."

"How do you know?"

"Believe me, we know."

I called Charlie Allen. He couldn't confirm whether the terrorists were still in Egypt, but he hadn't seen any evidence to indicate they had left.

Just before the morning staff meeting, I told McFarlane what I had learned from Simhoni's colleague.

"He could be right," Bud said. "Check it out with all our sources."

When the morning staff meeting ended, I was back on the phone to the Israeli embassy. Simhoni was in. "Uri," I said, "where are the four thugs?"

"Still in Egypt," he replied.

"Please keep an eye on them," I said, although they were undoubtedly doing that anyway.

Jim Stark was standing next to me when I hung up. "They're still there, aren't they?" he said.

I nodded. "Why don't you call around and see what else you can find out?"

A few minutes later, Jim brought in additional confirmation that the terrorists were still in Egypt. He had also learned that the Egyptians were planning to fly them out of the country that night, and by now it was already late afternoon in Egypt. Jim called Art Moreau and Charlie Allen while I ran upstairs to grab McFarlane. Bud was about to leave for a trip to Chicago with the President, who was scheduled to give a speech on tax reform. I found him just as he was leaving to board the helicopter for the trip to Andrews. Admiral Poindexter was with him.

"Our friends say the terrorists are still in Egypt," I

said, half out of breath from running up the stairs. "We've confirmed it. They're flying out tonight. Do you remember Yamamoto?"

Admiral Isoroku Yamamoto was the man who had led Japan's attack on Pearl Harbor. During World War II, after our intelligence had uncovered his flight plans to visit a naval base in the Solomon Islands, we ambushed his plane and destroyed it in the air. The idea that we might try something similar had just occurred to me.

"We can't just shoot them down, Ollie," said Poindexter.

"No," I said, "but we can intercept them and force them down at a friendly base, transfer them to one of our planes, and fly them back here for trial."

"It's a possibility," said Bud, as he ran off to board Marine One on the White House lawn. "Work out the details," he called back. "Call me in Chicago."

Over the next few hours, Jim Stark and I were on the phone continually—with the Israelis, the Pentagon, and our own intelligence services. With remarkable speed, Art Moreau began to pull together a plan for the Navy to intercept the hijackers. Meanwhile, we had only a few hours to learn exactly when, where and how they were leaving Egypt.

By mid-morning in Washington, we knew that the Egyptians had prepared a commercial airliner to fly the terrorists to Tunis that night. Once again the Israelis came through, providing us with the takeoff time, the tail number of the EgyptAir 737, the air base (Al Maza, outside of Cairo), and the information that a false flight plan would be filed for Algiers.

While Jim worked with Admiral Moreau, who was in touch with the Sixth Fleet through the Joint Chiefs' Communications Center, I drafted a message for President Reagan to send to President Habib Bourguiba of Tunisia, asking him to deny landing rights if the plane came to Tunis. Similar messages were drafted for Athens and Beirut, and the Sit Room readied all three for transmission after the Egyptian plane was airborne.

In the Mediterranean, Sixth Fleet ops officers, working directly with Admiral Moreau, had already come up with a plan for the intercept. Meanwhile, the Israelis called with dramatic news: Abul Abbas, the mastermind of this whole event, was flying out of Egypt with the terrorists!

Poindexter called Bud McFarlane in Chicago, and found him with the President at a Sara Lee bakery plant in Deerfield, Illinois. Bud had already briefed the President on Moreau's plan: F-14 Tomcats from the U.S.S. *Saratoga*, backed up by E-2C surveillance/command and control planes, would intercept the terrorists' plane and force it down either at Akrotiri, the British base on Cyprus, or at Sigonella, a joint Italian-NATO base in Sicily.

"The President likes it," McFarlane said. "Keep working on it."

Stark and I were euphoric. Although there were still many details to work out, at least we had a chance.

In approving the plan, the President had made clear that no innocent people could be hurt. The rules of engagement had to be airtight. But what if the Egyptian pilot refused to obey the instructions to land at Sigonella? Shooting down the plane wasn't an option. Even if the terrorists didn't deserve to live, there was a pilot, a copilot, and possibly a flight attendant on board. Innocent people should not have to die in order for the terrorists to be punished.

Somehow we had to make the pilot believe he had no choice but to land at Sigonella. And so one of the rules of engagement that Moreau developed allowed the Tomcats to fire warning shots across the nose of the Egyptian plane.

Stark and I were utterly amazed that Moreau was able to get the intercept plan through the Pentagon without Caspar Weinberger's coming unglued. We learned later that Weinberger had objected, and had tried to talk the President out of the operation on the grounds that it would harm our relations with Egypt. But the President wasn't buying it.

Nothing happens in government without paperwork, and at Admiral Moreau's request, Jim and I quickly prepared a directive for the President to sign. This document, which was faxed to Air Force One, ordered the intercept of the EgyptAir flight and outlined the rules of engagement that Moreau had drafted. President Reagan was flying back to Washington, and as soon as he signed it, he called Secretary Weinberger and told him he had ordered the intercept. Weinberger, who was en route from Ottawa to his summer house in Maine, called Admiral Crowe at the Pentagon and confirmed the order.

As the Navy jets scrambled off the darkened flight deck of the *Saratoga*, Moreau, Poindexter, Stark, and I began working out the final details. Our Special Ops forces, already in the air and headed for home, were diverted to Sigonella. We hadn't yet informed the Italian government of our plans for fear that the information would leak, but we would soon need permission to land. With Simhoni's help we had worked out a back-up plan: if Sigonella couldn't be used, the plane would be diverted to an Israeli military base.

The EgyptAir plane took off at 11:15 P.M. Cairo time. By midnight it was just south of Crete, where the F-14s were waiting in an ambush. With their lights off and their cockpits dark, the four Tomcats throttled back to follow the Egyptian airliner. About a hundred miles behind them sat Commander Ron Sims (a pseudonym) in his E-2C Tracker. When it was time to make radio contact with the Egyptian plane, Sims would do the talking.

As Sims listened in, the Egyptian pilot requested landing rights in Tunis. Permission was denied. He tried Athens—same answer. With no place to land, the pilot, unaware that he was now flanked by two F-14s, requested permission to return to Cairo.

That's when Sims made contact with him. "EgyptAir 2843. This is Tigertail 603, over."

There was no answer. Sims repeated the message three more times before he received a reply: "Tigertail 603. EgyptAir 2843. Go ahead."

"EgyptAir 2843. Tigertail 603. Be advised you're being escorted by two F-14s. You are to land immediately—immediately—at Sigonella, Sicily. Over."

The Egyptian pilot must have been astounded. "Say again. Who is calling?"

"Roger. This is Tigertail 603. I advise you are directed to land immediately, proceed immediately to Sigonella, Sicily. You are being escorted by two U. S. Navy interceptor aircraft. Vector 280 for Sigonella, Sicily. Over."

The pilot tried to radio Cairo for instructions. But Art Moreau and the Sixth Fleet planners had anticipated this, and had directed Sims's plane to jam him up and down the radio frequency spectrum. Now the only communication the pilot had was with Sims.

"You are to turn immediately to 280," Sims repeated. "Head 280 immediately."

The two F-14s turned on their lights and flew close enough to peer into the cabin. They dipped their wings in the aviation symbol for "follow me." And to show they meant business, they blasted the EgyptAir plane with their afterburners.

The pilot got the message. "Turning right, heading 280," he reported, and followed through. The poor guy must have been scared witless. "I'm saying you are too close! I'm following your orders. Don't be too close! Please!"

"Okay, we'll move away a little bit." Sims spoke as if he himself were flying one of the F-14s, rather than trailing them miles behind in the slower E-2C. By now the four original Tomcats had been airborne for hours and were running low on fuel. On another frequency, Sims requested new planes to replace them.

There was quite a parade heading for Sicily: in addition to the Egyptian plane, the four replacement

Tomcats, and Sims's Tracker, there were also a couple of C-141s carrying General Stiner and the special ops unit. Once the EgyptAir plane was on the ground, our plan was to remove the hijackers and Abul Abbas, transfer them all to one of Stiner's C-141s, and continue on to the United States.

It was finally time to get permission to land in Sicily. Everything else was in place, and Poindexter, Stark, Moreau, and I were elated that it all seemed to be working. But now that we had to notify Prime Minister Craxi in Italy, our embassy in Rome was unable to locate him. An officer at our Rome embassy finally found him, but no one from the State Department could get through.

I remembered that Michael Ledeen and Craxi were old friends. Frantically, I called Mike at home. "We need your help," I said. Violating all kinds of security precautions, I quickly brought him up to speed. "You've got to get hold of Craxi," I said. "Otherwise those planes can't land."

Ledeen asked the White House switchboard to put him through to the Hotel Raphael, where Craxi lived. One of the prime minister's aides picked up the phone.

"He's not here," Ledeen was told.

"You'd better find him," Ledeen said in Italian. "I'm calling from the White House, and lives are at stake. If anyone dies because you won't put me through, tomorrow morning your picture is going to be on the front page of every newspaper in the world."

Unlike all the rest of our government agencies, Mike knew the right button to push. Prime Minister Craxi was on the line in less than a minute.

"Why Sicily?" Craxi wanted to know.

"Well," said Ledeen, thinking fast and taking quite a risk, "no other place in the world offers such a combination of beautiful weather, history, tradition, and magnificent cuisine. "

Craxi laughed and said he would arrange it. But it wasn't that simple. Connections between Rome and the base on Sicily were less than efficient, and Craxi's order was late getting through. The Italian air traffic controllers didn't give permission for the planes to land until the Navy aircraft declared a midair emergency. Then, in quick succession, the Egyptian 737 and the American C-141s touched down on the airfield. The Egyptian plane, still buttoned up and with one engine still running, was quickly surrounded by General Stiner's special ops unit.

At first the pilot refused to open the doors or even turn off the engine. Then General Stiner had a portable stairway brought over. Stiner, one of the braver men on this planet, laid down his weapon, climbed up the stairway, and opened the door.

He was met by an Egyptian commando officer who pointed his submachine gun straight at the general.

"I don't want you," Stiner said. "I want *them*."

After a few moments of hesitation, the commando lowered his weapon. Down the stairway came the four terrorists, together with their ringleader, Abul Abbas.

This is where the story should have ended, but events rarely turn out exactly as planned.

While Stiner's men were surrounding the plane, they, in turn, were surrounded by a team of Carabinieri—the Italian national police—who now demanded custody of Abul Abbas and his terrorists. From the Sit Room, we listened in on a live, running account of the events at Sigonella, including the confrontation between Stiner's men and the Italian police. Reluctantly, Admiral Poindexter made the only possible decision—that we couldn't risk a shootout with the Italians.

Over the course of the next few hours, the Craxi government assured us that the terrorists in their custody would be brought to trial. We, of course, wanted them to be extradited to the United States, and we continued pressing that point. The White House sent Craxi a strongly worded message, reminding him of the extradition treaty between the United States and Italy, which spelled out that a suspected terrorist could be held for up to forty-five days while evidence was collected against him.

The *Achille Lauro* incident ended in a tremendous anticlimax. In order to put the four terrorists on trial, the Italians needed evidence of their crimes. For the past three days, the Task Force had worked this operation from the seat of its pants. It had succeeded brilliantly, and we were exhausted. But the legal battle had only begun.

Attorney General Meese and a deputy from the FBI came down to the Sit Room to help us prepare the necessary paperwork for a warrant to be drawn up. The Justice Department had to show a federal judge that there was enough evidence against the terrorists to present a reasonable case. But most of the evidence consisted of extremely sensitive intelligence that had been gathered by our own agencies as well as the Israelis. The Israelis were willing to help us in a variety of practical ways, but they weren't willing to expose their sources and methods—and neither were we.

But with the help of the Israelis, we were able to collect enough evidence to take before a judge. It was during the process of building this evidence for extraditing the terrorists that I had extensive contact with Amiram Nir, Prime Minister Peres's coordinator for counterterrrorism. Over the next fourteen months, I would get to know Nir much better.

Not everyone was as euphoric about the outcome as we were in the Task Force. George Shultz was angry about the damage that had been done to our relations with Egypt and Italy. Despite his pique, the State Department was helpful in the extradition work, and by early the next morning we had the paperwork in order. Although the situation required haste, we took care to abide by both the letter and spirit of Italian and American law.

But we didn't succeed. In the end, the four terrorists

were tried and convicted in Italy. Although the state prosecutor bravely asked for life sentences, the terrorists got off with terms of twenty to thirty years. Yussef Molqi, who admitted to killing Leon Klinghoffer, was so grateful for the lenient judgment that he called out in the courtroom, "Long live Italian justice, long live Palestine."

And what about Abul Abbas? Incredibly, the Italians actually helped him escape! After bringing the five men to Rome, they separated him from the others, dressed him in a pilot's uniform, and put him on a plane to Yugoslavia. We immediately prepared extradition papers and had them served in Belgrade, but by then the battle had been lost. Yugoslavia had diplomatic relations with the PLO, and Abbas was protected under diplomatic immunity. (No, I'm not making this up.) In the days that followed, we tracked him as he fled from Belgrade to Baghdad, where he became a permanent guest of that great human rights advocate Saddam Hussein. As far as I know, he's still there.

Not that there was any doubt, but the trial made clear to the world that Abul Abbas had indeed planned the entire operation. He and three of his lieutenants were tried and sentenced in absentia to life terms.

But the big fish got away. Compared to Abul Abbas, the four terrorists who had carried out the hijacking and the murder were just two-bit trigger men. We knew we'd never make a dent in the worldwide terrorist threat simply by capturing a few foot soldiers. We had to get the ringleaders.

It was infuriating to lose Abbas. Despite the brilliant success of this dramatic operation, we were unable to convince the Italians to let us have the main criminal—or even to prosecute him themselves. The Italians knew full well that Abbas was the mastermind of the entire operation, but they apparently wanted the rest of the world to believe that he just *happened* to be on that unscheduled EgyptAir flight.

It was an enormous betrayal, but in retrospect it isn't

all that surprising. The Italians, like the Egyptians, lacked the resolve to fight terrorism, because they feared the consequences of capturing and trying the terrorist leaders. Although we could never confirm it, I believe that both governments had made commitments to the PLO that Abbas would be released. That way, the operation couldn't be linked directly to Arafat.

Five years later, Abul Abbas surfaced again. In the spring of 1990 he planned an operation in which Palestinian commandos would land on a Tel Aviv beach and start shooting everyone they saw. The terrorists who intended to carry out this act were captured by the Israelis, and no civilians were hurt.

In March 1991, there was more news about the *Achille Lauro* terrorists. Abdulrahim Khaled, one of Abul Abbas's lieutenants, was arrested in Greece in connection with a planned terrorist event in Athens. Khaled was originally on the *Achille Lauro*, but he apparently left the ship in Alexandria just before his comrades seized it. When his true identity was revealed, the Italian government asked Greece to turn him over.

Although we were bitterly disappointed about losing Abul Abbas, the American people were jubilant when the intercept was reported. "WE BAG THE BUMS," wrote the New York *Daily News* in a banner headline. In an amusing footnote to the whole event, I was in Pat Buchanan's office, working with him on the President's announcement that the terrorists had been captured, when a call came in from Niles Latham, an editor at the *New York Post*. "We need a great headline," Niles said. "We'd like to use 'YOU CAN RUN BUT YOU CAN'T HIDE.' If you can get the President to use it, we'll put the whole line in quotes."

It was a little unusual for a journalist to suggest language for the President, but Pat and I had to acknowledge that this was a much better conclusion for the

President's remarks than the ending we had written. The President used the new line, and the reaction was terrific. Niles has been telling that story for years; maybe now people will believe him.


A lot of people have given me the credit for our success in the *Achille Lauro* affair. I'm proud to have been part of it, but the praise belongs to the Navy flight planners and pilots, and a host of others. Bud McFarlane should be acknowledged for authorizing the planning for the capture, and getting the President to override Weinberger's objections. But the bulk of the credit should go to Art Moreau. He hated the Washington bureaucracy, but he was a master at cutting through it. A few months later, he was named commander of NATO's naval forces in the Mediterranean. As soon as he arrived he was targeted by the Red Brigades and several Palestinian terrorist groups. He and his wife spent that year under heavy guard. Art Moreau died of a heart attack the following year without ever being recognized for the enormous contribution he had made to the fight against terrorism.

As the old saying has it, no good deed goes unpunished. Angry voices were raised in Egypt, where Mubarak was attacked both by moderates, who thought he should have apprehended the terrorists, and by Muslim fundamentalists who were convinced he had tipped us off and enabled the capture to succeed. In Italy, Prime Minister Craxi's coalition suffered the fate of so many previous Italian governments: it collapsed.

With all of this diplomatic fallout, our Secretary of State must have felt a fair amount of pressure. One afternoon, shortly after the fall of Craxi's coalition, George Shultz was leaving McFarlane's office as I was coming in. He looked up, glared at me, and muttered, "So here's the man who brought down the Italian government."

"Good afternoon, Mr. Secretary," I replied with a smile.

On Capitol Hill, there were others who objected. Senator Dave Durenberger, the ranking Republican on the Senate Intelligence Committee, was apparently upset that the President had supposedly violated the War Powers Resolution! Other members were outraged that we didn't consult with them before committing our Special Ops units. If we had, we'd *still* be looking for the killers of Leon Klinghoffer.

But these were exceptions. All over America, the response was overwhelmingly positive. The cooperation had been marvelous—among various branches of government, our intelligence services, and between us and the Israelis.

As successful as it was, the *Achille Lauro* episode did not end the problem of terrorism. Libya, the prime sponsor of international terrorist activity, showed no inclination to stop. On the contrary: when other supporters of terrorism closed down their training camps, Qaddafi moved in to fill the gap.

In late December 1985, Qaddafi was linked to Abu Nidal's deadly terrorist attacks at the Rome and Vienna airports. Over the winter, we watched as Qaddafi planned other terrorist events aimed at the United States. Within the administration, there was a growing sentiment in favor of a military response against Libya.

On March 28, 1986, Qaddafi made a statement calling on "all Arab people" to attack anything connected to the United States, "be it an interest, goods, ship, plane, or a person." Around the same time, our intelligence sources picked up instructions from Tripoli to various Libyan People's Bureaus—the Libyan equivalent of an embassy—to prepare for action. We didn't know what target they had in mind, but these were the same kinds of instructions that had been given to Libyan offices abroad prior to Libya's 1984 killing of anti-Qaddafi protesters in London.

A few days later, on April 5, 1986, a bomb went off at La Belle discotheque in West Berlin, a popular gathering place for off-duty American servicemen. Although we had compelling proof of Libyan complicity, there was no way to disclose the evidence without revealing sensitive details of our intelligence-gathering operations. Critics of the administration charged that we were inventing the Libyan role, but several years later, after the Berlin Wall came down, the East Germans admitted what we had claimed all along: that the orders for the bombing had come from Tripoli.

On April 14, American planes responded by bombing terrorist-related targets in Libya. As with the *Achille Lauro* incident, the Task Force coordinated the various bureaucratic requirements for the raid. But, because this action was going to be significantly more prolonged in its planning, the chair shifted from Bud to Don Fortier, by then deputy national security adviser. The strike was one of several possible responses we had considered against Libya. But it wasn't our first choice. Unfortunately, our "allies" were unwilling to support us in other measures against Qaddafi.

The action against Libya was essential in our fight against terrorism, but it wasn't undertaken lightly. There were numerous discussions about the bombing targets, and we made every effort to avoid killing innocent people. But we also knew that civilian casualties were probably unavoidable. A surgical strike is a nice concept, and while it may be achievable under test conditions when nobody is shooting at you, it rarely works as well when the air is full of antiaircraft fire. When a pilot is dodging antiaircraft missiles at six hundred miles per hour, pinpoint accuracy is an illusion.

In the old days, the United States would have found a way to assassinate Qaddafi. But despite what Seymour Hersh and other journalists have claimed, killing him was never part of our plan. On the other hand, we certainly made no attempt to protect him from our bombs.

By law, we couldn't specifically target him. But if Qaddafi happened to be in the vicinity of the Azziziyah Barracks in downtown Tripoli when the bombs started to fall, nobody would have shed any tears.

While no single military strike can end the problem of terrorism, our bombing raid on Libya destroyed Qaddafi's command post and communications center. But its greatest effect seemed to have been psychological. Qaddafi immediately went into hiding in the desert, and for over a year he initiated no terrorist action of any kind. While he is still in no danger of winning the Nobel Peace Prize, it appears that the bombing raid on Tripoli taught him a lesson.

# 10

## THE CONTRAS

I RARELY MET A CONTRA I DIDN'T LIKE. AND I NEVER met one at all until 1983, when I was introduced to Juan. Like many members of the Nicaraguan resistance, Juan was a former Sandinista officer who had fought for years against the hated Somoza regime. This is the story he told me of how he joined the resistance.

In July 1980, on the first anniversary of the day the Sandinistas came to power, an enormous victory parade was held in Managua. In honor of the occasion, the old cathedral and the square around it were draped in red and black, the Sandinista colors. An enormous poster of a hammer and sickle was flanked by huge portraits of Marx, Lenin, Castro, and Augusto Cesar Sandino, the legendary guerrilla leader who had fought against the U.S. Marines in the late 1920s and early 1930s.

Juan was marching in the parade along with his men, and he was shocked by what he saw. After all, the Sandinistas had always denied they were Communists. He turned to his commanding officer and asked, *"¿Qué es éste?"* ("What's all this?")

*"Es verdad"* ("It's the truth"), said the officer.

258

*"No por mío"* ("Not for me"), Juan replied.

That night, Juan and eleven men from his unit start-ed walking north to Honduras to join the resistance.

He was one of thousands who became what the Sandinistas called *contrarevolucionarios*—counterrevolu-tionaries—or contras. The resistance never liked that term, because it implied that they wanted to restore the old Somoza regime. In fact, most of the contras had supported the revolution against Somozoa. They just weren't willing to live in the totalitarian society that the Sandinistas were building.

But the name stuck—one of many public relations victories for the Sandinistas. The administration pre-ferred to call them freedom fighters, but "contras" was so widely known that even their supporters came to use that word.

To this day, I still hear it said that the contras were a creation of the CIA. Not true. And they certainly weren't created by me, or Dick Secord, or Dewey Clarridge. To the extent that anyone "created" the con-tras, it was the Sandinistas.

When the Sandinistas came to power, it was with the support of the United States. The Carter administration was so intent on getting rid of the brutal Somoza regime—which was certainly a worthy goal—that nobody wanted to look too closely at how that was being done, who was doing it, or where it might lead.

The Sandinistas came to power with grand declara-tions of freedom and democracy. They promised a soci-ety marked by free enterprise, free elections, a free press, freedom of religion—and just about everything else the United States wanted to hear. In return, our govern-ment became their main source of support. During the first few months of the new regime, we sent Nicaragua thirty-nine million dollars in emergency food aid—a considerable sum for a country of three million people. Just stay out of El Salvador, we told them, and we'll keep those dollars flowing. In 1980 our contribution to

Nicaragua was raised to seventy-five million dollars.

But as soon as they came to power, the Sandinistas began breaking their promises. Within months, anyone who wasn't a "scientific socialist" was driven out of the leadership. We know today that the Sandinistas had no intention of creating a free society—and every intention of trying to overthrow the governments of El Salvador and Honduras.

In the face of irrefutable evidence, President Carter came to have second thoughts about the Sandinistas. In the final weeks of his presidency he suspended all U.S. aid to Nicaragua and resumed support for the government of El Salvador, which was now fighting for its life.

By the time I became involved in Central American issues, I was shocked at how long it had taken us to recognize the Sandinistas' true colors. In July 1980, at their first-anniversary celebration, the guests of Nicaragua's new regime had included Fidel Castro and Yasir Arafat, and delegations from such freedom-loving states as Vietnam, North Korea, and East Germany. Meanwhile, the glowing promises of freedom had turned to dust.

Instead, the Sandinistas began organizing Nicaragua along the same lines as Cuba. President Daniel Ortega even named his younger brother Umberto as defense minister, just as Castro had done with his own brother, Raul. And like the Cubans, the Sandinistas began searching for opportunities to export what they themselves called a "revolution without frontiers."

Before long, they had replaced Somoza's dictatorship of the right with their own dictatorship of the left. They seized radio and TV stations. They herded farmers into state-run farms. They created an elaborate system of block wardens—or neighborhood spies. They censored *La Prensa*, the country's largest newspaper, and shut down the Catholic radio station. They fought against the Church, and forbade broadcasts of the Mass on radio or television. They established a secret police force and began confiscating private property. They killed, jailed, and exiled their political opponents. They started a nationwide conscription, drafted children into their youth movements, and sent the "elite" off for indoctrination in the Soviet Union, Cuba, East Germany, and Bulgaria.

And like their mentors in other Communist dictatorships, the new rulers of Nicaragua set themselves up in the finest houses, which they stocked with the best French wine and Russian caviar. It's a cliché, but that doesn't make it any less true: even the most ardent capitalist would be hard-pressed to match the material appetites and amenities of a privileged Communist. On my first trip to Managua, one of the regime's few remaining internal political opponents passed on a joke that became popular when Tomás Borge, the son of a peasant family, was named interior minister. Like many of his fellow Sandinistas, Borge had appropriated the enormous mansion of a former Somoza official. When his mother came to visit, he proudly showed her around: the swimming pool, the huge kitchens, the visitor's suite, the fountains, the patio, the splendid gardens, the maids, the butlers, and all the rest.

Halfway through the tour, she turned to her son in tears.

"¿Mama," he said, "qué pasa?"

"Oh, Tomás," she replied "It's so beautiful! But tell me—what will happen to all this when the revolution comes?"

When Ronald Reagan became President in 1981, he offered the Sandinistas one last chance to withdraw their support for the rebels in El Salvador and to make the promised democratic reforms at home. The Sandinistas didn't even blink. By now they were supported by a long list of governments: Cuba, the Soviet Union, the Communist bloc in Eastern Europe, Iran, and even France. And let's not forget Libya. During the Ortega years, the Libyans gave Nicaragua several *hundred* million dollars in economic assistance, not to mention technical support, weapons, and military assistance.

In March 1981, President Reagan authorized the CIA to begin supporting the growing army of Nicaraguan rebels, mostly in Honduras, who were opposed to the Sandinista regime. Congress provided funding to enable these fighters to interdict weapons and supplies on their way from Nicaragua to the FMLN guerrillas in El Salvador.

In the summer of 1981, Casey appointed Duane Clarridge, an experienced clandestine service officer and former CIA station chief, to be the CIA's link to the resistance. Officially, Clarridge's new title was head of the Agency's Latin American Division.

"I told Casey that sounded fine," Dewey told me later. "Then I got out my atlas to see what countries we were talking about."

Dewey Clarridge was a master spy who had been almost everywhere and done nearly everything. His experience in the clandestine service was so extensive that it was rumored that his résumé consisted of his name—followed by three blank pages. He had a great sense of style, and was known around Washington as an elegant dresser. One of the few times I saw Dewey get really angry was when a reporter described him in print as having shown up at a congressional hearing in a polyester suit. You'd have thought he had been called a Communist.

Clarridge and Casey had a lot in common, including an unmistakable lack of affection for the Congress. But unlike most people who had to testify on Capitol Hill, Dewey didn't even try to hide his attitude. I was with him on several occasions when senators, congressmen, and staffers asked inane questions based on farfetched newspaper stories about what the CIA was allegedly up to.

Washington is a city of rituals, and the ritual response is to say, "Thank you for the question, Senator. I'm not aware of any indication of that, but I can assure you, sir, that I will look into it closely as soon as I return to my office. I will be sure to give you a full report by tomorrow morning. You can be confident that we at the CIA share your concern about that article."

Dewey Clarridge's answers were more succinct: "That's absolute bullshit."

In the summer of 1981, Bill Casey asked Dewey to come up with some recommendations about Central America. "We can try to interdict the Nicaraguan arms shipments to El Salvador," Dewey said. "But we won't be able to cut it off completely. If the resistance can create a backfire to keep the Sandinistas busy, that will make it harder for them to concentrate on El Salvador. In other words, we've got to take the war to Nicaragua."

When Casey heard that, he knew he'd found his man.

At the time, the fledgling anti-Sandinista resistance movement along the Honduran-Nicaraguan border was being supported by a small group of Argentine officers and senior enlisted men. The Argentine military had just fought a particularly brutal war against the Montoneros, a Communist insurgency. Some of the rebels had taken refuge in Nicaragua, which had already become a kind of World's Fair for terrorists from all over the planet: the Red Brigades from Italy, M-19 from Colombia, the Baader-Meinhoff Gang from Germany, Libyans, Chinchoneros from Honduras, the *Sendero Luminoso* (Shining Path) from Peru, the IRA, and several factions from the PLO. One of the first reports I ever read about Nicaragua described a firefight between two rival Palestinian terrorist groups.

Casey met with General Leopoldo Galtieri, head of the military junta that ruled Argentina, and suggested that the United States join in supporting the anti-Communist guerrilla activity. Galtieri was delighted. But he was wary of America's reputation for abandoning its friends, and he gave Casey a prescient warning: "Don't get involved in this unless you're prepared to see it all the way through."

A month later, President Reagan signed a top-secret

Finding that authorized the CIA to begin helping the rebels directly. In 1982, primarily because of the war in the Falklands, Argentina withdrew its support. From then on the Nicaraguan resistance was in the hands of the CIA.

Even so, nobody in our government was under any illusions about the Nicaraguan resistance. After all, the Sandinista military was larger than all the other armies in Central America put together. And the Soviets were equipping them with tanks, attack helicopters, long-range artillery, armored personnel carriers, and sophisticated communications equipment.

Later, as the resistance grew, the administration's goals for the resistance grew with it—to the point where we believed they could exert enough pressure on Managua to bring about a democratic outcome. And in the end, that's exactly what happened.

My own involvement with Central America began in the spring of 1982, when Roger Fontaine, who headed the Latin America section of the NSC, asked me to provide a military perspective for an NSC policy paper on Central America. Bill Clark liked the results, and he asked me to start attending a Saturday morning study group on Central America. These informal meetings were held at the CIA, and were hosted by Bill Casey in his conference room on the seventh floor of the Agency's headquarters. Jeane Kirkpatrick used to attend, along with Dewey Clarridge, Fred Ikle, General Paul Gorman, Tom Enders from the State Department, and several others. I knew little about Central America when I arrived at the NSC, but I had been reading like crazy and paying close attention to the speeches and writings of Jeane Kirkpatrick and others. The more I learned, the more reason I saw for our involvement.

I wasn't shy, and at the Saturday meetings I started asking questions and making occasional comments. Some of my ideas must have had merit, because I was soon invited to other meetings and events, including seminars at various CIA sites on the training of anti-Communist resistance movements.

Early in 1983, when Pope John Paul II was scheduled to visit Central America, I was asked to serve as a liaison from our government and to provide information on potential death threats. The Pope was not harmed in Nicaragua, but when he addressed a crowd in Managua, a "spontaneous" demonstration drowned him out. For the Sandinistas, this turned out to be a domestic and international public relation disaster.

Events like the Sandinistas' treatment of the Pope convinced Casey, Kirkpatrick, Clark, and Weinberger that the situation in Central America required more from the United States than mere containment. It was clear to them that the Soviets and the Cubans were using Nicaragua as a secure base for the attack on their next target: El Salvador.

It was also apparent that a strategy of using an indigenous resistance movement to reverse the Communist gains in Nicaragua was going to take time. In the interim, El Salvador was in jeopardy of succumbing. Judge Clark had me prepare several position papers and legislative requests in support of increased American military presence in the region—especially El Salvador.

At the time, El Salvador was squeezed between the Communist guerrillas on the left and brutal death squads on the right. Under the guise of anti-Communism, the death squads terrorized the entire country—murdering nuns, teachers, labor organizers, political opponents, and thousands of other civilians. Some officials, both in Washington and in San Salvador, preferred to sweep this problem under the rug, and tried to dismiss reports of the death squads as Communist propaganda. But a lot of it was real.

I made several trips to El Salvador, and in the summer of 1983 I wrote a paper about the death squads. From talking with our ambassador, our military liaison personnel, and with CIA people who knew the area, it was clear there were numerous allegations that the murders were connected to a leader of the right-wing Republican National Alliance Party, also known as ARENA. Back in Washington, I met with those who were lobbying the Congress on behalf of El Salvador. "Stay away from this guy and his cronies," I'd tell them. "Don't try to white-wash the problem. The death squads are real, and they must be stopped. Yes, we have to support the fight against Communism, but our ultimate goal isn't just to prevent Central America from going Communist—it's to help these countries become real democracies."

I made the same point in briefings to congressmen and senators, and to their staffs. Most of them were open to the evidence, although two or three congressional staffers advised their principals that I was soft on Communism. I've been called a lot of things, but that was a first.

On Capitol Hill, the prevailing view was that the way to combat the death squads was to withdraw the American military presence in El Salvador—which consisted of only fifty-five advisers. I disagreed. I have always resented the view that the American military contributes to an atmosphere of violence and repression. Are American soldiers known for engaging in criminal acts against the civilians of other countries? Is the United States so full of human rights abuses that our soldiers are a menace to other countries?

In places like El Salvador, American military advisers are a moderating influence. There are ways to defeat a Communist insurgency without killing innocent people, but the Salvadoran military was lacking in both discipline and experience. At the time, this was an army that was used to doing only two things: marching in parades on national holidays, and organizing palace coups. My son's Boy Scout troop had been on more camp-outs than some of these guys.

The administration's opponents in Congress argued that we shouldn't be training the Salvadoran military because it was so undisciplined. But one reason it *was* so undisciplined was that we weren't allowed to train them.

In December 1983, I was assigned to be the NSC representative on a trip to El Salvador by Vice President Bush. It was clear that unless something was done to stop the death squads and to guarantee the long-promised transition to democratic rule, U.S. military aid to El Salvador would soon be terminated.

The Vice President was given the unenviable job of delivering this message, and along with Tony Motley, the new Assistant Secretary of State for Inter-American Affairs, I was tagged to accompany him. From Andrews we flew straight down to Argentina for the inauguration of Raul Alfonsin, Argentina's democratically elected president. Then we headed north, to Central America. During the flight, Tony and I typed up the talking points for the Vice President's scheduled meeting with President Alvaro Magaña in El Salvador, and we briefed the Vice President on the situation there.

On the way to El Salvador we stopped in Panama, where Mr. Bush held a brief airport meeting with President de la Espriella and General Manuel Noriega. The Vice President reminded Noriega that he had just returned from a democratic transition in Argentina and urged that same thing had to happen in Panama.

Noriega sat there like a sphinx. In retrospect, it was clear that he didn't get the message.

I had met with Noriega before, and I would meet him several times more. Whenever I accompanied a high-level visitor to the region, whether it was Casey, Weinberger, or another senior official, we would invariably stop in Panama for a meeting with Noriega. The message from our side was always the same: democracy must prevail.

I once met with him in London after an intermediary told us that Noriega wanted to help the Nicaraguan resistance. But that meeting went nowhere. We were looking for tangible support for the contras, while he was more interested in things like bribery and murder. Sitting in the lobby of a London hotel, I admonished him that despite our antipathy to the Sandinista leadership, we could not get involved in assassinations. But if he were willing to help train contra units, provide logistical support, and even use his assets to destroy Sandinista targets in Managua, we would certainly compensate him for his efforts.

In arranging for this meeting, the intermediary had emphasized that Noriega wanted our help in "cleaning up his image." But I was blunt with him. There were reports that he was involved in drug trafficking and murder, and had ties to Cuban front companies operating in Panama. This had to stop. The best thing he could do, I told him, was to step back and allow a real democracy to emerge in his country. But he didn't listen to me, or to anyone else with that same message.

For me, one of the ugliest aspects of the whole Iran-contra affair was the way my meetings with Noriega were described in some quarters as though the two of us had some kind of alliance. We didn't. Noriega was probably the single most despicable human being I ever had to deal with. After a meeting with him, you just wanted to go home and take a shower.

After the meeting with Noriega, the Vice President's plane flew directly to San Salvador, where we landed right after a rainstorm. The air was oppressively hot, and the humidity felt like 150 percent. We stood at attention, dripping with sweat, as the band played what seemed like all two hundred verses of the Salvadoran national anthem. Then it was off to the President's residence, where the meeting rooms were right out of a movie—dark and cool, with high ceilings and slow-turning fans.

At his initial meeting with Vice President Bush,

President Magaña asked if Vice President Bush would object to giving President Reagan's message on human rights directly to the Salvadoran field commanders.

The Vice President agreed.

During a break, everyone except the two leaders went upstairs, where we guzzled down glass after glass of Coca-Cola with lemon. Meanwhile, the Vice President met alone with Magaña. This was vintage Bush: long before he became President, he had a knack for developing a personal, effective working relationship with foreign leaders.

As the two men talked in the conference room, we could hear a commotion in the hallway below. I was standing beside Admiral Dan Murphy, the Vice President's chief of staff, when the head of the Secret Service detail came running upstairs. "The commanders are here," he said. "And they are *armed*. We can't let them go in with guns."

The Secret Service agent was right to be worried. Latin America wasn't the most stable place on earth, and the Vice President of the United States was about to have an unscheduled meeting with about thirty armed field commanders. It was possible that some of these guys had connections to the death squads, and that they wouldn't be too happy with the message that Bush was about to deliver.

It got so noisy outside the conference room that the Vice President came out. "What's the problem?" he asked. "We're trying to talk in here."

"These guys have guns," said Murphy. "It would be dangerous for this meeting to take place."

"Look," said Bush. "This meeting is absolutely necessary. President Magaña wants to hold it, and we're going to do it the way they've asked."

The Vice President spoke bluntly, without notes and without any diplomatic cushioning. He made it clear that if El Salvador had any interest in receiving additional American aid, the death squads had to stop and the murders of American nuns and labor leaders had to be solved. Although it was very tense in that room as Bush delivered his message, he came across as calm, strong, and determined. Some of the commanders who met with him that day were angry and defensive. They felt humiliated that a senior American official was telling them what was wrong in their own country. This was not what they had expected to hear. The Grenada operation had occurred a few weeks earlier, and some of these guys hoped that American troops would be sent to help them fight the guerrillas, or their Sandinista sponsors. But Bush's message was very different: unless you clean up your act, it's all over.

Later, during the 1988 presidential campaign, when George Bush was called a wimp, I would look back on this moment. I know a wimp when I see one, and George Bush was no wimp.

The effect of the Bush visit to El Salvador was mixed. Though death squad activity did not stop completely, the State Department was able to begin an important judicial reform program to train and protect judges, prosecutors and investigators. Investigations were opened into a number of previous murders. And, perhaps most important, the elections were held as planned. Over 80 percent of the population voted, and Napoleon Duarte became El Salvador's democratically elected president.

Although I began working on Central American issues in 1982, my involvement increased dramatically the following year when Bill Clark asked me to serve as the NSC liaison on the Kissinger Commission.[1] He obviously respected my abilities, but one reason I was picked was that NSC staff members were not exactly standing in line to work on Central America. This was a no-win issue, because the government was deeply divided as to how to help the nations of Central America move toward democracy. Amidst all the turmoil and infighting, by 1983 only one thing was clear and steadfast: Ronald Reagan's support for the Nicaraguan resistance.

Henry Kissinger headed the presidential commission on Central America, and my initial encounter with him was downright embarrassing. At one of the commission's first meetings, which was held at the NSC, I was asked to deliver a briefing on anti-Communist resistance movements around the world. I often used slides to enhance a briefing, and in preparing for this one I must have picked up a slide carousel that wasn't completely empty.

As the slides were projected behind me, I cheerfully began my presentation without bothering to look over my shoulder at the screen. Everything went smoothly until a familiar voice with thick German accent boomed out from the back of the darkened room.

"Major North," said the voice. "I vas unavare of anti-Soviet resistance movements in Norvay."

I slowly turned around to face the screen, which indeed showed a huge color map of Norway.

"Oops. Sorry, sir, wrong slide."

I was apparently forgiven, because when the Kissinger Commission traveled to Central America and Mexico, I went with them and helped arrange meetings with opposition groups. One of our stops was Managua, which by then was a very depressing place. After forty years of plunder by the Somozas, a terrible earthquake, and four years of Sandinista "economics," Nicaragua

---

[1]In addition to Dr. Kissinger, who chaired it, the members included Jeane Kirkpatrick; Jim Wright, the democratic congressman from Texas and future Speaker of the House; Pete Domenici, Republican senator from Arizona; Michael Barnes, Democratic member from Maryland; Republican congressman Jack Kemp; John Silber, president of Boston University; William Walsh, head of Project Hope; Bill Clements, former (and future) governor of Texas; Robert Strauss, Democrat-at-large; retired Supreme Court Justice Potter Stewart; and several others.

had become the second poorest country in the Western Hemisphere. Only Haiti was worse.

Our meetings with the Sandinistas were a complete waste of time. They would expound for hours on their grievances against us, and we would ask them embarrassing questions about human rights, freedom, and their support for the guerrillas in neighboring El Salvador and Honduras. We were clearly talking past each other, and we couldn't even agree to disagree.

During one of these sessions, Miguel d'Escoto, Nicaragua's foreign minister and a former Catholic priest, harangued us at length about the many heinous crimes the United States had committed against Nicaragua and the rest of the Third World. He had just said something about Nicaragua's being a peace-loving country—I don't recall exactly what, because I had stopped paying attention—when Senator Pete Domenici, who was sitting next to Kissinger, jumped to his feet with such energy that his chair fell over. Pete virtually exploded.

"You lying s.o.b!" Pete yelled, which immediately woke up several members of the commission. "When you came to see me in 1978, you were wearing your collar. You said you were a persecuted priest. I took you to meet my colleagues, and you swore to us that you and your buddies only wanted to get rid of Somoza. We helped you, and *now* look at what you've done. You're arresting your opponents. You're threatening your neighbors. You're building up an enormous army. You're nothing but a damned hypocrite! You lied then, and you're lying now!" D'Escoto went white. As he sat there with his hand on his chest, he seemed to be on the verge of a heart attack. It wasn't until Pete stormed out of the room that d'Escoto began to regain his color.

Sitting just behind d'Escoto and not even batting an eyelash during Pete's tirade was the infamous Nora Astorga. She was a household name in Nicaragua, and a heroine among the Sandinistas for her role in killing one

The Clancy clan was a big part of growing up. Uncles John, Larry, and Joe are standing behind Mom, Gram Clancy, and Aunt Mary during World War II.

Dad was a lieutenant when this picture was taken right after the war started. By the end of the war he was a major.

Grandma and Grandpa North with the two older North boys. Grandma North is holding Jack and I'm sitting on my grandfather's lap. They had a farm we came to love.

Every summer the North family took a vacation. My brother Jack and sister Pat accompanied me to my first congressional appearance at age twelve.

The 1967 Naval Academy boxing champions. Emerson Smith, the head boxing coach, at far right, was a legend at Annapolis. He's one of the finest men I've ever known. When he retired in the 1980's, I got President Reagan to send him a letter.

Major Reid Olson, my last company officer at Annapolis, taught me much of what was expected of a Marine officer.

When Betsy and I got married at Quantico, my Basic School classmates formed the traditional arch of swords as we left the chapel.

Both Grandmothers made it to our wedding. Betsy's grandmother Nan (on my right) and Gram Clancy (on my left) both lived into their nineties.

Sergeant Hue was one of our Kit Carson Scouts. A former NVA soldier, he helped me find an NVA position inside the DMZ in May 1969.

The Command Group of 2d Platoon, Company K, 3d Battalion, 3d Marines. The sign says: "Welcome. Now that you're here, this is the rear. Courtesy of Blue's Bastards."

Not everything in Vietnam was terrible. Betsy sent me this photo of herself with our new daughter, taken just hours after Tait was born at Bethesda Naval Hospital. I carried it with me everywhere.

Almost everything we ate, wore, or fired arrived by helicopter. This CH-34 evacuated our wounded from a bomb crater landing zone after an operation on Mutter's ridge.

Bill Haskell lost his eye in May 1969 during a terrible battle on the DMZ. We got together in 1970 for the Marine Corps Birthday Ball after he had been medically retired.

Betsy came to see me in Okinawa and joined me for rappeling down the face of a cliff. I used this photo to encourage reluctant marines.

When Sarah was born in 1976, I got to be in the delivery room. We called her "Sarah Sunshine" because she smiled so much.

*Top:* In 1983, while I was with the National Security Council, I was assigned to work with the President's Bi-partisan commission on Central America. Here, Lane Kirkland, head of the AFL-CIO, Robert Strauss, then chair of the Democratic Party and now our ambassador to Moscow, and Senator Pete Dominici, all members of the commission, agree on Washington's approach to the Sandinista government in Managua: hear, see, and speak no evil.

*Bottom:* Henry Kissinger, head of the President's commission, wanted to meet with Daniel Ortega. Perched beneath a large photo of Sandino, Ortega put nearly everyone to sleep with his rambling soliloquy on American imperialism.

John Grinalds, shown here in his white dress uniform, knelt in the sand and prayed for my back to be healed. It was. John remains one of the closest friends I have on this earth.

Two days after the Beirut terrorist attack on our Marines, President Reagan ordered U.S. military units ashore on Grenada. Five Caribbean democracies participated with us in this operation, and several of their leaders came to Washington to commend the President. Here, Eugenia Charles, the prime minister of Dominica, talks with President Reagan in the Oval Office before going out to meet the press. (The White House)

This is the last photo of my whole family before Dad died in 1984. Tim was still in college, Pat came in from California, Jack took leave from the Army, and I made it up from Washington.

In the spring of 1985, the President asked to meet with the leaders of the Nicaraguan resistance. During the meeting, Adolfo Calero presented him with a pin that read, "I'm a contra too." (The White House)

On his way to Camp David one afternoon, President Reagan secretly commended this Nicaraguan Catholic priest for opposing the Communist regime in Managua. (The White House)

The *Achille Lauro* cruise ship as it pulled into Egypt just after the terrorists had fled. Confined to a wheelchair, Leon Klinghoffer *(inset)* was shot by the terrorists and thrown overboard. Capturing the perpetrators became a contest of persistence and endurance for all involved. (both, AP/Wide World Photos)

One of the Israeli counterterrorist agents snapped this shot as I was calling Washington to let them know we had arrived safely in Tel Aviv from Tehran. Ami Nir is standing next to Bud. We had to black out the faces of the CIA officers and the communications equipment in order to have the photo released.

*Above left:* President Reagan inscribed this Bible, which I gave to our Iranian intermediary at a meeting in Germany. A few weeks later, Rafsanjani claimed that McFarlane had brought the Bible with him to Tehran. (AP/Wide World Photos)

*Above right:* Eugene Hasenfus was shot down over Nicaragua in October 1986. (UPI/Bettmann)

The contras never would have survived without the help of Saudi Arabia's King Fahd. The President wanted the contras kept alive "body and soul." The king made it happen with his secret assistance. (UPI/Bettmann)

Two great old Irishmen: Bill Casey and Ronald Reagan at the CIA headquarters in Langley, Virginia. On his deathbed in 1987 Casey reportedly said, "He'll never get away with it." I've often wondered if he was talking about the President. (UPI/Bettmann)

The Iranians we met with knew so little about the U.S. government that I had to bring a photo with me to show them who the players on our side were. I took this picture of an Oval Office meeting with me to Tehran, showing, from left to right, Bud McFarlane, me, David Chew (assistant to Don Regan), Bob Sims (Bud's press spokesman), Admiral John Poindexter, President Reagan, and Don Regan. (The White House)

Endgame: Cap and George in November 1986. These two great adversaries never seemed to agree on much of anything until after I was fired. Then they agreed that they were both opposed to the Iran initiative. Somehow their opposition had been muted enough to allow it to continue for over a year. (UPI/Bettmann)

Within months of this 1986 Oval Office meeting on combating terrorism, the three of us in the background—John Poindexter, me, and Don Regan—would be gone. The two men in the foreground, George Bush and Ronald Reagan, would be hounded for years by what had been set in motion in this room. (The White House)

Early in 1987, the FBI informed us of a new and very serious terrorist threat. In response, the government assigned more than thirty-five federal agents to protect my family and me. The white Cheverolet was armored from top to bottom to stop bullets. It also stopped the questions of reporters at the front gate. (©Greg E. Mathieson/MAI)

The press overwhelmed us like locusts, stripping our privacy from us at home, at the office, on the way to work—everywhere and every day for more than seven months. (©Greg E. Mathieson/MAL)

Manachur Ghorbanifar was brought to us by the Israelis as a man who could deliver. Although he couldn't pass a polygraph test, he did deliver hostages. The Reverend Ben Weir and Father Marty Jenco were both freed while "Gorba the Greek" acted as intermediary among the Iranians, Israelis, and the United States. (AP/Wide World Photos)

At their joint White House press conference on November 25, 1986, Ed Meese and the President announced that Admiral Poindexter had been "reassigned." As I watched from my office, the nation was told that I been relieved of my duties. In other words, *fired!* (Bob Daughtery/Associated Press)

I wasn't the only one at the table who got angry at the way the congressmen and senators behaved. Brendan was so outraged when they sent us a six-foot stack of documents just before we were to appear that he took a picture of it and showed it to the world. (Associated Press)

When it became apparent that the hearings were going to drag on, my best friend came to be with me. I had wanted to spare her the humiliation of congressional efforts to smear her husband. Betsy insisted that a loyal wife belonged at her husband's side. I'm glad she was there. (©Greg E. Mathieson/MAI)

After the hearings, numerous groups and organizations used my name and face to raise funds, claiming that a check to them would somehow help me. Sometimes it was even true—if my attorneys could catch them. In other cases, there was outright commercial exploitation—some of which, like this full-paged ad in a British newspaper, was enough to make you laugh.

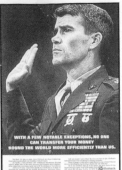

When he was campaigning for President, the press speculated that George Bush was a wimp. If he was, I never saw it. It took personal courage for him to invite Admiral Poindexter, me, and our wives to his home for this Christmas party in 1986. (The White House)

The day Tait graduated from high school in 1987, our extended family, including my mother, Betsy's sisters, and our nearby nephews, gathered along the famous fence in front of my house. The federal security agent in the background was not related but was much appreciated. (©Greg E. Mathieson/MAI)

In 1989 Joe Fernandez and I founded Guardian Technologies International, Inc., "The Life Saving Company." At our plant in Virginia we make high-technology life-protective equipment for law enforcement personnel and the military. In our business it's good to have the parking lot filled with police cars. (©Greg E. Mathieson/MAI)

Jim Lehnert, my radio operator in Vietnam more than two decades ago, had never been to the Vietnam Veterans Memorial. When he came for a visit we went together to pay our respects to our fallen brothers from Blue's Bastards. (©Greg E. Mathieson/MAI)

Throughout our long ordeal, the members of our Bible study group sustained Betsy and me with prayers, encouragement, and tangible support. Most of the group was there the evening we took this photo with Harold Morris, who was in Washington with Jim Dobson's Focus on the Family.

Much of the last five years has been like this white-water raft ride that Betsy, Stuart, Sarah, Dornin, and I took in Colorado in 1990 when we were on retreat with the Officers' Christian Fellowship. It reminds me of the caption a Marine friend has on a photo in his office: "God doesn't promise you a smooth passage—just a safe delivery."

An American family. My best friend and me and the children that the good Lord loaned us. They have been my island of tranquility in a stormy sea. (©Greg E. Mathieson/MAI)

of Somoza's top generals. She had lured him into her bedroom, where he was ambushed and brutally murdered by Sandinista guerrillas. According to the story, after slitting his throat, they cut off his genitals and stuffed them into his mouth. She had actually been proposed as ambassador to the United States, but the Reagan administration had refused to accept her credentials. This became the subject of some nervous laughter among a couple of the Sandinistas' supporters in the Senate, with whom Nora Astorga was said to be on very close terms.

This was the same woman who later became the Sandinistas' human rights advocate at the United Nations.

We also met with Danny Boy himself, who unrolled his own litany of complaints about the evils of American imperialism. Ortega struck me as a dull and humorless little clerk, hunched over his papers. As he droned on from his prepared text, it was hard to imagine him as a former guerrilla leader. He reminded me of the joke about the man with "negative charisma": when this guy enters the room, it feels like three people just left.

But he sure knew how to work a crowd. When his followers were out in force, leading the chants— *"Ortega, Ortega, Ortega"*—he became a different man: proud, self-confident, and fully in charge.


Although the Reagan administration had the right approach with regard to Nicaragua, we did a lousy job of selling it. In view of the President's rock-hard commitment to the contras, why couldn't the Great Communicator rally the public to join him?

For one thing, not everybody in the administration shared the President's views. George Shultz believed the problem could be solved through negotiation. Richard Wirthlin, the White House pollster, saw Nicaragua as a no-win issue, and encouraged the President's advisers to leave it alone. With the exception of Casey and Clark, most of the President's inner circle viewed the contras as a political liability, as indeed they were. Others just didn't believe Nicaragua was a serious threat—despite the fact that the Soviets were pumping in two and a half billion dollars in military aid.

Over at the State Department, there were those who couldn't entirely give up their earlier sympathy for the Sandinistas. They refused to admit that the Sandinistas were Communists, and continued to insist, long after the evidence was in, that the new rulers of Nicaragua were merely democratic socialists and land reformers. They felt that almost any government in Nicaragua was preferable to the ruthless and corrupt regime that the Sandinistas had overthrown. And they were right: almost any government was. But not this one.

American voters had little interest in Nicaragua, especially when they were told repeatedly by the news media that the contras consisted of thugs, drug dealers, and former members of Somoza's National Guard. Besides, Central America was seen as far away, unstable, and dangerous. One survey showed that 38 percent of the American public believed that Nicaragua was in the same part of the world as Vietnam.

And for many Americans it was. President Bush was correct when he declared, following the war with Iraq in early 1991, that the Vietnam syndrome had finally ended. The specter of Vietnam was so powerful during the Reagan years that many people—including some in the administration—believed that any help we gave the Nicaraguan resistance would only bring us closer to sending our troops into a protracted jungle war.

Opponents of the resistance preyed on this fear, and brought up Vietnam at every opportunity. We have no business interfering in other countries, they said. Nicaragua has a population of three million, so how could it possibly be a threat to the United States? Even a minimal amount of support to the contras is dangerous.

Remember—*this was how we got started in Vietnam*.

Those were scary words, but they just weren't true. On the contrary: supporting the contras was the best possible guarantee *against* our ever having to send American troops to Central America. Alfonso Robelo, one of the resistance leaders, said it best when he met with President Reagan at the White House. "All we want is your support," he told the President. "This is our country we're fighting for, and we're willing to shed our own blood to get it back."

Most of the contras never wanted us to send troops, and nobody in the administration who had the President's ear ever had that in mind.[2] But there were some right-wingers who cynically suggested that it might be best if we let the Sandinistas prevail so that the left could be blamed for "losing Central America." Then we would send in the Marines.

On the left, there were those who came to a similar conclusion through a different route: we shouldn't help the contras, they don't deserve it, and if things get bad enough down there we can always send in the Marines.

No matter which side it came from, I was horrified by this attitude. Send in the Marines? I was a Marine, and this sounded crazy to me. Sure—if war is the only alternative, send me. I'm good at it. But as long as Nicaraguans themselves were willing to risk their lives by taking on the Sandinistas, and all they wanted from us were the resources to do it, wasn't that a far better option?

Today, when support for Marxism is confined to a handful of poverty-stricken countries and certain

---

[2] Neither did President Reagan, despite the belief among many congressional Democrats that he was continually looking for a pretext to invade Nicaragua. At a news conference in February 1982, the President was asked about the possibility of sending American troops to Central America. He replied: "Maybe if they dropped a bomb on the White House, I might get mad."

American college professors, it's difficult to understand the popularity of the Sandinistas among American opinion leaders. But in some circles the equation was simple: if the United States government opposed the Sandinistas, then the Sandinistas must be the good guys. Moreover, the Sandinistas were revolutionaries. They appeared to be idealistic. Some had been imprisoned by the Somoza regime and had been treated terribly. Many were good-looking, and most of them were young. They had glamour and sex appeal. On their visits to the United States, Sandinista officials, and especially Ortega, were the darlings of the Hollywood and New York jet sets. *El Presidente* liked to go on shopping sprees along Rodeo Drive and Fifth Avenue, buying up that great staple of revolutions everywhere—designer sunglasses.

With few exceptions, the Sandinistas received unusually gentle treatment in the American press. Very few reporters took the trouble to examine the truth behind their claims, especially their allegations of human rights violations by the contras. Certainly there were some, as there are in any war. But the Sandinistas frequently circulated outright fabrications, and reporters who were normally skeptical would report these stories as if they were true.

The public relations effort on behalf of the resistance could have been far more successful if the contras had produced a charismatic leader (ideally, with a beard or a mustache) who could have effectively symbolized their struggle as an anti-Communist Ho Chi Minh, or Fidel, or Che. The resistance offered up several candidates who were brave fighters and fine leaders, but none of them could command a large following. One possibility was Mike Lima. He was a fierce combat leader who had been wounded half a dozen times. Mike was young and handsome, and with the help of a friendly reporter in Honduras, we were able to set up a press conference for him.

The first question was harmless enough: "When did you join the resistance?"

"Well," said Mike, "when I was at the National Guard Academy..."

CUT! Mike Lima had been fighting the Sandinistas for five years, but that was the end of his brief media career.

The most persistent rap against the contras was that they consisted of former members of Somoza's National Guard. In the early years of the resistance, there was some truth to that claim. When the Somoza regime collapsed, somewhere between a thousand and fifteen hundred Guardsmen escaped to Honduras, where they formed a government in exile that nobody recognized. This group became the formative nucleus of the resistance, and was quietly supported by Argentina.

Certainly there were some bad men in the National Guard—just as bad as the dictator they supported. But not all of them fit that profile. There were also young officers in the Guard, including some who graduated from West Point and other American military academies, who cared about democracy and believed in it.

Besides, former Guardsmen were only one segment of the resistance. By early 1983, there were around ten thousand contras, which meant that the Guard consisted of no more than 15 percent of the total. They were easily outnumbered by disenchanted Sandinistas—like Juan, who brought his entire unit to Honduras to fight against his former colleagues. Most of the contras were young *campesinos*, simple farmers who had fled from Communism and wanted land and freedom for themselves and their families. By the end of 1984 they had become the largest peasant army in Latin America since the Mexican revolution.

The American public may have been apathetic about Nicaragua and the contras, but it was a hot issue in Congress all through the Reagan years. This was especially true in the House of Representatives, where the Democrats formed a strong majority—and held some strange views on the funding of anti-Communist resistance movements. The farther away the insurgency, the more willing Congress was to fund it. It was relatively easy to get support for resistance forces in places like Cambodia and especially Afghanistan, which were halfway around the globe. Angola was a little closer, and therefore more problematic. Central America, right next door, was nearly impossible.

In the fall of 1983, after lengthy and acrimonious debate, Congress narrowly approved an allocation of twenty-four million dollars for the CIA to spend on the Nicaraguan resistance. But this money didn't go as far as we had expected. Much of it went to the CIA itself, for salaries, travel and living expenses for their trainers, logistics personnel, technicians, communicators, and other employees who were involved with the resistance.

Meanwhile, the contra base camps along the Honduran border were being overwhelmed with volunteers—far beyond the CIA's fondest hopes. And these volunteers rarely came alone. Often they showed up with their entire extended families: a wife, three kids, a couple of grandparents, an uncle, and two cousins. All of them had to be fed, clothed, and cared for, which meant that a lot of money went for food, shelter, clothing, blankets, medicine, baby formula, and training. That didn't leave as much as we'd hoped for guns and ammunition.

So early in 1984, the administration went back to Congress for an additional appropriation.

It was around this time that Dewey Clarridge came up with his plan to mine the harbors of Nicaragua. The contras had already hit several Sandinista bridges, warehouses, oil facilities, and power stations, but they hadn't yet matched the damage done to Nicaragua's economy by the Sandinistas' own policies. Dewey's mandate was to increase the pressure on the Sandinistas—particularly their state-controlled economic infrastructure. But so many volunteers had joined up that he was quickly running out of money for the insurgency.

Mining the harbors was Dewey's way of getting more bang for the buck. The idea came to him late one night while he was reading about the Russo-Japanese War of 1904–1905. The Japanese had enjoyed great success in mining some of the Russian harbors, and Dewey proposed that the CIA could do the same with Nicaragua. Except that instead of a real mining campaign, which would lead to foreign and civilian casualties, Dewey suggested using "firecracker mines," which created a loud explosion but caused little damage. Our hope was that Lloyd's of London and other insurers would stop insuring ships that were bound for Nicaragua, which would make it difficult for the Sandinistas to receive oil and other supplies necessary to keep their enormous army in the field.

Casey loved the idea, and so did the President. Even George Shultz went along. Bill Casey and Dewey Clarridge went up to Congress to meet with the relevant committees, where they mentioned the mining plan as part of their review of covert operations in Nicaragua.

In terms of damaging the Nicaraguan economy, the mining program was only a limited success. But the political damage in Washington was enormous. When details of the mining were revealed in the *Wall Street Journal*, all hell broke loose in Congress. Normally, when the President signs a Finding authorizing a covert operation, the congressional intelligence committees are briefed on it in detail within a matter of days. But most committee members swore they knew nothing about the mining. Their memories were so selective that even Senator Patrick Leahy of Vermont, no friend of the resistance, rebuked his colleagues for their deceit. One classified report to the intelligence committees had spelled it out in plain English: "Magnetic mines have been placed in the Pacific harbor of El Bluff, as well as the oil terminal at Puerto Sandino."

It got so bad that Bill Casey actually went up to the Hill to apologize to the members of the Senate Intelligence Committee. He must have gagged on his words, but he would have done anything to protect the CIA. "You shouldn't be here to apologize to us," said Senator Jake Garn of Utah. "We should be apologizing to you for pretending we weren't briefed." When Casey left the room, Garn exploded at his colleagues—using such colorful language that it raised a few eyebrows when word got back to his constituents in Salt Lake City.

The mining led to a spate of hearings. When Tony Motley was called before the House Intelligence Committee to answer questions about the mining, the congressmen jumped all over him. "This is terrible," one of them said. "We're involved in illegal, covert actions, and we're killing innocent sailors from other countries."

"Just a minute," Tony replied. "Let me put this thing in context. Fewer people were killed by these mines than died at Chappaquiddick."

Maybe that's why Tony didn't last too long in the job. As good as he was, you can't talk like that and stay very long at the State Department.

For many in Congress, the mining of the harbors was the last straw. Instead of providing additional money for the resistance, the House of Representatives gave us a new Boland Amendment.


In all, there were five separate so-called Boland Amendments passed by the House between 1982 and 1986. These became an annual rite of summer in Washington: the cherry blossoms would come out, the administration would ask for more funding for the resistance, and Congress would respond with another Boland Amendment.

The Boland Amendments were named for Edward Boland, chairman of the House Intelligence Committee, who proposed them. Although each of the amendments was different, all of them were restrictions on the use of appropriated funds, and were therefore attached to large appropriations bills. None of the Boland Amendments was by any stretch of the imagination a criminal statute, and none of them included any civil or criminal penalties. And despite what some Democrats—and even Bud McFarlane—claimed later, none of them applied to the President, or to his staff at the National Security Council.[3]

Shortly before Boland One came into being, several members of Congress had tried to ban aid to the contras from *every* branch of the government, including the White House and the National Security Council. This amendment, proposed by then-Congressman Tom Harkin, an Iowa Democrat, would have prohibited any government agency from "carrying out military activities in or against Nicaragua." This was very different from the language of any of the Boland Amendments, and especially from Boland One.

---

[3] The first Boland Amendment (or Boland One, as it came to be known), covered the period from December 1982 to December 1983, and outlawed the use of funds by the CIA or the Department of Defense for the purpose of "overthrowing the Government of Nicaragua."

Boland Two (which covered the period from December 1983 to October 1984) specified that no more than $24 million could be spent "by the CIA, the Department of Defense, and any other agency or entity of the United States involved in intelligence activities" to support military operations in Nicaragua.

Boland Three (which covered the period from October 1984 to December 1985) was the most restrictive. It specified that "no appropriations or funds made available" to the CIA, Defense Department, "or any other agency or entity of the United States involved in intelligence activities" could be spent to support "directly or indirectly, military or paramilitary operations in Nicaragua by any nation, group, organization, movement or individual."

Boland Four (covering the period from August 1985 through March 1986) outlined the same restrictions on military assistance, but allowed $27 million in "humanitarian aid, communications support, [and] intelligence sharing."

Boland Five, which ran to October 1986, allowed the Nicaraguan resistance to receive a very specific and limited amount of CIA support, and authorized the State Department to solicit humanitarian aid for the resistance from other countries.

The administration hit the roof when it heard about Harkin's proposal. It was obviously unconstitutional, because Congress has no right to limit the President's authority to carry out foreign policy. The President let it be known that if Congress approved the Harkin Amendment, which was unlikely anyway, he would promptly veto it. It was then that Congressman Boland offered his own amendment *as a compromise*. Boland himself called the Harkin Amendment "not necessary," and "a bad precedent."

Later, there would be an enormous controversy as to the exact meaning and scope of the various Boland Amendments. I don't pretend to be a legal authority, but common sense tells me that if a Congress that was known to be deeply divided on this issue nevertheless voted for Boland One *by a margin of 411 to zero*, there's no way on earth that this amendment could have been understood as forbidding all aid to the contras.

Not that everybody was happy with Boland One. It was criticized in the Senate—not by supporters of the contras, but by Senator Christopher Dodd. He complained that it gave a "green light" to continued support of the resistance—and indeed it did.

The mining operations in Nicaragua left us with Boland Three, which forced the CIA to withdraw all of its support for the resistance. If the Reagan administration was going to continue funding the contras, we would have to find another way.

# BODY AND SOUL

When Congress cut off the CIA's support for the contras, a lot of people expected the resistance to wither on the vine and disappear. But President Reagan had no intention of abandoning the contras, and he made that clear in both word and deed. He compared them to the Founding Fathers and the French Resistance. He met with their leaders at the White House. "I'm a contra, too," he announced. As he later wrote in his memoirs, "I wanted the contras maintained as a force, to the fullest extent that was legal, until I could convince Congress to appropriate new funds for the freedom fighters."

Within the administration, there was no doubt that the resistance would continue to be supported. The only question was how.

Even before the spring of 1984, when congressionally appropriated funds for the resistance began to run out, there were serious discussions within the administration, and even on Capitol Hill, about asking foreign governments to help support the contras. Later on, this approach would be referred to contemptuously as "tin-cup diplomacy." But Casey, McFarlane, and others saw it as a logical way to broaden the anti-Communist coalition. The Reagan Doctrine, after all, went beyond mere "containment." It also meant enlisting the help of our allies— not only against Communism itself, but against the entire Communist empire. This was already being done in Afghanistan, where several other governments had quietly joined us in supporting the rebels. Casey believed the Nicaraguan resistance deserved a similar effort.

Back in the fall of 1983, McFarlane had asked me to draw up a list of countries that might conceivably be approached. My nominations included the United Kingdom, West Germany, Taiwan, Singapore, Saudi Arabia, and Israel. But when I gave the list to Bud, he pointed out that we had to rule out Israel, as well as any other nation that received American aid. If a country we were helping then turned around and sent money to the contras, it would look as if we were simply laundering our foreign aid.[1] Besides, although almost nobody knew about it, Israel was already helping the contras in a very different way.

Operation Tipped Kettle had been Casey's idea. In 1982 and 1983, the Israelis had captured vast quantities of PLO arms in Lebanon. Much of it was Soviet-bloc weaponry that was intended for a guerrilla army, and the Israelis had little use for it. But if these arms could somehow be passed on to the contras, it would be a godsend.

The Pentagon sent a team of experts to Israel to examine the captured supplies and to make the appropriate arrangements. Twice—in May 1983, and again the following year—the Israelis shipped hundreds of tons of PLO weapons to Department of Defense warehouses. From there, most of the weapons were transferred to the CIA and distributed not only to the contras, but to anti-Communist resistance movements in other countries as well.

---

[1] I learned later that McFarlane had asked my colleague Howard Teicher to approach the Israelis to help. They declined.

Operation Tipped Kettle came off without a hitch or a leak. One reason it succeeded so brilliantly was that the man in charge of the Pentagon team really knew what he was doing. He was a major general in the Air Force with extensive experience in covert operations. His name was Richard Secord.

After McFarlane asked me to draw up a list of potential supporters, I heard little more about the idea until the following spring. But Bud must have been discussing it with Bill Casey, because in late March 1984, Casey sent him an EYES ONLY memo telling Bud that he, Casey, was "in full agreement" that McFarlane should "explore funding alternatives with the Israelis and perhaps others."

It wasn't long after he received the Casey memo that Bud made a rare visit to my office. As I rose to greet him, he came in and quietly closed the door. Sitting on a chair next to the coffee table across from my desk, Bud said, "I want you to have the resistance open up an offshore bank account so that a foreign contributor can make deposits directly into it."

Naturally, I wondered who that foreign contributor might be. But McFarlane clearly didn't want to tell me, and I knew better than to ask. He knew I would be going to Casey for advice on how to set this up, and I assumed he didn't want to put the CIA director in an awkward position. Casey was continually being called up to Capitol Hill to answer questions, and life was a lot easier if he didn't know those kinds of answers.

I walked down the hall to Casey's office in Room 345 of the OEOB.

"I've been told to have the resistance set up an offshore account," I told him, "and I could use some help."

Casey leaned back on his chair. He was chewing on a yellow wooden pencil. "Is it the Saudis?" he asked.

"I don't know."

"Come on, don't bullshit me. It's the Saudis, right?"

"Honestly, I don't know."

Casey smiled. "Well, it must be. How much are we talking about?"

"I don't know that either."

He peered at me skeptically over his glasses. Then he picked up the secure phone and asked for a number. When somebody picked up at the other end, Casey asked, "If a third party wanted to help our friends down south, who can we trust to handle the money?"

When Casey hung up the phone, he looked at me and said, "Calero's your man."

Adolfo Calero was a prominent figure in the resistance, and we had already met a couple of times.

"Go see Calero," Casey said. "He should set up an offshore account if he doesn't have one already. The money shouldn't come all at once. Have it arrive in regular payments, every month. That will give us more control."

Casey got up and motioned for me to join him over in the sitting area. Then he held school.

"Here's what to do," he began.

I took out a notebook.

"Put that away," he said. "If you have to write everything down, you don't belong in this business. The money should go directly from a foreign account into Calero's offshore account. It shouldn't come into this country at all. Do it with a wire transfer."

"What, exactly, is a wire transfer?"

Casey sighed before explaining. He had spent most of his life in the financial world, and had even served as chairman of the SEC. Asking Bill Casey about a wire transfer was a little like going up to Einstein and saying, "Excuse me, Professor, but what is a square root?"

"Why does it have to be an offshore account?" I asked.

"Two reasons," he replied. First, he explained, all Nicaraguan bank accounts in the United States had been frozen. Second, the Treasury Department monitors large transfers of funds in and out of American banks. Someone was bound to notice these transactions and start asking questions.

It wasn't until months later that I learned that Casey was right about Saudi Arabia. On the afternoon of June 25, 1984, the President and his top national security aides met in the Situation Room to discuss ways to keep the resistance alive. Casey spoke in favor of soliciting contributions from other countries. Shultz opposed it, but suggested that the Attorney General look into whether it was legal. Ed Meese agreed to check with the Justice Department. Everyone agreed that the matter had to be handled with great discretion. "If such a story gets out," President Reagan said as the meeting ended, "we'll all be hanging by our thumbs in front of the White House until we find out who did it."[2]

Shultz didn't know it at the time, and neither did I, but the President had already authorized McFarlane to see Prince Bandar bin Sultan, the Saudi ambassador to Washington, to ask for a contribution from his government. The first deposit, in the amount of one million dollars, arrived in early July, and over the next seven months the Saudis continued helping the contras at the rate of a million dollars a month. While this wasn't enough to cover all that an army needed, it did help buy food, clothing, weapons, and ammunition.

It was enough, in other words, to do what the President had told McFarlane he had wanted done—to hold the resistance together "body and soul" until Congress could be persuaded to change its mind and allow the CIA back in.

In February 1985, King Fahd of Saudi Arabia arrived in Washington on a state visit. During his meetings with the President at the White House, he agreed to provide

---

[2]From the declassified minutes of the National Security Planning Group meeting, June 25, 1984, p. 14.

additional funds to the resistance. I wasn't there, but Bud McFarlane said later that he gave the President a note card on the matter. Knowing how President Reagan felt about the resistance, I never doubted that he'd be willing to ask King Fahd outright for another donation.

Later, there were those who concluded that the Saudis' generosity came in return for an expedited delivery of Stinger antiaircraft missiles that was being held up by Congress. While the missiles may have figured into it, this explanation ignores the honest-to-God affection that the Saudis, like many of our allies, had for President Reagan. They truly liked him, and they also liked what he stood for—especially after four years of Jimmy Carter. If Ronald Reagan cared about supporting the contras, they were happy to help.

In addition, the Saudis have always been strongly anti-Communist. They knew what it meant to have a Communist presence in the neighborhood, which is why they were already supporting the Afghan resistance to the tune of *hundreds* of millions of dollars.


Armed with McFarlane's instructions and Casey's advice, I flew down to Tegucigalpa, the capital of Honduras, to meet with Adolfo Calero.

Calero, who looked like a silver-haired bear, was easily the most visible leader in the resistance. He had a law degree, and had been a successful businessman in Managua, where he had run Coca-Cola's operations. He had a special rapport with Americans, and had even gone to college in the United States. After graduating from Notre Dame, he returned to Nicaragua committed to both free enterprise and American-style democracy. His political views got him in trouble with the Somoza regime, and he was jailed more than once. But when the Sandinistas came to power, Calero's public opposition to Somoza didn't stop the new government from seizing his property and sending him into exile.

I thought Space Mountain at Disney World was a pretty good ride until I flew into Tegucigalpa. The airport's only runway is stretched between a mountain on one end and the edge of a cliff on the other. In order to land, the pilot has to fly in over the mountain; then he makes a sudden, deep dive, pulling up just as he hits the runway. He practically has to stand on the brakes until they smoke. You find yourself praying that the plane will be able to stop before it drops off the cliff and into the ravine—which is littered with the wrecks of planes that didn't stop in time.

I had pretty much stopped shaking by the time I got to the contras' safe house, which was located in one of the city's residential neighborhoods. About a dozen senior people from the resistance were waiting for me, including Enrique Bermudez, who was wearing his fatigues. From the way they greeted me, it was clear that even a visit from a relatively junior White House official meant a lot to them. In addition to the standard contra fare of black beans and rice, Adolfo proudly served chicken, which he had barbecued on the back porch.

Most of the table talk centered on recent cross-border operations by the Sandinistas, and on the inevitable topic that marked almost every discussion about the contras the deplorable conditions in the camps. When the meal was over, I spoke to the group with the help of a translator and delivered the message that McFarlane had instructed me to communicate: "Our goals and yours are the same. Like you, we want to see a democratic Nicaragua. Although the Congress has cut off the CIA, President Reagan wants you to know that we will find a way to help you. I can promise you that you will not be abandoned."

We finished dinner around ten. When most of the others had left, Calero motioned for me to step out on the porch. He tried not to show his disappointment, but it was clear that he felt let down.

"Colonel," he said, "I was led to believe that you would be bringing us something more than promises."

"I am," I said. "But I couldn't talk about it in front

of the others. There is a benefactor."

"Who is it?"

"I can't say. I've been told to tell you to set up an offshore bank account. I'll need the account number, a telex code, and a wire transfer address."

"How much will be deposited?"

"A million dollars a month."

Adolfo was silent for a moment, and I wasn't sure whether he was pleased by this figure or disappointed. Finally he said, "Yes, that will help."

"You can't let anybody know that I am involved in this," I said. "And we'll also need careful records of how the money is spent."

We talked on for a while. As I was leaving, Adolfo said, "We appreciate this help. I'll come up soon with the information you want. Some day, I'd like to thank President Reagan in person."

I spent that night at the ambassador's residence and flew back to Washington the next morning.

Calero came to town about a week later. McFarlane was nervous that somebody would learn about our arrangement, so instead of having Adolfo come to the White House, we met in a town house overlooking Lafayette Park. Without referring to notes, Calero gave me the information I asked for: The account was in the name of Esther Morales, a member of the resistance directorate. The number was 541–48 at the Miami branch of BAC (Banco America Central) International Bank in the Cayman Islands. As I jotted down the details, I noticed that Adolfo was smiling. He must have been amused that this American who was supposed to be an expert in covert operations had to put it all in writing.

Calero returned to his hotel, and I went back to my office, where I typed the information on an index card for McFarlane. Then I called Bud to let him know I had the information he was waiting for. "As long as Adolfo's in town," I said, "would you like to meet him?"

"Sure. But not here."

"Why don't I pick you up in the Military Office station wagon? You two can talk in the back."

(I could have used my own car, but it was parked on the Ellipse, half a mile away. Besides, I didn't want to surrender a parking space unless it was absolutely necessary.)

I arranged to pick up McFarlane on West Executive Avenue, and then turned right on Pennsylvania, where Calero was waiting in front of the Treasury. While I took them on an impromptu tour of the city's monuments, Bud and Adolfo talked in the back. Bud seemed to get a real kick out of meeting this way. This wasn't exactly high adventure, but it must have been a welcome break from the endless mundane meetings and paperwork he had to deal with. He reminded Adolfo that the monthly payments from the anonymous benefactor were meant as a bridge to tide over the resistance until Congress once again changed its mind and resumed funding the contras. He mentioned the need for regular accounting and stressed the importance of secrecy. No one at the CIA or the State Department, or anywhere else in the U.S. government, was to know the details of this arrangement.

When the Saudi money began to arrive, Calero used it to buy weapons and supplies for the resistance. He often called me for advice, which inaugurated a deepening level of confidence and contact between us. As time went on, we conferred about almost every aspect of the resistance movement—from where the contras could buy surface-to-air missiles to the need for more obstetricians in the base camps.

One afternoon, Casey called me from his office at the Intelligence Community Staff Building on F Street.

"Can you come over and see me right now?"

I threw on my coat, ran over to F Street, and took the creaky old elevator to Casey's office. This old building, with its high ceilings and peeling paint, was a relic from another era. Every time I entered it I was reminded of the dingy, cramped offices in London where George Smiley and his colleagues worked in the novels of John le Carré.

Casey was alone in his office. When I sat down, he said, "You're talking too much."

"What do you mean?"

"On the phone. How often are you talking to your pal in Honduras? Three, four times a week?"

"Something like that."

"All in the clear, right?"

"Yes."

"Well, it's got to stop," he said. I already knew that both U.S. and foreign intelligence services spent most of their time watching each other. Casey emphasized that these telephone calls made it too easy for the Soviets to listen in on my conversations with Calero.

He handed me a small black book. "Have you ever used one of these before?"

I opened it. Inside was a series of little pockets.

"No. How does it work?"

He shook his head, as if to say, Do I have to explain *everything*?

"It's a code book," he said. "You get one, he gets one. You change the code numbers on a set pattern. Now you can talk to each other without giving away the store."

It was a simple, do-it-yourself encoding/decoding device. All you had to do was enter the relevant words—Honduras, Nicaragua, guns, ammo, medicine, planes, whatever—and then line them up with the code numbers in the book, which could be changed every day. It was low-tech but effective. Even if somebody was listening in, he'd have virtually no idea what you were talking about.

These black books, a variation of a "onetime pad," were the first of several efforts on Casey's part to improve the security of our contacts with the resistance. Later, when more people were involved, he called me in again. "What are you doing about security?" he asked. "Your COMSEC [communications security] stinks."

Casey was concerned about the Soviets' ability to monitor telephone calls from their listening post in

Lourdes, Cuba. What had begun as a simple link between Adolfo and me soon involved over a dozen people on at least two continents. Adolfo and I were still using the original code books, but that didn't protect the rest of the group. Casey suggested the Phillips PX-1000, a European-made encryption device, but when that turned out to be inadequate, he recommended a brand-new American-made device manufactured by TRW, called the KL-43. I didn't even know these incredible machines existed until Casey had a few of them sent to my office.

The KL-43 resembled what later became known as a laptop computer, except that it came equipped with an encryption chip. You'd type in your message, which would appear on the tiny screen in plain English. After reviewing what you had written, you'd push the "encode" button on the keyboard, whereupon everything on the screen would turn to gibberish. Then you'd call the person to whom you intended to send it. After confirming that you were both using the same code, you'd put your telephone receiver in the modem. At the sound of the beep, you would push "transmit," and another beep would sound, locking both machines into sync. Within seconds, the recipient received the encoded message. For added security, he would hang up the phone before decoding the text with the push of a button.

In open conversation we referred to these machines as typewriters. Once a month, an intelligence officer would deliver a new cassette of codes, which looked like a tape dispenser. Every day you'd tear out another code, enter it into the machine, and burn the previous day's code strip. Even if a KL-43 fell into the wrong hands, there was little risk; the code would be obsolete within hours.

The KL-43, which came with its own little printer, was completely portable. I rarely left home without it.

The code books and secure communications equipment may have helped keep the Soviets and the Cubans from knowing the details of what I was doing to support the resistance, but it didn't keep the secret from spreading within our own government. Over time, the circle of knowledge inevitably expanded beyond Casey, McFarlane, Poindexter, and the President.

In part this was because of the Restricted Interagency Group, or RIG, which acted as a "compartmented" coordinating body for U.S. diplomatic, military, and covert activities throughout Central America—and especially for the actions we took to deal with the growing threat posed by the Sandinistas. The RIG, which was chaired by the Assistant Secretary of State for Inter-American Affairs, reviewed and cleared scores of covert operations proposed by the CIA, including the mining of key harbors, attacks on strategic targets inside Nicaragua, and measures to improve the support the contras received from the neighboring governments.

The process functioned reasonably well until late in 1984, when the RIG was caught up in the Washington game of musical chairs. By the middle of 1985, Tony Motley had been succeeded as chairman by Elliott Abrams, and the CIA's Dewey Clarridge was replaced by Alan Fiers. Eventually, Admiral Art Moreau from the Joint Chiefs of Staff was replaced by General John Moellering. Throughout this period, I remained as the RIG's NSC representative.

Like their predecessors before them, Abrams and Fiers became key players in the administration's effort to sustain the resistance. They were both enthusiastic about the need to keep military pressure on the Sandinista regime, and both men had access to their respective bosses, Shultz and Casey. We met frequently, traveled together to the region, and talked almost daily on the phone.

Elliott Abrams became the front man for the resistance, speaking out forcefully and articulately to Congress, in the media, and within the administration. Fiers, although less visible, was also very helpful. Inevitably, both men came to know more and more about what I was doing to support the resistance, in part because they had separate and accurate reporting channels from Central America. I came to count on them as allies in the struggle, and they were, at least until I was fired.

The personnel changes in the RIG also meant increased exposure for the various actions that the RIG reviewed. In all, there must have been well over a hundred people in our government (including State, Defense, CIA, the White House, and Congress) who knew at least some of what was being done to support the Nicaraguan resistance. As the CIA phased out its involvement and I became the focal point for the resistance, we tried to tighten that circle. But it could never be closed completely.

By 1986 a number of individuals, both in and out of government, were actively seeking me out to provide help, offer advice, ask questions, or request that I provide specific assistance to one or another of the resistance factions. Senator Jesse Helms urged me to do more for Eden Pastora and his group. Congressman Dave McCurdy prodded me to arrange for additional deliveries to the Atlantic Coast Indians. Bernie Aronsen, who replaced Elliott Abrams as Assistant Secretary of State for Latin America, suggested several new leaders for the resistance. Don Gregg, Vice President Bush's national security adviser, suggested Felix Rodriguez as a good contact in El Salvador. For a covert operation, there sure were a lot of people who knew about it—at least until the great plague of amnesia that hit Washington in the fall of 1986.

It soon became apparent to everyone that simply replacing the CIA's funding wouldn't be enough to sustain the resistance. For one thing, the initial Saudi contribution was quite modest. For another, the CIA had provided the resistance with far more than money. They had also found the weapons, bought them, and delivered them, and had provided training, communications, intelligence, command and control, and various other administrative services.

Critics of the resistance have argued that when the CIA pulled out, the contras should have been able to manage these tasks on their own. Ideally, that's true. But the CIA had never been particularly eager for the contras or any other resistance movement to learn these skills. For it was precisely by providing various support services that the Agency was able to maintain control and encourage a certain amount of unity among competing factions within the same general movement. As one clandestine services officer told me in Honduras, "I taught them everything they know. But I didn't teach them everything *I* know."

With the CIA out of the game, the contras had to learn how to run their own show. But for now they needed people who knew how to do these various jobs. In most aspects of life, OJT—on-the-job training—is a great way to learn. In war, however, it's a great way to get killed.

It wasn't until the CIA started pulling out that both the contras and their supporters in Washington came to appreciate just how much the Agency had been doing. The CIA had provided everything from standard propaganda techniques like running a radio station and dropping leaflets to far more delicate tasks, such as providing liaison between the resistance and the governments of neighboring countries. These governments were willing to help, but only if they could do so discreetly. They, too, were threatened by the Sandinistas, and they insisted on deniability.

As the CIA began to withdraw, Calero and other resistance leaders began calling on me for everything from intelligence and communications support to weapons and liaison with neighboring governments. It wasn't hard for the contras to buy most of their nonmilitary requirements, such as food, clothing, and some medicines. But without the CIA, they didn't have the necessary contacts to purchase Soviet-bloc weapons and ammunition. In a guerrilla war, it's always better if the insurgents use the same weapons as the government they're fighting. Anything else creates logistical problems, and prevents the guerrillas from effectively using and integrating whatever weapons and ammunition they manage to capture.

As the summer of 1984 came to an end, I felt like I was straddling a canyon. On one side was the resistance, always expanding, always needing more. On the other was the CIA, which was steadily withdrawing its support. The canyon was growing wider by the day. Unless I had help, and soon, I was going to fall in.

But Casey could see what was happening, and he asked me to come out to Langley on a Saturday morning to discuss the state of the resistance. He was wearing his golf clothes, and he looked a little incongruous in his bright yellow sweater.

I described the long list of problems that were developing in the wake of the CIA's withdrawal. "Money alone isn't enough," I said.

He nodded. "I know. And it'll only get worse in October, when all our people will be gone. You need somebody who can help you out."

He leaned back and looked up, as though the answer was written on the ceiling. Whenever he did this, it was all I could do to restrain myself from looking up there with him.

"Do you know Dick Secord?" he asked.

"The Air Force general? I know who he is. I talked to him a couple of times during the AWACs project."

"That's the guy," said Casey. "He's got the right experience for this sort of thing. He knows the right people, he gets things done, and he keeps his mouth shut. Why don't you call him?"

At the time, practically all I knew about Secord was that he had been a major general in the Air Force, a Deputy Assistant Secretary of Defense, and a key player in getting the AWACs package through Congress. In fact, he had a much wider reputation than I realized. He was known as an expert in unconventional warfare and a master of covert operations.

In the early 1960s, Dick Secord had been a key player in the CIA's secret war in Laos. People said he had ice water in his veins, and having later read one of his citations for bravery, I can easily picture him leading a squadron of aircraft through enemy flak without breaking out in a sweat.

Later on, all kinds of people came forward to allege that Dick Secord was unsavory and nefarious, and that despite his high position in the Department of Defense, he was somehow "shadowy." But I sure didn't hear any of that at the time. Not only did Casey recommend him, but Bud McFarlane was more than happy to have him involved. As I recall, the only person who raised any objection to Secord at the time was Clair George, Casey's deputy director for operations.

"What are you using *him* for?" he asked me.

"Because he was recommended by the director," I replied. Objection overruled.

Later on, the press raised Secord's previous association with the notorious Edwin Wilson, a renegade CIA officer who was jailed for selling arms to Qaddafi. But Secord had never been charged with any wrongdoing, and Casey, who yielded to nobody in his hatred for Qaddafi, did not seem troubled by any of this. But as I would eventually learn for myself, once you're under suspicion, evidence has nothing to do with it. If you're in the government and someone thinks you're guilty, you can kiss your job good-bye.

Dick had retired in the spring of 1983, leaving in disgust over the derailment of what had been a brilliant career. Albert Hakim, a businessman who had known Secord when Dick served in Iran, brought him into Hakim's trading company—Stanford Technology Trading Group International.

When I first met with Secord and asked him to become involved with the resistance, he wasn't especially eager. When he finally agreed, he made it clear that the only way he could help was if he set aside his other business activities. Casey, McFarlane, Secord, and I all agreed that he would be compensated from the proceeds of his activities. He had many contacts, and to the extent that he called upon them to help the contras, they, too, would have to be paid.

Let me be absolutely explicit on this point: by the time we involved Dick Secord in helping the contras, he was a businessman. He came in on that basis. While he genuinely believed in the cause of the Nicaraguan resistance, he was not coming to us, or to them, as a volunteer. Everybody understood that he would be making a profit.

I didn't know how much money Dick Secord made—if any—and I still don't. But I do know this: everything he was asked to do, he did. In retrospect, Secord and I should have agreed then and there on a set fee for his work. We never discussed exactly what fair and just compensation would entail—an omission that eventually led to major problems for both of us.

When Iran-contra erupted, critics of the operation pointed to this administrative failure as one of my major shortcomings. And it was. If the CIA had still been running the show, and Dick Secord had come in, they would have set him up with accountants, lawyers, communicators—a whole support staff. We didn't have this kind of help, and given the restrictions of time, secrecy, and budget, and the desperate needs of the contras, the choice I faced was between helping the contras imperfectly or not helping them at all. To me, the answer was obvious.[3]

Perhaps I should have gone to McFarlane and said, "Look, either I get five or six people to help me, or we'll have to stop. God simply did not put enough hours in the day for me to do everything necessary to supervise this."

But I was a junior staff officer, and the circle was supposed to be small, and nobody was eager to create a bureaucratic structure that would be dismantled when the Congress turned the CIA money back on. Besides, I loved the work, even if it was a little overwhelming. I was constantly on the phone—with McFarlane, Secord, Casey, and Calero and other contra leaders, as well as the State Department, our ambassadors in Central America, and our friends around the world. All this was in addition to the counterterrorism projects with the Task Force, and, starting in November 1985, the Iran initiative.

I had some reservations about the Iran initiative, as I have explained. But I had absolutely no qualms about doing all I could to sustain our commitment to the Nicaraguan resistance.

After Dick Secord agreed to help the resistance, he sent Raphael "Chi Chi" Quintero, a former Cuban freedom fighter who had once worked for the CIA, down to Honduras to meet with the resistance leaders. Quintero visited the contra camps, wrote up a detailed analysis of what the guerrillas needed, and provided a report back to Secord.

As Dick's involvement grew, he started hiring more people. In addition to Quintero, he brought aboard several men with whom he had worked in Southeast Asia: Tom Clines, Richard Gadd, and Bob Dutton, along with pilots, air crews, logisticians, and maintenance technicians for airdrops into Nicaragua.

Following the CIA's standard practice for a far-flung

---

[3]There were times when I was simply overwhelmed by all that had to be done. On June 10, 1986, I sent a PROFS message to Admiral Poindexter in which I expressed my frustration that I couldn't possibly accomplish all that the CIA had done for the resistance: "An extraordinary amount of good has been done, and money truly is not the thing which is most needed at this point. What we most need is to get the CIA re-engaged in this effort so that it can be better engaged than it now is by one slightly confused Marine Lt. Colonel."

covert operation, Secord and his people set up shell corporations in Portugal, Switzerland, Panama, and elsewhere. Using the money that went from the Saudis to Calero, they bought weapons, planes, ammunition, and just about everything else the resistance needed. They hired pilots, leased and bought planes, paid foreign agents, and built warehouses and even a runway—all of this in several different countries.

Much of this activity was simply an attempt to replicate what the CIA had been doing since 1981. Some of it was frustrating and wasteful, because the CIA had already created an infrastructure that Dick and his people weren't allowed to use. Several warehouses and other facilities in the region were just sitting there, gathering dust. But because of the Boland Amendment, everything the CIA had built up to help the resistance had to be done all over again. Working within the private sector, but with only a fraction of the Agency's resources, Secord and his team tried to create a mirror image of the CIA's earlier support.

Obviously, they couldn't do it all. One job they couldn't handle was the liaison and coordination that was necessary with government officials in neighboring countries. That task became mine. In order to base Secord's "private benefactor" planes at the Salvadoran Air Force Base at Ilopango, I met with President Duarte and received his personal permission. I had similar meetings with other leaders in the region.

Ilopango was a risky place to conduct such operations because American officials were always coming in and out of the base, while the resistance support aircraft, warehouses, and maintenance facilities were just sitting there, in plain view. Later, when the congressional inquiries began, the collective amnesia was amazing. Suddenly, almost nobody could remember that the resistance airplanes had been based at Ilopango. American officials throughout the region somehow forgot that I had been there often, and had even stayed in some of their homes and met there with resistance leaders.

Lewis Tambs was an exception. He and I had known each other at the NSC, and we stayed in touch when he served as the American ambassador to Colombia. After he was threatened with assassination, he was reassigned to Costa Rica. Even before he moved to San Jose we had talked about the need for a southern front against the Sandinistas.

Lew Tambs believed in the resistance, and he also believed in the power of prayer. He insisted that Joe Fernandez, the CIA station chief, notify him of every resupply mission. Every night there was an aircraft on a run over Nicaragua, Lew Tambs would light a votive candle at a little shrine in the embassy for the success of the mission and the safety of the crew. And with one exception, his prayers were answered.

Over time, Dick Secord was called upon to do more and more—both by me and by the resistance. When contra leaders came to me with their requests, I often put them in touch with Dick, who made purchases from arms dealers all over the world. By 1986 his operation had a small air force delivering supplies, a ship called the *Erria* to make overseas pickups, a construction company building a secret runway in Costa Rica, warehouses in El Salvador and Honduras, and communications and maintenance facilities around the region. Without Dick Secord, the resistance would have ceased to exist.

Dick wasn't the only retired general who helped the resistance. General John Singlaub came to me several times and asked what he could do for the contras.[4] When I described some of the problems they were having, Singlaub contacted a European arms broker and obtained several thousand Polish AK-47 assault rifles and ammunition. The price was terrific, much lower than what Secord was charging, but Casey was furious at the amount of "noise" that the sale generated. For

Casey, control and discretion were more important than price, and at Casey's direction, my active involvement with General Singlaub came to an end.

Throughout this period, I kept reporting to McFarlane to make sure he was comfortable with both my own expanded mission and with Secord's increasingly prominent involvement in providing arms and services to the resistance. On several occasions he made it clear that both he and the President were more than satisfied with the results.

The hardest part of supplying the contras wasn't buying the weapons, but delivering them to the resistance forces inside Nicaragua. After the CIA pulled out, the entire contra "air force" consisted of half a dozen aging, rundown transport planes flown by former National Guard pilots. They had neither the training nor the equipment to make nighttime drops, which are absolutely essential in this kind of war. Although this was Secord's area of expertise, it wasn't a problem that could be fixed overnight.

The people and the planes that Dick Secord brought in were the same kind he had used years earlier in Laos. Many old C-7s and C-123s were still around, collecting dust in desert boneyards. But it took months to find the necessary parts and to get the planes—and the pilots—back into shape. Everything took longer and cost more than we expected, but I wasn't about to second-guess a renowned Air Force general with Secord's experience.

---

⁴John K. Singlaub was a retired army major general, a short, tough-talking hero from both World War II and Korea. He had been the commanding general of U.S. Forces in Korea until President Carter decided to withdraw our troops. Singlaub made a statement in congressional hearings saying, without quite using these words, that the President's plan was just about the stupidest idea he had ever heard. President Carter didn't think it was so stupid, and although Carter later changed his mind, Singlaub decided to retire. In 1984, when Congress pulled the plug on the contras, Singlaub was furious. He felt so strongly about maintaining our commitment to the resistance that he volunteered to do whatever he could to make sure they were not abandoned.

Looking back on it now, however, it certainly looks as if the air-support team that Dick assembled was still fighting the last war. Moreover, they were trying to do so without the extensive infrastructure that the CIA had provided in Laos—and not even Dick Secord could replicate that.

Invariably, there were problems. During a flight to El Salvador, one of the C-7s developed engine trouble. As it lost altitude, the crew started pushing out anything that wasn't alive. It must have been a hell of a sight, with suitcases, boxes, and even a refrigerator tumbling out of the sky. The plane made an emergency landing on a road—and then sat there for days until somebody came out to fix it. Nobody was hurt, but this little episode became widely known among the small circle of people who were involved in supporting the resistance, and was the subject of considerable laughter. It was a textbook case in how not to run a covert operation.

To be fair to Dick, the team he assembled flew many dangerous missions over Nicaragua, and made numerous airdrops to resistance units. It's easy to dwell on the problems, but if I had to do it all over again, Secord is still the man I'd call.

Airdrops are inherently difficult, especially at night. If you were dropping eight bundles, you'd consider yourself fortunate if six were recovered. The supply plane would fly in ever-widening circles as the pilot looked for bonfires on the ground. But if the ground was wet, or the plane was half a mile off, the drop might never occur. The contras didn't have the kind of sophisticated electronic equipment that would make this process easier, and the airdrops didn't always go smoothly.

Before Secord came in, all of this had been handled by the CIA. But even they had screwed up a few times. To the bewilderment of the contras, one drop had consisted of nothing but sanitary napkins. Fortunately, the resistance was able to use them as battle dressings.

This brings to mind a story I heard years later from a

CIA official who had convened a strategy meeting in Florida with some of the resistance leadership. The Agency had booked a hotel suite in Coral Gables, which had been paid for in cash. When everybody was assembled, the group decided to order lunch from room service. One of the CIA officers picked up the phone and called down to the kitchen. "What's that?" he said. "No room service? *What?* Because we're CIA? You're kidding me, right?"

By now every man in the room was on his feet, scooping documents into briefcases and heading for the door.

"Wait a minute," the officer called out. "Come back! They just told me that CIA stands for 'cash in advance.'"

Militarily, the biggest challenge the contras had to face occurred when the Soviets introduced HIND helicopters into the region. These devastating attack helicopters were armed with gun pods, rockets, and infrared sensors that could detect movement on the ground. The Soviets used them in Afghanistan, too, where the rebels referred to them as flying tanks.

A normal helicopter is vulnerable to small-arms fire from the ground, but the armor-covered HINDs were virtually indestructible. We developed a variety of plans to deal with them. We even printed up handbills, which were circulated all over Nicaragua, offering a reward of a million dollars to anyone who would fly one to Panama, where the CIA and the Pentagon could take it apart and have a good look.

One response to the HINDs was suggested by a brave, former British SAS officer who had provided several discreet services to Her Majesty's government. After looking into the problem, he concluded that the best solution was to attack these helicopters on the ground.

We finally agreed on a plan to attack the military air facility where the helicopters were assembled. But this was an extremely complicated arrangement, and we never did work out all the details. Sending in a group of commandos to do the job wouldn't have been all that difficult, but getting them out again was another story.

As the Soviets delivered more of these attack helicopters to Nicaragua, the resistance implored us to help them with portable surface-to-air missiles. There were three possibilities: American-made Stinger, or Red-Eye missiles; British Blowpipes; and Soviet-bloc SA-7s. American missiles were politically impossible. Besides, the Sandinistas might retaliate by providing Soviet antiaircraft missiles to the rebels in El Salvador. After a futile effort to obtain Blowpipes, we finally settled on the SA-7s which we bought from China—of all places.

Officially the missiles would be shipped from China to Guatemala, and I flew down to Guatemala to make the arrangements. (In order for the Chinese to have deniability, Guatemala had to issue end-user certificates for the missiles.) Back in Washington, I met with a Chinese military officer assigned to their embassy to encourage their cooperation. Before our meeting, I made sure that the FBI was aware that our discussion was sanctioned by the national security adviser. The last thing I needed was for anyone on our side to wonder if the Chinese were trying to recruit me as a spy.

The Chinese officer was a short, gray-haired man who, according to our records, had fought against the U.S. Marines in the Korean War. Only now, instead of meeting as adversaries on a frozen hilltop overlooking the Chosen Reservoir, we enjoyed a fine lunch at the exclusive Cosmos Club in downtown Washington. Most of the conversation centered on "Soviet hegemonistic designs" on the Third World—one of the few subjects we could agree on.

Oddly enough, the Sandinista government had never bothered to establish diplomatic relations with China. Despite all their revolutionary rhetoric, they maintained the old Somoza government's connection to Taiwan. While there may have been some intricate explanation behind it all, I suspect it had less to do with politics or ideology than with simple bureaucratic ineptitude.

On the surface, it was certainly odd for us to be asking a Communist government to help us in supporting an anti-Communist resistance movement. But for the Chinese, this was another way to stick it to the Soviets. The sale of the missiles served two of their interests at once: better relations with the United States, and worse relations with the Soviet Union. They certainly weren't doing it for the money, which in this case was fairly trivial.

The shipment of missiles took so long to arrive in Guatemala that Calero started referring to it as "the slow boat from China." Like many covert operations that go on too long, this one began to generate reports in CIA cable traffic. Several reports specifically referred to Dick Secord's role in the delivery. So many cables were coming in that Casey ordered his stations to stop reporting on this shipment.

When the boxes containing the missiles and their firing mechanisms finally reached the military port of San Jose, Chi Chi Quintero was there to receive them. The twenty-truck convoy rolled through Guatemala, protected by an army contingent, complete with helicopters, to guard against an ambush by Salvadoran guerrillas. After all, how would it look if a shipment from a Communist country ended up in Communist hands?

But like so many other aspects of supporting the resistance, what should have been the easiest part became the most difficult. When the shipment finally reached Honduras, where the Honduran army was supposed to deliver it to the resistance, they diverted the missiles to a military base and refused to release them.

This was just another example of the terrible bind that the struggle over Nicaragua had created for the Honduran government. Emotionally and philosophically, they supported the contras. But they were also terribly afraid of antagonizing the Sandinistas, who crossed the border at will to strike at the resistance. Whenever this happened, Honduran civilians ended up getting killed. And so officially, as far as the Honduran government was concerned, the contras in Honduras did not exist.

Because Honduran support was so critical to the resistance, I had several meetings over the years with President Roberto Suazo Cordoba. Suazo was a popular politician who was widely revered for his medical work in the Honduran back country and his strong opposition to Communism. He was an enormous fellow, who seemed to gain weight before your very eyes—in spite of the fact that he was also a physician, who presumably understood the risks of obesity. He was a man of prodigious appetites who reportedly didn't hesitate to indulge them. I can still picture him in his huge sombrero, sitting on the veranda with his feet up and his hands stretched over his ample stomach.

When the Chinese missiles arrived in their country, the Honduran military was dumbfounded. "For years we've been begging you for surface-to-air missiles," they said. "The whole world knows you're providing them to the Afghan resistance. Now you're sending them to the contras. Why don't you have any for us?"

This shipment of ammunition and weapons had come halfway around the globe, but now it was being held up just a short drive from the contra camps along the border. We needed action—and quickly. I wrote a memo to McFarlane, urging that President Reagan call President Suazo in Honduras to ask him to release the shipment at once.

President Reagan made the call that very afternoon, and I monitored their conversation from the Sit Room. The weapons and ammunition were released that same day for delivery to the contras.

The Hondurans exacted a price for allowing the contras to remain in their country, and in 1985 the Reagan administration agreed on several incentives: the prompt release of thirty-five million dollars in economic support funds, and an expedited delivery of military assistance, including trucks, boots, radios, and weapons. We also agreed to supplement our CIA Honduran programs.

In 1989, when some of these details were documented at my trial, there were various claims and counterclaims as to whether there had been any quid pro quos for the Honduran help. There is no doubt about that. Prior to a meeting that President Reagan had with President Suazo on May 21, 1985, a routine NSC "meeting memo" for the President included the following paragraph:

"In your meeting it will be important to reiterate to Suazo the importance we attach to his continued cooperation in enabling the FDN [the contras] to remain a viable element of pressure on the Sandinistas. Without making the linkage too explicit, it would be useful to remind Suazo that in return for our help—in the form of security assurances as well as aid—we do expect cooperation in pursuit of our mutual objectives. In this regard, you could underline the seriousness of our security commitment, *which the Hondurans seem to regard as the main quid pro quo for cooperating with the FDN*." (Italics added.)

Later, at my trial, the story of American efforts to entice Honduran assistance to the contras became a key element in my defense. Following public disclosure of the Iran-contra operation, I had been described repeatedly as a loose cannon who acted pretty much alone. While I certainly got things done, reports of my "power" were greatly exaggerated. Obviously, there was no way that I could have helped get those missiles all the way from China to the Nicaraguan resistance without both the knowledge and the extensive help of senior officials in the United States government. At one point, when the Chinese were dragging their heels on the missile delivery, General John Vessey, Jr., chairman of the Joint Chiefs of Staff, was asked to "encourage" them to speed it up, which he did. The story of the Chinese missiles, together with the extensive documentation that exists on this and other efforts by the administration to help the contras, was more than enough to destroy the myth that I was a lone, unsupervised cowboy, off on my own.

Despite the enormous workload, my efforts on behalf of the contras were extremely satisfying. My original project was by now well under way and I had begun counting the months until I could leave the NSC and return to the Marines. But when I began working with the resistance, I started feeling productive again. Whether it was watching Secord find the right Soviet-bloc weapons for the resistance forces, or arranging for medical supplies to be delivered to the contra camps, the feeling of actually accomplishing something was enormously gratifying. At last I was doing something more useful than pushing paper from one side of my desk to the other.

There was, however, a heavy price to pay. Although I spent almost all my free time with my family, there wasn't that much of it to begin with. At home, the phone would ring at all hours of the night. Sometimes it was the White House calling about a terrorist attack. Occasionally, Adolfo or Dick Secord or one of my contacts in Central America would call to discuss an operational problem. Or it might be Ami Nir in Israel, who could never seem to remember that Tel Aviv and Virginia were located in different time zones. Ami was a captain in a reserve armor unit, and one night, during a particularly sensitive negotiation with the Iranians, he actually called me from his tank. He simply drove up to a telephone pole, hooked up to the line, and placed the call.

When I first came to the NSC our telephone was on Betsy's side of the bed, but as these nocturnal interruptions increased she put her foot down. "I know you *like* sleeping on that side," she said, "but if your friends are going to be calling you in the middle of the night, you'll have to answer it yourself." And so, after fifteen years of marriage, I started sleeping on the other side of the bed. It sounds trivial, but that little change took me months to get used to.

# 12

## IMAGE PROBLEMS

My enduring memory of the contra base camps is the savory smell of wood smoke. Fires were burning constantly—not only for cooking, but for warmth, too, especially on chilly mornings in the mountains. Yamales, Las Vegas, Las Trojes, Bocay, Cifuentes, Las Manos, El Paraíso, Rus Rus, Aguacate—I visited the camps on several occasions to learn for myself what was going on there, and what the people needed. Looking back, it was probably these visits that motivated me to put so much energy into supporting the resistance. You couldn't help but be moved by the plight of these people, who had left their homes, their modest farms, and the land they were born on to make the long trek north to Honduras.

During the day, the camps were a hub of activity. As the men trained for incursions back into Nicaragua, the women washed clothes in the river, collected wood for the fire, and carried water from the purification system. They also prepared the meals—black beans and rice in the morning, and then, for variety, rice and black beans at night. The dining area was often no more than an open pavilion with a plastic sheet overhead to keep out the rain. By the end of the day, everyone was exhausted from the spartan labor of survival.

When times were good, the soldiers had boots. For everyone else, it was bare feet, sneakers, or sandals. The fighting men wore whatever would pass for a uniform: it wasn't unusual to come across a formation that included Honduran army fatigues, Guatemalan khakis, U.S. Army–type camouflage outfits, and even Cuban army clothes, captured from a warehouse in Nicaragua. Some of the best uniforms were dark-blue work suits that Calero had ordered from Sears—right out of the catalogue.

Many of the camp residents wore clothes donated by American philanthropic organizations, and I would see kids wearing the most incongruous T-shirts: Alcatraz Prison, Minnesota Twins, Esprit, Harvard University, even "Kiss me, I'm Irish."

No matter how often I visited the camps, the resistance fighters were always younger than I expected. At Yamales, the largest of the camps, I met a dark-eyed ten-year-old named Tomás who had arrived at the camp with his teenage brother. Their parents were described as "missing"—probably detained, or worse, by the Nicaraguan authorities. Tomás had a child's eagerness for what his older brother was doing, and when he insisted that he, too, wanted to fight the Sandinistas, the officers allowed him to tag along with his brother during the training. He was quite a sight with his heavy AK-47, which was almost as big as he was.

When his brother's unit left the camp and went back into Nicaragua, Tomás had to be restrained from going with them. He was crushed: the only real connection he had left in the world was leaving, and Tomás knew that his brother might never return. That night, Tomás ran away from the camp. They found him in the morning, safe—but still furious that his brother had gone off without him.

In one respect, however, Tomás was fortunate. At least he and his brother were fighting on the same side.

As in any civil war, there were families in Nicaragua where brothers were actually shooting each other.

The White House and the State Department's Office of Public Diplomacy did what they could to make Americans aware of the conditions in the camps, but it was never easy. In 1991, when the Kurds starting fleeing Iraq, I was reminded all over again of what the contra camps were like. Americans are a generous people. We send relief to earthquake victims and refugees all over the globe. But the contras, most of whom were refugees from Sandinista oppression, were largely ignored.

The ignorance among Washington's decision-makers included an almost willful denial of the true size of the resistance movement. From a handful of former Guardsmen in 1980, the resistance had grown steadily. By the time U.S. government funds were running out in the spring of 1984, there were thousands of fighters spread out in half a dozen camps along the Nicaraguan-Honduran border. By then, a small southern front of the resistance had sprung up along the Nicaraguan–Costa Rican border.

In most guerrilla wars, if ten men go out on an operation, they consider themselves fortunate if nine come back. With the contras, a group of ten would disappear into Nicaragua, and two months later they'd return with a net gain of two or more men. They didn't have to work very hard to round up volunteers; when a contra unit moved into an area, disenchanted Nicaraguans would almost invariably seek it out and join.

But while actual numbers might have been in dispute, there was no question that the resistance was still conducting major operations deep inside Nicaragua—without any apparent support. Naturally, the survival of the resistance after the Boland cutoffs led many people to wonder where the support was coming from. The Saudi funding, which started in 1984, was a well-kept secret, as was a gift of two million dollars that General Singlaub solicited from the government of Taiwan.[1]

The invisible support for the resistance solved the most pressing problem: survival. The people in the camps were hungry, but they weren't starving. The guerrilla army needed more arms and better weapons, but at least they had rifles and some ammunition. The contra "air force" was a joke, but at least there were planes.

On Capitol Hill and in the press, the question kept coming up: who was paying for all of this? There was a lot of speculation about third-party support, and reports of donations coming in from Israel, South Africa, and elsewhere. There were also rumors that the Saudis were involved, as indeed they were.

Some people, who disliked the contras to begin with, concluded that the resistance was being supported by the drug trade. "They're not getting any help that we can see," people said. "They've got to be running drugs."

We heard these stories, too, and we continually probed these allegations and their origins and acted on them as best we could. When the CIA believed that two associates of Eden Pastora, the colorful but erratic southern front commander, had ties to the drug trade, word was put out to have nothing more to do with them. Aside from that, however, we found no evidence of any drug connection. There was enough animosity among the various contra factions that if drugs *had* been involved, somebody would have blown the whistle.

---

[1]Later on, the resistance received a third foreign contribution, although this one never actually reached the contras. In the summer of 1986, after being approached by the State Department, the Sultan of Brunei (whose full name was Haji Hassanal Bolkiah Mu'izzaddin Waddaulah) gave ten million dollars to the resistance. In a rare mistake, Fawn Hall accidentally reversed two digits while typing the account number of Lake Resources in Geneva: the money went to account number 368-430-22-1 instead of 386-430-22-1, and never reached its intended destination. By then, however, the resistance had two additional sources of income: private money raised by the National Endowment for the Preservation of Liberty (NEPL), which was headed by Spitz Channell, a conservative activist; and the "secret within a secret"—profits from the sale of arms to Iran.

Bill Casey believed that the drug rumors constituted a classic case of disinformation. He was convinced that these stories originated in Cuba and circulated from Havana and Mexico City to Capitol Hill, where they were eagerly spread by opponents of the resistance. There was irrefutable evidence that the Cubans themselves were involved in the drug trade, and what better way to deal with the issue than to focus attention on the other guys?

The Sandinistas, too, were involved with drugs. In 1984 I helped coordinate an elaborate interagency sting operation which involved a convicted drug dealer named Barry Seal. In return for a reduced sentence, Seal agreed to help the DEA. Part of his mission involved flying from Colombia to Nicaragua in a special plane that was equipped with hidden cameras and microphones. In April he flew to an airfield north of Managua, where he was met by Federico Vaughan, an aide to Tomás Borge, Nicaragua's interior minister. Vaughan helped Seal load seven hundred and fifty kilos of cocaine—an operation that was documented by a series of vivid black-and-white photographs. In July, Seal returned to Nicaragua. He again met with Vaughan, who agreed to set up a cocaine processing center in Nicaragua.

Based on various intelligence sources, we believed that the Sandinistas were setting up a program to process Colombian cocaine in Nicaragua and ship it to drug dealers in the United States. The Sandinista regime was going to help by providing security, personnel, airfields, and transportation support.

We had hoped to use Seal to run this operation long enough to capture Pablo Escobar, the infamous Colombian drug lord (who later surrendered to Colombian authorities after being assured that he wouldn't be extradited to the United States), as well as any Sandinistas who might be working with him. But this plan had to be terminated when a story about the operation and Sandinista involvement with Colombian drug dealers appeared in the *Washington Times*. The operation was immediately shut down.

Barry Seal then became a government witness against the drug dealers who had received his shipments. But he refused to accept the federal protection available to a witness in these circumstances. In February 1986, he was ambushed outside a halfway house in Louisiana, and he died in a hail of bullets. The three-man hit team was caught, convicted, and sentenced to life without parole. The C-123 transport plane that Seal had flown on his covert missions to Nicaragua was later purchased by General Secord, who used it to help the contras. Stripped of its surveillance equipment, this was the same plane that was shot down by the Sandinistas in October 1986, with Eugene Hasenfus on board.

No matter how hard we tried to disprove the rumors about the contras and drugs, the stories never really went away. Some are circulating to this day, despite the fact that all of us involved with the contras did everything we could to identify any possible violators.

Very little in my life has angered me as much as the allegations that I or anyone else involved with the resistance had a drug connection. I hate to put it in these terms, but since December 1986, the office of the special prosecutor has spent tens of millions of dollars investigating us—and me in particular. If there was even a grain of truth to these stories, it surely would have come out.


As part of the effort to unify the Nicaraguan resistance, Casey asked me to bring together the various factions in a single umbrella organization. Adolfo came up with the name: the United Nicaraguan Opposition—UNO. (Fortunately, the Spanish version yielded the same initials.)

To help UNO become a reality, Casey wanted Dick Secord's role expanded. Until now, Secord had simply served as a foreign purchaser of arms, ammo, and military matériel that the resistance was unable to purchase locally. Casey wanted Secord to become the sole provider of supplies to all the factions, not just Calero's FDN. In retrospect, we probably should have gone this route from the start, rather than putting the whole burden on Adolfo. It would have made it easier to implement the unity effort, and it would have prevented Adolfo from becoming the target for wild rumors.

During an all-night meeting in Miami with Adolfo, Enrique Bermudez, Dick, and others, we agreed on the need to encourage the departure of some thirty or forty American soldiers of fortune, whose increasingly conspicuous presence was unacceptable to the Honduran government. We also discussed the need to end the involvement of several Central American arms dealers who were selling weapons to the contras. Although their prices were generally good, and occasionally *very* good, most of these dealers had unsavory reputations, and one of them was suspected by the CIA of having been involved in the transfer of restricted American technology to the Soviets.

From now on, Secord would be the only source of arms. "Tell the resistance to stop dealing with these other guys," Casey had told me. "They have enough problems. I gave you the name of a reliable man. Use him."

And so Dick Secord emerged with a greatly enhanced role. He was now charged not only with the purchase of weapons, but with the entire resupply effort. Later on, congressional investigators and the press referred to this operation as "the Enterprise"; we knew it as Project Democracy. It consisted of airplanes, a ship, warehouses, flight crews—the works. The financial side of the operation was run from a master account called Lake Resources, a shell corporation in Geneva that was controlled by Dick Secord and Albert Hakim. When private money was raised for the contras, this was where it was sent.

As a result of that meeting, Secord created an airlift operation that could deliver supplies to resistance units deep inside Nicaragua, regardless of which faction they were from.

* * *

When I wasn't traveling in connection with the contras, or the Iran initiative, or counterterrorism projects, I gave a number of briefings about Central America. These talks, which were essentially narrated slide shows, were normally held in Room 450 of the OEOB, where the audiences ranged from a small handful of people to several hundred, and usually consisted of church groups or grassroots political organizations.

I would reveal as much as I was allowed to say about the Soviet and Communist bloc involvement in Central America. I described how the Soviets and their Cuban and bloc allies intended to create turmoil in the Caribbean basin to divert our attention and resources away from NATO, and from various Third World trouble spots. I pointed out that the Soviets were outspending us by a ratio of four to one *in our own hemisphere.*

Early in the presentation, I showed a series of slides in which we tracked the movement of a single weapon, a rocket-propelled grenade launcher that was manufactured in China. During the Vietnam War, the Chinese had sent it to Hanoi, where it was stamped by the North Vietnamese Army inventory control system. The weapon was subsequently captured by American forces in Vietnam, and left behind when we abandoned Vietnam in the spring of 1975. The grenade launcher was once again in Vietnamese hands. From Vietnam it went to Cuba, and from Cuba to a warehouse in Grenada, and from Grenada to the Sandinistas in Nicaragua—who passed it on to the insurgents in El Salvador. The Chinese grenade launcher was subsequently captured by the Salvadoran Army, which was how it ended up in our hands.

Sophisticated Americans used to snicker at any reference to an international Communist conspiracy. But documents found in Grenada, as well as our own intelligence reports, made clear that many weapons, like this RPG launcher, had definitely been around the bloc.

In these briefings, I would also describe the 1983 Grenada rescue operation. Here was a tiny island in the middle of the Caribbean where we discovered enough guns to arm every man, woman and child three times over. We also found an enormous archive of documents that was brought back to Washington to be analyzed. It offered the first detailed case study of a Soviet takeover of another country that we had ever seen. One of the experts assigned to study these documents was Michael Ledeen, which was how I met him.

Among other things, the Grenada documents revealed a massive indoctrination program for the island's population. Selected individuals from Grenada were sent to study and train all over the Soviet empire: Moscow, East Berlin, Ho Chi Minh City, Prague, Sofia, Havana. Could anybody honestly argue that there was no evidence of an international Communist connection?

The Grenada documents also included an item that McFarlane would not allow me to mention—not because it was classified (it wasn't), but because Bud didn't want to risk antagonizing the Congress. The document in question was a letter from a top aide of Congressman Ron Dellums of California to Prime Minister Maurice Bishop of Grenada. (Bishop was a protégé of Castro who was assassinated in 1983 by an even more extreme group, which precipitated our rescue operation.) "He really admires you as a person," Dellums's aide wrote to Bishop, "and even more so as a leader. Believe me, he doesn't make that statement often about anyone. The only other person that I know of that he expresses such admiration for is Fidel."

In 1991, Congressman Dellums was named to the House Intelligence Committee.

This wasn't the only information that I couldn't use in these briefings. We also had evidence of disturbing connections between other U.S. government employees and leaders in the Central American Communist movement. One such individual was a senior staffer for a powerful member of Congress. Casey had reliable information that this man was providing advice to the Sandinistas—coaching them, in effect, on how to improve their standing with Congress. But Bud wouldn't let Casey confront anyone on the Hill with this information, and he told me not to mention it in my briefings.

Finally, my briefings would include an explanation of why the Sandinistas posed a threat—not just to Central America but to the United States as well. Staff members at the NSC are paid to think about contingencies, and I would spell out what was admittedly a worst-case scenario. If the Communist regime in Managua succeeded in exporting its "revolution without frontiers," the entire region could turn into one mass migration of people fleeing north.

Historically, when Communists take over a country, almost anybody who can flee does. It happened in Cuba, in Vietnam, in Cambodia, and again in Afghanistan, where more than 25 percent of the population had fled to Pakistan, India, and Iran. The same thing was now going on in Nicaragua, the only country in Latin America whose population was actually declining. Four hundred thousand people—over 10 percent of the population—had already left for Honduras, Costa Rica, Guatemala, and Panama. Some made it as far as Mexico, and a few walked and hitchhiked all the way to Texas and Florida.

If the Sandinistas succeeded, I explained, and Communism took hold in the region, the tide of people heading north would be overwhelming. It was conceivable that millions of refugees would arrive at our borders, hoping to get in. What would it cost to provide food, clothing, housing, and medical treatment for five or ten million immigrants?

Later on, I was accused of using these briefings as fund raisers. I did give similar presentations to wealthy members of the National Endowment for the Preservation of Liberty (NEPL), a nonprofit foundation in support of President Reagan's agenda that was headed by Carl

"Spitz" Channell, a veteran conservative political activist. But I was careful never to ask for a contribution, and I always left the room before Spitz brought up the matter of money. McFarlane had told me not to ask for contributions, so I didn't. (I assumed that as a government employee, I simply wasn't allowed to solicit funds from private citizens. I learned later that this wasn't true.)

There were times when people just walked in and volunteered their help. One summer afternoon, Joseph Coors, the beer company executive, was sitting with his old friend Bill Casey in Casey's OEOB office, and he asked Bill how he could help the Nicaraguan resistance. "The guy to see is Oliver North," Casey told him. "His office is just down the hall."

Coors is a tall, self-effacing man who certainly didn't fit my image of what a multimillionaire would look like. When he asked what various amounts of money would buy for the resistance, I described the Maule M-7 airplane, a little four-seater that was used mostly by bush pilots and oil workers. Secord had already bought two of them, and used them for both med-evacs and resupply. The Maule was a STOL (short takeoff and landing) single-engine aircraft that didn't even require a landing strip. All you really needed was a straight stretch of dirt road.

A couple of days later, Joe Coors sent a check for $65,000. Dick Secord used it to buy another Maule, and for the rest of the war it flew with a Coors label on its tail.

Project Democracy became the operator of a seven-plane air force, consisting of three Maules, two C-123s, and two C-7s. Later, during the investigations, one of the few questions that nobody ever asked was what happened to those planes. It wasn't until much later that I learned the answer. After the Hasenfus incident, when Casey told us to shut down the whole contra supply operation, all the pilots, maintenance men, and mechanics whom Dick Secord had hired returned home on commercial flights, leaving the planes and equipment behind.

Later, in an effort to tidy up the loose ends from Project Democracy, the CIA undertook an extraordinary operation. First they had the little air force flown to a remote airfield. Then an enormous crater was dug with bulldozers. The planes were pushed into the pit, covered with explosives, and blown up. The remaining wreckage was saturated with fuel and then cremated. The fire burned for days.

When the smoke finally cleared, the charred remains were buried. It was probably the only time an air force had ever been given a funeral. One might call it the ultimate cover-up.

Around the end of 1984, I had gone to see Casey about the overall problem of funding a growing number of resistance activities. He recommended that I set up an "operational" account that would be run out of my office. He gave me a ledger, an accountant's notebook with a spiral binding, and told me to keep meticulous records of all the money I received from Calero (and later, from Secord), and all my disbursements on behalf of the resistance. "Keep good books," he said. "You've got to be able to answer for every penny."

I did as I was told. I kept careful records, including the serial number on each of the traveler's checks. I kept the ledger in my office safe, along with the cash and the checks. Some of the money went for emergencies, like the time Eden Pastora showed up broke and presented me with a bill for his five-day stay at the Four Seasons, one of the most expensive hotels in Washington, or the morning I was called by a member of Congress, who told me that several members of the Nicaraguan Indian resistance were in town and couldn't pay their hotel bills. Rob Owen, Jonathan Miller, and I had to go out to nearby banks and stores to cash traveler's checks for the Indians. Rob met them at the corner of Seventeenth and Pennsylvania and handed them the money.[2]

Fawn Hall cashed some checks, too. And once, on a weekend, when the banks were closed, she asked me for a loan of sixty dollars. I gave her three twenty-dollar traveler's checks, and she repaid the account the following Monday.

Around this same time, McFarlane was getting nervous about all the traveling I was doing. Many of my trips were covert, and Bud didn't want any record of them at the NSC. Besides, I was traveling so often that I was using up most of the NSC travel budget. The CIA maintains operational accounts for just these purposes, but the NSC has no such funds. McFarlane, and later, Poindexter, authorized the use of the Calero operational account for trips I took to both Central America and Europe, and to support hostage rescue efforts, an activity for which I also had Calero's approval.

Sometimes, when I was short of traveler's checks, I would use my own money to travel. The next time checks came in from Calero, I'd reimburse myself—just as I reimbursed resistance leaders for their hotel bills. That's why some of the checks were cashed at Giant Food, a local supermarket, and other stores near our house. Another check was made out to a store called Parklane Hosiery, which became the subject of great titillation during the hearings until Betsy reminded me that this was where we bought leotards for our daughters.

In all, over $100,000 in traveler's checks passed through the operational account. Like almost everything else about my work for both the contras and the hostages, the operational account was kept secret.

We certainly could have done more to hurt the Sandinistas economically. Despite the fact that they were virtually in a state of war against their neighbors, the

---

[2]During the hearings, Jonathan Miller was working at the White House. When his name came up as one of the people who had cashed traveler's checks, he was immediately fired, and ordered to leave the premises within the hour.

State Department was opposed to any economic restrictions that went much beyond a cutback in the coffee quota. As they saw it, a serious economic embargo would result in hardships for the Nicaraguan people. While that was certainly true, some of us, including Casey, Weinberger, and Ray Burghardt at the NSC, believed that with a well-mounted propaganda campaign, we would be able to demonstrate to the people of Nicaragua that their economic problems were the fault of their own government's policies.

The debate raged on within the administration, where everybody knew that if the President exercised his authority and imposed an embargo, this would infuriate Congress. Finally, Don Fortier, the number-three man at the NSC, urged Ray Burghardt and me to sit down and draft an Executive Order for the President's signature freezing all of Nicaragua's assets and implementing a full-scale economic embargo. With McFarlane's blessing, we sent copies to State, Defense, the CIA, Justice, Commerce, and the Treasury. Each agency was asked to concur quickly, because the draft Executive Order was being sent on to the President that same night. The other agencies either "concurred" or "interposed no objection," but we heard nothing at all from State. Late that evening, in one of the rare occasions when he was willing to confront the State Department openly, McFarlane sent the draft executive order to the President at Camp David. The President signed it the next morning, and the embargo began.

But for some supporters of the resistance, this didn't go far enough. They just couldn't understand why we still had diplomatic relations with Nicaragua. They blamed the State Department, but this was one time when State was not guilty. While the boys at Foggy Bottom were certainly horrified at the prospect of reducing our diplomatic presence anywhere on the planet, in this case they were right. True, the Nicaraguan embassy in Washington had its share of spies, and yes, its officials met regularly with congressional opponents of contra aid. But on balance, it was still to our advantage to maintain a presence in Managua. In addition to serving as an important symbol of liberty, our embassy was a vital source of reliable information.

It was also well protected. Although the U.S. embassy in Managua was often the target of angry demonstrations against the United States, these protests were tightly controlled by the authorities. In fact, Nicaragua was the one country in all of Central America where our diplomats didn't really need bodyguards. If the American ambassador so much as tripped on the curb, three Sandinistas would be there to catch him before he hit the ground. Certainly our embassy was a lot safer than the one in El Salvador, which was periodically hit by rockets, or our embassies in Honduras or Costa Rica, which were occasionally fired on with mortars and machine guns. The Sandinistas were careful not to provide us with any reason to take direct action against them.

One plan we discussed, but never implemented, was the possibility of establishing a Nicaraguan government in exile. During World War II, several countries, including France, Poland, and Yugoslavia, had established "free governments" in Britain. And in 1990, after Kuwait was invaded by Iraq, the Kuwaiti leadership set up a government-in-exile in Saudi Arabia.

In the case of Nicaragua, however, there were some fairly big obstacles. Unlike World War II, or Kuwait in 1990, there was no surviving head of state who could lead such a government. And what country in Central America would be willing to serve as the host? "Terrific idea," said Nicaragua's neighbors. "But please, not in our backyard. Say, why don't you try down the street and ask Costa Rica?"

These countries had good reason to be afraid. With the large and powerful Sandinista army so close, it would have taken an enormous dose of testosterone for any nation in the region to allow an official resistance presence within its borders.

Another possible site for a government-in-exile was Miami, which was both safe and convenient. But politically, Miami was a terrible idea. If the Free Government of Nicaragua were based in Florida, the rest of the world would regard it as nothing more than a pawn of the United States.

If it wasn't feasible to establish a government-in-exile, another possibility was to do essentially the same thing—inside Nicaragua, on a section of land that the resistance would seize. We actually looked into the possibility of having the contras capture one or two of the islands along the Atlantic Coast, or perhaps the northeast corner of Nicaragua, which included the port of Puerto Cabezas, where the Sandinistas were vulnerable. President Suazo in Honduras thought this was a fine idea—assuming that the new government was recognized and immediately supported by the United States. In El Salvador, President Duarte told me the same thing.

I even wrote a paper on how such a plan might work, and the idea was discussed at the Restricted Interagency Group. McFarlane thought it was worth pursuing, but here again there were numerous obstacles. Would any other countries recognize and support the new government? For that matter, could we be absolutely sure that the United States would? And who would head this new entity? Naturally, each of the three leaders of the United Nicaraguan Opposition saw himself as the ideal candidate. Was it really possible for them to share the spotlight?

Militarily, it could have worked. If the contra forces had taken over a section of northeast Nicaragua, it would have been difficult for the Sandinistas to dislodge them. The risk was that such a step might bring in the Cubans, which in turn would lead to the sending of American forces. That would have been serious indeed—although after Grenada, it was unlikely that the Cubans were looking forward to another military encounter with American troops.

Another idea that didn't quite materialize came up in

February 1985. The CIA alerted me to a Nicaraguan arms ship, the *Monimbo*, which for years had been wending its way around the Soviet bloc, picking up artillery, surface-to-air missiles, mines, ammunition, and other weapons for the Sandinistas. The ship was loaded with military supplies that could have been enormously helpful to the resistance, and I sent McFarlane a memo proposing several means by which the *Monimbo* might be intercepted, including seizing it on the high seas and removing its cargo. If that wasn't possible, perhaps there was some other way to prevent these arms from reaching the Sandinistas.

I received permission from Poindexter to see if we could prevent the *Monimbo* from reaching its intended destination. Poindexter even put his response in writing: "We need to take action to make sure [the] ship does not arrive in Nicaragua," he noted at the bottom of my memo.

In the end, it did not prove possible to seize the ship. But oddly enough, the *Monimbo* ran aground off the coast of Nicaragua, where its cargo was thoroughly ruined by seawater.

# 13

## THE SECOND CHANNEL

WHEN THE MCFARLANE DELEGATION RETURNED FROM
Tehran in the spring of 1986, one thing was certain:
Ghorbanifar had to go. Although he had been helpful in
opening up the connection to the Iranians, and had
played a major role in the rescue of two hostages, Gorba
had also given us plenty of evidence—more than he
knew—that he couldn't be trusted. As soon as the
Tehran meetings began, it was obvious that he had been
overstating to each side what the other was willing to
do. Now it was more important than ever that we find a
replacement.

It was Albert Hakim, Dick Secord's partner, who
made the connection to the man who replaced
Ghorbanifar and became known as the Second Channel.
Hakim and Secord are one of the all-time great odd
couples. Whereas Dick is a gruff, cold, aggressive,
straight-to-the-point military man, Albert is a warm and
fuzzy, courteous and courtly Iranian Jew who fled Iran
shortly before Khomeini took over. They had met in
Tehran during the mid-1970s, when Secord was stationed there as head of the U.S. Air Force programs.

329

My first encounter with Albert occurred under some-what ridiculous circumstances. In February 1986, Secord and I were in Frankfurt for a two-day meeting with Ghorbanifar and the Iranian government official known as the Australian, who later played a major role in our Tehran meetings. These talks, at the airport Sheraton Hotel, were the first direct contact in years between American and Iranian representatives.

The meeting had been convened fairly quickly, and the CIA officer who was with us couldn't speak Farsi. Nor could the Agency come up with a Farsi-speaking translator on such short notice. Gorba could have han-dled the job, but we had already spent enough time with him to realize that we couldn't rely on him in this role. It was Secord who suggested that we bring in his partner, Albert Hakim. (Secord himself spoke Farsi, but not fluently enough to be the translator.)

When Ghorbanifar learned that Hakim would be translating, he was outraged. "We know who he is," Gorba said. "Hakim is an enemy of the state. He opposed the revolution, and we cannot accept him."

Hakim was our only choice. But what if Gorba recog-nized him? And what if the Australian did? We hadn't yet met the Australian, and we weren't even sure exactly who he was. This was one of the great frustrations in dealing with the Iranians. With virtually every other nation in the world, you could pretty well assume that one of today's junior men would emerge as tomorrow's leader. When Gorbachev came to power in the Soviet Union, the whole world was surprised. But at least he had been part of the political establishment.

Iran was different. Khomeini's revolution resulted in a government without a history, and a regime led by men with no political background. Assuming the Australian really was a high government official, as Gorba had insisted, it was possible that in an earlier incarnation he was Hakim's barber, or his car mechanic. In fact, he turned out to be a former tailor—although not Hakim's.

Albert's version of how we solved this problem is simply irresistible:

> And so I'm sitting there and said to the group, "I certainly would remember Ghorbanifar. There is no reason that he would not remember me. So how do you want me to go into this meeting?"
>
> So they turned to the CIA official and said, "Do you have somebody that can disguise Albert?" And the guy said, "By the time I go through the bureaucracy it will be the end of the meeting."
>
> So Oliver North turned around to me and said, "I've heard from Richard [Secord] that you're very resourceful. Why don't you go and disguise yourself?"
>
> I said, "Thanks."
>
> So I left the hotel, came down to the concierge, and said "I need to buy a gift for my father and I want to get a wig for him. Where is the best place to go?"
>
> So a lady is looking at me, gave me a couple of addresses, recommended one. I got a cab. I went to the place and the lady started to go through all kinds of salesmanship to sell me the best wig and if I wanted to swim, I didn't want to swim, and I'm sitting there knowing that the meeting is going to start very soon and I cannot—"Lady, let's get on with it, I don't give a damn, just give me a wig."
>
> So she goes and brings me a number of wigs to select from. This has that advantage, this one this. Finally, to make a long story short, I said, "This is beautiful, just let's try it on." And so we tried it on and I looked at myself, I said, "Oh, this is not good enough." I said, "I don't like the style of this. Do you have a barber?" They sent me to the basement. There was another lady. I said, "I would like my hairdo in this form." We managed to shape it in such a way that it doesn't look like me.
>
> And I normally don't wear eyeglasses, but I have a pair of folding eyeglasses that I carry in my briefcase. I put that on and walked into the room and those three guys were just shocked, amazed. They didn't think that there was a chance for Ghorbanifar to know who I was.[1]

He certainly had *me* fooled. Hakim is nearly bald, and if I hadn't been expecting the disguise I would never have recognized him. At the meeting, we introduced him to the Iranians as Ibrahim Ibrahimian, a Farsi-speaking Turk of Armenian descent. They didn't have a clue as to his real identity. Later, I was asked whether Albert did a good job as our translator. I think he did—but then, how would I know?

Months later, following our trip to Tehran, two of Hakim's business associates put him in touch with one of Speaker Hashemi Rafsanjani's many nephews in Tehran. The Nephew, as we called this young man, became the so-called Second Channel who eventually replaced Ghorbanifar.

In late August, 1986, the Nephew flew to Brussels to meet Secord and Hakim. Dick called me right afterward, and for the first time in months he sounded enthusiastic about the Iran initiative. He was convinced that we had finally broken out of a web of duplicity. He was also impressed with the Nephew, in part because the Nephew had been candid in acknowledging that Iran did not really control the Hezballah hostage-takers in Beirut. Those of us who had gone to Tehran had already heard this, but Dick saw it as a positive sign.

Back in Washington, the conventional wisdom was that the Iranians *did* control the hostage-takers. Ghorbanifar certainly encouraged us to think so, and at first, I too had believed this. But the more intelligence reports I read, the more I began to believe that the link between the two groups was less a matter of control than of influence, especially on financial and religious matters. Although the question is still open, this wasn't

---

¹Deposition of Albert Hakim in Appendix B of the Report of the Congressional Committees Investigating the Iran-Contra Affair, B-13, pp. 591–92.

a simple case of a division commander in Tehran sending orders to his officers in Beirut.

Months before the Second Channel came along, Gorba had told us that some of the money from the earlier arms deals had gone to pay off Hezballah officials in Lebanon. The Nephew said the same thing and added that while the Iranians couldn't actually order the release of the hostages, they had been able to bribe the Hezballah leaders to gain the freedom of both Weir and Jenco. Unlike Gorba, the Nephew conceded that his contacts could *not* arrange what we really wanted, which was to get all the remaining hostages released together.

In just about every respect, the Nephew was a pleasant and welcome contrast to Ghorbanifar. Whereas Gorba was a fat cat who lived in Paris, the Nephew was a family man living in war-torn Iran with a brand-new baby. While he wasn't part of the government, he apparently had good connections. He had fought with the Rev Guards in the war against Iraq, and he struck both Secord and me as someone who wanted to improve his country's situation and to give his children a better and more peaceful life. In short, he was idealistic—a quality I had certainly never observed in Ghorbanifar.

And while Gorba never hid the fact that he was in it for the money (although he certainly tried to hide how much he was making), the Nephew didn't appear to have a financial motive. That, at least, was my impression; it's entirely possible that Hakim had warned him not to mention money in my presence. Albert knew that what I cared about was freeing the hostages and trying to achieve an opening with Iran. While Albert was certainly willing to work toward those ends, he was primarily a businessman who saw the initiative as an opportunity to make money.

It didn't take long for Gorba to discover that we were trying to open a second line of communication with Iran that would exclude him. Not surprisingly, he was furious. By this time, his incessant wheeling and dealing had apparently caught up with him. He had been dealing with the French, trying to deal with the British, and hoping to deal with the Irish—all of whom had hostages in Beirut. He was also angry that we still hadn't delivered the second shipment from our May visit to Tehran. Gorba maintained that he'd had to finance this one himself, and was therefore in debt. As he described it, he'd had to raise the money in short-term loans from various sources while he was simultaneously working any number of deals with other governments, ranging from soybeans to oil wells. He said he owed money to several parties, including Adnan Khashoggi, the flamboyant Saudi businessman.

While we waited to see if the Second Channel would work out, Charlie Allen from the CIA remained in touch with Ghorbanifar. Charlie had already called to warn me that if we dropped Gorba without either delivering what he had paid for or at least reimbursing him to the tune of four or five million dollars, we ran the risk of having Gorba expose the entire initiative. In other words, we should make sure to buy him out before dropping him.

Charlie was right, and we should have taken his warnings more seriously. But the trouble with someone like Ghorbanifar is that you're never really prepared for when he might be giving it to you straight. In retrospect, two of Ghorbanifar's statements turned out to be all too accurate. He had warned us that if he wasn't handled properly, the whole Iran initiative would come crashing down. He had also promised us that as long as he was involved, there wouldn't be any more kidnappings.

We should have paid more attention to that one. Soon after Dick made contact with the Second Channel, two more American hostages were seized in Beirut: Frank Reed, an educator, and Joseph Ciccipio, the comptroller at the American University in Beirut. I was sick. Throughout the Iran initiative, our worst fear was that the Hezballah would send around a videotape of the hostages being executed. Our second worst fear was that additional hostages would be taken—and now that fear had been realized. While the Iranians couldn't necessarily get all the hostages released, until now they had at least been able to discourage further seizures.

The two new kidnappings led to a number of meetings in Washington, where we seriously considered shutting the whole thing down. But while there was a risk in continuing, there was also a risk in stopping. We decided to go ahead.

I suspected that at least one of these new kidnappings had been orchestrated by the Australian's faction. He and his cronies must have been furious when they learned of the Second Channel, which presumably left them on the sidelines, and they surely knew that the Nephew had been authorized to leave Iran to meet with us. Later the Nephew confirmed my suspicions.

Shortly after Secord returned from his first meeting with the Nephew, we invited the young Iranian to Washington to meet with George Cave, Secord, Hakim, and myself. This was a quick way to determine whether the Second Channel was real: If the Iranians let this guy visit the land of the Great Satan, they probably meant business. Besides, we had already been to Tehran, and we weren't all that eager to go back.

On September 19, 1986, the Nephew arrived at Dulles Airport with two escorts. One was Hakim's business contact who had made the introduction, and the other was the Nephew's keeper, a combination of bodyguard and commissar. Unlike the Communist world, where the commissars reported to their political bosses, the Iranian keepers answer to the religious authorities.

When the Iranians landed, they were met by officials who had been sent by the CIA, and who sped them through customs and immigration and delivered them to their hotel. The previous day, I had run around

Washington getting the necessary authorizations to conduct surveillance on them while they were here. These things are not done casually. Surveillance on foreign nationals in the United States requires very senior level approval, the request for which had to be submitted with the signatures of four government officials or their principal deputies: the head of the FBI, the director of the CIA, the Attorney General, and the national security adviser. After collecting the necessary signatures, I had a courier deliver the request for final approval.

Throughout the time they were here, the surveillance was maintained—just as the Iranians had undoubtedly done for *our* visit to Tehran. One good turn deserves another.

I liked the Nephew as soon as I met him. He was a cheerful and friendly guy who had obviously put on a little weight since his time on the Basra front. He had lost several friends in the conflict with Iraq, and he seemed to be truly disgusted by what the war was doing to his country.

Despite the fact that Gorba had always shown up with fine Iranian caviar, the talks with the Second Channel were far more pleasant than our meetings with Gorba's group—if only because we didn't have to sit through hours of revolutionary diatribe. For the most part, however, the issues were not new. The actors had changed, but the script was the same.

Unfortunately, the Second Channel didn't move any faster than the First Channel. These meetings, too, lasted for hours at a stretch, and continued (at intervals) over a period of months. Our negotiations with both groups of Iranians were so interminable and frustrating that I actually developed some empathy for employees of the State Department.

Later, people who read or heard about the Iran initiative couldn't quite understand why it took us so long to accomplish so little. It's a good question, and there are several answers.

First, our goals were extremely ambitious: not only to recover the hostages, which was difficult enough, but also to reopen a relationship with a closed and hostile society. Second, there were years of acrimony and layers of distrust that had to be overcome. Third, everything had to be done through translators. Fourth, the Iranians have a different concept of time than we do, and life moves much more slowly in their world. Finally, it's clear, at least in retrospect, that there was an enormous gap between what each side wanted and what was actually possible. They wanted us simply to turn on the spigot of American aid; we wanted them to snap their fingers and get the hostages released. Neither feat was possible for either side.

During the Nephew's three-day visit to Washington, we met both in my office at the OEOB, and at Secord's in suburban Virginia. As always, we spent a lot of time discussing the hostages. I explained yet again that the hostage problem had to be resolved before there could be normal relations between our countries, that this was a hurdle to be overcome before we moved on to bigger issues.

At the same time, I didn't want the hostages to seem overly important. "We want them out," I said, "but let me put this problem in perspective. Fifty-two thousand Americans die each year in highway accidents. Well over a hundred thousand die of lung cancer. In a country of our size, five hostages are not very many. But the American people would be outraged if President Reagan helped Iran without first resolving this obstacle."

In reality, the hostages were on my mind more than ever. By the time we made contact with the Second Channel, I had been to any number of meetings with the hostage families. (The hostage problem fell under the rubric of counterterrorism, and McFarlane had asked me to meet with the families of the men who were held in Beirut.) A few family members, like Peggy Say, the sister of Terry Anderson, and Eric and Paul Jacobsen, the sons of David Jacobsen, came to my office regularly.

These visits would increase whenever there was news of any kind about the hostages. From time to time, the hostage-takers in Beirut would release a videotape or a letter from the hostages in an effort to put more pressure on our government. I can't speak for the rest of the administration, but they sure worked on me.

On one occasion, David Jacobsen's sons brought me a letter from their father that the captors had allowed to be smuggled out. Despite the deplorable conditions and the terrible uncertainty he was enduring, Jacobsen's letter was full of love for his family and concern for their welfare. Long before I finished reading it, my eyes had filled with tears. The hostage-takers also sent out occasional photographs of their prisoners, who were usually portrayed holding a contemporary periodical to show that they were still alive. These photos reached us from various sources, but we never made them public unless they had already been released to the press. The successive photos of Terry Anderson, Ben Weir, Father Jenco, and David Jacobsen were graphic illustrations of the effects of stress, poor diet, lack of sunlight, and the general debilitation caused by their confinement. For me, these pictures always provided additional incentive to push on, no matter how exhausted or disillusioned I might have been.

When the family members met with me and other government officials, they were understandably angry and impatient, and they demanded answers. "What have you heard? What are you doing to get them out?" They were dying to know what we were up to, but I couldn't reveal anything. They were convinced that our government wasn't doing enough, and I couldn't tell them otherwise. Despite everything I knew, part of me agreed with them.

And yet our government was actually doing a great deal, far more than we could ever make public. There were many unsung heroes in this effort: officers of the

CIA, DEA, and our embassy staff in Beirut had all risked their lives in efforts to recover the hostages. None of this could be revealed to the long-suffering families, and the Iranian initiative, too, was a well-kept secret. Meanwhile, both the State Department and the White House were quietly working through a variety of other channels to gain access to the hostage holders.

Poindexter and I had several meetings with foreign diplomats both in Washington and in Europe to seek their help in the name of the President. We traveled to France and England to try to determine whether there might be other approaches that could work. Our government had several other diplomatic initiatives under way, any one of which could have become that rare long shot that actually paid off. At least four other heads of state were actively and energetically trying to help, and so were the Vatican and the Anglican Church. Although none of these approaches succeeded, they were all time-consuming and emotionally exhausting.

For the most part, these foreign governments were acting in their own self-interest. Governments are made up of people, and generally behave like people. Favors are expected to be reciprocated: If Harry lends me his lawnmower today, I shouldn't be surprised if he wants to borrow my pickup truck next Saturday. If our government asks for another country's help on the hostages, nobody is shocked when they ask us for our vote in the U.N., or some military hardware, or even a new economic aid package. These terms are rarely articulated up front, and they're generally negotiable. But eventually the chits are called in.

The Nephew appeared to be well briefed on what had transpired with the First Channel, and he arrived in Washington with a long list of military hardware that Iran wanted to buy. But guns weren't the only items on his agenda. He wanted medical equipment and supplies for Iranian soldiers and civilians who had been wounded in the war. He was also desperate for chemical decontamination equipment for the Basra front, where the Iraqis were using chemical warfare weapons. And, just like the First Channel, he asked for our help in freeing the seventeen Da'wa prisoners in Kuwait.

Another topic on our agenda was Ghorbanifar, who was complaining that he was in debt to the tune of millions of dollars, sometimes he said as much as fifteen, sometimes as little as four. He said he couldn't even afford the interest payments. Although we believed that the figures were inflated, we urged the Nephew to keep him quiet by paying him off. Presumably, we weren't the only ones who wanted to keep Gorba happy; the Iranians, too, had a lot to lose if the initiative became public. But when it did, they certainly made the most of it.

During one of our Washington meetings, the Nephew brought up a new topic: getting rid of Saddam Hussein. I regret that there wasn't more willingness within our government to take that one seriously. I said flat out that we couldn't make any commitments about Saddam, but he brought it up again the next day. "The Arab nations can do it," he said, "and the United States can use its influence to make that happen."

In subsequent meetings, I assured the Nephew that the United States recognized that Saddam was the real problem in the region. "President Reagan told me that he thinks Saddam is a shit," I said. Albert Hakim, who was translating, couldn't bring himself to render that line into Farsi. "Go ahead," I told Albert. "That's the President's word, not mine."

Unfortunately, everything I told the Nephew about our attitude toward Saddam Hussein was a lie. I say "unfortunately" not because I lied to the Iranians, which I did whenever I thought it would help, but because our government's attitude toward Saddam Hussein should have been more along the lines I described.

Despite our loud declarations of neutrality in the Iran-Iraq conflict, our government was quietly siding with Iraq. It wasn't just a diplomatic tilt, either; we took affirmative steps to ensure that Iraq would not lose this war it had started. Operation Staunch was a major U.S. diplomatic effort to stem the flow of weapons to Iran, and with the obvious exception of the secret Iran initiative, it was quite effective. Iraq, however, continued to receive a steady supply of arms from the Soviets, the French, the Chinese, and anyone else who wanted a piece of the action. The Kuwaitis helped Saddam pay for what he bought in the international arms bazaar—an act of generosity they would later regret.

When Operation Staunch proved insufficient, President Reagan authorized our intelligence services to pass military information to the Iraqis. And even after the war was over, our pro-Iraq tilt continued. In the summer of 1990, just days before the invasion of Kuwait, the State Department was still trying to convince Congress to grant financial credits and other aid to Iraq.

The American tilt toward Iraq and antipathy toward Iran were two of the few things that Shultz and Weinberger ever agreed on. "We wouldn't want to see" an Iranian victory, George Shultz told a news magazine in 1984, and so "we have been deliberately working to improve our relationship with Iraq. . . . We have been cooperating with the Iraqis to a certain extent."[2]

While that was certainly true, it was also an understatement. Back in 1982, Shultz had instructed the State Department's Near East Bureau and our embassy in Baghdad to offer "incentives" if Saddam renounced terrorism. Eager to obtain American computer technology and other embargoed machinery, Saddam informed the State Department that he had "expelled" Abu Nidal. In fact, Abu Nidal and his henchmen had simply departed to work for a higher bidder—Muammar al-Qaddafi.

[2] *U.S. News & World Report*, March 12, 1984.

Despite the objection of the State Department's own Office for Combating Terrorism, and several of us at the NSC, State's Near East Bureau prevailed and Iraq was removed from the list of states sponsoring terrorism.

Weinberger showed similar leanings. Toward the end of his tenure at the Pentagon, he told a network television interviewer that he looked forward to a "totally different kind of government" in Iran, and called the Khomeini regime "irrational" and "fanatical."[3]

What disturbs me about the positions of Shultz and Weinberger is not that they were necessarily wrong about Iran, but that they were so *totally* wrong about Iraq.

"I felt strongly then and do to this day," Weinberger wrote in his memoirs, "that the conduct of the kind Iran exhibited during the seizure of our embassy completely disqualified it from any civilized intercourse with other nations."[4]

It's funny, but I don't recall Weinberger saying anything like that about Yasir Arafat, or Saddam Hussein. And yet it was Iraq that had started the war by invading Iran. And it was Saddam Hussein who was using chemical weapons against his own people, and who "accidentally" fired an Exocet missile into the U.S.S. *Stark*, and who, despite his disclaimers to the contrary, continued to provide a haven to some of the world's most notorious terrorists.

I certainly don't excuse the Iranian seizure of our embassy in 1979. But every new administration in Washington brings with it the memory of the worst catastrophes that affected its predecessors. Weinberger and Shultz were so obsessed with how Iran had humiliated us under Carter that they ignored the sins of Iraq, which were less visible, but in many ways, far worse.

As this book goes to press, the United States is making a similar mistake by cozying up to Syria. Hafez al-

---

[3]On "This Week with David Brinkley," September 27, 1987.
[4]Caspar Weinberger, *Fighting for Peace* (New York, 1990), p. 354.

Assad is cut from the same bolt of cloth as Saddam Hussein. He, too, is a brutal leader with dangerous delusions of grandeur who imagines himself as a modern-day Saladin. This is another "friendship" that may well come back to haunt us.

In one of our early meetings, the Nephew came up with a startling and dramatic proposition to free the hostages: he would learn, and then pass on to us, the details of exactly where in Beirut they were being held. We, in turn, would be free to mount a rescue operation to free them. While I thought the idea had possibilities, the dangers were immense. I remembered Desert One, when President Carter's attempt to rescue our hostages in Tehran had turned to dust and ended in death.

Secord was more optimistic. "Think about it, Ollie," he said. "They're giving us a gift. Imagine what a successful hostage raid would signal to the world. If we could get some collateral intelligence, Beirut is a beautiful place for something like this. It's perfect for helicopters at night."

I dutifully circulated the proposal to the Task Force, but it was met with a decided lack of enthusiasm. Even General Carl Stiner, the hero of the *Achille Lauro* operation, said, "Forget it, Ollie, it's a no-go." I'm not necessarily averse to taking risks, but on this one I agreed with Stiner.

Both Casey and Poindexter told me to keep the idea alive with the Second Channel, if only to see what would come of it. But I knew that a raid was extremely unlikely. Nobody wanted our rescuers to get caught in a trap, and there was no sure way to eliminate that threat.

Then Nir came up with an intriguing variation. If the United States didn't want to take this risk, maybe the Israelis could. Nir even suggested an insurance plan. To "facilitate" the Israeli rescue, which would include the two missing Israeli soldiers, Nir would arrange for Israeli intelligence agents to grab the Nephew, together with any other Iranian officials who might be wandering around Europe. To guard against the possibility of a double cross, they would all be held until the rescue was completed.

"Now you're talking," said Casey. And no wonder: if anything went wrong, the Israelis would take the blame. But the idea of an armed raid into Beirut never got past the talking stage, and it was probably just as well. The Nephew was too nice a fellow to throw into a dungeon. Besides, none of us could be sure just how much affection his uncle Rafsanjani had for him, anyway.

At several points during his visit to Washington, the Nephew asked for a brief intermission so he could pray. He hadn't brought his prayer rug, so one of my colleagues offered his multicolored gym towel. All this praying led me to make several references to Abraham, the biblical father of three great religions: Judaism, Christianity, and Islam. I also stressed that President Reagan was a man of God, but I apparently pushed the religious comments a little too far.

At one point, the Nephew's keeper took Secord aside to complain about me. "General," he said, "what's with this guy? We just *left* a country full of mullahs. And what do I find here but another lousy mullah!"

Someone in the delegation must have been looking forward to his brief escape from the strict religious environment of Tehran, because that night, when the Iranians returned to their hotel, there was a concerted effort to scare up a little female companionship from local escort services. Someone ended up making dozens of tries, not only because the hotel was well out of the city, but also because the Iranians could barely speak enough English to order room service—let alone ladies of the evening. These efforts went for naught, and our visitor spent the night alone.

The next night I took the Nephew on a tour of the White House, with Albert Hakim as our translator. Later, people wondered how I could possibly bring a secret Iranian contact into the White House, as if this somehow compromised national security. But it wasn't all that different from taking my cousins from Oswego, or visiting firemen from Oshkosh, or old classmates from Annapolis. I had taken dozens of visitors through the White House—including my parents, my brothers, my sister, my kids, and even the cousin of the secretary who worked down the hall. In the evening, especially when the President was out of town, such tours were actually encouraged, and the West Wing was always bustling with staff members showing people around. As for secrecy, I simply wasn't important enough for anyone to wonder whom I was with.

Foreign visitors were part of the atmosphere. At the request of a CIA colleague, I once took a group of Afghan resistance fighters on a White House tour, although I don't think they had the slightest idea where they were. After hours, and on weekends, when the President and First Lady were at Camp David, there were visiting pooh-bahs wandering through the White House from every planet in the solar system.

The Nephew brought along his camera, and he asked Albert and me to take a few pictures of him in the White House—presumably to show the folks back home that junior had made it to the top. That night, I took him through the West Wing—the Press Room, the Cabinet Room, and up to the doorway of the Oval Office, which is always guarded by a Secret Service agent and is closed off with a rope whenever the President isn't there. But what I really wanted to show him was President Theodore Roosevelt's Nobel Prize, which is displayed, appropriately enough, in the Roosevelt Room. "This is the Nobel Peace Prize," I explained. "It's the first one ever awarded to an American. It was given to President Roosevelt for his success in ending the war between Russia and Japan in 1905. Although that war had no direct impact on the United States, and took place thousands of miles from here, President Roosevelt brought the leaders of these two countries to Portsmouth, New Hampshire, where they negotiated an end to the fighting.

"President Reagan feels the same way about the war your country is fighting with Iraq," I added. "He wants to do whatever he can to bring peace."

Before the Nephew left Washington, he asked if the United States could issue some kind of public signal that would prove to his contacts in Tehran that he had indeed been meeting with high-level Americans. Obviously, I couldn't get President Reagan or Secretary Shultz to stand up and say anything nice about Iran. What we needed was an American statement that would satisfy the Iranians, but which nobody in our country would even notice.

Once again, history provided an answer. I recalled that during World War II, the Free French government in London used to broadcast coded messages to the French Resistance in their occupied homeland by inserting previously agreed-upon phrases in routine radio broadcasts. I wondered if we could arrange something analogous through the Voice of America. Perhaps the United States could thank Iran for its help in resolving the recent hijacking of a Pan Am plane. (The Iranian "help" had consisted of not allowing the plane to land in Tehran, but even that was appreciated.) The Nephew and I agreed on the wording, and he wrote it down. With the permission of Admiral Poindexter, I asked the Voice of America if they would include our brief insert in an upcoming Farsi-language editorial, and they agreed. Shortly after the Nephew returned home, the phrase was used in our broadcasts.

As soon as the Nephew left Washington, I sent a summary of our talks to Admiral Poindexter. He responded with an enthusiastic PROFS message to Bud

McFarlane at home. "Your trip to Tehran paid off," the admiral wrote. "You did get through to the top. They are playing our line back to us. They are worried about the Soviets, Afghanistan, and their economy. They realize hostages are an obstacle to any productive relationship with us. They want to remove the obstacle.... If this comes off, may ask you to do second round after hostages are back. Keep your fingers crossed."

The following day, October 4, McFarlane responded in kind: "If you think it would be of any value, I might be able to take a couple of months off and work on the problem," he wrote. "No guarantees and no need for any sponsorship (except for airfares and hotels) but I might be able to turn something up. Think about it."

McFarlane claimed later that after our May 1986 trip to Tehran he had wanted nothing more to do with the Iran initiative. But in the fall of 1986, he evidently still shared our belief that a strategic opening to Iran was both important and possible. Admiral Poindexter was suggesting a "second round"—meaning another trip to Tehran—*after* the release of the hostages. Cynics may scoff, but our goals with Iran went well beyond the hostage problem.

The optimistic sentiments expressed by McFarlane and Poindexter were apparently felt in Tehran as well. After hearing the VOA broadcast, the Iranians agreed to have the Nephew meet us again, three weeks later, in Frankfurt.

As always, this meant that we had to arrange for the meetings to be recorded. Because it wasn't always possible to have the hotel rooms where we met wired in advance, I often ended up doing the job myself. In addition to the KL-43 encoding device, I normally traveled with two machines that had been provided by the Agency: an audio recorder that was hidden in a briefcase, and a tiny video camera concealed in a gym bag. (Both recorders utilized special long-lasting batteries and tapes.)

I tried to make sure that all our meetings were taped. After all, I often promised the Iranians far more than we were prepared to deliver, and I told them things that clearly were not true. I wanted my superiors and anyone else with a need to know to be aware of exactly what each side had said. Secord urged me to run my tape recorder even when the room was already bugged. "Just in case," he would say. I didn't share his worries, but I went along with his request. Just in case.

Shortly after the Iranian initiative began, Casey had told me to get an alias identity to provide an added layer of security. I had been issued a black diplomatic passport, but he was concerned that my name was becoming too well known, and that an alias would provide deniability in the event that my missions were detected. I was issued a standard blue passport with my photograph, in the name of William P. Goode. I was now a businessman.

To authenticate Mr. Goode's identity, I was provided with appropriate "pocket litter"—business cards, receipts, and credit cards. While the credit cards couldn't be used to charge anything, the business cards were slightly more functional: the phone number listed on them was supposed to ring somewhere in the bowels of Washington, where it would be answered by somebody who would verify that Mr. Goode was indeed who he claimed to be.

Like me, Mr. Goode worked for the NSC. But whereas my NSC stood for the National Security Council, his NSC was a private business known as the National Security *Company*. When anyone asked, Mr. Goode explained that he sold a line of security equipment to companies in Europe which required special machinery to protect their secret work on the Strategic Defense Initiative. That would explain the two recording devices.

My only regret is that William Goode never bothered to sign up in a frequent-flyer program. When I think of the places he could have taken his wife and family, assuming he ever had the time...

Each time I left Dulles, I carried the two hidden recorders and my KL-43 secure communications device. To my surprise, the concealed recorders would pass right through the security X-ray machines without a flicker of concern on the part of the guards. I had my cover story all prepared, but nobody asked.

Except once. And then all the pocket litter and false identity papers and even my cover story still weren't enough for the skeptical authorities at London's Heathrow Airport. When I landed overseas, I was normally met by an embassy official who would clear me through customs. But this flight had arrived early. Passing through customs, I was stopped by the ever-vigilant and humorless British customs officials, who asked me to explain, and then demonstrate, all the electronic equipment I had with me—and that I was supposedly offering for sale. George Cave, who had gone through in another line, waited for me a few yards away, trying in vain to suppress his glee as I tried to talk my way out of this one.

The customs officials were fascinated by all this unusual equipment. I believe they knew very well that I was an American government official trying to pass as a businessman, but they insisted on hearing my entire cover story—several times. Why was I there? With whom would I be meeting? What were these toys I had brought along, and how did they work? Exactly what is the National Security Company? What other equipment does your company make?

It was awful. I had carefully memorized my story, but I soon had sweat rings from my armpits down to my belt loops. I felt like I was onstage as part of an improvisational theater troupe where the rest of the cast had been working together for years. Although Mr. Goode's performance did not quite live up to his name, after about twenty minutes of fun our man from the embassy finally showed up, and they let me go. George and I flew on to Frankfurt, where we were met by somebody from our embassy in Bonn in plenty of time to alleviate the need for another song-and-dance routine from the inexperienced (but not altogether untalented) Mr. Goode.

In Frankfurt, the Nephew showed up with a new keeper, whom Cave and I had already met in Tehran. Although we weren't able to confirm it, we believed he was an intelligence officer with the Rev Guards. But here again, we never learned exactly who he was or where in the power structure he fit in.

But one thing was clear: the new keeper was obviously more important than the guy who had accompanied the Nephew to Washington. He was also a lot less friendly. Because of his gaunt, severe appearance, and the intense, scowling way he looked at us, Secord and I referred to him as the Monster. Hakim called him the Engine, because he also seemed able to make things happen and keep them moving.

Prior to the Frankfurt meeting, the Nephew had told us he would be bringing along a Koran, a gift for President Reagan. To reciprocate, I brought an elegant, leather-bound Bible for Speaker Rafsanjani. I had thought it would be appropriate if, in addition to signing the Bible, the President would also write out a suitable biblical verse in his own hand. Recognizing the Khomeini government's prejudice not only toward Israel but also toward Jews, I chose a passage from the New Testament. With the help of a concordance, I turned to Galatians, which includes several references to Abraham as the progenitor of three different faiths. I selected Galatians 3:8, which reads: "And the Scripture, foreseeing that God would justify the Gentiles by faith, preached the gospel beforehand to Abraham, saying, 'All the nations shall be blessed in you.'" I asked Admiral Poindexter to have President Reagan inscribe the Bible with this verse and his signature, and it was done.

When I presented the Bible to the Iranians, I said that President Reagan had authorized me to tell them that the United States accepted their revolution. Throughout our discussions with the Iranians, it seemed terribly important for them to hear that. We had already made it clear in Tehran, and I thought it would have been obvious from the fact that ever since Khomeini had come to power, the United States and Iran had been negotiating at the International Court of Justice in the Hague about the disposition of Iran's frozen assets. But these men hadn't spent many years in government, and perhaps they felt insecure in their new identities. Whatever the reason, they needed to hear of our acceptance again and again.

The Nephew never did bring that Koran he had told me about. But at our next meeting he offered me a gorgeous, deep red Persian carpet that must have measured at least ten feet by fifteen. "I would like you to have this," he said. "I believe you are sincere, and that you want to help your country. I know that as a military man, you could never afford something like this."

He was certainly right about that. But there was no way I could accept his gift, and I tried to explain that as politely as I could.

Later on I asked George Cave, "How on earth was he able to bring that huge rug out of Tehran?"

"It probably came out years ago," George replied. Shortly after the revolution, he explained, the new government of Iran had removed an enormous quantity of valuables—carpets, gold, silverware, paintings, and even chandeliers—from the Shah's palaces in Iran, and shipped them to warehouses in Frankfurt. Periodically, the Iranians would sell off some goods to raise hard currency.

By the end of the first day in Frankfurt, it looked like the Second Channel might lead to some real movement on the hostages. But what I didn't know was that thousands of miles away, the entire contra initiative had just come crashing down. Literally.

I didn't learn about this until we broke for dinner,

when I went to my room and turned on CNN—just in time to see a disheveled-looking American being paraded past the wreckage of a C-123 transport plane. His hands were tied behind his back, and he was guarded by a Sandinista soldier. Looking straight at the camera, the American said: "My name is Eugene Hasenfus. I come from Marinette, Wisconsin."

My heart stopped. I didn't recognize the name, but I certainly knew what this meant.

I immediately called my office, where Bob Earl responded with a KL-43 message that he'd already drafted. Bob confirmed everything CNN was saying, and gave additional details. This flight, as I already knew, was part of Project Democracy's aerial resupply to the resistance deep inside Nicaragua. Three other men on that plane had been killed, including Buzz Sawyer, whom I had come to know and admire, and Bill Cooper, the chief pilot, whom I had met. I did not know the third man, who was a young communicator and logistician from the resistance. Hasenfus was the "kicker," the crewman who rigged the parachutes on the payloads and literally kicked them out of the plane during an airdrop. Like the other two Americans, he had been recruited by Secord's team.

Their plane had taken off from Ilopango, El Salvador, and was carrying a full load of supplies for the resistance: rifles, grenade launchers, medicine, and boots. At 12:45 in the afternoon, it was hit by a Sandinista antiaircraft missile and had exploded in flames. Hasenfus was the only one with a parachute, and as he floated to the ground, he watched the plane crash and burn. It must have been a terrible experience, and I can't blame him for talking. When he was captured a few hours later, the poor bastard must have thought it was all over.

The Hasenfus episode gave the Sandinistas what they'd been hoping for: concrete proof that American mercenaries had been flying over Nicaragua. They had been claiming for months that American planes were dropping bombs on their country, and while they were wrong about the bombs, the rest of it was true.

I immediately left Frankfurt to return to Washington. Dick left, too, to deal with the firestorm. Cave, who was under orders from Langley not to carry on discussions with the Iranians without me, flew back to the States. That left only Albert to stay behind with the Iranians, which was a big mistake.

We left Albert behind not to negotiate, but to stay with the Second Channel and hold the fort until I returned. When I left Frankfurt, I naïvely expected to return in a couple of days. But I had no idea what awaited me in Washington, and it turned out to be three weeks before I came back.

Meanwhile, Albert continued the negotiations. During the next day or two, he made concessions that the rest of us would never have agreed to. Among other things, he promised the Iranians that we would approach the government of Kuwait and urge them to release some of the Da'wa prisoners. He also agreed to sell five hundred more TOW missiles to Iran—at a considerable discount from previous prices.

When Nir learned about that, he was beside himself. "It makes us look terrible," he said, referring to his own government. "And where does it leave Ghorbanifar?"

Nobody was pleased with Hakim's negotiation. But it wasn't such a big deal at the time, and none of us could imagine just how unhappy it would make Congress nine months later, during the hearings. Although I didn't like the so-called Hakim Accords, I went along with them because I would have promised the Iranians just about anything to free more hostages. "You want the next ride on the space shuttle? It's yours, baby."

Later, in the midst of all the inquisitions, I was asked whether I had any qualms about lying to the Iranians. The answer is no. My only reservation was that one of my lies might be discovered, and that the hostages would pay the price. I lied to them not because they were Iranians, but because lives were at stake.[5]

As soon as I returned from Frankfurt, Casey asked me to come out to his office in Langley for a long, serious talk. The administration was denying any link to the Hasenfus flight, but sooner or later the real story was going to come out. "It's over," Casey said, referring to Project Democracy. "Shut it down and clean it up. Bring everybody home. We're going back in."

Fortunately for the contras, Congress had finally approved the allocation of one hundred million dollars for the CIA to resume helping the resistance, and soon the money would begin to flow. The Hasenfus flight went down less than two weeks before the CIA began resuming its support for the resistance.

But Nicaragua wasn't the only thing on Casey's mind. He also described a disturbing conversation he'd had with an old friend named Roy Furmark. Furmark, who was said to be a business partner of Adnan Khashoggi, told Casey that Ghorbanifar was deeply in debt to Khashoggi and two Canadian investors. Gorba had threatened to go public with both the Iran initiative and the "diversion" unless he recovered his losses. But Ghorbanifar was only part of the problem. Casey was also unhappy to hear that Furmark, an outsider, had detailed knowledge about Lake Resources, the use of the residuals, and my own involvement in all of this.

Casey's admonition to "clean it up" meant more than just bringing back the pilots and others who had worked for Secord. Between the Hasenfus problem and Furmark, we were facing the strong possibility of the imminent exposure of all our operations, including the hostage recovery effort. My office was littered with files and documents that, if exposed, would jeopardize the lives of people we had worked with in Nicaragua, Europe, and Iran. Among other things, I had detailed

---

[5]In the Bible, in the second chapter of Joshua, Rahab lies to the authorities in order to save the lives of the two Israelite spies. I don't recall reading about her trial.

financial statements from Adolfo showing how the Saudi money was spent—which included sensitive payments to individuals still inside Nicaragua. If there were leaks, these people would be in real danger.

And so I began to shred more than the routine excess paperwork from the office. A paper shredder is an essential piece of equipment in any office that deals with classified material. These papers can't be disposed of in the regular trash; they must be destroyed to protect legitimate secrets. Casey's warning got my attention. Although I normally shredded every day, during my final weeks at the NSC I shredded more than ever.

It wasn't a matter of staying late at the office and shredding documents into the wee hours, although at the very end I did that, too. I tried to destroy all documents that mentioned the "diversion," or the names of people who might conceivably be at risk. I also destroyed the ledger that Casey had given me the previous year, in which I had kept records of all the money and traveler's checks flowing in and out of my office. The ledger, too, was filled with names of individuals and organizations whose public exposure would have been a disaster.

It took three weeks before the Frankfurt meeting with the Second Channel was resumed. We met again on October 29, this time in Mainz, a university town outside of Frankfurt. I arrived in an optimistic mood: although the contra project had come unraveled at the end, at least we had been able to keep the resistance together until the CIA could get back in the game. And now the Second Channel seemed to be leading somewhere: we seemed close to a deal that would result in another hostage release in Beirut.

But the Nephew and the Monster arrived in Mainz with alarming news. Pamphlets were being circulated in mosques in Tehran and Qum which disclosed both the arms sales and the McFarlane trip to Tehran. Although several of the key details about the trip were wrong, we were horrified to learn that any news of that visit was being discussed openly.

According to the Nephew, the pamphlets had been distributed by a rival faction in the government which wanted to stop the initiative. But the source hardly mattered. No matter where the pamphlets had come from, we were now living on borrowed time. We figured it might take as long as a month for the stories circulating in Tehran to be picked up in the United States. In fact, it took about a week.

I immediately sent a KL-43 message to Admiral Poindexter, telling him the news and recommending that we press on and do everything possible to get out more hostages before the Iran initiative met the same end as Project Democracy. In his reply, the Admiral okayed what would be our final transaction.

It was later alleged that my frantic attempts in late October and early November to get the remaining hostages released were related to the upcoming midterm elections. There *was* a connection, but it wasn't what it seemed. Nobody in Washington ever told me to get the hostages out by Election Day. Had this been a presidential election, a timely release of the hostages might have had some effect. But the outcome of these races, for the House, the Senate, and for governor, wouldn't have been changed in the slightest by a hostage release.

The Iranians saw it differently. They assumed, with some justification, that the seizure of hostages from our embassy in Tehran had led to the defeat of President Carter in 1980, and they thought that our hostages in Lebanon were similarly important to this campaign. I knew better, but because of Hasenfus and the pamphlets, I didn't want to set them straight. If anything was going to develop, it had to happen soon. I went along with their premise, and insisted that we had to get the hostages out before Election Day, November 4.

"We've got to move quickly," I told them. "If the Democrats win big on Tuesday, we won't be able to send you any more shipments."

It could have been the elections that finally made

them move. It could have been the pamphlets. Perhaps it would have happened anyway. But before we left Mainz, the Nephew promised us that by the end of the week, in return for five hundred TOWs, two or three hostages would be released in Beirut.

I passed on the good news to John Poindexter, who directed me to go to Cyprus to make the necessary arrangements with our embassy. I then flew back to Washington—losing Bill Goode's luggage in the process (but, thankfully, not the KL-43 and the recorders)—to await word from the Iranians.

On Friday afternoon, I heard from Hakim that a hostage release was imminent. When Charlie Allen at the CIA confirmed that at least one hostage would be released on Sunday, I immediately flew to London, where, as William Goode, I boarded a British Air flight to Cyprus.

I couldn't fly directly to Beirut. The Beirut airport is in West Beirut, the Moslem section of the city, and just about the only Westerners who end up there have been hijacked from somewhere else. My plan was to fly into Cyprus and then make the rest of the trip in a U.S. Army helicopter. And while a long overwater helicopter flight into a city full of gunfire was not my idea of a good time, it was still safer than flying into the Beirut airport.

On Saturday night, when I landed at Larnaca Airport in Cyprus, the place was teeming. I looked around for Harry, my contact from the CIA, but there was no sign of him. I was standing in line to get change for a phone call when I finally noticed Harry standing near the exit. He nodded, and I followed him out to the car.

Harry was already in the vehicle when I came out. "Hurry up!" he yelled. "Get in!" I looked up to see three men running toward me. They were all carrying something, but I couldn't tell what it was. I ran for the car. I stood there, trying to open the right rear door at the same time that the driver was trying to unlock it for me. For a long moment or two the door was stuck as both of us kept fumbling with it. When it finally opened, I tumbled in as the driver hit the gas.

As we pulled away, I looked back at the men who had been coming toward me. They weren't a hit team after all. They were a film crew, and their camera was still running.

Later that night, Harry turned on a local news broadcast. To my horror, I saw myself falling into the car like a scared rabbit. Harry had his face in his hands. "I can't believe it," he said. "They've just identified you as being from the CIA. They said you're working on the hostage release."

I immediately wrote up a detailed account of the incident and sent it to Admiral Poindexter on the KL-43. To this day, I still don't know how the film crew knew I was coming in. We learned later that they were associated with a PLO news organization. There had been rumors in Beirut about an imminent hostage release, and Harry and I assumed that the camera crew had simply been waiting at the airport. But that still didn't explain why they had focused on me. Had they tailed Harry's car? Or was there a security leak in our communications?

Late that night, I called John Kelly, our ambassador in Beirut, to tell him that we expected a hostage release the following day, although we still didn't know who it would be—or how many. I asked him to arrange for a pickup and a quick medical check, and not to tell anyone—not even the State Department. Those were Poindexter's instructions.

I spent that night on Harry's couch. Early Sunday morning, I spoke to Ami Nir in Tel Aviv. He, too, had seen the film of my little dance recital at the Cyprus airport. "Nice going, North," he said. "Real nice."

That morning, I got the word from Bob Dutton, Secord's man, who was in Beirut, that David Jacobsen had just been released.

The Second Channel really worked!

"Keep a lid on it," I told Dutton. "Keep it quiet." If Jacobsen's release was announced too early, it could prevent the other hostage we expected from getting out.

I spent that day pacing in a room at the Golden Bay Hotel outside Larnaca as Chi Chi Quintero and I waited for additional good news. It never came. As the hours passed, it became increasingly clear that it was Jacobsen—and only Jacobsen.

Talk about mixed feelings! I was elated and depressed at the same time. I returned to the embassy and called the admiral to tell him what had happened.

"Okay," said Poindexter. "Go get him."

Early Monday morning, before dawn, I boarded a U.S. Army helicopter for the flight to Beirut. It was cold, damp and windy at the airfield, and I could see we were in for a rough trip. But I didn't know the half of it. We tried to avoid several line squalls blowing in from the west, but it was impossible to dodge them all. The weather was so bad that the two helicopters couldn't see each other, and the "chase" bird had to turn back to avoid a possible collision. Our pilot, a young Army warrant officer, took a compass fix in the general direction of Beirut, which was somewhere off in the distance, beneath the clouds.

We landed at the provisional embassy compound in the hills above East Beirut. Fortunately, there was no gunfire to welcome us, although in Beirut that was always a possibility. When we touched down, the security team rushed us off the Landing Zone—a scene vaguely reminiscent of Vietnam. Once we were safely inside, I was introduced to the man we had worked so hard to recover.

David Jacobsen was skinny and pale, but he looked to be in reasonably good health. He was, to say the least, enormously grateful to be free. As the helicopter was being refueled, he told me how he had been released the day before. At about nine in the morning, his guards had driven him through the pockmarked streets of West

Beirut to the old American embassy, which we had abandoned in 1983 after a car bomb destroyed the building. I apologized for keeping him waiting an extra day, and explained that we had been anticipating the release of another hostage. He brushed it aside. He couldn't stop praising the convoy of volunteers from the embassy who had driven into West Beirut, risking their lives to pick him up.

The small sitting room was crowded with men who had prayed along with Jacobsen for this moment: Ambassador John Kelly, who held the least-wanted post in the entire diplomatic corps; the Deputy Chief of Mission, who had led the convoy of cars to recover Jacobsen; Bob Dutton, who had flown to Beirut a couple of days earlier; and Terry Waite, the special envoy of the Archbishop of Canterbury. Terry had risked his life to gain the release of all the hostages, but not long afterward, in January 1987, he too would become a hostage.

As soon as the helicopter was ready, we climbed aboard. David was dying to talk, but it was simply too noisy. He settled for writing a note in which he made clear that despite everything that had happened to him, his sense of humor was still intact. "Is it true," he wrote, "that the in-flight movie will be *Bedtime for Bonzo?*"

The flight back to Larnaca was not much smoother than the flight into Beirut, although at least we were flying in daylight. When we landed, Jacobsen was greeted by an official American delegation. Having already been spotted by one news team, I remained in the helicopter as Jacobsen, Waite, and our ambassador to Cyprus met with the press. As soon as the cameras were turned around to cover the press conference, I got out and boarded the waiting Lear jet that Secord had leased. In a few minutes we would be taking off for Wiesbaden, West Germany, where Jacobsen would be debriefed and checked over by the doctors. His two sons would be meeting him there, and he couldn't wait to see them.

I could hear Jacobsen's press conference from the plane. When David described how he had taken comfort in the words of Psalm Twenty-seven, I opened my Bible and looked it up. I was wearing a baseball cap, and I took it off and wrote a passage from that psalm on the bill: "I will see the goodness of the Lord in the land of the living." As soon as David came on board, I gave him the cap.

On the flight to Wiesbaden, we finally had a chance to talk. The poor guy was so starved for human discourse that the words just poured out of him. While he was angry at those who had taken him, he was even more grateful to be free. He also accepted the fact that he couldn't know all the details that led to his release.

He told me the whole story, which he repeated again, more than once, in Wiesbaden. On May 28, 1985, he had been kidnapped and shoved into a small, hidden compartment under the floor of a van. He thought he was about to be killed. Instead, his captors brought him to a cold basement, where he was chained to the floor and blindfolded.

Over the next year and a half, David was moved to several different locations. These were no ordinary prisons. There were many times when his guards wouldn't even let him use the bathroom. At one point they forced him to make a videotape, and then beat him severely when an American network anchorman speculated that David might be using the opportunity to send coded messages. (He wasn't.) On several occasions his captors told him he was about to be released. It was painful to learn that one of those times had coincided with our May visit to Tehran.

He told me he survived the ordeal through his faith. They let him have a Bible, where he found great comfort in the patient message of Ecclesiastes, and in Psalm Twenty-seven, whose opening line is "The Lord is my light and my salvation. Whom shall I fear?"

He also described some of the mental exercises that helped pass the time and keep him sane. In his imagination, he drove slowly down the main street of Huntington Beach, California, his hometown. He recalled every store, every cross street. He spent hours thinking about his past, including his brief tenure as director of Beirut's American University Medical Center.

Later in his captivity, he was held in a room with other American hostages. They prayed together, talked, and argued, too, as they often took out their anger and frustration on each other. There were also moments of levity, like the day they composed a handy phrase book for travelers in Lebanon:

> *Fekr cabul cardan davat paeh gush divar.* I am delighted to accept your kind invitation to lie down on the floor with my arms above my head and my legs apart.
>
> *Auto arraregh davateman mano sespaheh-hast.* Thank you. It is exceptionally kind of you to allow me to travel in the trunk of your Mercedes. It is so much nicer than other trunks I have been in.

In sharp contrast to Benjamin Weir, Jacobsen was eager to share every bit of information he could recall that might conceivably help us know more about the hostages. He was terribly disappointed when I told him that Weir had refused to answer our questions. He angrily pointed out that he and the other hostages had been kept in the same location for twenty-nine days after Weir was released. He was anxious about the fate of the remaining hostages, and was determined to say nothing to the press that might possibly add to their danger.

On November 7, three days after the midterm elections, David Jacobsen arrived at the White House to meet with President Reagan. I brought him into the Oval Office for what became a very emotional meeting for both of them. The President wanted to know firsthand what the experience had been like, and David described his confinement in vivid detail. It was incredibly moving and satisfying to see these two men talking together after all this time. Weir and Jenco had also met with the President, but it just wasn't the same.

When President Reagan took Jacobsen out to the Rose Garden for a photo opportunity, the press was in an uproar. The story of McFarlane's trip to Tehran had just been reported in the United States after appearing in *Al-Shiraa*, a Beirut magazine. But even so, the way they went after Jacobsen was unbelievable. Although he had just been through a long and terrible experience, the reporters were shouting at both him and the President, demanding answers to their questions. I stayed behind in the Oval Office, watching from the window as the assault began: "How did you get him out, Mr. President? What truth is there to these stories out of Lebanon?"

One reporter asked, "Why not dispel the speculation by telling us exactly what happened, sir?"

"Because," the President replied, "it has to happen again and again and again until we have them all back."

The whole scene infuriated Jacobsen. He knew all too well that this speculation could cause the terrorists to harm the hostages, and he pleaded with the press to show restraint. When a reporter asked a particularly delicate question about the details of his release, Jacobsen let him have it: "Irresponsible speculation like your question nearly resulted in my death," he said. "You have endangered the lives of hostages remaining in Lebanon. I don't want that to happen and I don't think you want that on your conscience. So in the name of God, would you please just be responsible and back off?"

I have no doubt that David was speaking for the President, too. He was certainly speaking for me.

When the two of them returned to the Oval Office, Jacobsen was incredulous. "They really don't care, do they?" he said to the President.

President Reagan gave one of his famous headshakes. "Well—" he began. Then he stopped himself.

I know how I would have finished that sentence.

\*   \*   \*

David was so angry at the press that I recommended that we leave via the ground-floor portal to the West Wing, and that we stop by my office long enough to let the press corps filter out through the northwest gate. I had an ulterior motive: I wanted to introduce him to some of my coworkers who had done so much to gain his release. Bob Earl, Craig Coy, Fawn Hall, and Barbara Brown had all worked long hours for months, and here, at last, was a hostage who genuinely appreciated their efforts. It was a joyous experience for us all.

Later that afternoon, the admiral and I talked about the possibility of continuing the initiative. Although Rafsanjani had confirmed the details of McFarlane's visit to Iran, and had even added some new distortions of his own, the Nephew made it clear that he wanted to meet again. I left for Geneva the next morning.

While I was angry at the Nephew for not delivering what he had promised, I was still hopeful that we could work something out.

"What happened?" I asked him.

"Please," he said. "We did the best we could. You know that we don't control these people. We offered to tell you where the hostages are being kept."

"So tell us."

He never did.

"Get them out now," I pleaded with him.

"We'll do everything we can," he said.

I have no idea whether he was telling the truth.

The meeting ended inconclusively, with promises on both sides. But nothing came of it, and I returned to Washington to face the music. I never saw the Nephew again.

In December, several weeks *after* I was fired, there was one last meeting in Frankfurt between American negotiators and the Second Channel. Charles Dunbar, a State Department official, and George Cave represented the

United States. The Monster represented Iran, but the Nephew didn't show. When the Monster brought up the Hakim Accords, Dunbar replied that the United States was no longer interested in selling arms to the Iranians.

The Iran initiative was finally over.

# 14

## ENDGAME

When I returned on November 11 from the final meeting with the Second Channel, Washington was in an uproar. The wreckage from the Hasenfus shoot-down had spread well beyond the immediate problems of trying to recover the bodies of the downed airmen, paying their death benefits, and negotiating the release of Hasenfus himself. On Capitol Hill, the Democratic leadership was howling for political blood. In El Salvador, inquisitive reporters—possibly, as Bill Casey believed, with help from the Cuban intelligence service—had been provided with phone records that linked the house in San Salvador where the air crews lived to the CIA station in Costa Rica, my office in the OEOB, and Secord's office in Virginia.

Meanwhile, both the FBI and the Customs Service were investigating Southern Air Transport, the Miami-based company that handled the maintenance on the planes belonging to Project Democracy. Years earlier, Southern Air had been a CIA proprietary, and it still provided contract services to several U.S. government agencies—and to Dick Secord's operation. Now questions had been raised as to whether Southern Air had been shipping weapons from the United States to the contras, as some in the media had claimed. While they hadn't done that, they had transported TOW missiles from U.S. Army depots to Tel Aviv, where they were transferred to Israeli planes and sent on to Iran. We were hoping to stop this connection from being exposed.

And that wasn't the half of it. By mid-November the press was full of stories, leaks and speculations, not only about the contras, but about the Iran initiative, too. My name was starting to show up a little too often, and I knew I was in trouble when the ABC evening news named me "Person of the Week." I missed the original broadcast, but Dornin, our youngest daughter, who was five, told me about it with great excitement. "Daddy, I saw you on television. You were the week of the man!"

Sarah, who was ten, and old enough to read the newspapers, was similarly confused. After seeing a reference to the religious tensions in Lebanon, she said, "Dad, what's the difference between the Sunis and the Shitties?"

The disclosures in *Al-Shiraa* about the meetings in Tehran became even more interesting when Rafsanjani himself held a press conference in Tehran to discuss the McFarlane visit. He confirmed that an American delegation had indeed arrived in Iran, but his account of the trip was as colorful as a Persian carpet.

As Rafsanjani described it, McFarlane and four other Americans had flown to Tehran illegally, disguised as members of an airline crew. The five of us were then supposedly locked up in a hotel while the Ayatollah was consulted on what should be done with us. "Iman Khomeini instructed us not to talk with the Americans and not to accept their gifts," Rafsanjani said, adding that these gifts included a cake that was decorated with a key, to symbolize the new opening to Iran. Unfortunately, he said, the cake was eaten by the security "boys." Rafsanjani also displayed the Bible inscribed by President Reagan that I had given to the Nephew in

Frankfurt just a month earlier, claiming that this, too, had been brought to Tehran by our little group. The visit ended, he said, when the American intruders were expelled from Iran by the Revolutionary Guards.

Other than the fact that the security guards really did eat the cake, virtually nothing else in Rafsanjani's announcement was true. Yet some of the details he cited are still accepted as the conventional wisdom about our trip to Tehran.

Back in Washington, the administration did its best to put a more positive spin on the McFarlane visit. Several high-level officials provided both on- and off-the-record interviews with key members of the press, and at Admiral Poindexter's request, I did, too. On November 13, following a speech by President Reagan, Bud McFarlane appeared on ABC's "Nightline" with Ted Koppel. In sharp contrast to Rafsanjani's version, Bud explained that the Tehran trip had consisted of "four days of talks that went reasonably well." He added, "We were received hospitably and treated with the normal practice that surrounds meetings like this."

"Did you bring in a cake?" Koppel asked.

"I didn't have anything to do with a cake," McFarlane replied.

True. The cake was for Gorba's mother. It's possible that Bud didn't even know about it.

"Bible?"

"No Bible."

"Pistols?"

"I don't operate that way, Ted."

Bud may have forgotten about the pistols, but the rest of his account was generally accurate. I think it's sad that the American press was more willing to believe Rafsanjani than the President's former national security adviser. But for once I couldn't really blame them. From the President on down, the administration was putting out so many versions of the Iran initiative that nobody knew what was coming next. And in case things weren't confusing enough, just a week after Rafsanjani's disclosures, Iran's ambassador to the United Nations came out and backed President Reagan's position by denying that his country had been involved in *any* arrangement with the United States to trade arms for hostages.

Meanwhile, Secretary Shultz took it upon himself to denounce the Iran initiative during an appearance on "Face the Nation." This was hardly the time to break ranks with the President, and some of Shultz's cabinet colleagues were outraged. Rumors were flying that Shultz was about to resign, and that his job would be given to one of the Baker boys—probably James, but maybe even Howard. Things got so bad that Larry Speakes, the White House press secretary, felt compelled to go out and assure the press corps that the President didn't want Shultz to resign.

Weinberger, who had also opposed the initiative, at least had the decency to say nothing. But Cap was in an awkward position, because it was his own Pentagon that had shipped the weapons and sold them to the CIA for the explicit purpose of having the Agency sell them again, through private channels, to Tehran.

Casey was furious, and thought Shultz was being disloyal to the President. A few days after Shultz appeared on television, Casey sent a personal letter to President Reagan recommending that Shultz be fired and replaced by Jeane Kirkpatrick. "Dear Mr. President," he wrote. "On Friday I spent over five hours discussing and answering questions for the House and Senate Intelligence Committees on *our* effort to develop a relationship with important elements in Iran.... The public pouting of George Shultz and the failure of the State Department to support what we did inflated the uproar on this matter. If we all stand together and speak out I believe we can put this behind us quickly.

"Mr. President," Casey concluded, "you need a new pitcher."

But Shultz had no intention of leaving the game. In

fact, as I learned while preparing for my trial, the Secretary of State was hoping to play two positions at once: he wanted to replace John Poindexter as national security adviser while continuing to serve as Secretary of State.

On November 13, President Reagan had gone on television to give his version of events. In the wake of all the leaks and unattributed sources, he promised to tell the whole story. "You are going to hear the facts from a White House source," he promised. "And you know my name."

He continued: "The charge has been made that the United States has shipped weapons to Iran as ransom payment for the release of American hostages in Lebanon; that the United States undercut its allies and secretly violated American policy against trafficking with terrorists.

"Those charges are utterly false. The United States has not made concessions to those who hold our people captive in Lebanon, and we will not. The United States has not swapped boatloads or planeloads of American weapons for the return of American hostages, and we will not.

"We did not—repeat, did not—trade weapons or anything else for hostages, nor will we."

As I explained earlier, President Reagan wasn't exactly lying, but he wasn't telling the truth, either. He believed what he said, and he *still* thinks we didn't trade arms for hostages. After all, he reasoned, the people we were dealing with were Iranians, not the hostage holders themselves. Technically, he was correct.

In his speech, the President insisted that the arms we shipped to Iran could have fit in a single cargo plane. He took a lot of heat for that remark, but it wasn't wrong. Before the speech, Admiral Poindexter had asked me to determine whether what we had shipped would, in fact, have fit into a single plane. I called the Pentagon to check on the size and the weight of two thousand TOWs, plus the electronic parts, and I calculated that yes, they would have fit in a C-5A, the largest cargo plane in our Air Force. Regardless of how it was portrayed, this was not an enormous quantity of arms.

Hindsight is always easy. But I still wonder how events would have turned out if, having decided to put aside the ongoing rescue efforts and address the nation, President Reagan had made a somewhat different speech that evening—which might have gone something like this:

> My fellow Americans: The charge has been made that the United States has shipped weapons to Iran as ransom payment for the release of American hostages in Lebanon. Let me tell you what we did—and why.
>
> In an effort to open a relationship with the revolutionary government of Iran, we sold two thousand TOW missiles and some electronic parts to Tehran. We had reason to believe there were moderate, or pragmatic, individuals in the government of Iran who were not hostile to the United States. In an effort to reach these people, we worked secretly through two different channels. We also worked to free the American hostages in Lebanon, and three of them were in fact released.
>
> Two members of my cabinet were opposed to this initiative, but they were willing to see it through. All of us understood that this was a very high-risk venture, but we believed it was a risk worth taking.
>
> As you now know, our effort to open a relationship with the current government in Iran did not succeed. Tonight, I call upon the government of Iran to begin an open dialogue with the United States—a dialogue that could lead to a better relationship between our two countries, and, possibly, an end to the fruitless war between Iran and Iraq.
>
> We know that the government of Iran has some influence over those who hold the American and other Western hostages in Beirut. I call upon Iran to use its influence so that the hostages are released.

In other words, President Reagan could have tried to make a virtue out of a necessity.

Although it was true as far as it went, even this speech would not have revealed the whole story. It would have made no mention of the "diversion," for example, or of the American role in the 1985 HAWK shipments from Israel to Iran. It's possible that this speech might have revealed enough to contain the damage and make a constructive difference, but not necessarily. As things turned out, nothing we did during those days made much difference at all. We only made things worse.

Shortly after the *Al-Shiraa* revelations, Admiral Poindexter asked for a chronology of the Iran initiative. He assigned the task to my office, and gave instructions to work with the CIA, the Pentagon, and anybody else who could help in preparing it.

Because my own operational involvement in the Iran initiative had not begun until I heard from Rabin in November 1985, I relied on Michael Ledeen, Bud McFarlane, and Ami Nir for some of the earlier details. Invariably, people remember things differently, and there were several discrepancies in their recollections that had to be talked through and synthesized. The chronology started out as two pages, but it soon expanded into twenty.

On Tuesday, November 18, at about eight in the evening, Bud McFarlane came to my office to "lend a hand" in reworking a draft of the President's opening remarks for the press conference scheduled for the following night. In a PROFS message to Admiral Poindexter, he proposed several changes in the text, including a denial that the United States had approved of any shipments to Iran before the January 1986 Finding. When he had finished working on the President's remarks, Bud turned to the chronology and made these same changes on my draft.

By now, President Reagan, Admiral Poindexter, and Don Regan had met with various congressional delegations to discuss the Iran initiative, and all of them had studiously avoided any mention of our involvement in the 1985 shipments. On November 12, when President Reagan and his senior foreign policy advisers met with the congressional leadership at the White House, the President pointedly omitted any reference to his okay for the Israeli TOW shipments in the summer of 1985 or to his December 1985 Finding retroactively authorizing the Iranian initiative activities. And although the senior government officials who were present knew about it, no one mentioned our involvement in the November 1985 HAWK shipment.

From then on, the President and his senior advisers were committed to this version of events. In his speech to the nation from the Oval Office on November 13, the President made no mention of U.S. government approval for or involvement in these early shipments.

By the time McFarlane sat down at my computer to type his rendition of the 1985 events, his account coincided with the President's. In his description of the HAWK shipment from Israel to Iran, Bud totally altered the facts about the delivery and our role in facilitating it, and made it appear that we didn't even know about it at the time.

To this day I don't know McFarlane's reasons for these changes. I have mine, and at the time, that was enough; we knew from our intelligence and from meetings with the Iranians that the HAWK shipment of November 1985 had infuriated the Iranians. They had been led to expect a long-range system that could shoot down high-altitude Soviet and Iraqi aircraft. But HAWK is a low-altitude, relatively close-in, antiaircraft system. To make matters worse, there was the awkward problem of the Israeli markings on several of the missiles when they arrived in Iran.

When the Iranians had confronted us with these problems, we had assured them that we'd had nothing to do with that particular shipment. With the agreement of the Israelis, we presented ourselves as the good guys. "Deal with us from now on," we said. "You can return those HAWKs, and we'll help you get what you need."

Now, in November 1986, I still didn't want us to reveal our connection with that 1985 shipment. I was concerned that if the United States was perceived as having played any role in that transaction, the hostage-takers in Beirut might take out their anger on the hostages. As David Jacobsen had told me earlier in the month, that sort of thing really *did* happen. We also worried that additional hostages might be seized. That had happened when we switched from the First to the Second Channel, which had apparently infuriated somebody in the Iranian government.

We were also concerned that any revelation of our role in the 1985 shipment could harm the Nephew. He might end up being targeted as the fall guy in Tehran, especially if it was revealed that even the most recent shipments to his country had gone through Israel. Although by that time I fully expected to lose my job at the NSC, at least I had a career in the Marine Corps to look forward to. The Nephew might find himself in a more difficult situation. In Iran, after all, the word "firing" was often followed by the word "squad."

There was still another reason for not disclosing the American role in the 1985 shipment from Israel. The original Presidential Finding which Reagan had signed in December 1985, authorizing the covert shipment of arms to Iran, had been worded in such a way as to make the Iran initiative sound like nothing more than arms for hostages:

Scope: Hostage Rescue—Middle East.

Description: The provision of assistance by the Central Intelligence Agency to private parties in their attempt to obtain the release of Americans held hostage in the Middle East. Such assistance is to include the provision of transportation, communication, and other necessary support. As part of these efforts certain foreign materiel and munitions may be provided to the Government of Iran which is taking steps to facilitate the release of the American hostages.

Any disclosure of this Finding would have been enormously embarrassing for the administration, especially since the President had insisted in his speech, and continued to insist, that the Iran initiative was *not* about arms for hostages.

On the afternoon of November 21, John Poindexter and I sat in his office and discussed the problem. In January 1986, the President had signed a second Finding, which made clear that the Iran initiative was much broader than simply arms for hostages. This second Finding spelled out the President's goals: to create an opening to Iran, to help bring about an end to the Iran-Iraq war, *and* to recover the hostages. The admiral believed that the poorly worded first Finding had been effectively superseded by the second Finding.

If that first Finding was ever revealed, the President would be humiliated. The admiral asked Paul Thompson, his lawyer, to bring in the signed original 1985 Finding. Admiral Poindexter then tore it in half and placed it on the coffee table. This was one of the charges on which the admiral was later indicted and convicted.

In changing the chronology and in destroying the superseded Finding, Bud and the admiral had taken steps to preserve lives and to protect the President. But there were other matters, too, that we didn't want anyone to know about. No version of the chronologies mentioned the secret within a secret. We were trying to avoid the political explosion that such a revelation would entail—and we were certainly right about *that*. We also knew that the Iranians would be furious if this story came out. They had been taken to the cleaners, and charged enough for the weapons to fund the Nicaraguan resistance and other projects as well. If it was revealed that these funds were used to support the contras, the Iranians might well go ballistic. After all, they had been supporting the Sandinistas. While the government of Iran had no great sympathy for Communism, they apparently believed that the

Sandinistas qualified for that old Middle Eastern proverb: the enemy of my enemy is my friend.

Meanwhile, back in my office on the night of November 18: When McFarlane finished making the changes in the President's press statement and the chronologies, he pushed himself from my computer terminal. As he stood up, he said, "What did you do about that stuff from the NSA?" He was referring to a PROFS message he had sent me a few days earlier, in which he had stated his hope that certain National Security Agency intelligence files on the Iran initiative had been purged. Bud, it seemed, believed history could be rewritten by deletions and alterations. When I explained that these files were in various government agencies, and probably could not be recovered, he changed the subject. "Did you ever take care of that other stuff—way back then?"

"Other stuff?"

"What did you do with *that*?" He gestured toward my computer. There, taped to the monitor, was a list of six NSC document control numbers that Bud had written out and given to me more than a year earlier. The numbers referred to memos I had written to Bud back in 1984 and 1985, seeking his approval for some of my efforts in support of the Nicaraguan resistance. In the fall of 1985, Bud had directed me to change these memos, removing any reference to my support activities and his knowledge of them. But I still hadn't done it.

In the summer of 1985, after a number of stories had appeared in the press about secret support for the Nicaraguan resistance, two prominent members of Congress started asking questions about the NSC's involvement in the resistance. Congressman Michael Barnes, chairman of the Western Hemisphere Subcommittee of the House Foreign Affairs Committee, was a leading opponent of the President's policies in Central America. Congressman Lee Hamilton, chairman of the House Intelligence Committee, was less vocal than Barnes, but he too was opposed to military aid for the resistance.

After the news stories appeared, both Barnes and Hamilton wrote letters to McFarlane, asking whether the NSC had indeed been supporting the resistance. The letter from Barnes specifically asked about press reports of contact between me and the contra leaders.

There are two ways to protect a secret when you're asked about it directly. One is simply not to answer. The other is to lie.

I preferred the former, and I argued with Bud that we shouldn't answer these letters. As I saw it, this was precisely the kind of situation that executive privilege was invented for. After all, the Executive Branch is not compelled to answer every question that Congress asks.

Bud disagreed. He said he had talked to the President about it, and that my approach was too confrontational. McFarlane refused to accept my input. Instead, Bud invoked his own form of executive privilege. He lied. In letters[1] to Barnes, Hamilton, and others—and in meetings with still other congressmen—he flatly denied that the NSC in general, and Oliver North in particular, were involved in these activities: "Dear Mr. Chairman," he wrote to Barnes,

I can state with deep personal conviction that at no time did I or any member of the National Security Council staff violate the letter or spirit of the law. At no time did we encourage military activities. We did not solicit funds or other support for military or paramilitary activities, either from Americans or third parties.

At the hearings, Bud would describe responses such as this as "too categorical." That's putting it mildly.

On September 30, 1985, Barnes again wrote to McFarlane. This time he specifically asked to see NSC

---

[1]Because of these letters, McFarlane pled guilty to withholding information from Congress.

documents. I again argued that we should simply tell
Barnes that we weren't going to answer his questions. I
even went up to the law library on the top floor of the
OEOB to research the history of executive privilege.
When I returned to my office I drafted a letter for Bud
to send:

> These internal documents are the appropriate purview of
> the Executive Branch, which must abide by its commitments
> to other governments not to compromise sensitive informa-
> tion. The Executive Branch cannot delegate this responsibil-
> ity to the Congress and maintain its credibility with those
> entrusted to govern in other countries. The right of the
> Executive to maintain confidentiality of information impor-
> tant to the conduct of our foreign policies must be sus-
> tained.
>
> This principle dates back to the time of our first
> President, wherein he refused to lay before the House of
> Representatives the instructions, correspondence, and doc-
> uments relating to the negotiations of what came to be
> known as the Jay Treaty. This long-standing principle has
> been consistently upheld by the Supreme Court in a num-
> ber of cases, including the *United States* versus *Curtiss-
> Wright Export Corporation*.[2]

Whether simply to placate me, or to get a second
opinion from a real lawyer, Bud forwarded my letter to
Fred Fielding, the White House counsel, for his comments. But Fielding, too, preferred not to confront
Congress, and as far as I know, the letter was never
passed on to the President—the only person who could
actually invoke executive privilege.

McFarlane knew that Barnes and his allies were not
going to stop their fishing expeditions, and he was wor-

---

[2]The Curtiss-Wright case was decided in 1936, when the Supreme
Court upheld the right of the President to prohibit the shipment of
arms to Bolivia and Panama.

ried that Congress would somehow succeed in getting
its hands on our documents. When the first letters had
arrived from Barnes and Hamilton, an NSC security
officer had gathered our permanent record files dealing
with aid to the contras and delivered them to Bud's
office. Now, months later, Barnes was demanding to see
them. Apparently confident that Barnes wouldn't sum-
mon the energy to do any of the hard work himself, Bud
invited Barnes down to his office. With the pile of
memos sitting in plain view, he invited Barnes to review
them on the spot. Barnes refused, and asked for copies
to be sent to his staff for their review. That was out of
the question. We had serious concerns about a member
of Barnes's staff who was close to the Sandinistas, and
McFarlane had no intention of allowing these papers
out of his office.

After Barnes renewed his request to see documents,
Bud called me in. "Ollie," he said, "some of these need
to be fixed." Bud explained that the memos, all of which
I had sent to him, were inconsistent with what he had
said and written to Congress, and that they were "problematical." He handed me a piece of paper on which he
had written the numbers of six NSC documents.[3] He also
cited several other documents whose numbers I wrote
down on the back of that same piece of paper. In "fixing" them, Bud said, I should remove all references to
my operational role, and make the memos consistent
with what he had said and written to Congress.

If these memos ended up on Capitol Hill, the resistance
would be finished. Any hope of restoring CIA funding for
the contras would evaporate and sensitive operations would
be jeopardized. We knew that Congress had two ways of

---

[3]One of these memos described my meeting in Washington with a
Communist Chinese official in our effort to obtain antiaircraft missiles
for the Nicaraguan resistance. Another outlined my proposals to take
action against the Monimbo, the Sandinista arms ship. The rest dealt
with specific resistance activities and operations, and the support we
were providing for them.

dealing with something they didn't like. They could legislate against it—and with the Boland Amendments they had already gone about as far in that direction as they could. Or, in the case of a secret operation, they could leak it. Still, I didn't understand why McFarlane had selected only certain memos, when I had written *dozens* of memos that were equally "problematical."

"Just take care of it," McFarlane said, showing me a document he had already changed. "And from now on, no more memos with this kind of detail. And no more PROFS notes about it, either."

Now, I'm not normally a procrastinator. But until Bud came to my office on November 18, 1986, I still hadn't gotten around to revising these papers. With so many other NSC memos that revealed similar information, I just didn't see the point. But that Tuesday night, when Bud brought it up again, I dutifully started changing the memos to make them appear more benign. Specifically, I removed references to my operational role, and to McFarlane's knowledge of it—just as he told me to.

But it was too late. I was still working on these papers when I was fired. Later, they were published for the whole world to see, which was an odd way of shutting down a covert operation.

It wasn't until 1989, during my trial, that I finally understood why Bud had selected these particular documents. Whether or not there were other memos in the same category, Bud knew that these six documents all revealed his detailed awareness and approval of my activities, and perhaps, to his way of thinking, the President's as well.

By November 1986, it was far too late to hide *my* role. By then, ambassadors, military officials, CIA officers, members of Congress, and scores of individuals in foreign governments all knew what I had been doing. But that night, when McFarlane told me again to change those memos, I did.

This was the third time in the space of a year and a

half that the NSC in general, and I in particular, had become the focus of attention. The first spate of press reports, in the summer of 1985, had prompted congressional inquiries and McFarlane's subsequent letters to Barnes, Hamilton, and others, leading to Bud's directive that I change the six memos.

The third, and by far the most serious, was the current imbroglio.

But there had also been a second go-round with the press and Congress in the summer of 1986, a few months after Bud had resigned. Following another spate of news stories about the NSC and the contras, the House of Representatives took the highly unusual step of drafting a Resolution of Inquiry, specifically directing the President to tell Congress what Lieutenant Colonel Oliver L. North had been doing on behalf of the resistance. To my knowledge, this was the only proposed resolution in the history of the United States that directed the Commander-in-Chief to do anything about a lieutenant colonel.

The Resolution of Inquiry was offered on the House floor by Representative Ron Coleman of Texas. But word quickly spread that the real originator was his congressional colleague Michael Barnes, who was evidently trying a little covert operation of his own.

Like all proposed legislation, this draft resolution was submitted to the White House legislative affairs office for comment. They, in turn, passed it on to the NSC legislative office. When Ron Sable, senior director of legislative affairs at the NSC, told me he wasn't sure what the administration was going to do about the resolution, I was livid. I went to the admiral and said, "I certainly *hope* we're going to oppose it! And since I'm the one who's named, you ought to let me write the response."

"Come on, Ollie," the admiral replied. "I know what you'll say. The whole world knows how you feel about this. You'll just want to cite executive privilege and tell them to go to hell."

That was certainly true.

"Well, that's not going to work," he said. "If we start throwing up roadblocks, that will only make things more difficult." As it turned out, the admiral was right. At the time, we didn't know that one of the congressional staffers had written a memo explaining that the Resolution of Inquiry was designed solely to embarrass the administration by forcing the President to invoke executive privilege. But we didn't learn this until three years later, during preparations for my trial.

After several days of bureaucratic wrangling, Sable's office drafted letters for the admiral's signature, telling the appropriate committee chairmen that the administration opposed the Resolution of Inquiry. Unfortunately, Sable also wrote that the admiral was standing by McFarlane's 1985 responses to Barnes and Hamilton. For signing these letters, which included the references to McFarlane's earlier correspondence, the admiral was later indicted and eventually convicted. This was another first: McFarlane sends two letters to Congress, and two other men are indicted for what's in *his* letters. The ways of justice can be very strange.

Congress was less than satisfied with the admiral's letters. In July 1986, Congressman Hamilton called the admiral. "We need to talk to North about this Resolution of Inquiry," he said.

"No, you don't," said Poindexter. "The White House isn't in the business of sending its staff up there to testify, and we're not going to start now."

But Hamilton insisted it all could be handled much more casually. Instead of appearing before a congressional committee, I could simply sit down with some of the members of his intelligence committee and answer their questions during an "informal off-the-record" meeting in the White House Sit Room.

Calling it a meeting instead of a committee appearance and moving it over to our turf certainly made it more palatable. So did the fact that, as I understood it by the time we met the Resolution of Inquiry was dead anyway, because the House Armed Services Committee had voted it down. But I still didn't think it was a good idea, and I said so to the admiral. We both knew that there was a great deal of information that I couldn't reveal, including the Saudi donation to the resistance, my role in the delivery of military supplies, and, of course, the fact that by then, the Ayatollah was unwittingly helping us to fund the resistance.

"You can take care of it," the admiral said.

The Sit Room meeting took place early on the morning of August 6, 1986. The President was in California, and the admiral had taken some well-deserved leave. Congress usually isn't around during August, either, but unfortunately for me, several members of the intelligence committee were in town and attended the meeting along with two of their staffers.

Some of the congressmen had never been to the Sit Room before, and I could see them looking around in astonishment, just as I had when I first arrived at the NSC. Entering the Sit Room for the first time, I had expected to find something ultramodern and high-tech, like the situation rooms depicted in movies, and I was disappointed that this place seemed so ordinary. For a moment it had actually occurred to me that maybe this wasn't the Sit Room after all. Maybe *this* room was nothing more than a gigantic elevator, and when somebody pushed a hidden button on the wall, it would lower us down to the *real* Sit Room, in the seventh sub-basement, hundreds of feet underground. If that's what the congressmen expected, they were disappointed.

I, too, was disappointed that morning. I had been hoping that the committee members who supported the contras would be able to steer the conversation away from the really tough questions. I was wrong.

Somebody asked if I had ever given military advice to the Nicaraguan resistance.

My answer was something like, "Look. Enrique

Bermudez is a colonel. I'm a lieutenant colonel. It's inconceivable to think that a couple of military guys sitting down to talk about a war they both feel strongly about won't also talk about military things. But do I give him military advice on day-to-day operations? Even if I thought I could, we both know that you can't run this war from Washington. The war is being fought and planned right down there in the region."

At best, this was a nonanswer. It was meant to be evasive, and it was. While it was true that this war, like all guerrilla wars, was being planned and fought at the small-unit level, that wasn't the whole truth. In fact, I had given the resistance all kinds of advice.

That morning, in the Sit Room, I tried to avoid telling outright lies. But I certainly wasn't telling the truth. I knew that full and truthful answers would have destroyed the Nicaraguan resistance. And some of the congressmen knew that, too.

By the time this meeting was held, the House and the Senate had each appropriated one hundred million dollars in covert CIA military support for the resistance. We all knew that it was just a matter of time before Speaker O'Neill would have to "conference," or reconcile, the two bills, and nobody in the administration—least of all me—wanted to rock that boat. The admiral and I also wanted to avoid the kind of political firestorm that would hit us with full force less than four months later.

Despite my anxieties, the Sit Room meeting was surprisingly cordial—perhaps because I wasn't the only one there who knew I was avoiding direct answers to their questions. I had already given numerous briefings about the resistance to several of these men and to dozens of their congressional colleagues. Many of them had been to the region, visited the camps, met with resistance leaders, and seen the close quarters at Ilopango Air Force Base, where the resistance planes were stationed. For years, they had been asking CIA briefers about the sources of contra support, and they had all seemingly accepted the Agency's claims of ignorance. One of the committee members, Dave McCurdy of Oklahoma, had even called me late one night to ask that supplies be provided to the Atlantic Coast Indians. I had done as he asked. I was certain that McCurdy didn't want me to talk about that, and I didn't.

I look back on that meeting today knowing that what I did was wrong. I didn't give straight answers to the questions I was asked. When the admiral sent me a PROFS note a day or two after the meeting, he wrote, simply, "Well done." But I didn't feel that way then, and I don't now.

I know the difference between right and wrong, and I can tell good from bad. But I also know that the more difficult decisions come when we have to choose between good and better. The toughest calls of all are those we have to make between bad and worse. That was the choice I was faced with on August 6 in the Sit Room. Later, I was indicted for lying to Congress during that meeting. Although I admitted what I had done openly in the hearings, and again during my trial, I was not convicted.

Maybe that's because in two hundred years of sparring between the Executive Branch and Congress over the control of foreign policy, no one else has ever been charged with such a "crime." Until special prosecutors came along, these kinds of informal, unsworn exchanges between the Executive and the Congress had always been treated as part of the political process. Regardless of whether it was morally right or wrong—and I knew it was wrong—I certainly never imagined that anything I was doing was a crime.

Looking back on it today, it's clear to me that the best thing I could have done was not to have gone to that meeting at all. I should have said, "Admiral, I can't do it. You and I both know what these guys are going to ask, and we also know that I can't answer those questions without destroying the resistance."

But I didn't say that to the admiral, and I don't blame him for what happened.

After McFarlane left my office on that Tuesday evening in November, I had less than a week left at the NSC. I didn't know it at the time, but I could sure see where things were headed. I began to expedite the process I had started in October of "cleaning things up," and every evening that week I went through more of my personal files. It took days to go through the scores of individual files from which I pulled a memo here, a letter there, and various notes that could put people at risk. The documents that I removed from my files included the names, addresses, and phone numbers, and in some cases account numbers, of people who had worked with our government in both the hostage initiative and the contra support project. In a number of cases they were people who had received money from me in support of these efforts.

These were people who had trusted us in general, and me in particular, to keep their names and identities secret. I shredded these papers, along with letters and reports that I had received from them, detailing what was going on in a particular operation or event. Despite all the jokes and accusations, the amount I actually shredded was far, far less than people imagined. Most of the "shredding" time was spent looking through my files.

Later on, the investigators asked whether the "risks" I had spoken of included political risk. And I can't deny that I also tried to find documents like the "diversion" memo that would not only endanger lives, but also put the President at risk. But there wasn't a wholesale effort to destroy everything. I knew that even if I wanted to, I couldn't change the record.

Within weeks, those who survived the blowup of late November, 1986, started a wholesale declassification and exposure of the files in my office. As the Tower

Commission, the congressional panels, and the special prosecutors pressed their inquisitions, nearly everything in my office was laid open for anyone to read. I watched in horror as a top-secret presidential Finding was reproduced in dozens of American newspapers. Publishing the text of classified documents was bad enough, but in the case of the Finding, and numerous other documents, it wasn't just the text. These were photocopies, which revealed the *format* of these documents—allowing the KGB or any other adversary to know exactly what a classified presidential document looked like. From now on, anyone could create an authentic-looking presidential Finding, and could use it as "proof" that the U.S. government was involved in some alleged misdeed or another.

As the week wore on, press speculation about what had been shipped to Iran, how it had gotten there, and why it had been sent became even wilder. On several occasions, Ami Nir and I talked and confirmed that both governments, as we had previously agreed, were going to stick with "no comment" when we were asked about U.S.-Israeli cooperation in the Iran initiative. Nir reaffirmed that the U.S. role in the 1985 HAWK shipment should be "protected" because of possible harm to the hostages in Beirut. Understandably, he was still concerned about the two Israeli soldiers.

On Thursday afternoon, November 20, several of us sat with Bill Casey in the admiral's office to discuss his upcoming testimony on the Iran initiative. His staff at the CIA had been preparing various drafts of what he would say. But as usual, Casey, who had been on a secret visit to Central America until that morning, insisted on preparing his own testimony.

After the meeting in the admiral's office, Casey and I walked back to the OEOB together. As we stepped up the ramp that led into the building, he said to me, "It's over. You know that, don't you?"

I nodded. When we got to his office, we talked for a few minutes about the testimony he would be giving the next day on the Iran initiative. As I started to leave, he said, "It's going to be okay down there."

I gave him a puzzled look.

"You know, Nicawogwa. You did a good job. We're back in. But you kept them going."

Although I saw him briefly later that week, this turned out to be the last real conversation we ever had.

On Friday, November 21, both Casey and the admiral met with members of the congressional intelligence committees. The admiral, meeting with a handful of legislators at the White House, apparently stuck with the cover story that the administration had adopted over the preceding weeks: that the United States had not learned of the 1985 HAWK missile shipment from Israel to Iran until January 1986. Casey, giving testimony on Capitol Hill, claimed that the CIA hadn't learned until sometime in 1986 that their proprietary airline had transported HAWK missiles from Israel to Iran. Neither statement was true.

What *was* true were several references that Casey volunteered about me in his testimony. Although this hearing was about the Iran initiative, Casey pointedly suggested three different times that *the committee might be fascinated to know what Oliver North had been doing operationally to help the Nicaraguan resistance*. By bringing this up, Casey was doing what he and I had already discussed: he was ready to throw me out of the boat in the hope that the rest of the administration would stay afloat. But at the time, the committee wasn't interested in this particular diversion.

Because of all the conflicting stories, the President asked Ed Meese to "pull the facts together" and produce a coherent account of what had happened, and when, in the Iran initiative. Admiral Poindexter told me about the Meese mission on Friday afternoon. He mentioned that Don Regan wanted this information by Monday afternoon, and that some of "Ed's guys" would be coming by on Saturday. Could I come into the office to give them a hand?

I assured him I would.

When I arrived at my office on Saturday, two men from Meese's office—William Reynolds and John Richardson—were already there, looking through the red file folders that Bob Earl and I had left out for them. I showed them how to work the copy machine, and they continued reading through documents and copying some of them. I went to work: taking and making phone calls, reading cables, and generally taking care of business. On several occasions I got up and shredded some of the papers I was finished with. Later on, the press accused Meese's aides of incompetence (or worse) for allowing me to use the shredder while they were there. That's unfair. Shredding was a standard part of our office routine. Besides, this wasn't a raid, and I hadn't been accused of anything. They were working on their projects; I was working on mine.

Shortly before two o'clock, Reynolds and Richardson left for lunch, where they met with Ed Meese and Charles Cooper, another of Meese's aides, at the Old Ebbitt Grill on Fifteenth Street. I went upstairs to the admiral's office, where I found Poindexter and Casey having lunch. When I mentioned that two members of Meese's staff were going through my files, Casey said, "That's not so bad. We've got congressional staffers all over the place, poking into things that are none of their business."

Richardson and Reynolds returned to my office around three-forty-five. I assumed they wanted to ask me some questions, but no, they said, they were only there to review documents. Although I didn't know it then, I would be seeing them again the following afternoon, when I went to meet with Ed Meese.

I arrived at Meese's office in the Justice Department shortly after two o'clock on Sunday. Reynolds, Cooper, and Richardson were with him. Ed opened the meeting by asking me to try to recall everything that had happened on the Iran initiative. "Don't worry about trying to protect the President or anyone else," he said. "Just tell me the story."

This may sound strange in view of what happened at this meeting, but the tone of our discussion was friendly and casual. I had known Ed for more than five years. I first met him in connection with the sensitive project at the start of my tour. We worked together on counterterrorism and in several other areas. He personally detailed two DEA agents to help me with hostage recovery efforts, and when I had to arrange for wiretaps and FBI surveillance of foreigners, he was one of the officials I had to call.

I didn't expect this meeting to be especially dramatic. I thought we were still trying to put the best possible face on what happened—to reveal enough to satisfy Congress and the press, but not so much as to endanger the hostages.

About an hour into the meeting, Meese said, "Is there anything else that can jump up and bite the President on the ass?"

"Not that I can think of," I replied.

"How about this?" he said, handing me a nine-page document. It was an April 1986 memorandum from me to Admiral Poindexter, which detailed a planned arms shipment to Iran and included a specific mention of twelve million dollars in residuals from the arms sale that would go to the Nicaraguan resistance.[4]

*Oh, shit*, I thought.

This was precisely the kind of document I had shredded. Or so I thought.

"Where did this come from?" I asked.

"That's not important," said Meese. "Did this happen?"

---

[4]The critical part of the memo read as follows:

"$2 million will be used to purchase replacement TOWs for the original 508 sold by Israel to Iran for the release of Benjamin Weir. This is the only way that we have found to meet our commitment to replenish those stocks.

"$12 million will be used to purchase critically needed supplies for the Nicaraguan Democratic Resistance Forces. This material is essential to cover shortages in resistance inventories resulting from their current offensives and Sandinista counter-attacks and to 'bridge' the period between now and when Congressionally-approved lethal assistance (beyond the $25 million in 'defensive' arms) can be delivered."

"No, that particular shipment never took place," I said. This was true, but the next question was inevitable.

"Well, did anything *like* this ever take place?"

I paused. This was the secret within a secret that was never supposed to be revealed. But there was no way I was going to lie to Ed Meese. After what seemed like an eternity, I said, "Yes."

Nobody screamed. The earth didn't shake. The walls didn't come crashing down. Nobody fell out of his chair. Nobody said, "Get out the handcuffs! This man has violated the Boland Amendment!"

Ed Meese was certainly *interested*, but there was no hint in his reaction of what was to come just two days later, at the November 25 press conference.

"Was there a cover memo?" I asked. A cover memo would have indicated whether this particular document had been forwarded to the President—and I still didn't know where this memo had been found.

"No," said Reynolds. "There was no cover memo."

"Should we have found a cover memo?" said Meese.

"Not necessarily," I said. "I was just wondering."

Meese and his assistants asked a number of other questions. Had I ever discussed this arrangement with President Reagan? No, I said, but if anyone had, it would have been Admiral Poindexter.

The meeting ended shortly before six o'clock, when Meese left to pick up his wife at the airport. As he was leaving, I expressed my concern about the safety of the hostages. "I certainly hope this won't be made public," I said.

Famous last words.

After the meeting, I drove to the White House to find Admiral Poindexter. He wasn't in his office, or at home, either. The Sit Room watch officer told me he was at RFK Stadium, where the Dallas Cowboys were playing the Washington Redskins. "Do you want us to beep him?" he asked.

"That's all right," I said. "It can wait." I thought I'd

let him get home before I gave him the bad news.

When I finally reached the admiral, at home that evening, I told him that Ed Meese and his people had shown me a memo from April which was explicit about the "diversion."

The admiral was silent for what seemed like a long time. "Well," he finally said, "what did you tell them?"

"I told them the truth," I replied. "I explained that this particular transaction hadn't occurred, but that other transactions had."

Another long silence. "You did the right thing," said the admiral.

I stayed in my office very late that night. I knew it wouldn't be long now, and I had stacks of material to straighten out before I left.

I also took the time to redraft a farewell letter that I had previously prepared for Admiral Poindexter:

> There is that old line about you can't fire me, I quit. But I do want to make it official so that you know I sincerely meant what I said to you over the course of these last several difficult weeks. I'm prepared to depart at the time you and the President decide it to be in the best interests of the Presidency and the country.
>
> I am honored to have served the President, you and your predecessors these past five and a half years. I only regret that I could not have done so better. My prayer is that the President is not further damaged by what has transpired and that the hostages will not be harmed as a consequence of what we now do. Finally, I remain convinced that what we tried to accomplish was worth the risk. We nearly succeeded. Hopefully when the political fratricide is finished there will be others in a moment of calm reflection who will agree.
>
> Warmest regards, Semper Fidelis, Oliver North

I sent that letter on Monday. By Tuesday I was gone.

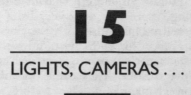

# 15

## LIGHTS, CAMERAS . . .

I HAVE ALWAYS BEEN AN EARLY RISER. THE MORNING
after I was fired, I left the house, as usual, at six o'clock,
and held the front door open so that Max, our Labrador
retriever, could go out for his morning ritual. It was still
dark, and at first I didn't notice anything out of the
ordinary. But as soon as I closed the door behind me, all
hell broke loose: klieg lights lit up the yard, cameras
flashed, and dozens of reporters started shouting to me
from the fence along the road in front of our house.

Max was not amused. He's a tough-*looking* dog, but
he's actually a wimp. He didn't even object when
Dornin climbed on his back and rode him like a horse.
But Max has one great talent: a ferocious bark that
belies his basic cowardice.

And that morning, as soon as those lights came on,
Max let loose. The press panicked. "Run for it, Bob! It's
an attack dog!" Light stands came crashing down, car
doors slammed, and reporters scrambled for their cars.
Poor Max just stood there, quivering in fear with his tail
between his legs—but barking like crazy.

But when they really want to, journalists learn fast,

and it didn't take them long to break the code on Max. He was a pushover for a 7-Eleven doughnut, and over the next few months that dog must have gained about twenty pounds. But for those first couple of mornings after the firing, there was only very brief footage of Oliver North leaving his house.

From November 26, 1986, until after the hearings the following July, the press was at our house every morning at five o'clock. They came on Sunday. They showed up on Thanksgiving. They were even there on Christmas.

Christmas! That really shocked me. With four children, we get up early on Christmas morning. First we take pictures of the kids sitting on the stairs. Then we sing "Silent Night." After the kids open their Christmas stockings, we all go into the kitchen, where Daddy makes blueberry pancakes. When breakfast is over, we gather around the tree to hand out the presents. That's when I noticed that Dornin, our five-year-old, was missing.

Just then the front door opened, and in walked Dornin with an empty tray.

"Where were you?" I asked. "It's time for the presents."

"I went outside to give the 'porters some Christmas cookies," Dornin said.

"I thought I told you never to talk to them," I said.

"But Daddy," she said. "It's Christmas, and they were cold."

Only months later, when I looked back on this incident, did it occur to me that Dornin's Christmas spirit was a lot better than mine. I realized that those reporters and cameramen had been sent there by their editors and producers. I'm sure it wasn't their choice to spend Christmas morning standing outside our house. At least I hope not.

But even today, nearly five years later, I can't quite get over the fact that the press showed up on Christmas morning. They also came on Easter and on Passover.

The only morning they missed was New Year's Day. Was *that* their religious holiday?

Thanks to these daily visitors, I must have been the most photographed commuter in America. Anyone with a television must have thought I *lived* in my car. Soon Johnny Carson was doing routines where he put on a uniform and answered questions through a car window:

> *Reporter:* "Colonel North, sir, is it true that you secretly sold arms to Iran and used the money to help the Nicaraguan resistance?"
> *Carson (looking up at his questioner):* "Say, did you know you had a very long hair growing in your left nostril?"

By then, of course, I was no longer driving to the White House. The night I was fired, I received a call from General P. X. Kelley, commandant of the Marine Corps. "You've been reassigned," he said. "Put on your uniform and report to headquarters tomorrow morning."

General Kelley posted me to the Plans and Policies division at headquarters, and I appreciated his vote of confidence. He could have assigned me to some far less visible job, or even asked me to resign. Instead, he had me working right down the hall from him. I offered to leave the service, but he wouldn't hear of it. "Come in tomorrow," he said. "If anyone doesn't like it he can talk to me."

Late that night, I got out my uniform and dusted it off. I had rarely worn it at the NSC, probably no more than half a dozen times in five and a half years. At one point, somebody at the White House had decided that every Wednesday, all the military people on the White House staff should wear their uniforms. This lasted about a month, until some of the civilians started looking around and muttering, "My God, there are so *many* of them!" And there were. It wasn't long before we were back in civvies.

*    *    *

That first morning after I was fired, the reporters chased me all the way to Marine headquarters in Arlington, following me in vans, cars, and motorcycles. Every morning thereafter, the press was waiting as I left the house.

They descended on us like a plague of locusts, intent on devouring our privacy and scouring the neighborhood for tidbits of information about our family. We couldn't go to the store, or to church, or the gas station without being watched. We couldn't get the newspaper, fetch the mail, wash the car, or mow the lawn without being observed, filmed, videotaped, photographed, tape-recorded, or written about. They followed me to work, to the dump, to the baby-sitter's house. They chased our children to the bus stop and pumped them with questions. When Betsy and I started driving them ourselves, they interviewed the neighbors' children. When my pickup had a flat tire on the way back from the dump one Saturday, they stopped and jumped out of their "chase car"—not to help me change the tire, but to film me doing it.

We soon developed a morning routine. I'd get into my car, and as I drove out to the road, a flock of reporters and photographers would be standing there, blocking the driveway. I'd wave them aside with a smile. They'd shake their heads. I'd slowly ease forward, always keeping in mind the admonition of Brendan Sullivan, my lawyer: "Whatever you do, don't run them over."

They'd signal for me to roll down the window—my ticket out of the driveway. As soon as I did, they'd start shouting questions: "Colonel North! What do you have to say about reports in the press that you sold pieces of White House china and silverware to raise money for the contras?"

Brendan and his colleagues had given me strict orders to remain silent, and no matter how provocative the questions, I did everything I could to comply. Although I chafed at this restriction, I knew there were good reasons for it. When you're facing the kind of inquisition I was, anything and everything you say in the press can, and probably will, be used against you. Unlike some of the attorneys who represented other Iran contra defendants, my lawyers maintained a strict code of silence. They didn't talk about the case with *anybody*—and they expected the same from me.

Every day, Brendan would be given a pile of phone messages from the press, but he never returned the calls. As he came in and out of the law firm, reporters continually asked him questions. But he refused to confirm or deny anything, no matter how absurd the allegation.

"How did it go this morning, Mr. Sullivan?"

"No comment."

"Are you worried about this case?"

"No comment."

"How's the weather today?"

"No comment."

I didn't have quite as much will power, and there were a couple of times when I surrendered to over whelming temptation. One morning, a reporter from CBS asked me how I felt about people like Maureen Reagan, who had said publicly that I should stop "hiding" behind the Fifth Amendment and start telling my story.

"I don't believe the President really wants me to abandon my individual rights under the Constitution," I said. "How many of you are willing to give up your First Amendment rights?"

Then somebody asked: "How do you feel about some of the things your erstwhile friends are saying about you?"

"On that one," I replied, "I would refer you to Psalm Seven, verse one."

"What does it say?" somebody shouted as I drove off.

"Look it up!" I yelled back. "It'll be good for you."

That night, on the "ABC Evening News," Peter Jennings actually read the verse on the air:

> O Lord my God, I take refuge in you;
>> save and deliver me from all who pursue me,
> Or they will tear me like a lion
>> and rip me to pieces with no one to rescue me.

Okay, I thought, this isn't a total disaster. At least I was able to get a verse of Scripture onto the network news.

Despite everything, I tried to retain some of my morning routine, which normally included reading at least a few verses from the Bible before I left for work. Occasionally, if I came across a line that seemed especially appropriate, I would quote it. The reporters liked to tease me about this, and sometimes I teased them back. "I try to read two things every morning," I told them. "The Bible and the *Washington Post*. That way I know what both sides are thinking."

My father had died in 1984, but my mother, living alone in upstate New York, was besieged by the press. Reporters used to ring every buzzer in her apartment building until somebody finally let them in. TV cameramen stood outside her door for hours, and there were times when she didn't dare leave. When the press couldn't get to her, they started in on her neighbors: "Do you know Mrs. North down the hall? Tell me, how often does her son come to visit? Does she have any strange habits?"

I had tried to prepare my own family for what was about to happen, but none of us could begin to imagine the full scope of it. The night I was fired, we all assembled on the living room floor where we normally played Scrabble and Trivial Pursuit. "I have been reassigned back to the Marine Corps," I said. "Although I haven't done anything wrong, there may be a lot of negative stories about me on television and in the newspaper." I didn't go into much detail, and I couldn't foresee then how brutal all this would be.

Looking back, I can see how much this whole thing has intruded on the lives of our children. In addition to the teasing, the questions, the rumors, and the wild allegations, the kids have also suffered on a more basic level. They were no longer allowed to be just Tait North, or Stuart North, or Sarah North, or Dornin North. From now on people would see them as Oliver North's kids. Even today, wherever they go, they start out either bigger or smaller in other people's eyes, depending on how those people feel about me. No matter what they accomplish on their own, it can never compete with Daddy's fame—or his notoriety. They don't deserve that, and I feel terrible about it.

Each of our children has reacted differently to these pressures. Tait, a senior in high school, a cheerleader, and head of the honor society, was furious when I was fired. She blamed the President and his whole administration. As she saw it, Ronald Reagan abandoned me after I had worked so hard for his policies, and to this day she is bitter about him. She and I have had some long talks about Iran-contra, and my role in it, and I have tried to put my own situation in a larger context. "Keep this in mind," I told her. "In many other countries, if something like this happened, your father could well have left for work one morning and you'd never have heard from him again."

Stuart, a sophomore in high school, responded with questions. I could answer some of them, but much of the information was either classified or had been declared off-limits by the lawyers. Naturally, this was hard on Stuart. Try telling your sixteen-year-old boy: "I'm sorry, but I just can't talk to you about that."

"What do you mean?" he'd say. "I'm your *son!*" He was reading all these articles in the paper, and watching news stories on TV. "Dad, what am I supposed to say when kids in class ask me questions about all the things you did?"

"Just tell them that you know your dad is a good Christian who wouldn't knowingly break the law," I told him.

Fortunately, Stuart was in a relatively protected environment at Woodbury Forest School in Orange, Virginia, where he was surrounded by supportive friends and teachers. But the long arm of the investigation reached him there, as federal agents showed up at the school to determine how Stuart's tuition bills were paid. (He was on scholarship.) Stuart knew generally what was going on, but Emmett Wright, the headmaster, made every effort to shield him from it.

Sarah, who was ten, probably suffered the most. She developed a rash on the back of her hands from nervously rubbing them together. She was hounded at school—not only by her classmates, but even by a couple of the teachers. She once asked one of her teachers what to do with a paper she had written. "Why don't you shred it?" the teacher replied. "If you don't know how, just ask your father. He's an expert at it."

But most of her teachers were far more supportive. One of them gave Betsy a pair of notes that she had confiscated from Sarah and one of her friends in class. Sarah's note breaks my heart: "Dennis says, 'Your dad's going to jail,'" she wrote. "And I was like, 'No, he's not.' I wish my dad was *normal*. You know what I mean?" But even in this there was a ray of sunshine. The response from her friend Cindy read, "No he won't. God won't let that happen."


Five-year-old Dornin, fortunately, was too young to fully grasp the content of what was being said and written about her father. We had established a family rule about not watching the news, but sometimes Dornin would see my face on television. She'd run up to Betsy and say, "Mommy, Daddy's on television. Again!"

"Cover your ears, child," Betsy would say, "and turn that thing off."

The avalanche of publicity brought the two younger girls much closer together. But even with a new and far less demanding job, I was rarely around to spend much time with them. I would arrive at Marine headquarters around seven-fifteen. At four in the afternoon, I'd drive over to Williams & Connolly to spend the next six to eight hours with the lawyers. It was like working two jobs.

Had Betsy not been a strong, devout, God-fearing woman, I shudder to think what would have happened to our family. But somehow she managed to keep us relatively sane, which was itself a full-time job. Every morning, for example, she would go through the *Post* and perform surgery on it, cutting out every article about Daddy and his legal problems so the kids wouldn't see them.

During those difficult months, Betsy and I went through a wide range of emotions. She was extremely supportive, but there were moments when the strain got to us both. "What have you done to my children?" she blurted out one night.

"Wait a minute," I said. "*Your* children?"

Obviously, the conversation didn't end there. Some of the stories in the press were just ludicrous. That Fawn Hall and I had planned to run off together to a desert island. That a private jet had stood by all through 1986, waiting to take me wherever I wanted to go on a moment's notice. That I was involved with drug-running for the contras. That I was behind an assassination attempt on Eden Pastora. That I was a compulsive liar. That I was, above all, a loose cannon on the gundeck of state.

A number of leaks clearly came from the White House. Once it became obvious that my lawyers wouldn't allow me to respond to any allegation, no matter how absurd, it seemed that a few individuals worked overtime in an attempt to divert attention away from the White House and other administration officials who had been involved in, or at least aware of, my activities. Story after story detailed operations I had supposedly conducted all on my own. "Anonymous sources" made a concerted effort to portray me as an unreliable renegade, and the press lapped it up, never stopping to ask how I could possibly have done all this on my own. Even now, many Americans believe that I sold arms to the Iranians *by myself*, and that no one in the U.S. government knew what I was doing in Central America! I believe that many of these stories originated with Don Regan's staff. He had apparently put out the word that my credibility was to be destroyed, and that I was to be depicted as some kind of deceitful wild man. (That way, nobody would believe me if I implicated the President.) Strangely, I didn't hear any of these accusations before I was fired. In fact, some of these same anonymous sources used to come up to me and tell me what a great job I was doing.

Many of the negative stories about me were based on true events, but were twisted to cast them in a nefarious light. I had indeed been supporting the resistance and meeting with Iranians, and had even used traveler's checks from the contra account in supermarkets, tire stores, and to buy leotards for my daughters at Parklane Hosiery. Because of this, it was implied that I had violated the Arms Export Control Act, broken neutrality laws, stolen money, and carried on an affair with Fawn Hall. There were also stories about my hospitalization in Bethesda, including one report that I had been found running around naked—waving a gun!

Almost all of these articles and news stories were attributed to unnamed or anonymous sources—mostly government insiders with their own axes to grind. But the media dutifully and uncritically carried them. There was a real mob mentality, and some people said things about me that they later came to regret. A couple of them even apologized.

Certainly I had made mistakes. But I had been a good staff officer. I was loyal to the President and his policies, and I bitterly resented allegations that I wasn't. I had worked my tail off at the NSC, and had kept my superiors informed every step of the way.

For me, the most offensive accusation was that I supposedly saw myself as being above the law, or that I "shredded the Constitution." That was terribly hurtful, because it was contrary to the way I was raised and educated, not to mention everything I had learned at Annapolis and as a Marine. Each time I was promoted, I had taken an oath to support and defend the Constitution of the United States. I meant those words, and I obeyed them. This tiger didn't change his stripes.

Perhaps the most disturbing story of all appeared on February 20, 1987, when it was suggested in the *Washington Post* that I had passed top-secret intelligence data to the Iranians without the permission of my superiors: "If he was acting entirely on his own," the article said, "North may have violated federal espionage laws, which for military personnel convicted of spying in peacetime carry the death penalty."

In reality, every bit of information we gave to the Iranians was prepared specifically for that purpose by the CIA and passed to the Iranians with the knowledge and approval of senior government officials. But that didn't seem to make much difference. On a Saturday morning, two days after the article appeared, Sarah and I got into the pickup truck and drove out to get some firewood. "Colonel North," one of the reporters shouted. "How do you feel about the article in the *Post* that said you might get the death penalty for treason?"

"If there's going to be an execution," I replied, "we ought to hold it in Yankee Stadium. That way we can sell tickets and send the proceeds to the contras."

As I was spouting off out the window, I couldn't see

the shock and the tears on Sarah's face. It wasn't until we were halfway up the hill that I noticed she was crying.

I pulled over, put my arm around her, and said, "Don't worry, honey. It's going to be all right."

"Daddy," she said, "they *can't* give you the death penalty. It's unconstitutional."

Some of the worst stories came from the congressional investigators and the Office of the Independent Counsel, where scores of attorneys and their agents had begun probing every aspect of my life. The investigators were especially interested in my financial situation, and they left no stone unturned. They even sent agents out to California to interview a friend of Stuart's who had helped us paint our fence. I had written him a check for the whopping sum of thirty dollars. His father called me one night and said, "Boy, it's nice to know you've got friends in Washington who care enough to come all the way out here to talk about you." Our tax dollars at work.

The congressional investigators and special prosecutors went after every single business and individual to whom I had written a check. They even interviewed our baby-sitter.

One Saturday afternoon, I drove down to the gas station to fill up the pickup truck. When the owner spotted me, he came out and said, "Well, your buddies were here this week."

"What do you mean?"

"You know, the G-men. They took my business records, my tax records, everything."

The same thing happened at the little sawmill where I used to buy slab wood for our wood stove, and again at the local hardware store. They went after our plumber and the electrician. They even sent agents down to Kentucky, because our tax return had included several hundred dollars from the estate of Betsy's father.

Nothing was off-limits. They actually tried to interview a pastor about our past contributions at church.

"I'm not totally familiar with the law," he told them, "but isn't there some provision for a pastoral privilege?" The agents left without answers.

Even if your neighbors like you, and ours were great, enough visits from enough investigators inevitably throw a little sand into the gears. It makes people wonder: if they're *that* interested in this guy, maybe there *is* something wrong with him. I might react the same way: when a federal agent knocks on your door and flips out his badge, it makes an impact. (It's *supposed* to.) We've all seen it on TV: the Feds are the good guys, right? And so, inevitably, people begin to ruminate: You know, he *was* gone a lot. He *was* a little secretive. Maybe there *is* something wrong....

Before the investigations were over, every one of our friends and neighbors was either interviewed or subpoenaed by congressional investigators, or the Office of the Independent Counsel, or both. I'm surprised they didn't bump into each other as they went around asking questions. Do the Norths ever fight? Do they go away on trips? Do they live beyond their means? Betsy's sister was asked, "How much does it cost to feed the horses, dogs, and cats when the Norths are away?" Later, they went after Betsy—fingerprints, mug shots, handwriting sample, grand jury, the whole bit. It was just awful.

It was a very strange situation, with the government I had worked for these many years now using its full bureaucratic firepower against me. The IRS called: they wanted to send three agents to my house for "three or four days" to conduct a "full field audit." I had better things to do, but I was about to say, "Sure, come on over. I've got nothing to hide."

By then, however, I knew enough to check with Brendan, who just about had a cow. "Not on your life," he said. "You're not letting anybody from any agency of the government on your property, and you're not giving them anything. Tell them to call me."

The congressional inquisitors and special prosecutors weren't the only ones after me. Early in 1987, the FBI learned that certain Libyans in the United States were collecting information on my location, travel routes, and work habits with the intention of making an attack or an assassination attempt on me and/or my family. But when the FBI called Brendan, they weren't nearly so forthcoming. I was with him at the time, and the conversation went something like this:

*FBI:* We have information that leads us to believe that your client, Colonel North, may be in some jeopardy.

*Sullivan:* You're telling me?

*FBI:* This has nothing to do with the Congress or the Independent Counsel. We have some information about the possibility that someone may be trying to kill him.

*Sullivan:* And who might that be?

*FBI:* I can't give you that information.

*Sullivan:* Then why are you calling me?

*FBI:* Because Colonel North ought to have some protection.

*Sullivan:* I agree. Can I count on you to provide it?

*FBI:* We're not in the business of providing protection. All we can do is notify you.

*Sullivan:* Exactly what is the threat?

*FBI:* I'm sorry, that's all I can tell you.

*Sullivan:* That's really great. What are we supposed to do?

*FBI:* I would suggest that you contact the Department of Defense. Your client is in the military, and they have people who can deal with this sort of problem.

*Sullivan:* Can you tell them about this?

*FBI:* Yes, if they've got the right clearances.

*Sullivan:* Okay, let me get this straight. North is the target of an attempt to kill him. You can't tell us when or where, or who it is—or anything more about it. And we're supposed to get hold of somebody I don't know at the Pentagon who might be able to get more information from you?

*FBI:* You've got it.

Well, by the end of the afternoon, Brendan had tracked down the right people at the Naval Investigative Service. We soon learned that certain members of a group called the People's Committee for Libyan Students (PCLS), based in Virginia, were planning their first annual commemoration of the American antiterrorist bombing raid on Libya in April 1986. After my involvement in that operation, I had been threatened with death by Abu Nidal, one of the world's most dangerous terrorists. But it seemed that Abu Nidal wasn't moving fast enough for Colonel Q., because now some of his own boys were trying to speed up the timetable.

That evening, the Naval Investigative Service (NIS) assigned a small protective detail at our house that they coordinated with the Fairfax County Police Department, the state police, and the Loudoun County Sheriff's office. Nobody said so directly, but I had the feeling that they hoped to catch these guys in the act. (I would have tried the same thing in my old counterterrorist job.)

One morning, shortly after the security detail was posted, I planned to stop by Tait's school on my way to work. As we left the house, the agent who was riding with me jotted down the license numbers of the cars parked along our street, most of which belonged to reporters. While I was at the school, a report came back that one of the cars parked in front of our house had apparently been stolen. The agent with me was immediately concerned, because he had noticed that the woman driving that car appeared to be of Arab descent. He quickly alerted the local police. "Quick," he said to me, "out the back door. We've got to get you out of here."

"Where are we going?" I asked.

"To Marine Corps headquarters. You'll be safe there."

"No, we're not," I said. "If there's a problem at home, that's where we're going."

From the car, I used his portable phone to call Betsy, who was home alone. There was no answer.

We raced back to the house. The red car was gone, but there were two police cars in the driveway—and a third one parked on the street. Betsy was in the kitchen, and a very apologetic police officer was standing out front. After I had left, Betsy had gone out to the barn to feed the horses. She was out there with her coat thrown over her nightgown when the officers showed up. When they saw someone moving in the barn, they did what any police officer in that situation would have done. They drew their guns and shouted, "You there! Freeze!"

I went nuts. "That's it!" I told the agents. "You guys please leave. Call off the helicopters, the dogs, the police cruisers. It's not your fault. I'm just grateful that nobody sneezed when that gun was pointed at my wife. But that's it, gentlemen. Good-bye."

The mysterious red car turned out to be driven by a reporter from a newspaper in Philadelphia. It belonged to her boyfriend, and it hadn't been stolen after all. Somebody had copied down the license number wrong, which shows that you don't have to work at the NSC to make that kind of mistake.

When I finally got to work, there was a note on my desk telling me to report immediately to General Tom Morgan, assistant commandant of the Marine Corps.

"What happened this morning?" he asked.

I told him the story.

The general reminded me that this protection had been put in place by the government, and that nobody had any interest in having a Marine assassinated. He agreed that there had to be some changes made, and he told me that this could best be done with our family quietly out of the area until the improved security arrangements were in place. We were to report to Camp Lejeune within twenty-four hours, where we would be sequestered for a few days. This wasn't a suggestion or a request. It was an order.

It could have been worse. Someone further up the line in the Pentagon actually suggested that I should be issued permanent-change-of-station orders to a secure military facility in the Aleutian Islands off the coast of Alaska! Brendan thought it might be difficult to defend a client four thousand miles away. General Morgan agreed, and the orders were never cut.

The next morning we loaded up the car and drove down to North Carolina with a security escort. As soon as we left, agents from the NIS moved into our house and began installing sophisticated security and surveillance systems. Later, I was indicted for having accepted a $13,000 security system in 1986. At that price, it couldn't have been all that good. The federal government spent close to a million dollars protecting my family and me from February 1987 until October of that year, when pressure from angry congressmen forced the Department of Defense to cut off the security.

At Camp Lejeune we were sequestered in a beach house on a remote corner of the base. Unfortunately, late winter in North Carolina is not the best time to enjoy the beach. I read stories to Sarah and Dornin, and we played board games for hours. (Stuart remained at school, and Tait stayed with a friend so she wouldn't miss classes.) We had some good times, but I felt like a caged lion.

After the NIS had secured our house in Great Falls, we returned to a totally new situation. We were now guarded by up to thirty armed security men in three eight-hour shifts. And I do mean *men*. I'm a little old-fashioned when it comes to accepting women in traditional male jobs, but as a man with a wife and three lovely daughters, it seemed to me that our security team wasn't particularly well balanced. I know how young men think, and when Tait got in the car, some of these guys were watching her instead of the road. It was also getting just a little ridiculous: Betsy and the girls would all go shopping, and they'd be followed by five husky young men with bulging pockets, all of whom looked to be about seven feet tall.

"Can you send some female agents?" I asked General Morgan. A few days later, five very attractive women showed up to join the security team. Stuart was overjoyed. Unfortunately, the male agents became even *more* diverted. But something good came of it: two members of our security team who met on the job later got married.

Having guards around me all day took some getting used to. I liked these people. They were professionals, good at their job, and I appreciated the safety they provided for Betsy and the children. They were also extremely considerate—or so I thought. If I had to drive to the grocery store for a gallon of milk, or to the laundry to pick up the dry cleaning, one of the agents would always volunteer to do it for me. "Please, Colonel, don't trouble yourself. You stay here. I'll take care of it." It made me uncomfortable, but these guys were on their feet and out the door in no time.

At first I assumed that these were simply favors, perhaps inspired by a "servant's heart," as the Christian phrase describes it. Being new to the security routine, it took a while before it finally dawned on me that something else was going on here. It wasn't just that nobody on our security team wanted anything to happen to me; it was that they *especially* didn't want anything to happen to me *on their watch.* After all, if you're in the security business it doesn't look all that great on your résumé when you're forced to mention that the last guy you were protecting is unable to provide a recommendation because he was gunned down while picking up his dry cleaning.

\*   \*   \*

Looking back on it, I can only laugh at my reaction to all the early publicity in the months after I was fired. Kid, you ain't seen nothing yet! Once the hearings began, everything that happened until then seemed trivial. It was one thing to be a household name, but after I appeared on television all day for six days, I became a household *face*. The July 9 issue of the *Washington Post* contained twenty-three pictures of me. Suddenly there were Oliver North T-shirts, buttons, and bumper stickers. There were even Oliver North dolls. Someone told me later on that after the dolls stopped selling, the manufacturer took the same mold, stuck on a new head, and replaced the Marine uniform with a fancy Italian suit. Voilà—the Mikhail Gorbachev doll. Say it ain't so!

There were Oliver North look-alike contests. In *People* magazine a celebrity dentist in Beverly Hills explained what was wrong with my teeth. On television, a plastic surgeon to the stars explained how my broken nose could be straightened and my ears pinned back so that I wouldn't look like Howdy Doody. (The shocking part about it was that my kids had no idea who Howdy Doody was.) There were cardboard cutouts, videotapes, and hundreds of editorial cartoons. There were even Ollieburgers, made of—what else?—shredded beef covered with shredded lettuce and shredded cheese. There must have been a million jokes about shredding. At least *Advertising Age* was a little more original when they suggested that I'd make a good pitch man for—warning, bad pun follows—contra-ceptives.

*Newsweek*, which never said anything nice about me, nonetheless ran a billboard ad showing me at the hearings, with the caption "Few things in life are as feisty as *Newsweek*." A company that made frames for eyeglasses ran an ad depicting me "wearing" their glasses, with the caption, "I've been framed." And a British bank ran a full-page ad in a London newspaper, with a photo of me and the caption, "With a few notable exceptions, no one can transfer your money round the world more efficiently than us."

The circus atmosphere eventually died down, but the memory lingers on. To this day, I'm still recognized wherever I go.

"You look an awful lot like Oliver North," people will say.

"You know," I reply, "people tell me that all the time."

Sometimes I actually get away with it. But usually they'll say, "You really *are* Oliver North, aren't you?" When I hear that, I reach for my pen.

People often have a preconceived idea of what I should look like, and they're not shy about telling me. "I expected you'd be taller," they'll say. Or a complete stranger will come up to me and say, "You've put on a little weight, Colonel." (The fact that it's usually true doesn't make me feel any better.)

At first I naïvely thought I could avoid being recognized. When our family went to Disney World, I wore a huge pair of sunglasses and an oversized hat. I even kept my head down so people wouldn't see my face. It worked, too—for about ten minutes. We were coming out of Space Mountain when a woman waiting in line called out, "Look, honey, it's Ollie North. Hey, Ollie, what's with that funny hat and the stupid glasses?" I spent the next forty minutes signing autographs while Betsy and the kids went on to the next ride.

In the summer of 1990, after sailing in an ocean race with Brendan, I showed up in Bermuda with a beard and long hair, happy in my imagined anonymity. But as soon as I walked into the hotel, somebody called out, "There's Oliver North. Nice beard, Ollie!"

One time, when I wanted to slip into Williams & Connolly without being identified by anticontra demonstrators outside the building, I donned an old gray wig that had once belonged to Betsy's mother. With a leather jacket and old jeans, I looked like an elderly Berrigan brother. Even my own lawyers didn't recognize me. When I bounded into Barry Simon's office, he jumped up and yelled, "How did *you* get in here?"

The biggest consequence of being recognized is that everything takes much longer than it used to. Whether it's leaving church, getting a haircut, or watching Stuart play football, people are always coming over to me, shaking my hand, taking pictures, asking for autographs. It got to the point where Betsy started asking me not to show up at certain events she was going to because it took us so long to leave.

Sometimes, when we're out together, Betsy has to remind me to be nice to all the people who come up to me. Somebody will ask for my autograph when I'm in the middle of a conversation. "I'm sorry," I'll tell them, "but I don't have anything to write on." Then Betsy kicks me hard on the ankle. "Wait a minute, I might have a card right here in my pocket."

"I realize how tiring it must be," she'll tell me later. "But the people who ask for your autograph have no idea that you've already been stopped fifteen times in the past hour." And of course she's right. Without the kindness, generosity, and prayers of so many Americans, we would never have been able to mount a defense. There's just no way we could have done this alone.

To my surprise, almost everybody who comes up to me is supportive and kind. I'm aware, of course, that lots of Americans disapprove of everything I did—or at least everything they *think* I did. But since the day I was fired, with the exception of congressmen and prosecutors, not more than half a dozen Americans have been unkind enough to say anything nasty or critical to my face. About the only time I encounter any hostility is when I'm out making a speech, especially at a political event. But even when people don't approve, they're usually polite.

Sometimes, on the street or in an airport, they'll say, "I watched your show," as though the hearings were some kind of soap opera or variety show. Or "I watched your trial," although the trial, which took place almost two years after the hearings, was never on television. But I can understand that, because the hearings certainly *looked* like a trial. I've even had people come up to say, "I read your book," although until now I had never written one.

When the news media showed up at our house every morning, they were able to capture—totally against our will—little vignettes of ordinary family life at our home in suburban Virginia: leaving for work, cutting the grass, or going out to buy a Christmas tree. People who saw these scenes on television started to think of us as a TV family and came to feel as if they knew us. It's *still* an odd feeling to have a perfect stranger come up and ask me about Betsy, or one of our kids, by name. They still ask me if Betsy still has the blue-and-white polka-dot dress she wore for one day at the hearings. People we have never met before invite us to stay at their houses. Maybe I'd feel differently if I were a rock star or a politician. While I certainly appreciate the support, I have never become comfortable with all the attention.

It happens at church, too, and a few people actually started attending our church because they wanted to talk to me. Several years back, I wasn't very sympathetic when President Reagan announced that he and Nancy had stopped going to church because their presence was simply too disruptive to the service. Today, after seeing the disruption even at my level, I can appreciate why he said that.

I miss having a free and totally spontaneous conversation with people I don't know. I used to enjoy talking to my seatmate on an airplane, or trading stories with the father standing next to me at a horse show where our daughters are participating. But these days, people usually ask questions or make comments about my activities, and when they don't, it's only because they're going out of their way to treat me as "normal."

To this day, our family receives a good deal of mail from people we have never met, who send us anniversary cards, birthday cards, and especially Christmas cards. Some of these cards are signed, simply, "an ordinary American," or with some other anonymous phrase. But most are signed by name, and each December, Betsy and I sort through thousands of cards in an attempt to figure out which ones come from people we actually know. Several correspondents have sent me photographs of the house in Philmont where I grew up, or of my father's wool factory. People send us cookies and cakes, which our security team tries to keep us from eating.

Let me add, however, that fame is not without certain advantages. One of the great benefits of this whole fiasco is that it put me back in touch with many of the men I served with in Vietnam. They write me letters, and some of them show up at my speeches. They have been steadfast in their support, and they knew that most of what they were reading in the papers and hearing on television just wasn't true.

It's great to see these guys again, but it's sobering, too. The last time we were together, well over twenty years ago, they were nineteen and I was twenty-five. Since then, all of us have grown fatter, balder, and older. They don't look quite as sharp as they did, and I hate to think how I must appear to them. Still, it's great to see them again, and to meet their families. We catch up as best we can, but we rarely talk about the war.

Another advantage to being known is that whenever I feel strongly about a particular subject, I can usually get myself heard. I have spoken out on a number of issues, but one of those I feel strongest about is the need to limit the number of terms that a member of Congress can serve. Most members of the House and Senate come to Washington with good intentions. They don't intend to abuse their trust, or to pillage the public treasury. But very quickly they become professional politicians whose overriding concern is getting reelected again and again and again. The President's tenure is limited; I think we should have a similar limit for Congress.

Yet another benefit of fame is that, ironically, all of this public exposure has actually strengthened my connection with my family. There have been some very difficult times, but we have emerged from that experience closer than ever. I'm home for dinner more often, and I spend more time with our children—which makes me realize how many special times I missed with our two older ones.

Finally, there's a certain financial advantage to fame. I'm not referring to my speaking fees, most of which go to cover my enormous legal and security bills. I have in mind something far more modest: these days, when I write a small check, there's at least some chance that the person I give it to may decide to keep it as a souvenir. This has messed up my checking account more than once, but I can live with that.

The first time it happened, I thought back to an anecdote about General Moshe Dayan that I once heard from Ami Nir. The story may well be apocryphal, but I'll tell it anyway in honor of Ami. Dayan was a well-known collector of antiquities, and he loved to poke around in little Arab shops in Israel. If he saw an artifact he needed for his collection that was selling for, say, a hundred Israeli pounds, he would always pay for it by check.

But the merchant wouldn't cash Dayan's check. Instead, he'd frame it and put it on display, with a note: "Check signed by Moshe Dayan. Two hundred pounds."

Before long, Dayan's check would be bought by an American tourist. As Nir explained it, everybody was a winner from this transaction. Dayan got the artifact for free. The Arab shopkeeper made twice what he expected. And some dentist from Milwaukee would be able to display Moshe Dayan's autograph on the wall of his den.

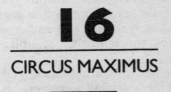

# 16

## CIRCUS MAXIMUS

IT WAS THE NOISE THAT TOOK ME BY SURPRISE. AFTER watching the Iran-contra hearings on television for seven weeks before my own testimony began, I thought I knew what to expect. But when I finally arrived at the Senate Caucus Room, the scene that greeted me was a lot more raucous than the calm and orderly image portrayed on TV.

Directly in front of me, in the narrow space between the witness table and my congressional inquisitors, well over a dozen photographers and cameramen were snapping and shooting like crazy. After so many months of the press hanging around "Scapegoat Central," as some of them referred to our house, I was amazed that anyone still wanted to take my picture. But on that first morning, the clicking and whirring of motor-driven cameras continued nonstop for what seemed like half an hour. Eventually the photographers settled down, but every time I shifted in my chair or scratched my ear, it was like stirring up a nest of insects. There were times when the commotion was so loud that I had trouble hearing the questions.

Just beyond the photographers, on an elevated, double-tiered dais, sat the twenty-six members of the Iran-Contra Committee and their innumerable staff. Peering down at me, they were closer than they appeared to be on television. This sea of faces was in constant motion, with senators, congressmen, and staffers walking in and out, whispering to each other, shuffling papers, and passing notes.

Directly behind me, seated at several long tables, were scores of reporters and commentators, like a crowd of jackals waiting for the flesh to come flying their way. They kept up a constant chatter, buzzing about everything from baseball and the weather to their opinions of my latest answer. Behind *them* were four rows of chairs for Executive Branch officials as well as the handful of American citizens in whose name all of this was ostensibly being done.

From watching the earlier witnesses, I had expected that the hearing room would resemble a theater, with everybody paying rapt attention and looking in the same direction. But this was more like the crowd at a sporting event. The only thing missing were the hot dog vendors and souvenir stands as you entered the stadium—although I was told that all of that and more could be found right outside the building on Constitution Avenue.

*Circus Maximus.* The hearing room, which looked so much larger on television, reminded me of a miniature Colosseum when the lions were about to be released. The committee members sat there proudly on their high platforms, like corpulent and powerful Roman potentates. They looked down their noses at the solitary gladiator while the crowd awaited the ritual slaying.

A lot of political blood had been spilled in this room. Back in 1912, the hearings on the sinking of the *Titanic* had taken place beneath these very chandeliers. Teapot Dome, the Army-McCarthy Hearings, Watergate—these walls had heard it all. Twelve months earlier, if anyone had suggested that I, too, would end up testifying here, I would have asked him what planet he was visiting from.

As I entered the arena on the morning of Tuesday, July 7, 1987, I had a fleeting thought: Who *are* these people, and what am I doing here? Taking my place at the witness table on that first morning, I was acutely aware that my mother was watching on television, that Betsy was watching at home, and that our kids would probably be seeing this, too—at least on the evening news and in the papers. (Other than that, it didn't even occur to me—on that first morning, at least—that millions of others might well be watching, too.) I was grateful that our family had just enjoyed a relaxing Fourth of July together: we had all gone sailing with Brendan Sullivan and his family, which was a lot more fun that sitting in his conference room and wading through documents. But little did I realize that our lives would never again be the same.

Even today, wherever I go, I meet people who "know" me from watching the hearings on TV. They're often surprised to find that I'm a "real" person—a fairly casual guy who loves a good laugh, and who turns out to be very different from that serious and confrontational Marine they saw on television. After six days of testimony, most people assumed that this must be my normal disposition.

Actually, I'm not like that at all. But this was a special situation. For months I had heard little but lies, distortions and innuendos about myself and my activities. No wonder I was angry.

I was well aware that some of the committee members were already convinced that I was the villain, or, as *Newsweek* put it in a colorful summary of the conventional wisdom, "the Rambo of diplomacy, a runaway swashbuckler who had run his own private foreign policy from the White House basement."

But if they believed the worst about me, that was fine, because I wasn't too crazy about some of them, either. To me, many senators, congressmen, and even staffers were people of privilege who had shamelessly abandoned the Nicaraguan resistance and left the contras on the battlefield, exposed and vulnerable to a powerful and well-armed enemy. And now they wanted to humiliate me for doing what *they* should have done!

But our differences were broader than that. Many of these people had done little in life but run for political office. They were supposed to be public servants, but far too many, in my view, were simply running reelection machines. They had turned Congress into a retirement home for professional politicians.

Unfortunately, some of my attitude seeped through in my answers. Toward the end of the hearings, one of the members said that I obviously held Congress in contempt. I don't. I have great respect for Congress as an institution, and I certainly acknowledge its right to gather information in a fair and honest manner.

But that's not what happened during the hearings. Few members came into that room with an open mind, and few questions were asked simply to elicit information. Despite all the pretense, this was not an open forum in search of the truth.

This was politics. Viewed in a larger perspective, these hearings were one more battle in a two-hundred-year-old constitutional struggle between the Legislative and Executive branches over the control of America's foreign policy. Congressional hearings are a constitutionally sanctioned way for Congress to try to nail the presidency, and even to humiliate a particular President. But to force the public testimony of witnesses who were also facing a special prosecutor created a whole new dimension. Taken together, the hearings and the special prosecutor became a way for the two branches of government—legislative and executive—to avoid resolving the broader issues of who would determine our foreign policy. By the summer of 1987, the White House was willing to give up just about anyone or anything that would permit the upper echelons of the administration to survive. By allowing the actions of those who had served the administration to be criminalized, the administration itself was able to back away from the real issues involved. This was fine with Congress, and a gift for the press.

In the hearings, as in the media, the same question kept coming up in a variety of forms: what did the President know, and when did he know it? But even this was a sham, for the committee members already knew the answers. Shortly before my public testimony began, Brendan had agreed that before I testified publicly, the committee could ask me one question in private. Not surprisingly, their most burning question was whether I had told the President about the "diversion." I explained that while I had never discussed it with President Reagan, I had always assumed that he was aware of what I was doing, and that he had, through my superiors, approved it.

The committee's infatuation with the "diversion" continued throughout the hearings. It served to distract attention from many other things that the President and his administration had done to support the contras during the Boland prohibitions. And it kept all the attention focused on me—which appeared to be just what the committee *and* the administration wanted. It was a very cozy relationship that persisted throughout—and it left John Poindexter and me out in the cold.

From the Tower Commission through the hearings, and later, the trials, the administration's approach was to give the investigators just about everything they asked for. The White House turned over tens of thousands of pages of my notes, records, and files to the committee and to the prosecutors, but wouldn't provide any of it to my attorneys. And there was a disturbing willingness on the part of the administration, the Congress, and the special prosecutor's office to spell out the intimate details of secret operations undertaken by our government while the entire world press was looking on. It didn't seem to matter that lives were at risk. Both the committee and the special prosecutor developed a charade of assigning numbers and letters to various countries and individuals, but this was merely an open invitation for the press to step in and clear up the ambiguities.

One possible victim of this process was General Gustavo Alvarez, the former commander of the Honduran armed forces who had been helpful to our government in supporting the contras. In January 1989, he was assassinated near Tegucigalpa. His direct connection to our government was certainly known by some of his own people. But until his support for American measures to aid the resistance was made public, he had been relatively safe.

Alvarez wasn't the only casualty. Several other individuals in foreign governments were hounded, harassed, and even purged because their numbers came up. Benjamin Piza, the public security minister in Costa Rica, was threatened with both violence *and* legal action because he had helped us build a secret airfield. In Israel, Ami Nir, who had risked his life in going to Tehran with us, was fired from his job in the prime minister's office. General Rafael Bustillo, the head of the Salvadoran air force, was humiliated by the special prosecutors, who had him grabbed and dragged before a grand jury when he arrived in the United States for medical treatment.

I was alarmed by the committee's willingness to reveal secrets. My inquisitors knew full well that on several occasions I had been sent to Central America to talk with heads of state and other senior government officials about support for the contras. I had promised these individuals that we would protect both their identities and the fact of their support. They didn't fully trust the United States to keep secrets, but we continually assured them that they could count on us.

The hearings made a mockery of these promises. What happened was tantamount to taking the secret archives of the NSC and dumping them out in the street.

People often ask if I was afraid during the hearings. I was certainly angry, disgusted, embarrassed, and occasionally contentious, but fear didn't enter into it. The one time in my life when I had experienced real fear was in Vietnam, which may explain why I didn't feel it in the Senate Caucus Room. Once you've been shot at and hit in combat, everything else tends to pale by comparison. What was the worst these people could do to me? As far as I could see, none of them had any hand grenades. I wasn't counting on enjoying my days in that room, but I fully expected to survive the experience.

The opening question came from John Nields, the arrogant, long-haired chief counsel for the House committee members:

*Nields:* Colonel North, were you involved in the use of the proceeds of sales of weapons to Iran for the purpose of assisting the contras in Nicaragua?
[The answer, of course, was "yes." But first there was a pre-arranged ritual to be played out:]
*North:* On advice of counsel, I respectfully decline to answer the question based on my constitutional Fifth Amendment rights.

A buzz of anxiety shot through the room, which I took to mean: wait a minute—does this mean that after seven months of silence, and the entire country watching on television, this guy isn't going to *talk*?

Months earlier, I had almost gagged when my lawyers had told me I'd have to take the Fifth Amendment. "What are you talking about?" I said. "The Fifth Amendment is for *criminals*. It's for cowards. It's tantamount to pleading guilty! I've seen mafia types take the

Fifth on television. I've got nothing to hide. I'll go in there and tell them everything. I'm *proud* of what I did."

"I know you are," Brendan calmly replied. "But that's not what you're going to do."

"Listen," he said, when I continued to object. "If you and I were in a plane that crashed in a jungle behind enemy lines, and we were fortunate enough to survive, I'd rely on you to get us out of there alive. Well, today you're in a different kind of jungle, and you've got to rely on me. You may not like everything I tell you to do, but as long as I'm your lawyer, that's the way it's going to be."

I *still* don't feel comfortable about taking the Fifth Amendment, but as usual, Brendan was right. From the very beginning, he and his legal team were looking ahead to the possibility of a criminal trial. They wanted to make sure that if Congress compelled me to testify, none of my answers could be used against me in court if I was later charged with a crime—as indeed I was. This arrangement is known as "use immunity." To put it into effect, I had to begin by publicly and formally claiming my constitutional protections against self-incrimination.

Senator Inouye, chairman of the Senate select committee, then spelled out the terms: that I was here because of subpoenas issued by the Senate and House committees, that I was being compelled to testify, and that "no evidence or other information obtained under the oath or any information directly or indirectly derived from such evidence may be used against you in any criminal proceeding."

I probably should have known better, but I believed him. Later, during my trial, the very first witness for the prosecution was Lee Hamilton, the cochairman of the Joint Iran-Contra Committee. But all that was yet to come. Now that the formalities were completed, the hearings could proceed.

The Fifth Amendment wasn't the only issue where I disagreed with my lawyers. We also had a brief but spirited argument over whether I should wear my uniform to the hearings. I was against it. I was a very unpopular person on Capitol Hill, and if I was dressed as a Marine, it wasn't hard for me to imagine that Congress might decide to "modify" the Corps' budget request.

My lawyers saw it differently. "You're still a Marine," they said. "You spend every day at the Marine headquarters, wearing a uniform. You ought to wear it to the hearings."

When I persisted, Brendan urged me to ask General Kelley, the commandant, for his opinion. "When I go up to testify," the general told me, "I always wear the uniform. All my Marines do, and you should, too."

That settled it. Here, too, Brendan turned out to be right. I had thought that the hearings were essentially political, and to a large extent, they were. But they were also about something even bigger.

Television.

Later on, people would come up to congratulate me, or to applaud my lawyers, for "putting the hearings on television." In some respect, the TV coverage worked in my favor, and it certainly helped me raise money for my defense. On the other hand, it also made it much easier for the special prosecutor's office to use my immunized testimony against me because so many people had heard it and seen it. But regardless of whether it helped or hurt, it wasn't my decision. This was the committee's call, not ours.

From the beginning, Brendan took the position that because of the special prosecutor's investigation, and the possibility of criminal charges, I shouldn't have to testify before Congress at all. Although he fully recognized that Congress could force me to appear, he told them in a twenty-seven-page letter that they had no statutory authority to make me testify more than once. "You have a choice," he told the committee. "You can question Colonel North in a closed session, or you can do it in public. It's up to you."

The Joint Iran-Contra Committee chose to have me testify in front of the cameras—a decision they surely came to regret.[1] But from their point of view it made sense. Because I had given no prior testimony, and hadn't granted a single interview to the press, there was, to say the least, a great deal of public interest in what I was going to say. For the committee members, the prospect of appearing before tens of millions of people on network television was apparently irresistible. They all remembered Watergate, when several relatively unknown politicians rose to national prominence, including Howard Baker, Lowell Weicker, Peter Rodino, Sam Ervin, and, of course, Daniel K. Inouye. You couldn't buy that kind of publicity, which was why the competition to serve on the House and Senate Iran-contra committees had been so fierce.

By March, when these two committees were merged into one panel for joint hearings, twenty-six members had already been appointed. But while almost everybody in Congress agreed that the joint committee was far too large, not a single member volunteered to step down.

Their goal, of course, was "face time"—a chance to pontificate before the cameras. The committee members didn't really want to ask the questions; they preferred to make speeches. And so they left the detailed questions to their two "designated hitters"—John Nields and Arthur Liman.

As chairman, Senator Inouye retained a major role. But he ruled against us at every turn, and millions of Americans concluded that he was unfair. The hearings didn't help his career, either. He was later defeated for Senate majority leader by Senator George Mitchell, who at least appeared to be far more reasonable.

---

[1] Nearly three-quarters of the nation saw at least part of my testimony on television. According to a *New York Times*-CBS survey at the end of the first week of my testimony, 43 percent of the public gave me a favorable rating. In a similar survey back in March, only 6 percent rated me favorably. (*U.S. News & World Report*, July 20, 1987, p. 19.)

Nields and Liman did not have an easy time of it. With the other witnesses, they had a script to follow. They or their staff had spent days in depositions, interviews, and private hearings, going through questions and producing a transcript. Brendan wouldn't allow that in my case. As a trial lawyer, he knew there was nothing more powerful in the hands of a cross-examiner than prior testimony taken under oath. My lawyers wanted me to go in there with a clean slate. Without their usual road map to show them the way, Nields and Liman were forced to think on their feet and to improvise.

For weeks before I testified, Brendan and his team had tried to prepare me for what the hearings would be like. Nearly every afternoon after work, I would drive from Marine headquarters in Arlington to Williams & Connolly in downtown Washington for the pleasure of spending the evening and half the night being grilled.

Typically, the lawyers would show me the text of one of the documents that had been referred to that day in the hearings: "Tell us about this memo."

"I sent that to McFarlane shortly before the trip to Tehran. Apparently I made a few typing errors. Is that the problem?"

"Come on, Ollie, don't be a wise guy. You have a natural tendency to joke around, but don't do that during the hearings. They will expect you to be apologetic and serious. At least be serious."

But the lawyers never asked me to apologize, and I had no intention of doing so. "You don't have to be defensive," Brendan said. "The way you explain things to us, minus the wisecracks—that's how you should talk to the committee. Just tell the truth."

It's hard for me to describe how close I feel to my lawyers, and especially to Brendan. I have spent so much time with Brendan and his team that they have come to know me better than anybody else except Betsy. As we worked together month after month, we developed an intensely personal relationship.

For them, this wasn't business as usual, and I ran up well over a million dollars before I could pay them anything. But it was clear from the start that my lawyers weren't in this for the money. They believed with a passion that what was happening to me was wrong, and there were times when they were even more outraged than I was. I came to admire and appreciate them so much that I almost stopped telling lawyer jokes.

Brendan's team of five was up against more than eighty lawyers and agents on the special prosecutor's staff, and over a hundred staff members and lawyers attached to the congressional committees. But each member of the Sullivan team brought a special gift to the party. They reminded me of a crack military unit, where each member has his own MOS—military occupational specialty.

Brendan, the field marshal, is a master of legal tactics and an expert at cross-examination. Later, at my trial, even the judge and the prosecutors conceded that he did a brilliant job with some of the witnesses. Brendan's face reveals nothing. I have watched him sit through the most difficult moments of the hearings and the trial without changing his expression. (He is considerably younger than he looks; he was only forty-five at the time of the hearings—just two years older than I.) Although I trusted him completely, he still checked every decision with me, and always allowed me to voice my opinions and occasional disagreements. Once or twice he even listened to me.

Barry Simon, who has worked closely with Brendan for years, is an expert on the law. He is also the smartest man I've ever met. (Barry is partly bald, and it wouldn't surprise me if he had burned off some of his hair by thinking so hard.) He's a former chemistry major who graduated from Harvard Law School, where he was president of the *Law Review*. While Brendan reminds me of an inscrutable elder statesman, Barry is far more direct and confrontational. He has a phenomenal memory, and I wouldn't dare contradict him unless I was actually holding a document in my hand that proved I was right—and sometimes not even then. It didn't take long before he knew more about Iran-contra than I did.

Nicole Seligman is a brilliant negotiator. She was also the youngest member of the defense team, and at one point was actually mistaken for my daughter. Nicole is a master of the art of the possible; where others see only problems, she sees possibilities and finds solutions. She is blessed with an unusually clear and logical mind, and a terrific sense of humor. She's also a fine writer—which may have something to do with her previous career as an editor on the Asian edition of the *Wall Street Journal*.

John Cline joined the team after I was indicted in 1988, and brought in a remarkable talent for research. Barry would cite (from memory, of course) half a dozen cases that might apply, and John would research them. He'd write a draft of the motion or the brief under discussion, and send it on to Barry for a quick review. Barry would send it back to John, who would revise it again and deliver it to Brendan. Brendan would make a few last-minute changes, and would send it to John, then back again to Brendan for a final review before a courier delivered it to the courthouse. They never missed a deadline.

Terry O'Donnell, the fifth member of the team, was an expert on the inner workings of government. He had served in the Ford administration, and he understood the intricacies and the legal aspects of covert operations. He also appreciated the mentality of many of the government officials we had to deal with in the bureaucracy. When the FBI alerted Brendan to the Libyan threat, it was Terry who found the right office to call in the Pentagon.

The case made tremendous demands on all of the lawyers, and on their families, and on the two paralegals and three overworked secretaries who struggled along with the rest of us. One young man, Chris Capozzi, gave up a year of law school to stay on the case.

I learned a great deal from my lawyers, and some of

their advice is indelibly etched in my memory. During my very first meeting with Brendan, he said, "We have a few rules here that you're going to get to know and love. The most important ones are these: Always tell the truth. Don't create anything, and don't destroy anything. Don't confirm or deny anything to the media, and don't talk to the press or anybody else. And that means *anybody* else—with the possible exception of Betsy."

He continued: "If one of your former colleagues contacts you, here's what you should tell them: 'First, tell the truth. Don't lie to anybody about anything—even if you think it will help me. Second, don't create anything and don't destroy anything. Third, get yourself a lawyer. If you don't know a lawyer, call Brendan Sullivan and he'll recommend one.'"

"Make absolutely sure your answers are truthful," Brendan told me early on. "You haven't broken any laws yet. Don't start now. Nobody will go to jail for what they did in this affair. But they might for what they do now. People could be indicted for perjury as the result of their testimony. Tell the truth—even about things you may have done wrong in the past. Call us crazy, but we have a little policy here at Williams & Connolly: we don't like to see any clients end up in jail."

Anyone who saw my testimony on television will recall that Brendan was at my side throughout the proceedings, sitting next to me at the witness table, or, as he called it, the bicycle built for two. One difference between a hearing and a trial is that at a hearing, the witness is allowed to consult with his lawyer at any point, which led to a number of quick, whispered conversations between us. The subject of these whisperings, I learned later, inspired all kinds of guessing games—and a few jokes, too. "If you keep giving him the answers," quipped one comedian, "how will he ever learn?"

On the afternoon of my first day of testimony, Brendan received an urgent message from a colleague back at the office. This lawyer's mother, who was partially deaf, had called her son to say that when Brendan covered the microphone and started whispering to me, it was possible to read his lips. From then on, Brendan held up his hand whenever we spoke.

Sometimes he reminded me to slow down. Once he pointed out that I had answered only the first half of a two-part question. Occasionally he suggested that I had not fully responded to a question, and should expand my answer. He pointed out a few traps. Once or twice, when he could see I was losing my temper, he actually told me a joke. But my favorite interruption was the time he leaned over and said, "Hi. It's been a while since you and I have had a chat, so I thought I'd just say hello. Look serious. If you smile now, I'll kick you so hard your ankle will bleed."

This was no idle threat. As we sat there at the witness table, our faces were scrutinized by a hundred cameras. But because the table was covered by a long red cloth, nobody could see our feet. Every time I said something dumb or sarcastic, Brendan would kick me—hard.

"I came here to tell you the truth," I told Nields that first morning. "The good, the bad, and the ugly."

*Ouch!*

And later.

*Nields:* Where are those memoranda?
*North:* Which memoranda?
*Nields:* The memoranda that you sent up to Admiral Poindexter seeking the President's approval.
*North:* Well...I think I shredded most of that. Did I get 'em all?

*Ouch!*

And a few minutes later:

*Nields:* Sir, do you remember the question?
*North:* My memory has been shredded.

*Ouch!*

I was far too insolent that first morning, and by the time we broke for lunch my ankle was killing me.

The hearings must have been terribly frustrating for Brendan. As a trial lawyer, he's used to making arguments before a judge and a jury. But during the hearings his visible role was reduced to occasional whisperings and periodic objections when the committee's unfairness became too flagrant—all of which were overruled by Inouye.

Late in the afternoon of the third day, things came to a head when Arthur Liman asked me a hypothetical question.

*Sullivan:* Those kinds of questions, Mr. Chairman, are wholly inappropriate, not just because of rules of evidence, not because you couldn't say it in a court, but because it's just dreamland. It's speculation.... Come on, let's have, Mr. Chairman —

*Inouye:* I'm certain counsel —

*Sullivan:*—plain fairness, plain fairness. That's all we're asking.

*Inouye:* May I speak, sir? May I speak?

*Sullivan:* Yes, sir.

*Inouye:* I'm certain counsel realizes that this is not a court of law.

*Sullivan:* I—believe me, I know *that*.

*Inouye:* And I'm certain you realize that the rules of evidence do not apply in this inquiry.

*Sullivan:* That I know as well. I'm just asking for fairness—fairness. I know the rules don't apply. I know the Congress doesn't recognize attorney-client privilege, a husband-and-wife privilege, priest-penitent privilege. I know those things are all out the window —

*Inouye:* We have attempted to be as fair as we can.

*Sullivan:*—and we rely on just fairness, Mr. Chairman. Fairness.

*Inouye:* Let the witness object, if he wishes to.

*Sullivan:* Well sir, I'm not a potted plant. I'm here as the lawyer. That's my job.

Who could have guessed that a throwaway line about foliage would capture the imagination of the American public? That afternoon, we returned to the law firm to find dozens of potted plants. By the next day, there were potted plants everywhere—in the lobby, in the corridors, and especially in Brendan's office, which now resembled a terrarium.

This botanical generosity represented just a fraction of an unimaginable outpouring of public support. At Williams & Connolly, the phones were ringing off the hook. On the building across the street, occupied by a staid old bank, the occupants of an upper story posted a scoreboard that changed each day. By the end of my testimony, it read, OLLIE 6, CONGRESS 0. In our neighborhood in Great Falls, my neighbors hung banners and flags from the trees on the road that ran past our homes.

During the hearings and shortly afterward I received over a million pieces of mail from people who had been watching on television. Some of the envelopes were simply addressed to: Oliver North, American Hero. They reached me anyway. Eventually, all of the mail ended up at Williams & Connolly, where it filled the mailroom and overflowed into the basement. The firm's regular mail was buried in the avalanche, and some of it wasn't found for weeks.

Edward Bennett Williams, who had established the law firm that bears his name, asked me if the security team could process the mail a little faster so that the place could resume some semblance of normalcy. But by then there was far too much for one bomb-sniffing dog to go through. To speed things up, the security guys arranged to bring in a few dogs from other agencies, including the Metropolitan Police, and the Bureau of Alcohol, Tobacco, and Firearms. But nobody thought to stagger their schedules, and when four huge German shepherds arrived within a few minutes of each other, there was one hellacious dog fight in the basement of Williams & Connolly. And I thought the *hearings* were noisy.

Many letters included donations for my defense fund, which my former classmates at Annapolis had established right after I was fired. Some correspondents enclosed a single dollar, with a note saying, "I want to help, but this is all I can afford." A few older people even signed over their Social Security checks, which we tried to return. The support was simply overwhelming, both logistically and emotionally.

A surprising amount of mail came in from people who described themselves as liberals. As one of them put it, "I may not like everything you stand for, but what you said at the hearings made a lot of sense. And it's obvious that the big guys have thrown you off the boat." As if to confirm that sentiment, actor Lee Majors sent me the jacket he had worn in his TV show, "The Fall Guy."

Then there were the telegrams—hundreds, thousands, and eventually tens of thousands after Western Union advertised a discounted price and set up a special toll-free number. Almost all of them were favorable:

> NEXT MALE CHILD WILL BE NAMED OLIVER.
> GOD LOVE YOU. MONEY TO FOLLOW.
> CONGRATULATIONS BUT QUIT QUOTING THE CONSTITUTION AND THE LAW. IT IS CONFUSING THE COMMITTEE.
> I CONGRATULATE YOU ON YOUR DECORUM IN THE FACE OF THOSE ILL-BRED HYENAS PUTTING YOU THROUGH THIS HELL.
> YOUR'RE DOING WONDERFULLY. CHIN UP. KISS YOUR WIFE, CHILDREN. PET YOUR DOG. I'M 81. FRIENDS HERE BELIEVE YOU.
> I CROWN YOU SIR OLIVER, SLAYER OF TOADS.
> CONGRATULATIONS ON TAKING CAPITOL HILL. HOLD POSITIONS UNTIL RELIEVED. AMERICAN PEOPLE ON THE WAY. SEMPER FI.

My biggest supporter was Betsy. She sat behind me during the questioning, and with me during the breaks.

Sometimes we held hands and prayed together. She would rub the back of my neck to help me relax, and would lighten things up with a smile or a joke. Betsy knows me so well that she could spot the occasional moment where I was groping for the right word so I could avoid using profanity on national television.

For the first two days of my testimony she had watched the hearings at home. We had some idea of what the sessions would be like, and Brendan and I agreed that there was no need for Betsy to suffer through this long and demeaning process. But on the second day, when I finally got home well after midnight from my daily posthearing stint at Williams & Connolly, Betsy was waiting up for me. She had saved some dinner, although I had already eaten at the law firm, where Brendan had ordered in yet another Domino's pizza.

"This isn't right," she said. "I should be in there with you."

"Do you really want to go?"

"I do. My place is with you. I wouldn't want anyone to think I don't support you."

It was two in the morning, but I called Brendan at home. "Can Betsy come with me tomorrow?

"Sure, if she wants to. Now get some rest."

But there wasn't much time for sleep. We had to get up at five to make it to the law firm in time for the brief morning meeting before we drove over to the hearings. Betsy got the children ready for day camp, fixed their lunches, arranged for them to go to a neighbor's in the afternoon, and reviewed their revised schedules with the security team.

I was running on adrenaline, but by the time we got to the Caucus Room, Betsy was exhausted. And for some inexplicable reason, unless you were sitting on the dais you weren't allowed to have coffee. At one point during the afternoon I noticed the cameras zooming in over my shoulder, but I couldn't figure out why. Was there a fly crawling on my ear? Only later did I learn that their target was Betsy—who had fallen fast asleep.

When we returned to Brendan's office, the networks were still showing scenes from the hearings. Betsy was mortified. She began to apologize to Brendan, but he assured her it was no problem. "In fact," he said, "when you come tomorrow, I want you to fall asleep again. It's the best thing you could have done. It shows that you're so confident in your husband that you don't even have to pay attention to all of this garbage."

During breaks in the hearings, the witnesses and their lawyers were allowed to take refuge in a small hideaway office across the hall from the Caucus Room that belonged to Senator Edward Kennedy's staff. There were French doors that opened up on a balcony, where somebody had set up a chaise longue and some deck chairs. During the lunch break on that third day, Brendan urged Betsy and me to step out on the balcony and wave to the crowd of supporters gathered on the street below. I didn't feel comfortable doing that, but Brendan literally pushed us out the door, saying, "These people came down here to see you and encourage you. They'll never get into the hearings. Let them know you appreciate their support."

Until that moment I had no real sense of what was going on outside the building. But as soon as we stepped out onto the balcony, a tremendous roar went up. I had expected to see a few dozen people, but there were *thousands*, and many of them were carrying huge banners supporting me. It was overwhelming, and I was too choked up to say a word. What a dramatic contrast to what was going on inside.

This extraordinary reception did not go unnoticed by the Senate authorities. The next morning, when our little group arrived in the holding room, we noticed that the doors leading to the balcony had been bolted shut with headless screws.

The visible signs of support weren't limited to the streets. As we walked down the long corridors of the

Russell Senate Office Building on our way to and from the Caucus Room, staffers and secretaries got up from their televisions and stood in the doorways with applause and words of encouragement and support: "Keep it up. Hang in there. Great job!"

On the third day, one of the congressional staffers started something that quickly became a daily lunchtime ritual. There would be a knock on the door of the holding room, and I would be asked to go back across the hall into the now-empty hearing room to pose for photographs with staffers, pages, and even some of their family members. The line grew to include the Senate and House security personnel, the Capitol Hill police, and few committee staffers. Even the Sergeant-at-Arms, an Inouye appointee who was anything but friendly, insisted on bringing me to his office to meet his staff and sign autographs.

But none of these sentiments penetrated the walls of the hearing room, where the atmosphere remained tense. As we expected, Nields asked me about the testimony of several previous witnesses. Albert Hakim had told the committee that he had set up a death benefit account called "Button" in case I didn't return from my trip to Tehran. ("Button," Albert explained, was short for "Bellybutton"—as if that cleared things up.) Albert had once assured me that he would make sure Betsy and the kids would be all right in case anything happened to me. "Don't worry," he had said. "I'll take care of them."

At his request, I asked Betsy to go to Philadelphia to meet with Hakim's lawyer. There was no mention of money, or bank accounts, and no funds were ever transferred to our possession. The lawyer merely wanted to know how many children we had and how old they were. Later, after I returned from Tehran, Albert's lawyer called Betsy a second time; she didn't return the call. But it wasn't until the hearings that I had ever heard about a fund being set up, or the names "Button" or "Bellybutton."

\* \* \*

Another topic that came up was the now-famous security system at our house. On the evening of April 25, 1986, eleven days after the American antiterrorist raid on Libya, I received a call from the FBI's counterterrorism office. The news was not good: in Lebanon, a spokesman for the Abu Nidal organization had announced that several American targets, including me, had been marked for assassination. The announcement had been recorded on videotape.

My first response was that it would be best if this announcement did not appear on television in Europe or the United States. Terrorist organizations often commit acts of violence simply to get attention, and to broadcast this threat would be to play into their hands. It could also attract the attention of unstable individuals who might see this as an opportunity for notoriety. During the next few days, Admiral Poindexter, White House press secretary Larry Speakes, and I made an effort to get the American networks not to run this tape on their news broadcasts.

When nothing happened for about a week, I assumed we were out of the woods. But then Betsy called me at the office to say she had just seen the videotape of the threat on the "CBS Evening News," which she had been watching with the children. They were not amused.

Bob Earl called down to the Sit Room and arranged to have the broadcast replayed so that I could see it. There, on the screen, was Abu Bakr, a spokesman for the Fatah Revolutionary Council. My fellow targets were General Jack Singlaub, Edward Luttwak, a Washington-based consultant on international affairs, and the Heritage Foundation, a Washington think tank. None of them had been involved with planning the attack on Libya, but curiously, all had in one way or another been publicly linked in the media to Central America and/or the contras.

Now, there are death threats and there are death threats. Abu Nidal has been called the world's most dangerous terrorist—and for good reason. He is responsible for the deaths of hundreds of innocent people. Some terrorist groups, like the Red Brigades in Italy, try to avoid killing women and children. But Abu Nidal's gang delights in it.

Among other atrocities, Abu Nidal had planned the Christmas 1985 massacres at the Rome and Vienna airports in which more than a dozen people were killed and over a hundred wounded by terrorists carrying hand grenades and assault rifles. One of their victims was an eleven-year-old American girl named Natasha Simpson.

I was deeply concerned about the safety of Betsy and our children. In addition to all my usual travel to Europe and Central America, I was planning to leave for what could have been a *very* long visit to Tehran. One of General Simhoni's officers at the Israeli embassy called to remind me that they were all too familiar with Abu Nidal's group, and that this was not a threat to be taken lightly. They confirmed FBI reports that Abu Nidal had operatives in the United States, and they urged me to take steps to protect myself and my family.

At the suggestion of the FBI, I contacted the Secret Service, my local police, and the Pentagon. The Fairfax County Police sent out an officer who did a site survey, and who briefed our family on the precautions we should take. They promised to increase their patrols in our neighborhood, and suggested that we install a security system immediately.

I knew that the Secret Service provided security for several White House officials including Admiral Poindexter and Bud McFarlane. I discussed the matter with the admiral and with Rod McDaniel, executive secretary of the NSC. But there wasn't much they could do: I was simply too junior to qualify for government protection.

I then called several private security companies, but nobody could come to our house before I was scheduled to depart for Tehran. At one of our planning sessions for the Tehran trip, General Secord asked me what I had done in response to the death threat. When I explained that I was having trouble getting any kind of immediate protection for my family, he told me not to worry, that he had a friend who might be able to help. A few days later he introduced me to Glenn Robinette, a former CIA employee who owned a security company. Robinette came out to the house, did a quick survey, and said he could install a system right away. And he did.

Glenn Robinette never sent me a bill, and I didn't ask him for one. In the chaos that surrounded our preparations for the trip to Tehran, I just didn't sit down and discuss the financial arrangements with Dick Secord.

I didn't think much more about it until just before I was fired. Realizing that I had never paid for the security system, I called Glenn Robinette. He was off in Central America, and when he finally called me back in December, I asked for a bill. In response, he sent me two back-dated bills.

And here I did a really stupid thing. In direct violation of Brendan's rule of "don't create anything," I continued the charade by sending two phony, back-dated letters responding to Robinette's back-dated bills. What I should have done, of course, was to tell Brendan what had happened. But I thought I knew better.

I should have shouted it from the rooftops: *"Dick Secord helped me get a security system to protect my family because there was a serious death threat and nobody in our government would help."*

Which was, in effect, what I told the committee:

*North:* I admit to making a serious, serious, judgment error in what I then did to paper it over and I'm willing to sit here and admit to that. But I'm also suggesting to you gentlemen that if it was General Secord who paid the bill...first of all, "Thank you, General Secord." And second of all, you guys ought to write him a check because the government should have done it to begin with.

While some of the committee members found it convenient to play dumb, I was convinced that certain members of Congress had known a lot more than they let on about my involvement with the contras while I was at the NSC. This was especially true of the House and Senate intelligence committees, who received regular intelligence reports from the region. They knew full well that the administration in general, and I in particular, had been helping the contras. They might not have known exactly *how*, but they certainly knew about it— which was why they had asked such detailed questions in their letters to McFarlane in 1985, and to Poindexter in 1986. Not all the members of the intelligence committees knew all the facts, but there weren't many people in Washington with an interest in the Nicaraguan situation who didn't know, at least in general, that Oliver North was up to his ears in aiding the contras.

But during the hearings, Nields and Liman questioned me about my contacts with Congress during this period on the assumption that no one in Congress had the faintest idea of what I had been doing. Not surprisingly, Nields focused on my August 1986 meeting with the intelligence committee in the Sit Room:

*Nields:* And this was you personally talking to them?
*North:* It was on instructions of the national security adviser. I was instructed to meet with Chairman Hamilton and, I believe, many of the members of the Committee.
*Nields:* And they were interested in finding out the answers to the questions raised by the Resolution of Inquiry—
*North:* Exactly.
*Nields:*—your fund-raising activities—
*North:* Precisely.

*Nields:*—military support for the contras —

*North:* That's right . . .

*Nields:* The beginning of this memorandum that appears to be a description of what you said during that meeting, it says "from Boland Amendment on, North explains strictures to contras." Is that true? Did you explain the strictures to the contras?

*North:* I explained to them that there was no U.S. government money until more was appropriated, yes.

*Nields:* And it says "never violated stricture. Gave advice on Human Rights Civic Action Program."

*North:* I did do that.

Nields: But I take it you did considerably more, which you did not tell the committee about.

*North:* I have admitted that here before you today . . . I will tell you right now, counsel, and all the members here gathered that I misled the Congress.

*Nields:* At that meeting?

*North:* At that meeting.

*Nields:* Face-to-face?

*North:* Face-to-face.

*Nields:* You made false statements to them about your activities in support of the contras?

*North:* I did. Furthermore, I did so with the purpose of hopefully avoiding the very kind of thing that we have before us now and avoiding a shutoff of help to the Nicaraguan resistance and avoiding an elimination of the resistance facilities in three Central American countries —

*Nields:* We —

*North:*—wherein we had promised those heads of state. On specific orders to me, I had gone down there and assured them of our absolute and total discretion.

*Nields:* We do live in a democracy, don't we?

*North:* We do, sir. Thank God.

*Nields:* In which it is the people, not one Marine lieutenant colonel, that gets to decide the important pol-

icy decisions for the nation.
*North:* Yes.
*Nields:* And, part of the democratic process —
*North:* And, I would point out that part of that answer is that this Marine lieutenant colonel was not making all of those decisions on his own. As I indicated in my testimony yesterday, Mr. Nields, I sought approval for everything I did.

There was no changing his mind. Nields, Liman, and most of the committee were intent on showing that one renegade lieutenant colonel had done all this on his own. I knew from the outset that the hearings were going to be anything but fair, and I suppose I shouldn't have expected otherwise. After all, it was Congress that set the agenda and made the rules. It was Congress that called the witnesses and decided on the questions. It was Congress that chose not to investigate itself for its fickle, vacillating, and unpredictable policy toward the Nicaraguan resistance.

The whole process, as I pointed out in my "opening statement,"[2] was like a baseball game in which one of the teams was also the umpire. It was Congress that called the balls and strikes, and decided who was safe and who was out. And it was Congress that added up the score and in the end, inevitably, declared itself the winner.

As if to prove my point, the committee did several things during my testimony that were just outrageous. During part of his questioning, Arthur Liman displayed a huge blowup of the text of one of the Boland Amendments, making it look as if this had been a separate, one-page document. In reality, the various Boland Amendments had been buried in government appropriations bills that ran well over a thousand pages each. But

---

[2]Which—talk about fair—I wasn't allowed to give until the third day of my testimony.

this display, which included the President's signature, gave the distinct impression that the President had read it over and said, "Oh, gosh, here's the Boland Amendment. Quick—give me a pen so I can sign it."

I wasn't the only one who felt this way. Congressman Henry Hyde of Illinois took the floor to object to this portrayal. It is "deceptive," he said, and he apologized for the way it was displayed. "If I tried this in a municipal court in Chicago," he said, "phonying up an exhibit to make a point that was half true—I'd be held in contempt."

Hyde then made a remarkable statement about the hypocrisy of the hearings. Referring to the Congress, he said:

> Now, if *we* don't like a law, Colonel, and you guys ought to learn this as the NSC and then the administration, you just exempt yourself. You see, we exempt ourselves from OSHA, the Occupational Safety and Health Act. We exempt ourselves from the Ethics in Government Act; no special prosecutors are going after us. We have our own committee of our own brethren that'll take care of that. We are exempt from equal opportunity, equal employment opportunity; none of that because we're political people. The Budget Act; waive it. Pass it, kid the people, and waive it. Every time something comes up that's in excess of the budget, pay no attention to it....
>
> Now, if we can't ignore the law or exempt ourselves from it, we play games with the process. Do you know how we got our pay raise?...you know what we did in the House? We waited, under the guidance of the stage director over there, the Speaker, until thirty days had elapsed, until it was vested, it could not be unvested and then we got a vote on it. We waited until it was locked in, and then we voted. And we could all tell our constituents, "I didn't vote for that pay raise." That's the way we do things. So there's much to be learned from watching us.

It was about then that the committee began to self-destruct. Brendan and I sat there in astonishment as the members turned on each other and their lawyers. Instead of focusing their undivided anger at me, they began to debate each other. During their internal squabble, Brendan leaned over to me and quoted the famous tag line of those Sergeant Preston radio shows we had both listened to as kids: "Well, King, this case is closed." Believe me, it's hard not to smile when your lawyer says something like that.

The Boland Amendment wasn't the only ill-advised exhibit. Although it was widely known that my family was at risk from terrorists who had threatened to kill me, a large blowup of a letter I had written was placed before the cameras, complete with our home address. Thanks, fellas.

There was also a farcical flap over the slide shows I had presented to various groups in Washington. Because this was the subject of some controversy, several of the committee members thought it would be appropriate for me to give this same briefing, complete with the slides, for the committee. The slide show soon became the subject of a raging debate by members of the committee, many of whom just couldn't tolerate the prospect of my being allowed to say a favorable word on behalf of the contras. And so it was claimed that for "security" reasons the lights could not be dimmed for the slides to be seen.

This was plainly ridiculous. The place was crawling with police and security agents. During the hearings, the Senate Caucus room was one of the best-protected rooms in the world.

In an inspired example of lunacy, the committee came up with a compromise: instead of showing the slides and giving the briefing, *I would hold each slide up in the air and discuss it*. This was absurd, and everybody knew it. But it was better than nothing.

I held up a slide of a Soviet HIND helicopter, and described its lethal power. I held up a slide of a textbook from a school in Nicaragua, showing how children learn arithmetic by adding up hand grenades and machine guns. I held up a slide showing several Miskito Indians, and explained how they had been driven out of their ancestral homelands. I held up a slide of the leadership of the FDN: of the sixteen men in that photograph, eleven were former Sandinistas.

The "slide show" and the two documents were only the tip of the unfairness iceberg. The whole proceeding was grossly unfair, which was one reason the American people responded as they did. But even the blatant unfairness that was captured by the cameras couldn't depict the full measure of the tilt. I can't recall a single instance in which Senator Inouye granted or sustained *any* of Brendan Sullivan's objections.

The unfairness continued right through to the very end, when it surfaced in Senator Inouye's shocking closing statement. Referring to the Uniform Code of Military Justice, which applies to all men and women in the armed services, Senator Inouye reminded his audience that the orders of a superior officer must be obeyed by subordinate members—so long as those orders are lawful.

This was certainly true. But then Inouye stepped over the line of decency and actually compared my responses to those of Nazi war criminals!

*Inouye:* The Uniform Code makes it abundantly clear that it must be the lawful orders of a superior officer. In fact, it says, members of the military have an obligation to disobey unlawful orders. This principle was considered so important, that we—we, the government of the United States, proposed that it be internationally applied, in the Nuremberg Trials. And so, in the Nuremberg Trials, we said that the fact that the defendant had —

*Sullivan:* Mr. Chairman. May I please register an objection —

*Inouye:* May I continue my statement?

*Sullivan:* I find this offensive! I find you engaging in a personal attack on Colonel North, and you're far removed from the issues of this case. To make reference to the Nuremberg Trials, I find personally and professionally distasteful, and I can no longer sit here and listen to this.

*Inouye:* You will have to sit there, if you want to listen.

*Sullivan:* Mr. Chairman, please don't conclude these hearings on this unfair note.... You may ask questions, but you may not attack him personally. This has gone too far.

Indeed it had. It's true that the Nuremberg Trials marked the most famous use of the "authorization" defense. But even if the reference to Nuremberg hadn't been disgusting and inappropriate, there was an enormous difference between then and now. Those defendants had been ordered to kill people. I had been ordered to protect them.

# 17

## A SMOKING GUN IN THE CLOSET

"OYEZ, OYEZ, OYEZ. THIS HONORABLE COURT WILL NOW come to order. The United States of America versus Oliver L. North. Judge Gerhard A. Gesell presiding."

That's how it started each morning, day after day, week after week, during my trial. That phrase sickened me: The United States v. Oliver North. Why not the Congressional Police v. Oliver North? Or Independent Counsel v. Executive Branch? Either one would have been more accurate.[1]

I have heard it said that a trial is like war, and for lawyers that analogy must ring true. But it's not that way for the defendant. In combat, after all, you're allowed to shoot back. But in this battle Brendan and his team did all the shooting for me. They performed brilliantly, but I found it agonizing not to be able to respond.

Each night, the defense team would regroup, replenish, and rearm as they prepared for the next day's clash. As soon as the daily transcript arrived, one member of the legal team would review it for holes in the enemy's line. Another would pore over the previous statements

448

of tomorrow's witness. A third lawyer would sift through the thousands of documents that were being introduced as exhibits in the case, while a fourth would focus on the documents and witnesses we planned to use as a rebuttal to the prosecution's arguments.

In theory, at least, the defendant is presumed innocent. But it sure didn't feel that way while the prosecution was making its case. As I had to be reminded again and again, in order to convict me of breaking the law the prosecution had to demonstrate criminal intent. "This isn't like breaking the speed limit," the lawyers explained. "They'll need to show that you were thinking and acting like a person *intending* to break the law."

Betsy tried to come to court every day, but that wasn't always possible. She was a volunteer teacher's aide in Dornin's and Sarah's classrooms, and she was also determined to keep our family life as close to normal as possible. On days when she could get there, she was accompanied by Brian Cox, the assistant pastor at our church, or by a friend. (Brian came so often that Brendan arranged for the kitchen at Williams & Connolly to prepare a sandwich for him, too.) When Betsy couldn't make it, Brian or one of the men from our family Bible study group would be there, and during the lunch break we would set aside a few minutes for a quiet prayer.

For Betsy the trial was a horror show. She was getting very little sleep, and outside of court we saw almost nothing of each other. In addition to attending the trial and wondering whether her husband and the father of her children would be sent to jail, she still had to manage the house and take care of the children. If the prosecutors had their way, at the end of this process she

[1]I wasn't the only one who felt that way. As two of the three Appeals Court judges wrote later in reversing my convictions, "We do not countenance political trials in this country, and this matter is not styled *Independent Counsel v. Executive Branch* or even *Congress* v. *Executive Branch*."

would have no husband, no income, and millions of dollars in debts.

People tried to help. Some of our neighbors and the members of our Bible study group pitched in to prepare casserole dishes that Betsy could heat up when she got home. But it was terribly difficult to maintain any semblance of normalcy for the children.

Not surprisingly, they were confused by the news reports of the trial. Although my story had already come out in great detail during the hearings, the media were now presenting each charge and every bit of evidence as though it were being heard for the first time. I remember when Congressman Lee Hamilton, the first prosecution witness to testify at the trial, "revealed" that in August 1986 I had met with members of the House Intelligence Committee in the White House Sit Room, and that he thought my answers were misleading. All this had been discussed in detail during the hearings, but here again it resulted in page-one coverage and lead billing on the evening network news.

During Brendan's cross-examination, Hamilton had to admit that no one had ever before been charged with lying to Congress in such a forum, that no transcript existed of the Sit Room meeting, and that I had not testified under oath. But these points rarely came out in the news. Neither did the fact that Hamilton had sat through my entire congressional testimony. When they had forced me to testify, I had been assured that nothing I said in the hearings could be used against me in a criminal prosecution. But here was the chair of the House Iran-Contra Committee, testifying against me at my trial.

After reading a newspaper account of Hamilton's testimony, our son, Stuart, called me from school late one night to ask if all this meant that I hadn't told the truth during the congressional hearings. No, I explained, this charge had nothing to do with the hearings. But Stuart wasn't the only one who was confused on this point. To this day, I hear from people who assumed I was on trial for having lied to Congress during the hearings.

One reason for the confusion may be that the special prosecutors had their own spin doctors who presided over regular briefings for the press. For most public prosecutors—U.S. Attorneys, district attorneys, and so on—a public affairs staff would be thought of as an unwarranted and inappropriate extravagance. But the special prosecutor answers to no one. At every break, and before and after each day of testimony, the special prosecutor's public affairs officer or one of his deputies would huddle outside the courtroom with members of the press to "clarify" prior or upcoming testimony and evidence. Brendan, still adhering to his no-comment rule, preferred to argue the case in front of the jury.

In addition to being longer than the hearings, the trial was far more tedious. As my lawyers already knew but I had yet to learn, a real trial is very different from the courtroom scenes on "Perry Mason" or "L.A. Law," which invariably depict the most sensational or dramatic scenes. There *are* fascinating moments in trials, but they're generally overshadowed by the drudgery of paperwork, procedure, and repetitive testimony. The congressional hearings were no picnic, but at least my part was over in six days.

And during the hearings, I was able to respond to questions and comments as soon as they were made. When other witnesses came in to testify, I could watch them on television or on videotape with Brendan in his conference room, where I could tell him exactly what I thought of each answer.

In the trial, by contrast, I had to sit there mute and impassive, day after day, as the prosecutors tried to get each witness to say terrible things about me. Just about all I could do was take notes. "North is scribbling away like a medieval monk," one reporter observed. With the exception of the jury, which had to sit through it all without uttering a word, just about everybody else had a specific task. The lawyers on both sides were busy examining and cross-examining the witnesses. The court stenographers had to type the thousands of words necessary to prepare the transcript, which ran to more than eighty-five hundred pages. The bailiffs and marshals walked around keeping order, and occasionally waking up a nodding juror. Even the judge could interrupt, ask questions, and make rulings. With so little to do, I often felt like a spectator.

For the prosecutors I felt only disdain. They had sought this job in a politically charged case that would give them enormous visibility. Unlike other public prosecutors, who are required to take cases as they come in, these guys were more like a lynch mob in pin-striped suits.

And so I especially enjoyed it when many of their own witnesses embarrassed them by saying kind things about me. Adolfo Calero was summoned by the prosecution to help make the case against me for supporting the resistance, and for setting up the operational account from which, it was alleged, I had stolen forty-four hundred dollars in traveler's checks.

During Brendan's cross-examination of Calero, he asked:

*Sullivan:* Would you try to tell the ladies and gentlemen of the jury as best you can who is this guy Colonel North? What did he do for you?
*Calero:* Well, for us he became a sort of a savior, I mean. We felt—as I said, we felt abandoned, we felt that we couldn't feed our people and that we had no way of getting support any place and then all of a sudden we were introduced to this man with whom we became more and more familiar as time went on....Our men, even though they were Nicaraguans and were not Americans, seemed to be as important for him as Americans, and he worried about us and felt like us. So we developed a very—a tremendously

human relationship....We are tremendously grateful
to him, and as I said before Congress, the Nicaraguan
people have a tremendous appreciation for this
man—so much so...that we're going to erect a mon-
ument for him once we free Nicaragua.

I don't know what the special prosecutors had been
expecting from Adolfo, but I doubt they had counted
on their witness wanting to put up a statue in honor of
the defendant!

Later, Brendan came around to the issue of the traveler's checks:

*Sullivan:* Do you trust him?
*Calero:* Absolutely. I would say that I trust Colonel
North with my life. I mean, that's the biggest thing I
have.
*Sullivan:* The prosecution in this case says that
Colonel North stole $4,400 of your traveler's checks.
Do you believe that that is conceivable?
*Calero:* No.

And still later:

*Sullivan:* Did anybody in the United States government indicate to you that North was not acting properly?
*Calero:* Never. I mean as I said before, and I was
showing in the picture [taken in 1985 in the White
House], it was Colonel North who took us to the
President.

Calero wasn't the only prosecution witness whose tes-
timony must have disappointed my persecutors. Chi Chi
Quintero described my "devotion to duty" and called it
"a work of art." Dick Gadd called me a "national hero."
Joseph Coors, whom Casey had sent to my office when
Coors offered to help the resistance, told the court that I

was, in his view, "a tremendously wonderful patriotic American." When Coors finished his testimony, he walked over to the defense table, gave Brendan a pat on the back, and shook my hand. The prosecutors cringed.

Had the prosecutors been less politically and personally motivated, they might have anticipated these problems. But then, these weren't regular U.S. Attorneys from the Justice Department. They had *asked* to be hired by the Office of the Independent Counsel, this strange entity created by the Congress for the sole purpose of going after members of the executive branch.[2]

In the regular criminal justice system, a prosecutor is normally presented with a crime—a robbed bank, a murder, whatever. His task is to find the perpetrator and bring him to justice. But in a strange perversion of that process, a special prosecutor has a much different task. First an individual from the executive branch is identified and chosen as a suspect; then the special prosecutor tries to identify a crime that this person may have perpetrated. The whole process is eerily reminiscent of that cynical line from the early days of the Soviet KGB: "First, bring us the man. We'll find the crime."

In theory the special prosecutor is accountable to the Attorney General, who can fire him only for cause. In practice, however, it's as if Congress had its own Justice Department. The Independent Counsel is independent, all right: independent of financial restraints, independent of time limitations, and independent of any obligation to show results within a given period of time. The Office of

---

[2]The position of special prosecutor was created in 1978, when Congress passed the Ethics in Government Act. Since 1982 the special prosecutor has been known as the independent counsel, but the original term strikes me as more accurate. In December 1986, Lawrence Walsh was appointed to the position by a special panel of judges. The Attorney General had asked for an investigation into the use of residuals from the Iran arms sales. But at the request of Congress, this narrow inquiry was quickly expanded to include just about everything short of fishing without a license.

the Independent Counsel has become a pervasive and powerful machine, a legalistic tank that can roll over and flatten its victims beneath its unlimited size, time, and money. It's hard to calculate just how much of the taxpayers' money the OIC has spent on this case, but as I write these words in the summer of 1991 the total is probably more than forty million dollars—and climbing.[3]

When the congressional hearings began, the special prosecutor was already in the midst of his own investigation of the individuals involved in Iran-contra. The first victim was Spitz Channell, and the pressure brought to bear on this poor man was intense. By April 1987, the special prosecutor had apparently convinced him that unless he pled guilty to a convoluted charge of conspiring to defraud the IRS through the National Endowment for the Preservation of Liberty (NEPL), a tax-exempt organization, he would face a jail sentence for personal income-tax violations.

On April 29, Channell appeared before a judge in a federal courthouse.

"You are charged with conspiracy in this case," the judge said, "and of course it requires two or more persons to have a conspiracy. Are you prepared to state the names of any of those with whom you conspired?"

"Yes, Your Honor."

---

[3]The Iran-contra special prosecutor constitutes the largest and most unaccountable prosecutorial staff ever assembled in the United States, and has included more than fifty lawyers, seventy-five investigators, and scores of support personnel. It is the only government office in America that is subject to no oversight and no budgetary restraints. Lawyers hired by the special prosecutor have been paid at the top of the federal pay scale—now in excess of $100,000 a year—including new attorneys right out of law school. At one point, Special Prosecutor Walsh had a press office about as large as that of the Attorney General of the United States. It's like a whole separate law firm being financed by the American taxpayers, who are powerless to limit it or stop it. The taxpayers are also footing the bill for Mr. Walsh's living quarters in the Watergate, his chauffeur-driven car, his air fare for his frequent trips to and from his home in Oklahoma, and some of the most expensive office space in Washington.

"Would you please do so?"

"Yes. Colonel North, an official of the National Security Council."

Brendan called me with the news of this ridiculous charge, but it wasn't quite the shock that the prosecutors had intended when they scripted this little dialogue. We were well aware of Channell's vulnerabilities, including his inability to pay the mounting expenses of his defense—something the prosecutors certainly counted on. And so Spitz Channell became the first of several defendants who, faced with an overwhelming debt and the destruction of their reputations and future careers, would plead to a lesser offense rather than continue fighting the monster. Although I made a different choice, I can't say I blame them.

My next few months had been taken up with preparations for the hearings, followed by tons of legal paperwork on both sides. In March 1988, Brendan called me at Marine headquarters and asked me to come to his office. "You'd better leave work early today," he said. "There have been some developments."

By now I knew that this phrase did not signal good news. When I arrived at Williams & Connolly, Brendan sat me down and explained that the special prosecutor had decided to indict four of us—Admiral Poindexter, General Secord, Albert Hakim, and myself—on a variety of counts.[4]

This was my worst moment in the entire case, and

---

[4]The indictments were returned by a federal grand jury on March 16, 1988. In all, there were twenty-three counts, including conspiracy to defraud the United States, obstruction of justice, false statements, theft of government property, wire fraud, making false statements to Congress and the Attorney General, and destruction and removal of documents. Sixteen of the counts applied to me. By the time my trial began, these had been pared down to twelve.

On June 8, 1988, Judge Gesell ruled that Poindexter, Hakim, Secord, and I would all be tried separately, so that in defending ourselves we could each make use of immunized testimony that the other three had given to Congress. Secord and Hakim later pleaded guilty to reduced charges. Admiral Poindexter went to trial and was sentenced to six months in prison.

one of the worst in my life. An indictment may sound like the end of the process, but it's really just the beginning. Although I should have known better, I just couldn't comprehend how the same government that Admiral Poindexter and I had served for so many years could have given birth to this creature, the Office of the Independent Counsel, which was ruining our lives. We had all hoped for months that it wouldn't come to this, and that fairness and justice would eventually win out. But the criminal investigation, like the hearings, was ultimately about politics.

I had already decided that if I was indicted, I would retire from the Marine Corps. Brendan had made it clear all along that he would do everything within the law to defend me—and that this could well include a subpoena to the President of the United States, as well as any other senior government official whose testimony might be necessary.

That left me no choice. Simply put, I had no intention of being the first serving officer in American history to cause the Commander-in-Chief to appear at a trial of a military officer. I had spent my entire adult life in an institution where the chain of command was an essential discipline, and this was a precedent I didn't want any part of. Not only was it degrading to the presidency, but it could erode or weaken the entire concept of the chain of command.[5]

And so I reluctantly announced my retirement. I cried that night, and so did Betsy, because she knew how much being a Marine had meant to me. It had been my identity every day for close to twenty years, and I had expected it would continue to be true for another ten or fifteen. I got up every morning as a Marine, and came home every night as a Marine. It was hard to imagine being anything else.

---

[5]As things turned out, the President fought having to appear, and the judge refused to compel him to do so.

General Kelley was no longer the commandant, and when word went out that I was leaving the Marine Corps, I could almost hear the collective sigh of relief from some of the higher-ups. My retirement was fast and abrupt; twenty-four hours after I submitted the paperwork, it was approved. Normally it takes weeks to get an appointment for a retirement physical, but I heard from the dispensary the very next morning: "Colonel North, we received your request. We have an opening this afternoon."

Today, I realize that it's not the Marine Corps that I miss. It's being with Marines. I loved getting up in the morning and going off to work with a group of men who were all headed in the same direction. It was a very structured life, but it offered enormous responsibilities and a full measure of adventure. I miss the camaraderie. I miss the hours of hard work in the company of tough, talented, and motivated men. I miss drinking black coffee in the middle of the night. And I miss being part of that society of risk-takers.

Now, for the first time in my life, I didn't have anywhere to go in the morning. The day after my retirement, I woke up as usual at five-thirty, shaved, got dressed—and drove to the offices of Williams & Connolly, where I spent a lot of time over the next few months. While it wasn't exactly like going to Marine headquarters, it wasn't altogether different, either. The lawyers worked like Marines, swore like Marines, and regarded their enemies with about as much compassion. Only instead of using rifles and grenades to defeat their opponents, they apparently intended to work them to death.

But soon the lawyers, too, had to shift to a different battleground. Shortly after the indictments, everyone who was working on my case had to leave the Williams & Connolly building and move to a special suite of offices on Connecticut Avenue. Because the lawyers on both sides and the defendants would have to review tens of thousands of highly classified documents related to the cases, we were all required to work out of a Sensitive Compartmented Information Facility. The SCIF, as it was known, was a suite of offices that were protected by sophisticated monitoring and alarm systems, and shifts of armed guards around the clock.

The SCIF had to be seen to be believed. We all were supposed to wear identification badges. Document control clerks and classified information guards kept track of every document that came in or out. The windows were always closed, and in order to prevent electronic and visual eavesdropping from surrounding buildings, the blinds were always drawn. Although the SCIF occupied most of the fourth floor of a modern office building, it had all the charm of a subway tunnel. We began to refer to ourselves as SCIF rats because we never got to see daylight. The walls were typical government gray, and we decorated them with memorabilia sent in by supporters all over the world: African masks, dolls from the Orient, photographs, and flags. Chris Capozzi, the paralegal in charge of collating and cataloging the documents, took an excerpt from one of my Marine Fitness Report duty station requests and printed it up on a big chart as a reminder of where I would rather be: "assigned to a forward-deployed unit at the edge of the empire, preferably in harm's way."

While this wasn't the edge of the empire, I was certainly in harm's way.

Even so, we had a few laughs. Barry Simon worked out a way to protect our defense strategy by having all our witnesses sign into the SCIF as "Mr. Visitor." And from the start the lawyers tried to keep things on an upbeat note. They even threw a SCIF opening party, where Admiral Poindexter and I were invited to cut the ribbon. The lawyers brought in champagne and—what else? a cake in the shape of a key.

Then we moved in. For more than a year, we ate nearly every lunch and dinner in the SCIF. We ordered in so many Domino's pizzas and Chinese takeout deliveries that Brendan finally arranged for a caterer to deliver a home-style meal one night a week.

We spent hours poring over the tons of material that the prosecutors delivered to the SCIF, including some of the documents I had worked on or written during my five and a half years at the NSC. It took us weeks to go through it all, in part because there was so much of it, but mostly because it was all so thoroughly mixed together.

I had maintained my office files by subject and, within a subject file, by date. And so, for example, all my files on Palestinian terrorist organizations were in one drawer of a safe, arranged in chronological order. But the files delivered to us in the SCIF were so jumbled up that they seemed to have been run through a blender. A 1985 document on the military situation in Afghanistan would be followed by a 1983 analysis of the Sandinista economy.

After several weeks of collating, sorting, and cataloging, I could see that we still didn't have it all. Many documents that I specifically remembered were still missing, along with tape recordings of meetings I had held with the Iranians. "There's more," I kept telling the lawyers. "I *know* there's more."

And indeed there was. Thanks to Barry Simon's tenacity and his constant haranguing, the prosecutors (after months of denial) suddenly found what we had been asking for. They had been working for more than eighteen months, but had apparently forgotten about this stuff. At last, we were allowed to go over to the OEOB. When we entered the room where my files were stored, we found *eighty cartons* of material that had been removed from my office. Astonishingly, no lawyer from the special prosecutor's office had bothered to review this material! Random documents were marked, and some boxes were identified as having been reviewed months earlier by FBI agents. But none of the highly paid lawyers from the enormous prosecution staff had taken the time to look through my files.

Barry, Nicole, John, and I sat there for days, wading through my files and jotting down the control numbers of documents we needed. Here were the tapes and transcripts I had been describing to my lawyers. Here, too, were the so-called Honduras documents, which showed how widespread the administration's support for the contras had been during the period covered by Boland. If I had shredded even half as much as people said, all of this material would have been long gone.

Meanwhile, time was running out. We found these boxes in July 1988, and the trial was scheduled to begin on September 20. The eighty boxes of documents were clearly grounds for a postponement—what lawyers call a continuance. We desperately needed time to review all these documents, and either get them declassified or receive permission from the judge to use them at the trial.

I had another concern about the schedule: if my trial began in late September, it was almost certain to hurt the Republicans in the presidential elections. The Democrats had already made *that* clear: on the opening night of their national convention, two of the principal speakers invoked Iran-contra. The publicity of a trial would only add fuel to that fire. Because the prosecution gets to state its case before the other side can respond, the defense might be forced to remain silent until after Election Day. "A trial at the height of the campaign," Brendan wrote to the judge, "transforms this case even more into an election-year issue at the expense of North's right to a fair and impartial trial."

On August 5, in light of the eighty boxes of new material, Judge Gesell agreed to postpone the trial. It finally began on February 21, 1989.

Those eighty boxes of documents proved to be invaluable to my defense. Among other benefits, they gave us critically needed ammunition to counter one of the special prosecutor's key witnesses: Bud McFarlane.

I have already discussed Bud McFarlane's appearance as a prosecution witness at my trial, where he was even more obtuse than usual. "You don't lie," he told the court at one point. "You put your interpretation on what the truth is." Huh? And when the chief prosecutor asked McFarlane whether his 1985 letter to Congressman Hamilton had been true, Bud replied in classic McFarlanese: "As written, no. In context, I think so, but it's wrong to write it, I agree. I'm wrong."

It was painful to sit there and watch as a man for whom I had once had enormous affection and respect was torn apart. The prosecutors, who had made Bud one of their star witnesses against me, couldn't resist attacking this unfortunate, broken man. They derided him for the letters he wrote at the time of his suicide attempt in early 1987, and even the judge joined the offensive as Bud made further efforts to distance himself from me—and from what he had asked me to do.

Although Bud had already pled guilty to several misdemeanor charges of misleading Congress in 1985 and 1986, and had even been sentenced, he still wouldn't admit that he had tried to cover up his knowledge and approval for what I had done to support the Nicaraguan resistance. Instead, he blew up at the prosecutor. It was after one such explosion on the witness stand that Judge Gesell referred to him as "an intensely unreliable witness."

Bud's testimony hurt me personally, and it hurt my case, too. His testimony about what he knew in 1985 was painful to hear. Brendan's task was to make clear that McFarlane had known about and authorized my actions. He started out by walking Bud through the written record, each step of which was designed to show the jury that Bud had not only known what I was doing, but had approved it, too. Then he had Bud sum up what I had been doing for the resistance—and why.

*Sullivan:* You had asked, indeed you had directed, that Colonel North keep the freedom fighters alive body and soul, correct?

*McFarlane:* Yes.

*Sullivan:* And you transmitted to him the direct order of the President of the United States in 1984 to keep them alive body and soul, correct?

*McFarlane:* Correct.

*Sullivan:* And you not only told him it was your order and your directive, but you told him that it was the President's order and the President's directive that he do what he could to keep them alive body and soul, correct?

*McFarlane:* Yes.

*Sullivan*: And during the period 1984 and 1985, up until the end of 1986, the Congress of the United States was not providing military money to the freedom fighters, were they?

*McFarlane:* No.

*Sullivan:* And the fact is that the mission of keeping them alive was accomplished by Colonel North and others during that period of time, isn't that true?

*McFarlane:* Yes.

*Sullivan:* They stayed alive during the years when Congress had abandoned them, didn't they?

*McFarlane:* Yes.

And a few minutes later:

*Sullivan:* Now, Mr. McFarlane, was the President angry when the Boland Amendment precluded the United States from fulfilling its commitment to the freedom fighters?

*McFarlane:* Yes.

*Sullivan:* Did he express that anger to you?

*McFarlane:* Yes.

*Sullivan:* And did you in turn express the President's anger to Colonel North?

*McFarlane:* Yes.

*Sullivan:* And what was the reason for the anger?

Was it because the United States had broken a promise to these people and had abandoned them?

*McFarlane:* Yes, in part.

*Sullivan:* What was the other part?

*McFarlane:* The President saw the behavior of the Congress, the cutting off of support to be not only breaking faith with people who we encouraged to risk their lives, but he saw an inconsistency between the Congress that could say yes, let's support freedom fighters in Afghanistan 12,000 miles away but let's don't do it right here in our own neighborhood. It didn't track. It was inconsistent.

And still later:

*Sullivan:* Mr. McFarlane, you received literally hundreds of memoranda from Colonel North over the course of the time you worked with him, didn't you?

*McFarlane:* Yes.

*Sullivan:* I dare say that he might have written more memoranda that any staff officer you had, is that correct?

*McFarlane:* It's likely, yes.

*Sullivan:* And I take it that when you carry out your responsibilities as the head of the NSC, that when you get matters of importance, you do read them, or have other staff officers look at them and apprise you of what's in them, correct?

*McFarlane:* Yes.

*Sullivan:* And it is also true, isn't it, that Colonel North, based upon your experience with him over the years, made extraordinary efforts to keep you advised on the work that he was doing in carrying out his assignment, isn't that correct?

*McFarlane:* Yes. Generally, yes.

*Sullivan:* And wouldn't it be fair to say that from your vantage point it may be that Colonel North gave you too much paper rather than too little?

*McFarlane:* Oh, I wanted to be informed.

For me, the entire trial came down to two fundamental issues. The first was that everything I had done was known about and approved by those I had worked for. Even without the testimony of President Reagan or Admiral Poindexter (who had not been granted immunity to testify at my trial), Brendan was able to make this point during his cross-examination of McFarlane. The other major theme was that I hadn't acted with criminal intent. In other words, I had no intention of breaking any laws. In fact, those of us involved in helping the resistance went to great lengths to avoid violating the Boland Amendment or any other statute.

On this question of criminal intent, the prosecutors based much of their argument on the testimony of Spitz Channell. During the trial, Channell told a story that he had related several times before: that in September 1985, he had chartered a plane to bring me to Dallas, Texas, for a dinner with Bunker Hunt, the well-known oil man and silver magnate. Channell hoped that Hunt would make another contribution to NEPL on behalf of the contras, and he had brought me down to describe the situation in Central America and the needs of the resistance. After dinner at the Petroleum Club, Hunt, Channell, and I had chatted while Channell's assistant went to find a cab to take me back to the airport.

But in describing this scene at my trial, Channell added an extraordinary new wrinkle: a conversation between Bunker Hunt and me, which, he now said, "just stuck in my mind." As Channell described it, Hunt had asked me, "What are you going to do? Do you mind getting in trouble for this?" To which I had supposedly responded, "No, I don't care if I have to go to jail for this, and I don't care if I have to lie to Congress about this."

Brendan had consistently told me not to show any reaction to other people's testimony, no matter how bizarre it was. But when Channell told this story, I just couldn't help myself, and I looked up at him in astonishment. The conversation he had just described clearly implied that I thought what I was doing might be criminal. Had it actually occurred, I would have been in real trouble.

But this conversation never happened. I knew it, Channell knew it, and Sullivan knew it. If the prosecutors didn't know it, for several reasons, they surely should have.

In any event, they certainly appeared delighted to have this new version from Channell as "evidence" of my criminal intent. For the past two years, the poor guy had been living with the prospect of jail hanging over his head. *But his actual sentence would not be determined until the prosecution evaluated the degree of his cooperation.*

When Channell came up with this new anecdote, Brendan saw it not as a problem, but an opportunity. In Brendan's view, if the prosecutors were willing to put on such testimony in order to "get" his client, he would expose the lie.

Why did Brendan believe so strongly that Channell was lying? For one thing, the prosecution had not listed Bunker Hunt as one of their witnesses, which presumably meant that Hunt couldn't corroborate Channell's story. But then, Channell couldn't even corroborate his *own* story. He had spent scores of hours in hearings, interviews, depositions, and in front of the grand jury, but not until much later, when the "deal" he would get depended on his testimony, did he mention this alleged conversation between Hunt and me about lying to Congress or going to jail.

Unfortunately, Brendan couldn't simply jump up and point out the inconsistencies in Channell's stories. He had to wait for the cross-examination, when he would have the opportunity to show why Channell's testimony was unreliable. During the break, the lawyers tore through the box containing the transcripts of Channell's previous testimony and quickly pulled out the pages that would show how this poor, intimidated man, threatened with jail, had finally succumbed to the pressure. As we walked back in, Brendan turned to me and said, "We've got 'em."

What followed was Sullivan at his finest. He started out by gently leading Channell back through the testimony he had just given. In the process, he pressed Channell on whether or not he had intended to commit a crime. No, Channell said, he hadn't. The prosecution had basically convinced him to plead guilty to what had never before been criminal: conspiracy to use a tax-exempt organization to support the Nicaraguan resistance.

Then Brendan reminded Channell of his many previous versions of the Bunker Hunt meeting, which had included no mention of this alleged conversation with Bunker Hunt. As Sullivan began reviewing Channell's previous testimony about that evening in Dallas four years before, he confronted Channell with the fact that his testimony had changed dramatically. After Brendan pointed out several inconsistencies in Channell's testimony, the judge intervened:

*The Court:* And how do you explain that you told the jury that this [conversation between Hunt and North] stuck in your mind and you had no doubt about it?
*Channell:* Because it has, and it was very interesting how long—
*The Court:* You've now got three versions already.
*Channell:* It has —
*The Court:* What stuck in your mind when you told the jury it stuck in your mind?
*Channell:* That Colonel North said what he did relating to these two questions, and it just stuck.

And now Brendan moved in for the kill:

*Sullivan:* What it points out, sir, is it is hard to remember what was said. It's hard.

*Channell:* Well, I understand that.

*Sullivan:* And this is important. And sometimes when you have such an urge to cooperate, there is a little danger that you might put words in somebody's mouth that really don't belong [there]? Is that fair to say?

*Channell:* Well, I'm sure there is that temptation, of course.

A moment later, after chastising poor Channell again, the judge turned to the jury and said, "My instructions are the same to you, ladies and gentlemen of the jury, as to each and every statement that has been pointed out. You may consider them in connection with your appraisal of the credibility of this witness."

In effect, the judge himself was advising the jury that Spitz Channell's testimony could not be trusted. We could only hope that the jury would be able to do what the judge had instructed. But the effect on the prosecution was visible. For them it was like a punch in the stomach—not a knockout, but enough to badly damage their argument about criminal intent.

By the time I finally took the stand it was almost anticlimactic. For me, this was "Hearings II—The Sequel." Only now, instead of looking up at congressmen, senators, and their aides, I was facing the special prosecutors. Judge Gesell was on my left, and the jury members sat in the jury box on my right.

Betsy was sitting in the first row behind the rail. Whenever I looked over at her she would smile, and each time we came back from a break she said, "I'm praying for you. It will be all right."

The courtroom looks different from the witness stand than it does from the defense table, and I was struck by the contrast in bedside manner between the chief prosecutor and Brendan. My antagonist tended to strut about and posture in front of the jury, much like the courtroom lawyers in the movies and on television. Brendan was more subdued and less affected as he leaned on the podium below the judge's bench.

During my cross-examination, the prosecutor would begin each session with "Good morning" or "Good afternoon." But I just couldn't bring myself to wish him the same. I really *didn't* want him to have a good morning or a good afternoon, and only a moment earlier I had taken an oath to tell the truth.

For some observers, the most dramatic point in a trial occurs when the defendant takes the stand. For me, however, the climax occurred during the closing arguments. The prosecutor closes first, as he tries to show that he has already proven beyond a reasonable doubt that the defendant is guilty. Then comes the defense counsel, who tries to demonstrate just the opposite.

These prosecutors claimed that they made no use of my testimony at the hearings, and that they hadn't watched it or even read about it. But oddly enough, the trial ended on the same sordid note as the hearings. In the Senate Caucus Room, Senator Inouye had ended his final remarks by comparing me to the Nazi war criminals at Nuremberg. At the trial, the chief prosecutor invoked the name of Hitler to describe what I had done. I'm not entirely sure what to make of these comments, but they certainly went far beyond the bounds of reason and civility. They remind me of the old Soviet mentality, where anyone opposed to any element of the state's domestic or foreign policy was immediately branded a "fascist."

Brendan was outraged by the prosecutor's effort to link me in the jurors' minds with Adolf Hitler, and I remember wondering what my father, who had gone to war to fight the Nazis, would have thought of that reference. "These people will stop at nothing," Brendan said.

Listening to Brendan's close was like watching a master carpenter putting the final touches on a beautiful house that he had been working on for months. Addressing the twelve individuals who would be deciding my fate, he carefully summarized all that they had seen and heard during the trial. He described my Marine Corps career, and my work on sensitive projects at the White House. He reminded the jury that there was ample proof that the people I had worked for had approved what I had done. Although I hadn't been able to articulate it well, Brendan was able to capture and describe my feelings of being abandoned by former colleagues and higher-ups.

He recalled the terrorist threats to my family, and pointed out how the lives of others had depended on what I had or hadn't done. He pointed out that criminal intent had never entered my mind. And in the end, he urged these twelve citizens to consider carefully whether or not they could convict me beyond any reasonable doubt.

By the time he was finished I was utterly drained. I remember almost nothing of the prosecutor's rebuttal, the judge's instructions to the jury, or the flurry of final motions that are so essential to a defendant. Now it was just a matter of waiting for the verdict.

With the understanding that we would return to court the moment a verdict was in, the judge had granted Brendan's request that we be allowed to wait at the law firm. That was a big relief, although it also meant that reporters and camera teams took up day-long watches at the courthouse, outside the Williams & Connolly building, and in front of our home. Brian Cox and the men from our Bible study group came by several times for lunch and prayer, and Betsy joined us when she could. Each afternoon, when the jury recessed for the day, I was able to go home and have dinner with the family.

The jury deliberated for more than eleven days. Early on the afternoon of May 14, Judge Gesell's clerk called Brendan to say, "We have a verdict." I was on my way out to meet Betsy for lunch at the nearby Army & Navy Club when one of the security agents gave me the news. Brendan had Betsy paged, and a few minutes later she joined us in Brendan's office.

As the reporters yelled out questions, we piled into the waiting van for the now-familiar trip to the courthouse. On the way over, Brendan said, "Remember, if it doesn't go our way on all counts, there will be an appeal."

As we entered the courthouse, Betsy spotted David Harper, our pastor, trying to make his way through the horde of reporters. She prevailed on Jerry Dimenna, the head of our security team, to get David into the courtroom. Once we were inside, Betsy and I stood together holding hands, and David said a quiet prayer with us. Then, glancing over at the defense table, David asked me to bring over the well-worn Bible I had brought with me to court each day.

This Bible had been around. Morton Blackwell in the White House Public Liaison Office had given it to me shortly after I arrived at the NSC, and I had carried it with me ever since. I took it with me everywhere—including Tehran.

Before I returned to my seat, David opened the Bible to Psalm Ninety-one and handed it to me. As we waited for the jury to come in, I sat there and read:

> Surely He will save you from the fowler's snare
> and from the deadly pestilence.
> He will cover you with His feathers,
> and under His wings you will find refuge;
> His faithfulness will be your shield and rampart.

Meanwhile, in the hallway outside the courtroom, all order broke down as the crowd of reporters tried to surge through the metal detectors and security that the federal marshals had set up for this trial.

It was shortly before two-thirty when the jury came in. I looked at their faces, but it was impossible to know what they had decided or what they had been through. The foreperson handed the verdict form to the bailiff, who gave it to the judge.

The room was silent while the judge read the jury's decision. After what seemed like a long delay, he started to read in a steady monotone, like the roll of a drum on some faraway parade field:

"As to count one, the verdict is not guilty," (Thank you, Lord) "both of the substantive count and aiding and abetting.

"As to count two, the verdict is not guilty," (Thank you, Lord) "of the substantive count and of aiding and abetting.

"On count three the verdict is not guilty" (Thank you) "as to the substantive count and not guilty" (Thank you) "as to aiding and abetting.

"As to count four the verdict is not guilty" (Thank you) "as to the substantive count and not guilty" (Thank you) "as to aiding and abetting.

"As to count five the verdict is not guilty." (Thank you.)

"As to count six, the verdict is not guilty" (Thank you) "of the substantive count, guilty" (Oh God, *why?*) "of aiding and abetting."

Later on, I was told that these words from the judge had been punctuated by a gasp from somewhere in the court. If so, I didn't hear it, and it did nothing to slow the judge's steady rhythm:

"As to count seven, the verdict is not guilty" (Thank you) "of the substantive count, and not guilty" (Thank you) "of aiding and abetting."

"As to count eight, the verdict is not guilty." (Thank you.)

"As to count nine, the verdict is guilty." (Oh God, not another one!)

"As to count ten, the verdict is guilty." (Lord, no more, please!)

"As to count eleven, the verdict is not guilty." (Thank you, Lord.)

"As to count twelve, the verdict is not guilty." (Thank you, Lord.)

The judge's reading of the verdict lasted little more than a minute. It seemed like hours. I was stunned, elated, crushed, and happy all at once.

The judge had said "not guilty" thirteen times and "guilty" three times. But there were only twelve counts, and for a moment I couldn't remember which ones were which. While I sat there trying to figure it out, a stampede of reporters raced for the door while Judge Gesell and the lawyers calmly took care of the final procedural obligations.

By the time they finished and the courtroom was quiet again, I had figured out what the three remaining charges were: helping to obstruct Congress, something about destroying, altering, or removing documents, and accepting the security system. And then it was over.

As the judge walked out, the courtroom again became chaotic. I walked over to Betsy and hugged her. I embraced David Harper, and shook hands with Brendan, Nicole, Barry, Terry, and John. Congressman Henry Hyde gave me a bear hug and turned to reassure Betsy.

The prosecutors left their minions behind to pack up their papers, and rushed out to the dozens of waiting microphones. As I returned to the table to retrieve my briefcase, Brendan came up behind me and gave me a pat on the back. "Let's go," he said. "It's not over yet. We're going to fight this until you are free of it *all*. Remember, you walked into this courtroom with sixteen counts against you. You went to trial on twelve, and now we're down to three. We're headed in the right direction. Come on, let's get on with the appeal. And by the way, are you having fun yet?"

On the way back to Williams & Connolly, Brendan had decided that when we arrived, he and I would each give a brief statement as a way of dealing with the horde of reporters who would be camped outside the office. Both our comments turned out to be prescient. Brendan ended his statement by saying, "You can be assured that we will never abandon Colonel North and his family in this legal battle." And they didn't.

I said, "We now face many months, perhaps years, fighting these remaining charges. [Little did I know!] Nevertheless, we are absolutely confident of the final outcome. As a Marine, I was taught to fight, and fight hard, for as long as it takes to prevail. We will continue this battle, and with the support and prayers of the American people, I will be fully vindicated."

I didn't know it at the time, but vindication would be long in coming. Brendan had already announced that there would be an appeal, and throughout the case the lawyers had carefully noted each legal issue that might later prove relevant.

One particularly sensitive point had to do with the jury. During the trial, we had all heard murmurings that I was being judged by other than a jury of my peers. Some people argued that Sullivan should have made an issue of the fact that I was a white, male, college graduate who had served in the military, had traveled extensively, and had worked in the upper echelons of government; that my background was radically different from that of the all-black, mostly female jury.

At the time, I didn't give this much thought. But a year later, in the summer of 1990, a member of the jury that convicted me was interviewed on television, and what she said came as a shock: "What were people going to think on the outside if we found him not guilty? Okay, what were they going to think of us being as blacks, finding a white man not guilty? They're really going to think that we're stupid."

I was stunned. Justice is supposed to be blind; the color of a person's skin should not determine their guilt or innocence. To this day, I don't quite know what to make of the juror's statement, which goes against everything I have ever learned and believed.

\*　\*　\*

Patience was never my strong suit, but mine would be sorely tested over the next seven weeks as the judge collected information to use in determining my sentence. While we waited, Stuart graduated from high school and I tried to resume a more normal family life while working with Brendan to prepare a presentencing report, which would outline all the reasons why the judge shouldn't send me to jail.

I was assigned a probation officer, Ralph Ardito, whose task was to act as my warden during this period and to make a recommendation to the judge as to my sentence. At first I was wary of him; I assumed he was another member of the prosecution that had been arrayed against me for so long. But I soon learned that Ardito was a real professional. He was charged with a difficult task, and he carried it out with great compassion and sensitivity.

As the day of sentencing approached, Brendan's office was besieged with calls and offers of help. People I had known well and men I had served with sent letters to the judge, asking for leniency. Some of the most moving letters were from Marines I had served with in Vietnam, most of whom I hadn't seen in twenty years

On the Fourth of July, the day before the sentencing, our family enjoyed a quiet picnic with a group of our neighbors. Afterwards, we went to watch the fireworks at the Great Falls firehouse. It was a wonderful day: we swam, played, and talked until after sunset. I didn't want it to end.

The next morning, I got up even earlier than usual and read from the Bible. As Betsy and I drove into Washington, we didn't know whether or not we would be riding home together after court. As always, the reporters and cameras followed us every step of the way. The Lone Ranger had Tonto, his faithful Indian companion. I had the press.

As we walked toward Courtroom Six, one of the reporters ran along beside me.

"You look awfully calm for a man on his way in to be sentenced," he said.

"That's because I know where I'm going," I replied. I was thinking in terms of a far larger context.

He looked astonished. "You do?  How many years are you going to get?" he asked.

"Eternity," I replied. He looked totally confused. He obviously had in mind a very different kind of sentence.

And so did the special prosecutor. He pleaded with the judge to send me to prison. And he wasn't alone, either. The *New York Times* editorialized in favor of a lengthy prison term. And people wonder why I don't like the press.

The sentencing hearing was as much of an emotional roller coaster as the day the verdict was announced. Hearing somebody argue in a court of law that you deserve to go to prison is an awful experience. But there was also Brendan's eloquent plea for the judge's compassion. Drawing heavily from letters he had received, interviews he had conducted, and everything he had learned about me, Brendan took almost a full hour to explain to the judge why I should remain free. He began with my military career and moved on to more contemporary events:

In December 1986 he was named the primary target in the named request for an independent counsel. He became the target of the longest, largest, independent counsel and grand jury investigation in the history of our country....

Throughout the two and a half year period [since the firing] he and his family have been subjected to the greatest and the most intrusive media interest perhaps of any citizen except a sitting President. The media generated literally tens of thousands of articles and op-ed pieces to which he cannot respond.... For months at a time the press camped outside his home and followed him to work and to the store and to church and to the city dump. At no time has he given an interview about the case, respecting counsel's advice that that's not the proper way in litigation. He and his family have also been plagued by the unauthorized books that purport to tell in intimate detail the story of his and his wife's life, his children's lives. They've been subjected to an offensive fictionalized TV mini-series without authority, without interviews, without permission. Just like he's some commodity that people use....

North has been likened to Adolf Hitler, the worst criminal and mass murderer who ever lived....

His family has felt the extraordinary impact. The assassination threat has not abated. It's been exacerbated by the world-wide publicity caused by one branch of our government.

Colonel North didn't ask to become known throughout America. He was thrust upon the TV of every person in the country.

The threat eats away at a person like a cancer. It's always there. It's always haunting. You don't know whether it will never happen or something will happen next month.

Maybe most of all, the thing that I've heard no one say is, what is his loss as a result of all of this? It's loss of peace of mind. We all go out to the car and we go to work and we don't think for a minute that we'll be assaulted on the way, much less killed. The loss of peace of mind—what a burden. It's an extraordinary punishment which he'll carry with him today and into the foreseeable future, which should be weighed when the court determines today what the appropriate sentence is.

What must it be like to wonder about these things? To wonder whether some group that doesn't think logically wants to even the score with America by getting Ollie North, or just some deranged person who wants to get on the front page of the newspaper by attacking North.

He's suffered enough. His family has suffered enough. He's been punished enough. A prison term on top of that would be fundamentally too harsh, wrong. It's a time for forgiveness. It's a time to say it's over."

And it almost was. The judge handed down a three-year suspended sentence, fined me a hundred and fifty thousand dollars, and assigned me to two years of probation and twelve hundred hours of community service in an inner-city drug-prevention program.

There were several points in Brendan's remarks when I had to choke back tears as I listened to him describe my life. Even so, Brendan didn't use everything. He didn't mention the call I had received late one night from Billy Graham, or the supportive letters from former President Nixon. Nor did he mention three laudatory letters I had received from President Reagan while I was working at the NSC—which he hadn't known about. They turned up two years after the trial, when we were moving to a new house. When I brought them in to show Brendan, he went bonkers.

By far the most interesting piece of evidence that Brendan didn't use was what we called the "smoking gun in the closet" tape. (The title comes from a deliciously mixed metaphor that appears in the first line of the transcript.) This tape was supposed to be nothing more than a routinely recorded telephone conversation between employees in two different Manhattan offices of New York's Citibank on June 17, 1987, about three weeks before I testified at the congressional hearings. But in a coincidence that is almost too bizarre to believe, leaking through the conversation between the two bank employees was a second dialogue between two men on the subject of the Iran-contra hearings. From their discussion, it's clear that one of these men had already appeared before the congressional committee.

The bank gave the tape to the FBI, and the following summer, Barry Simon found it in a pile of potential evidence that was finally provided to us by the prosecution. Although most of the conversation between the two men was remarkably clear, we were never able to determine who they were. But there was no doubt as to what they were discussing:

*A:* Yeah, there's a smoking gun in the closet. Reagan knows.

*B:* Listen…

*A:* I told the committee. There was no, I told the committee there was, I had nothing to do with those papers. Ollie North knows about it. Reagan knows…Reagan knows about it—

*B:* Listen, he ain't testifying.

*A:*—and the…and the other—the other people involved do know about that.

*B:* [Unintelligible.]

*A:* Well, you have to go to the Committee.

*B:* [Unintelligible]…the Committee.

*A:* You have to go to the Committee, not me.

*B:* Listen…

*A:* Somebody's got to bring this up.

*B:* [Unintelligible.]

*A:* I think somebody ought to go, somebody's got to be responsible for this.

*B:* [Unintelligible.]

*A:* Reagan…Reagan knows. Reagan has all the memos.

*B:* He's got all the memos? I thought he tore all that stuff up.

*A:* No. He's got all the memos, and there are copies.

*B:* Didn't you burn that stuff?

*A:* No.

*B:* Oh, jeez. I warned you about that.

*A:* Nobody…no…

*B:* It's going to hit the papers like crazy.

*A:* Nobody told me to.

*B:* [Unintelligible.]

*A:* [Unintelligible.] No.

*B:* What about your secretary? She couldn't get the stuff copied?

*A:* Not all of it.

*B:* [Unintelligible] about Reagan [unintelligible.]

*A:* Well…I'm getting out of this thing, and if somebody comes to me, I'm blowing the cover.

*B:* I'll tell you, if I go down, I'm taking you with me.

*A:* Well, me too.

*B:* You and your…secretary…[unintelligible.]

*A:* I'd better call you back. I think we're tapped.

*B:* I think so.

*A:* All right. 'Bye.

When he first heard the tape during preparations for the trial, Barry was flabbergasted. "Listen to this!" he called out, and we all gathered in the SCIF conference room to hear it. Barry played it over and over to see if I could possibly identify the voices. Two of my lawyers wondered whether one of the men was Don Regan, but that struck me as unlikely: it just didn't sound like him. Regan would have come across as more arrogant, whereas these men were clearly anxious. My own guess was that one of the participants was Ed Hickey, the President's military aide, who has since passed away. Hickey was interviewed around this time by the committee, and he had been involved, along with me, in a hostage rescue attempt by the Drug Enforcement Agency that was funded with profits from the Iran arms sale.

But that's just a guess. Whoever these men were, it was clear that somebody was in possession of important documents, some of which had been destroyed. But what? And how, exactly, did all this fit into the Iran-contra story?

When I was unable to identify the voices, my attorneys took the tape to the White House. On July 28, 1988, Brendan and Barry went to the White House to meet with Arthur B. Culvahouse, the President's counsel, and one of his aides to seek access to documents and to ask for an interview with the President. They took the tape along.

As Barry described it later, Culvahouse blanched when he heard the tape, and his aide appeared visibly shaken. Both men denied any knowledge of it, and as far as they knew, no other government agency had been asked about it either. And yet the special prosecutors had received this tape months earlier.

Well, said Brendan, would you help us get to the bottom of this and let us interview the President about it?

Culvahouse told Brendan he'd think about it. Two months later the answer came back: no.

Apparently the special prosecutor's zeal in pursuing John Poindexter and me did not extend to finding out who was on that tape, or what documents they were discussing. Nobody at the White House, the FBI, or the special prosecutor's office was interested in helping us. And it's safe to assume that nobody on the congressional committee heard this tape, either. If they had, it surely would have leaked.

Without being able to identify the voices, we were not able to use the tape in court. The special prosecutor might never have given it to us except that he was required to do so under the rules of evidence. But neither they, the FBI, nor the White House ever revealed its existence.

# 18

## LOOKING BACK

ACCORDING TO THE CONVENTIONAL WISDOM, IRAN-CON-
tra occurred because a small group of misfits and rene-
gades, working out of the White House basement, rose
above the law and carried out their own foreign policy,
whereupon their superiors where shocked—*shocked*—to
learn what they had done.

It makes for a good story, but that's not what happened. As I see it, the causes of Iran-contra lie in several
directions, with plenty of blame to go around.

I have already described my own mistakes, regrets,
and lapses in judgment. But I never saw myself as being
above the law, nor did I ever intend to do anything illegal. The argument over the meaning and constitutional
legitimacy of the Boland Amendments will continue for
years, but I have always believed, and still do, that these
amendments did not bar the National Security Council
from supporting the contras. Even the most stringent of
the Boland Amendments contained clear and substantial
loopholes which we used to ensure that the Nicaraguan
resistance would not be abandoned.

From 1984 on, I did my best to keep faith with two

groups whom I cared about deeply, and whose fate President Reagan had put at the top of his agenda: our hostages in Lebanon and the contras. While I worked frantically on behalf of both groups, I can see now that I was also motivated by my own pride and ambition. No matter how difficult or demanding the job was, I was sure I could handle it. I knew that if these missions were successful, only a very small handful of people would ever know what I had achieved. Paradoxically, I took pride in that, too.

I still have conflicting feelings about the Iran initiative. It ended in failure, but that's not to say it wasn't worth trying. Had we succeeded, not only would all the hostages have come home, but we would have opened a new relationship with a country that is still important to our national security.

But we didn't succeed. Not only were we unable to establish a connection to the moderates in Iran, but we also undermined a valid and well-established policy of not making concessions to terrorists. Although we didn't deal directly with the terrorists in Beirut, the perception that we did was so widespread that it almost didn't matter. And while we did rescue three of the hostages, two other Americans were seized. Moreover, our contacts with Iran ultimately caused great political damage and embarrassment to the United States, and especially to President Reagan.

While I recognize the liabilities of the Iran initiative, I continue to feel that saving a life—or trying to—is even more important than preserving a policy. Earlier, we condemned several European governments for making that same choice with regard to *their* hostages in Beirut, but in the end we did the same thing. However unwise our actions may have been in retrospect, I'm glad that I live in a country where the protection of human life can still outweigh the grand designs of government.

Our Nicaraguan initiative was more straightforward, and for me, at least, presented no great moral quandary.

Until Congress decided to resume its funding for the contras, we succeeded in fulfilling the mission assigned by the President: to keep the resistance alive, body and soul. Our goal was not military but political: to enable the contras to exert the kind of pressure on the Sandinistas that could ultimately lead to a free and democratic Nicaragua. Early in 1990, our efforts were vindicated when a coalition of anti-Sandinista groups, led by Violeta Chamorro, scored a decisive electoral victory over Daniel Ortega and the Sandinistas.

"Set your watches," Mrs. Chamorro had told her audiences. "Set them to the same hour as Poland, Bulgaria, and Czechoslovakia. Set them to the same hour as Chile, because this is the time of democracy and freedom."

These were lofty sentiments, but almost nobody in the United States thought she could win. And despite everything I knew and believed, I didn't either. I had begun to accept the views of the media experts who pontificated at length about the inevitable Ortega triumph.

But I underestimated the power of the secret ballot. That divine spark of liberty that exists in all of us made the difference in Nicaragua, just as it did in Berlin, Poland, Romania, and so many other places. Although I believed fervently in Ronald Reagan's messages of freedom and democracy that we had broadcast to the world, and had even helped draft some of them, I obviously missed the full magnitude of their impact.

With this global shift toward liberty, Ronald Reagan's presidency should have ended on a great victorious crescendo. But the aftermath of the Iran and contra initiatives distorted the real impact of his presidency. Brendan Sullivan had forecast this outcome when he wrote to President Reagan, urging him to pardon me, Admiral Poindexter, Joe Fernandez, and others involved in these initiatives. Brendan's letter was signed by the lawyers representing the government officials indicted in the controversy and hand-carried to the President. This letter, reprinted for the first time in the Appendix, was never acknowledged.

Brendan's assessment was correct—the controversy continues to this day. But while some of the blame goes to me, not all of it can be ascribed to those of us who carried out these policies.

Congress, too, bears some responsibility for what happened. Its vacillating support for the contras not only endangered their lives, but also broke faith with our nation's commitments.

As we've seen, both the special prosecutor and the hearings became ways for Congress to criminalize legitimate policy differences between coequal branches of government. But why were those differences so great to begin with? And aren't there *always* policy differences between the executive and legislative branches?

Yes—but rarely to the extent we saw during the Reagan years. What happened in Washington in the 1980s was the result of changes in both the legislative and executive branches during the preceding two or three decades. Ever since Lyndon Johnson's landslide victory over Barry Goldwater, which was followed four years later by the highly contentious 1968 Democratic National Convention in Chicago, the leadership of the Democratic Party has been moving steadily to the left. These days, when the reelection of Capitol Hill incumbents is now virtually guaranteed, House members and senators have become more beholden to their party's leadership than to the voters they ostensibly represent. This helps to explain why many have drifted so far from the center of the political spectrum.

As Congress was inching to the left, the American body politic reacted in 1980 by electing a true conservative to the White House. But unlike the slow and gradual permutation on Capitol Hill, the shift in ideology when Ronald Reagan came to the White House was both enormous and abrupt. Suddenly, the traditional adversarial relationship between the President and

Congress became more intense than it had in many years. And Nicaragua became the battlefield.

More than any of his recent predecessors, President Reagan came into office with clear philosophical goals. He favored less government and lower taxes, and he believed that private enterprise should replace the public sector in providing opportunities for the American people.

And in case his domestic vision wasn't shocking enough for the Democratic majority in Congress, Reagan wanted these same principles to be reflected in our *foreign* policy, too. He insisted that American foreign policy should exhibit the revolutionary and anti-tyrannical ideals of our forefathers. In practical terms, this meant that the United States would go beyond mere "containment" and would actively support anti-Communist resistance movements in Angola, Cambodia, Afghanistan, and Nicaragua. The Reagan doctrine not only traumatized the Congress; it also stunned large sectors of Washington's permanent bureaucracy.

This was, after all, a sea change in our international posture. Since 1945, Communism had prevailed just about everywhere it had tried its hand. But Ronald Reagan and Bill Casey insisted that if we could help an indigenous anti-Communist resistance movement inflict a single major defeat, the entire Communist house of cards would come tumbling down. After the invasion of Afghanistan, the Soviet empire was stretched so thin that Moscow simply couldn't afford to continue supporting all its proxies.

For the congressional Democrats, the first two years of the Reagan administration were an unmitigated disaster. After a long string of defeats on domestic policy issues, they focused their attention on Central America—one of the few areas where the President was vulnerable. Pointing to our long and shameful history of backing Latin American regimes with abysmal human rights records, they portrayed our policy of backing the contras as simply more of the same. Here they had some success, which culminated in the various Boland Amendments, each of which whittled away at our support for the Nicaraguan resistance.

Despite all my disagreements with the congressional Democrats, I find it hard to believe that most of them really wanted to see a Communist toehold on the mainland of our hemisphere. But they were willing to try almost anything in their fight against Ronald Reagan. In the process, they put the final nail in the coffin of Sam Rayburn's famous dictum that politics stops at the water's edge.

President Reagan, too, must accept some of the blame for what happened. Ironically, his greatest strength was also his primary weakness. He always focused on the big picture, and he knew exactly what direction he wanted to go. But in the process he neglected the details. He knew where he wanted to end up, but he didn't guide how he got there.

Later, when the whole thing blew up in his face, President Reagan claimed to accept responsibility for Iran-contra. But his professions rang hollow as he evaded real responsibility for what had happened by claiming that he just didn't know. It was a weak defense, and it reflected badly on him and his presidency.


Some commentators have tried to argue that Iran-contra occurred because the executive branch carried out both of these operations in secret. But some secrecy is essential in foreign policy. The problem isn't secrecy; it's how to protect actions that cannot be publicly disclosed without cutting Congress out of the loop.

After all, the Constitution reserves for Congress the right to advise and consent. As I see it, the Founding Fathers intended to follow the biblical precept that in the counsel of many there is wisdom. But the current system of five large committees (including two intelligence committees) in the House and Senate, each with dozens of staffers, overseeing American foreign policy is simply too unwieldy. Protecting secrets has become more difficult than ever, which discourages the executive branch from revealing important information. We have gone from the counsel of many to the counsel of *too* many.

There is an alternative. We know from other operations, such as the Manhattan Project during World War II, and the subsequent building of our nuclear arsenal, that Congress *can* keep secrets if the relevant committees are small enough. In the case of intelligence operations, we would be better off with a *very* small joint committee of perhaps five members, consisting of, say, three House members and two from the Senate, with both parties represented. This body would have an equally small professional staff.

Another lesson to be learned from Iran-contra is that the team of advisers around the President would more effectively serve him and the nation if it included members of Congress. In the past, presidents usually found a way to work with congressional leaders from both parties, but in the adversarial atmosphere of Washington in the 1980s, that just wasn't possible.

And what of America's role in the larger world? The threat of imperial Communism has collapsed with the Soviet Union. But we still don't live in a world of our own making. The resurgence of regional and ethnic nationalism everywhere from the Balkans to Quebec presents a host of new foreign policy challenges. While the broad threat of international terrorism seems to have diminished, at least for the moment, there are still leaders like Muammar Qaddafi and Saddam Hussein who offer havens and support for its perpetrators. And although his days are undoubtedly numbered, Fidel Castro continues to advocate the export of revolutionary Marxism.

The world must also grapple with the rise of radical Islamic fundamentalism, which is unalterably opposed to the values of individual liberty, religious freedom, and democracy that we cherish. With the twentieth century drawing to a close, Islamic fundamentalism poses serious threats to a number of nations: Saudi Arabia, Egypt, Sudan, Algeria, the Philippines, Indonesia, Pakistan, and even India. As one of the Iranian officials reminded us during our visit to Tehran, "The Ayatollah's picture is in all of these places, and we didn't mail it there."

Although the world we live in is now much smaller, this doesn't diminish the role the United States will have to play. But we must abandon our old tendency to support the status quo. In the past, this willingness to "deal with the devil I know" has only encouraged the very revolutions we hoped to avoid. For years we tolerated and supported repressive, right-wing, extremist regimes in places like Cuba, Nicaragua, Panama, Vietnam, and the Philippines, merely because they were anti-Communist. Some of the leaders who were advocates of change in these countries, including Fidel Castro and Ho Chi Minh, had come to us first but were rebuffed. We shouldn't have been surprised that they turned to the Soviet Union for help.

With our history and our values, the United States should never have allowed revolution and change to become the exclusive domain of the left. The ideals of our own revolution—freedom, tolerance, and individual liberty—were inspiring two centuries ago. They still are.

# POSTSCRIPT

BRENDAN AND HIS TEAM KEPT UP THE BATTLE AFTER THE trial—right to the end of this long ordeal. On July 20, 1990, a three-judge panel of the U.S. Court of Appeals reversed one of the three outstanding counts against me and vacated the other two. If the special prosecutor still wanted to convict me, he would have to show the judge that none of my immunized congressional testimony had been used against me by the grand jury that indicted me, or by the trial jury that later convicted me.

The special prosecutor chose to appeal this decision by asking the entire appeals court to reverse its own three-judge panel. On November 27, 1990, the Court of Appeals again decided in my favor by upholding the panel's decision. As a result of the *en banc* ruling, the Marine Corps restored my pension and I recovered something even more precious: my right to vote.

I had hoped the story would end here, but it was not to be. Lawrence Walsh, the special prosecutor, decided to take his appeal to the Supreme Court. On May 28, 1991, the Supreme Court reaffirmed the two earlier appeals court decisions by announcing that it would not hear the special prosecutor's appeal.

Although Walsh had assured Brendan that he would drop the case if he lost in the Supreme Court, he changed his mind. Instead, he apparently intended to start all over again. On September 11, 1991, only six weeks before this book was due to go on sale, we returned to court for an extraordinary session. The first—and only—witness was Bud McFarlane. The prosecution had obviously expected Bud to explain that his testimony at my trial had been unaffected by my congressional testimony. But the more the prosecutor pressed McFarlane on this point, the more Bud insisted that he had been immersed in watching my appearance at the hearings: "This was very explosive testimony," he said. "Tens of millions of Americans were blown away by it.... In watching four days of riveting testimony by a man who was like a son to me, how could I *not* have been affected?"

Clearly stunned by Bud's emotional outburst, the prosecutors finally conceded that their case had collapsed.

It ended very much as it had begun. On November 23, 1986, when Ed Meese and his assistants had shown me the "diversion" memo that marked the start of my legal problems, the Washington Redskins had been playing the Dallas Cowboys at RFK Stadium. The ending of my case took place under remarkably similar circumstances. On Sunday, September 15, 1991, I was listening to a Redskins game against the Phoenix Cardinals when Brendan called me at home with the wonderful news that Lawrence Walsh had decided to drop the two remaining charges. It was finally over.

The following morning, my family and my lawyers accompanied me to court for my last day as a defendant. The long ordeal that had begun nearly five years earlier in a White House press conference came to an abrupt but welcome end in less than ten minutes. Judge Gesell signed a two-line order granting the prosecutor's motion to dismiss and said, simply, "This terminates the case."

From the very beginning, Brendan had insisted that my compelled public testimony to Congress made it impossible for the prosecution to proceed. And now, five years after it all began, Walsh finally admitted that Brendan was right.

As I left the courthouse, Betsy, Sarah, and Dornin joined me on the steps. As usual, reporters were waiting. But this time I spoke to them:

"For nearly five years, my family and I have been under fire. Throughout this time we have been blessed to be supported by the finest attorneys in America, and by the generosity and prayers of the American people, and that is what has sustained us through this ordeal. Without this support and encouragement, we could not have prevailed."

And I meant it, with all my heart.

As for the other members of our cast:

Elliott Abrams, who had chaired the small, secret interagency group that had reviewed the activities of the Nicaraguan resistance, left government in 1988 to become a consultant. In October 1991 he pleaded guilty to withholding from Congress his knowledge of my activities in support of the contras.

Charles Allen, with whom I had worked on counter-terrorism, is still at the CIA. But rather than being rewarded for his hard work, he was passed over for promotion because he was too candid with his superiors with regard to the Iran initiative.

The Australian is apparently still a government official in Tehran.

Congressman Michael Barnes was defeated in his bid for a U.S. Senate seat in 1986.

Enrique Bermudez, the military commander of the Nicaraguan freedom fighters from 1981 to 1988, was murdered in Managua in the spring of 1991.

Congressman Edward Boland retired in 1988 after

serving for thirty-six years in the House of Representatives.

George Bush was elected President of the United States.

Adolfo Calero continued to serve as head of the United Nicaraguan Opposition after I was fired. Later, he helped organize the resistance coalition that nominated Violeta Chamorro as the opposition candidate for president. He's returning to Nicaragua.

William Casey died of cancer and pneumonia on May 6, 1987, during the second day of the congressional hearings.

George Cave was asked to participate in one final meeting with the Second Channel after I was fired. He continues to serve as a consultant to the CIA.

Carl (Spitz) Channell was working to establish a new conservative political action committee in Washington when he was struck by a car on March 15, 1990. He died on May 7, 1990.

Duane (Dewey) Clarridge was forced to retire from the CIA in 1988 and now works for General Dynamics. On the day before Thanksgiving 1991, the special prosecutor indicted him for his involvement in the Iran-contra affair.

Joe Fernandez, who served as a CIA clandestine services officer for twenty-one years, and whose last post was chief of station in Costa Rica, was indicted twice by the special prosecutor before all charges against him were dropped. He is today my business partner in Guardian Technologies International, Inc., the company we founded in 1989 to manufacture protective armor for law-enforcement officers and the military.

Alan Fiers, chief of the Central American Task Force, retired from the CIA in 1989. In the summer of 1991, faced with the prospect of indictment, he pleaded guilty to misdemeanor charges and agreed to cooperate with the special prosecutor's investigation.

Robert Gates, who served as deputy director of intelligence of the CIA, and then as deputy director of the

CIA itself under Bill Casey, was nominated to become CIA director in 1988. His nomination was withdrawn in the face of congressional opposition, whereupon he was named deputy national security adviser to President Bush. In the summer of 1991, he was again nominated to become director of the CIA, which once again resulted in political controversy.

Clair George retired from the CIA in 1988, where he had been deputy director for operations. In September 1991, he was indicted by the special prosecutor, who alleged that he had withheld information from Congress about my activities.

Manucher Ghorbanifar provided separate and extensive interviews to both the special prosecutor and the congressional investigators. Gorba continues to live in Europe, where he maintains several residences.

Albert Hakim pled guilty to a misdemeanor charge brought against him by the special prosecutor. He has since returned to California, where he has established another international trading company.

Fawn Hall lives in California. She is regularly required by the special prosecutor to return to Washington to testify.

Lee Hamilton completed his six-year tenure as chairman of the House Intelligence Committee. He remains a member of the Democratic congressional leadership.

Eugene Hasenfus was released by the Sandinistas at the end of 1986. When he returned to the United States, he unsuccessfully brought suit against Dick Secord and several other individuals involved in supporting the Nicaraguan resistance.

David Jacobsen returned to California, where he wrote a memoir of his ordeal as a hostage in Beirut.

Michael Ledeen continues to serve as a consultant in Washington, and has written a book about the Iran-contra affair.

Robert (Bud) McFarlane, who had pled guilty to several misdemeanor charges, was sentenced to probation and community service and is now a consultant in Washington. He was the only witness to be called in September 1991, during the final proceedings brought against me by the special prosecutor.

Admiral Art Moreau, the real hero of the *Achille Lauro* incident, became the NATO naval commander in Naples, Italy. He died of a heart attack in 1989.

The Nephew still resides in Iran, and travels on occasion to Europe.

Abu Nidal is reportedly living in luxury in Libya.

Ami Nir left his government position, and was killed in a plane crash in Mexico in 1988. In the summer of 1991, his widow's home was broken into by thieves who made off with Nir's secret files on the Iran initiative.

Manuel Noriega surrendered to American authorities in 1990. He now resides in Miami as a guest of the U.S. government.

Daniel Ortega was defeated in the election of 1990. He remains head of the Sandinista party in Managua.

Admiral John Poindexter was convicted in 1990 on six counts stemming from his involvement in the Iran-contra affair. In November 1991 the U.S. Court of Appeals reversed his conviction. The prosecutor is still mulling over what to do.

Ronald Reagan returned to California and wrote his memoirs.

General Richard Secord is in business in Virginia, and is writing his memoirs.

Brendan Sullivan and his legal team continue to protect the constitutional rights of those they defend.

Lawrence Walsh, the vigilante who rode into town in 1986 as the special prosecutor, remains at large.

# APPENDIX

THE WHITE HOUSE

WASHINGTON

November 4, 1985

Dear Ollie:

I have been told that on the door of your office is a passage by Thomas Merton which reads "We must be content to live without watching ourselves live, to work without expecting an immediate reward, to love without instantaneous satisfaction and to exist without special recognition." In today's modern world many would challenge Merton's statement and ask why we must be content to live this way?

Ollie, you and other great Americans throughout our nation's proud history have fully understood why some must live this way--it is because our nation was built by men who dedicated their lives to building our country for the sake of their children and countrymen, without taking the time to worry about receiving recognition for their efforts.

To fully acknowledge your contributions to our country would be extremely difficult even for those who know you well, because your own standards of conduct and performance are higher than those which others apply. You are a man who has devoted your life in the most unselfish manner to building our nation. As a heroic soldier in the field, as a military planner and as an aide to me on some of the most important issues of our time, you have proven yourself to be an outstanding American patriot. Please let this letter serve to speak to how much the

2

American people and I appreciate the patriotism and sacrifice of you and your family. I am proud to have LtCol Oliver North, United States Marine Corps, on my team.

Sincerely,

Ronald Reagan

LtCol Oliver North
Deputy Director for
  Political-Military Affairs
National Security Council
Washington, D.C.  20506

ov. NORTH T. North....
11-27-85

Dear Oliie,

As I head off to
Maine for Thanksgiving I
just want to wish you a
Happy one with the hope you
get some well deserved rest.

One of the many things
I have to be thankful for
is the way in which you have
performed, under fire, in tough
situations. Your dedication and
tireless work with the hostage
thing and with Central America
really gives me cause for great
pride in you and Thanks — Get some Turkey

Geo Bush

en route to Kennebunkport
11-27-85

Dear Ollie,

As I head off to Maine for Thanksgiving I just want to wish you a happy one with the hope that you will get some well deserved rest.

One of the many things I have to be thankful for is the way in which you have performed, under fire, in tough situations. Your dedication and tireless work with the hostage thing and with Central America really give me cause for great pride in you and thanks—get some turkey.

George Bush

November 10, 1988

The Honorable Ronald Reagan
President of The United States
The White House
1600 Pennsylvania Avenue
Washington, D. C.   20500

    Re:   Request That You Use Your Power to Grant Reprieves
         and Pardons as Provided in Article II, Section 2 of
         the United States Constitution

Dear Mr. President:

      Executive clemency by pardon is requested by three
former government officials:  Admiral John Poindexter, USN
(Ret.), LtCol Oliver North, USMC (Ret.) and Joseph Fernandez, CIA
Operations Officer (Ret.) before a trial begins.  These men have
devoted their entire adult lives to the service of their country,
but tragically, despite their good faith, they have been indicted
for carrying out foreign policy objectives of The United States.

      The decision to grant or deny this request is entirely
within your discretion; it is not a decision encumbered by legal
technicalities, or issues about whether you have the power to act
or not.  In matters of clemency there are no such issues.  You
have unlimited power which comes directly from Article II,
Section 2 of the Constitution.  For once, there are no judicial
decisions limiting your authority to grant Executive Clemency; no
requirement for legal opinions, no Congressional limitations or
notification requirements, and no obligation to confer with
Executive Branch Agencies or Departments.  The decision is yours
alone to make as Head of State.  It is a decision made after
reflection and prayer; a decision predicated on your sense of
what is right and what is not; a decision which takes into
account the interest of the nation as well as compassion for the

The Honorable Ronald Reagan
Page 2
November 10, 1988

individuals and their families who have become embroiled in this
controversy and suffered so much.*/

    1.   The National Interest Is Best Served by
        Exercising the Power of Executive Clemency

        We believe that it is in the national interest to
put an end to the Iran-Contra controversy after two years of
intense scrutiny.  The matter has been fully and repeatedly
investigated.  It has been probed by numerous governmental groups
including the Tower Commission, a joint committee of Congress,
and several Inspectors General.  Tens of thousands of man hours,
and tens of millions of dollars have been devoted to these
inquiries since November 1986.  Enough is enough!  The trials of
several individuals targeted by the Independent Counsel serve no
purpose except to prolong the agony for the country and the
people involved.

        The nation cries out for an end to this matter.
Since LtCol North's testimony at the Congressional hearings in
the Summer of 1987, millions of Americans have made known their
views through polls and petitions that a Presidential pardon
should be granted.  Never before in the history of our country
has there been such a spontaneous outpouring of support and
sympathy from the American people as that which followed the
televised hearings.  Many in Congress were against the
President's policies, but the American people understood and
sympathized with the President's goals.

        The victory of George Bush is significant because he
was elected by Reagan supporters who want a continuation of your
policies.  It turned out that Iran-Contra was not an issue on which
the Democrats could win the Presidency -- although they tried to
make it the cornerstone of their convention and a major campaign
issue.  Clearly, the American people did not disapprove of your

---

*/   Retired Major General Richard V. Secord and naturalized
     citizen Albert Hakim have also been indicted in this
     matter.  This letter consolidates the pardon request of the
     three government officials.  It is our opinion, however,
     that if a pardon is granted, it should include General
     Secord and Mr. Hakim.

The Honorable Ronald Reagan
Page 3
November 10, 1988

support for the Nicaraguan freedom fighters, or your efforts to
save American citizens held hostage, or your goal of opening a
dialogue with Iran. Had they disapproved, as the Democrats hoped,
George Bush could not have been elected.

The Administration of George Bush should be free to build
on the Reagan legacy of peace through strength and economic
prosperity; it should not be preoccupied with protracted trials of
former officials which will consume months and perhaps years. The
new administration should not have its energies diverted from the
accomplishment of its own objectives.

Between 1980 and 1988, Congress attempted to usurp the
powers of the Presidency. In opposing your aggressive support of
our national security interests, the Congress was willing to call
the administration a lawbreaker. But because you are the most
popular President of our generation, Congress was unable to inflict
real harm on you or on the Presidency. Instead the attack has
focused on others. The goal of your political adversaries was to
dismantle the Reagan legacy; and the indictment of Admiral
Poindexter, LtCol North and Mr. Fernandez was but one of the
boldest actions in a continuing confrontation. But Americans have
a keen sense of fairness. They see the prosecution of a few
individuals as unjust, and they understand the controversy is kept
alive by anti-Reagan forces who have always been on the other side
of the political fence.

Further damage to our national security could likely
occur if trials are permitted to go forward. During their
government service Admiral Poindexter, LtCol North and Mr.
Fernandez fought to protect the National Security and worked hard
to guard the secrets of the nation. Now they find themselves in
the bizarre position of being unable to defend themselves without
revealing many of those same secrets in open court. Even the
Independent Counsel has had to concede that the case deals with
some of the nation's most tightly held top secret, codeword matters
which, if disclosed, would cause severe harm to the national
security.

The concern about protecting classified material is so
great that defense lawyers were required to move out of their law
offices into another building with a specially constructed
Sensitive Compartmented Information Facility ("SCIF"), protected

The Honorable Ronald Reagan
Page 4
November 10, 1988

round-the-clock by armed guards and monitored by additional
government security specialists.  The "SCIF" contains hundreds of
thousands of documents with the highest compartmented classi-
fications.  Court records indicate that exposure of some of these
secrets could result in loss of life.  The nature of a trial is
such that some of this information is bound to become known.  We
were witness to the foolhardy attempt at the Congressional hearings
to designate countries by letters of the alphabet, believing that
such a code would give them the protection they deserved.  While
Congressional probers referred to "Country A" and "Country B," it
was not long before the press published the actual names.

The exercise of your pardon power would eliminate the
possibility of further harm to our national security interests and
would accommodate the desire of millions of Americans to put this
matter behind us for the good of the country.

> 2.   A Trial of Admiral Poindexter, LtCol North and
>       Mr. Fernandez Would be a Terrible Injustice

The proceeding pending in the District of Columbia is
nothing more than a political trial.  It is paid for by a
Democratically-controlled Congress, conceived by a special force of
volunteer prosecutors, supported by the Administration's
adversaries, and fanned by the media.  The chance of obtaining a
fair trial is seriously in doubt.  Never before has anyone been
compelled to testify on national television and later been
prosecuted for conduct which was the subject of that testimony.
Admiral Poindexter testified for five days and LtCol North for six
days.  Mr. Fernandez testified for more than two days in executive
session.  They were interrogated by numerous Committee lawyers,
Congressmen and Senators.  The Congress assured the widest
dissemination of the testimony by conducting televised hearings
over our strongest objections and in the process "tainted" all of
the prosecution's witnesses and, undoubtedly, the potential jurors
as well  Moreover, any jury in the District of Columbia (a
Democratic Party stronghold) will undoubtedly be hostile to a
Republican Administration.  These former government officials
should not be abandoned to a protracted fight in a criminal
courtroom where the jurors start off with a strong bias against the
Reagan Administration and its policies.

The Honorable Ronald Reagan
Page 5
November 10, 1988


These men are fighting for their freedom against an Independent Counsel who has assembled the largest and most costly prosecutorial force in the history of our country. It consists of more than 30 lawyers, 50 investigators, scores of staff members, with offices in New York, Oklahoma and Washington. It is the only entity in the United States Government which has an unlimited budget. It has spent significantly more than 10 million dollars of taxpayers' money to date. The goal of this prosecutorial army is to convict and imprison Admiral Poindexter, LtCol North and CIA Operations Officer Joseph Fernandez. Needless to say, these men receive <u>not</u> <u>one</u> <u>single</u> <u>penny</u> of government money to defend themselves against this adversary.

You are known to be a President of strength and of courage; a President who does what he believes is right. The American people elected you to guide this country for eight years. They look to you now to prevent injustice. These men should not be singled out for prosecution and subjected to a political trial aimed at destroying them.

As President, you demonstrated extraordinary concern for Americans held hostage and those victimized by terrorists. The fact that you cared about the anguish of those citizens and their families endeared you to the people of this country. Admiral Poindexter, LtCol North and Mr. Fernandez are no less prisoners, held captive here in Washington. Congressional hearings, investigations, and pretrial proceedings have already consumed two years of their lives. They have become pawns in a dispute between the Congress and the Presidency over the control of the foreign policy of the United States. Please end this matter now -- before they are subjected to further abuse for doing their duty as they saw it.

3.  Fairness, Equity and Compassion Warrant a
    Pardon Before Trial

The devastating personal and economic impact on these men and their families cries out for a pardon to terminate the proceedings.

A.  <u>Impact on Families</u>. Admiral Poindexter has been married for thirty years and has five children, ages seventeen to twenty-eight. LtCol North has been married for twenty years and has four children, ages seven to nineteen. Joseph Fernandez has

The Honorable Ronald Reagan
Page 6
November 10, 1988

been married for twenty-five years and has seven children, ages
five to twenty-two. The impact on their families has been
devastating over the last two years. What must it be like for
children to see their father vilified and attacked on the front
page of the newspaper and on television news shows night after
night, accused of criminal wrongdoing thousands of times? Perhaps
some of the older children can understand the nature of this
dispute which brings their fathers into the criminal courtroom, but
certainly the younger ones cannot. Several of these children have
observed their fathers under siege for a substantial period of
their lives. The wives and children of these men have been
permanently scarred by this experience. No courtroom victory years
away can make amends. Not even an acquittal can eliminate the pain
they have had to endure; pain which will only be exacerbated by the
lengthy and highly publicized trials they face. We are confident
that you understand the torment to which they have been
subjected. Only your intervention will allow them and their
families to resume normal lives.

      B.  **The Impact on Careers**. Admiral Poindexter served
with distinction in the United States Navy for thirty-three
years. Among his awards was the Legion of Merit. He worked at the
National Security Council and The White House for five and one-half
years, tirelessly carrying out the goals of your Presidency. As a
Naval officer, he was suggested for appointment as Commander, Sixth
Fleet and was considered a likely future candidate for Chief of
Naval Operations. The termination of his career fifteen years
before mandatory retirement was a tragic by-product of this case.

      LtCol North's service at the National Security Council
during the period August 1981 to November 1986 was characterized by
selfless devotion to his country, to your administration, and by
the expenditure of limitless energy to achieve the policy goals you
established. His devotion to duty and willingness to sacrifice all
in accomplishing an assigned mission has become an American
legend. He is a decorated Vietnam war hero having received the
Silver Star, the Bronze Star, two Purple Hearts, and numerous other
awards. His career goal has always been to simply serve his
country by being the very best Marine Corps officer. Though he was
considered a likely candidate for promotion to full Colonel and
then to General, he was forced into early retirement by the
indictment.

Joseph Fernandez is a twenty-year veteran of CIA. Throughout his career, Mr. Fernandez served in numerous overseas assignments where he endured the hardship of working undercover to facilitate the policies of the United States. Most recently, he served as CIA's Chief of Station in Costa Rica where he struggled against great odds to carry out the policies of this Administration in Central America. After leaving Costa Rica, Mr. Fernandez would have attended the prestigious Senior Seminar at the Foreign Service Institute in preparation for further assignments at the highest levels of CIA, both overseas and at CIA Headquarters. Instead, he, too, was forced into retirement.*/

All of these men served selflessly, often at risk of their lives. Their careers were ones of family hardship, long separations and frequent moves -- all for the benefit of this country. The termination of their service by indictment and early retirement is a travesty that will ultimately affect the morale and steadfastness of others in the service exposed to rigorous demands. Your pardon will not only help these three men and their families who have suffered so much, it will restore the morale and esprit of their brothers-in-arms.

C. The Economic Impact. None of these men can find normal employment so long as criminal charges remain pending. They are simply unavailable to work because of the enormous amount of time and energy that must be devoted to the preparation of their defense. LtCol North has accepted speaking engagements in an effort to help defray the cost of legal services and other extraordinary expenses. Admiral Poindexter has taken a part-time job and Mr. Fernandez is still seeking work. All have had to put their lives and futures on "hold." Without a pardon, they will have to spend the next years of their lives in the fight against this unjust prosecution.

As a result of the criminal litigation, they have incurred costs beyond what they could ever hope to pay themselves. They have had to deal with this devastation to their lives and to their families' economic security without any help

---

*/   The indictment of Mr. Fernandez was recently dismissed in the District of Columbia without prejudice. The Independent Counsel stated that he will reindict the case in Virginia.

The Honorable Ronald Reagan
Page 8
November 10, 1988

from the government they served for so many years. Simple fairness
justifies your intervention by a pardon to stop this process before
further damage is done to them and their loved ones.

     D.  <u>Safety and Security of LtCol North's Family</u>.  In
April 1986, LtCol North's life was threatened by the Abu Nidal
terrorist organization, but the government offered no assistance or
protection.  A year later, in 1987, LtCol North and his family were
protected by a large contingent of Naval Investigative Service
(NIS) agents because of additional foreign terrorist threats to his
life which were uncovered by the FBI.  His televised testimony in
the summer of 1987 created unsought worldwide visibility and
instant recognition which increased the dangers to him and his
family.  His photograph was even distributed on the cover of
<u>Pravda</u>.  Despite known dangers, the Congress televised LtCol
North's home address for the world to see during the hearings in
complete disregard for the safety of his family.

     Political pressure from some in Congress, shocked by
North's popularity after the hearings, resulted in the government
protection being withdrawn.  In place of more than a score of
government security specialists, LtCol North now must depend on the
charity of the American people to provide protection.  Even modest
security of this sort is extremely expensive but the government
provides no help.

     The continued visibility caused by a lengthy trial
increases the risk of harm to him and his family.  They should not
have to endure those risks, and he should not have to live in fear
that his family could be harmed.

               <u>Conclusion</u>

     A pardon at this time, prior to trial, is fair,
reasonable, and in the interest of the nation.  The country has had
enough of the Iran-Contra matter.  It is particularly unfair to
permit a legion of prosecutors to single out these former
officials.  Each one of them embarked upon a life of service to his
country knowing that he could be called on to sacrifice his life.
But not one of them could have anticipated this kind of
nightmarish, unending turmoil and disruption to normal life, to
families and to careers.  It is too much to ask of even the most

The Honorable Ronald Reagan
Page 9
November 10, 1988

devoted soldier and public servant. This matter should be ended, not only for these men but for the good of the country.

As your eight-year Presidency comes to a close, your impact on this great Country is clear. You will always be remembered for renewing our economic prosperity, for supporting freedom and democracy throughout the world, and for achieving peace through strength. You have shown understanding and compassion for people yet, time and time again, demonstrated remarkable strength. People know you as a President who does what he believes is <u>right</u>.

A pardon of these patriots would put an end to the Iran-Contra matter after two years of turmoil, would protect the national security, and would permit them and their families to resume a normal life. Put this matter to rest for the nation's sake so that we can build on the foundation of peace and prosperity you have given to all Americans.

Respectfully yours,

WILLIAMS & CONNOLLY

Brendan V. Sullivan, Jr.
Counsel for LtCol Oliver L. North, USMC (Ret.)

FULBRIGHT & JAWORSKI

Richard W. Beckler
Counsel for Admiral John Poindexter, USN (Ret.)

SEYFARTH, SHAW, FAIRWEATHER & GERALDSON

Thomas E. Wilson
Counsel for Joseph Fernandez, CIA Operations
Officer (Ret.)

# EPILOGUE

## I

IN AUGUST 1991, JUST A FEW WEEKS BEFORE THE manuscript for the hardcover edition of this book was due at my publishers, I met with Brendan Sullivan in his downtown Washington office. For more than a year, work on this book had been a closely guarded secret. Now it was time to make sure that no classified information inadvertently had been included in the nearly finished manuscript.

We certainly hoped by then that my long ordeal with Special Prosecutor Walsh was nearing a conclusion. In a matter of weeks he would have to decide whether to bring me to trial again or—as we hoped—drop the remaining three charges against me. Having weathered the storm thus far, I didn't want this book to create new vulnerabilities or to jeopardize someone else.

After hearing my concerns, Brendan responded: "Ollie, there is only one way to be certain that there's no classified information in the book, and that is to have it reviewed by the government. After all that's been said and released in this case, that's the only way to be really sure."

I knew he was right. That was one of the reasons why the work on the book had been conducted so secretly.

But now, nineteen months into the project, I was having second thoughts about having the same government that had prosecuted me review my book. It struck me as an invitation to leaks and delays. But I also knew we had to be certain.

The lawyers called the CIA's legal experts and explained the situation. They took the manuscript—and promised to get back to us as soon as possible. A few days later an Agency attorney called with both good news and bad. On the positive side, he had only a few changes. Several names had to go, and two or three others had to be disguised. In the photographs, several faces and pieces of equipment would have to be blacked out. All in all, these were problems I could easily solve before sending off the manuscript.

But then came the bad news: a handful of other government agencies wanted to review the text before the manuscript went to the publisher.

The way I looked at it, this was a sure sign of more bad news to come. The publisher's deadline was only weeks away. Even if these other government agencies could somehow review the book in a matter of days, which seemed highly unlikely, and even if they found no major problems, could they really do all this without a single leak?

From my perspective, a leak about the book would create extraordinary speculation in the media, which would prolong the security review and perhaps delay publication for months. This in turn, might encourage Prosecutor Walsh to try to stop the project altogether.

Now, some of my closest friends have told me that I'm absolutely paranoid about Mr. Walsh. Maybe they're right. But even paranoiacs have enemies, and Prosecutor Walsh and his merry minions had been anything but friendly for the past five years.

When I heard that several other government agencies would have to review the book, I launched into a lengthy complaint: "Walsh hauled Betsy in for fingerprints and mug shots and then threw her into the grand jury. When that wasn't intimidating enough, he dragged you, Brendan, before the grand jury. It took us a whole separate legal battle to stop these travesties. If Prosecutor Walsh is capable of trying to force a wife to testify against her husband and an attorney to testify against his client, surely he'll do anything he can to stop this book.

"He's already tried it once—he brought one of his own deputies into court to stop him from publishing a book about Iran-Contra."

Brendan let me finish and quietly replied, "Calm down. Walsh has no reason to stop this book. The review is the right thing to do. You have to trust these people to do their jobs with integrity. When they're finished, send off the manuscript and get on with other things."

As usual, he was right. The review was completed with a few additional changes and the fully "vetted" text went to the printer.

Later, people said we were lucky. But I don't believe in luck. Divine providence, sure, but not coincidence or luck. The events in the last few months of 1991 only reinforced my faith in God's willingness to intervene in the affairs of man, even when we least expect it or deserve it.

A few days afterward, on September 16, 1991, Judge Gesell accepted the special prosecutor's motion to drop the final three charges against me. After a brief statement to the press and a celebratory luncheon with Betsy, Sarah, Dornin, Brian Cox, Brendan and the rest of the defense team, I returned home to put the final touches on the foreword to this book.

Remarkably, virtually nothing about the existence of the book leaked until one day before the scheduled announcement, when a story appeared in the *New York*

*Times.* For nearly twenty months a handful of key people at HarperCollins in New York and at Zondervan in Grand Rapids, Michigan, had kept the project under a tight veil of secrecy. Those few individuals who worked on it had always referred to the book under the code name of *Mr. Smith Goes to Washington.* (In all dealings with our publishers, I was known as Mr. Smith, whereupon Bill Novak took to calling himself Mr. Jones.)

Finally, on October 17, less than a week before it appeared in the stores, the book was publicly announced by HarperCollins and by Zondervan. This time they used its real title: *Under Fire.*

The title, incidentally, came from a handwritten note that then–Vice President Bush had sent me just before Thanksgiving in 1985, which is reprinted at the end of this book. Those words turned out to be most appropriate to what subsequently happened.

In retrospect, I should have expected it. Still, the viciousness of the press reaction to *Under Fire* took me by surprise. Privately, a number of interviewers and reporters assured me that the book was well written, revealing, and a "good read." Publicly, they trashed it— and, of course, its author.

Many commentators seemed outraged that a book by Oliver North could be a commercial success, but *Under Fire* hit the best-seller lists immediately. And the more copies it sold, the angrier they became. During my book tour, reporters and interviewers demanded to know what gave me the right to profit from my "wrongdoing."

In our system of law, once you stand accused, no one ever declares you innocent. The best you can hope for is to be proclaimed "not guilty"—or to have the charges dropped. Now, I had certainly been accused of various "wrongdoings" by the congressional committees and the special prosecutor. But the jury pronounced me not guilty on nine counts, the courts dismissed all others but three, and Prosecutor Walsh dropped those himself.

That was all I could have hoped for.

The second area of criticism was clearly political, but it took on a personal dimension as well. By arrangement with the publishers, *Time* magazine published advance selections from the book in its October 28 issue. For the cover, *Time* selected a phrase that appeared in the first chapter: "Reagan knew everything."

Although the hardcover version of *Under Fire* ran 446 pages, these three words became the principal focus for almost every newspaper story, interview, and commentary about the book. Almost nobody pointed out, although I certainly tried to, that I had made this very same point about President Reagan at the congressional hearings in 1987, and again at my trial in 1989: that although I had never discussed the "diversion" with him, I always believed that the President was fully informed about my activities, and that he had approved of what I was doing.

I protested repeatedly that my statement about President Reagan was being made to sound as though it were a major revelation—which I certainly never thought it would be. But those who had hated Ronald Reagan when he was president used my book to attack him and then attacked me for implicating him—even though I was only repeating what I had said all along.

During the book tour, one of the most frequently asked questions from President Reagan's antagonists was, "Don't you feel betrayed by the administration you served?" I replied that I was certainly disappointed that Ronald Reagan didn't do what he could have done to spare me years of legal torment and enormous financial obligations. And that's where the "sound bite" would stop.

Almost invariably, journalists would edit out the remainder of my comments, in which I cited my deeper convictions about Ronald Reagan—views also expressed in my book: "Ultimately, I think of Ronald Reagan in terms of the four children that the Good Lord loaned my best friend and me. The world they are growing up in is a far safer place than it was in 1980. In his eight years in office, Ronald Reagan revitalized America's economy and transformed our future. The collapse of communism, the diminished threat of nuclear war, the improved opportunities for liberty and peace are the consequence of his tenure." I even quoted a line from the book: "If Karl Marx provided the stimulus for the first Russian Revolution in 1917, it was Ronald Reagan who inspired the second in 1991." The critics didn't want to hear it.

I still believe President Reagan led the whole world a few steps closer to freedom and prosperity. And for the better future he offered my children, I will always be grateful. I doubt his critics ever will be.

## II

When it came time for the book tour, I made some tough demands on the HarperCollins and Zondervan publicity departments. I explained that I wanted to be home every weekend, and that the entire tour, which was to begin in late October, had to end in time for Thanksgiving. They accommodated me the only way they could—by cramming a two-month book tour into twenty-five days. There were days when I appeared in three different cities, and stores where I autographed more than a thousand books.

It was grueling, but it wasn't all grim. My very first interview was on "Nightline" with Ted Koppel. The two of us had already met for a preliminary discussion, and when I called to ask Ted what I should wear on his show, he said, "Anything you like—so long as it doesn't clash with my blue paisley skirt."

I wasn't especially looking forward to appearing on "Nightline," because I assumed that Koppel and I came from totally different worlds. But I soon learned that he was still married to his first wife, and that they have four children, so at least we had *that* in common. And, like me, he works very hard and sees less of his family than he would like. (I sometimes wonder if either of us will ever do anything about it.) Although I disagreed with Koppel on virtually every point, I found myself liking him. At least I had a chance to confirm that his hair, which looks like an orange wig on TV, is real.

But I drew the line at Larry King. When he invited me to appear on his television show, I turned him down immediately. After five years of his unremitting hostility every time my name was mentioned, I couldn't imagine why he wanted anything to do with me. Then he wrote me a personal letter, urging me to reconsider. A number of people told me that he had a reputation for treating his guests fairly, and after talking it over with Brendan and Betsy, I decided to give him a try.

Despite all the things he had said about me in the past, Larry King turned out to be terrific, and he was easily one of the most gracious interviewers I met during my entire tour. Not only did he ask good questions, but during some of the commercial breaks, he showed me a few tricks that call-in-show hosts typically use to set up a guest whom the interviewer doesn't like. Believe me, those tips came in handy a few days later when I appeared on Phil Donahue's show.

Donahue acted as if I were the devil himself. I had the impression that he wanted to show that he could do a better job of attacking me than all those senators, congressmen, prosecutors—or even Ted Koppel, for that matter.

When he walked out into the audience, I decided to stand up on the stage instead of just sitting there passively while he pranced around. A moment later the producer came running out to say, "On this show the guests don't stand."

"They do now," I replied.

One of the callers, an older woman, started to berate Donahue for interrupting my answers, and for his undisguised hostility toward me. He cut her off, whereupon there was an awkward moment of stunned silence. In an attempt to extricate us from the discomfort, I said, "Thanks, Mom."

Well, as soon as the show aired in upstate New York, I received a message to call my mother. I believe I was in Philadelphia at the time, although it could have been Cleveland or Boston. When I finally reached her, she mentioned the woman who had called the Donahue show. "I just want you to know, dear," she said, "that wasn't me."

"I know that, Mom," I replied. "I was just trying to be funny."

But it didn't end there. "Well," she continued, "if you *knew* that wasn't me, why did you say, 'Thanks, Mom'? That's just the kind of thing that keeps getting you in trouble!"

The worst part is, she's right. Thanks, Mom.

One story I was asked to tell repeatedly during the tour had to do with the time our children took cookies out to the reporters who had staked out our house from morning to night for seven full months after I was fired in 1986. It was a Christmas morning, and unlike their father, they were acting in the spirit of the day.

I mentioned this incident to Ted Koppel before we went on the air, whereupon a voice boomed out from behind one of the large studio cameras: "I was there."

"Show yourself!" demanded Koppel.

"Now I can tell you the rest of the story," the cameraman said as he came out. "When your kids brought out the cookies, we weren't sure what to think. So before we ate them, we fed a few of them to your dog to make sure they were safe."

During my book tour, several reporters actually treated me like a human being. And not all of them asked about Ronald Reagan. I was asked about my favorite pizza and, by a woman in Canada, whether I had an unmarried brother. On a radio talk show, I was asked to sing "Happy Birthday" to the producer—on the air.

But too many of the interviews were almost identical. I kept explaining that *Under Fire* was not an attack book. I described it as part love story, part adventure, part political intrigue, and mostly a testament of faith. Yet, as I jetted around the country, the same question kept coming back at me, again and again: "What did the President know and when did he know it?"

In addition to the press, I also met real people—including literally tens of thousands of wonderful Americans who showed up at bookstore autographing sessions. By the end of January, I had already gone through more than a hundred and fifty blue Pentel Rolling Writer pens. Many of these sessions were so well attended that the stores simply ran out of books. Sometimes people at the end of the line would drive over to another store, buy the book, and drive back to get it autographed. In Florida, one woman came through the line with fifteen books for me to sign. Apparently that wasn't enough, because she showed up again weeks later with a dozen more. In Ohio.

As time went on more and more of the people at the bookstores had already read the book—including many who ended up reading most of it in line, or who discussed it with total strangers while they were waiting. When they finally got to the front, some of them laughingly blamed me for ruining their summer back in 1987, when they were glued to the hearings on television and didn't get to enjoy the sun or the beach. Others showed me photographs of their dogs, cats, birds, and other pets who were born or acquired during that time, and who had been named Ollie, or Oliver, in my honor. I was even introduced to some four-year-olds named Oliver, most of whom were not in a very good mood. These poor kids had no idea why they had been dragged to a bookstore to stand in a very long line that was barely moving. Duane Ward, the publisher's representative who handled logistics for this marathon and who accompanied me to every city and kept me sane, would patiently explain to these puzzled youngsters that the man writing his name in all these books was actually "Waldo."

Whereas the press had focused almost exclusively on Ronald Reagan, the people I met in the bookstores wanted to talk about the personal side of *Under Fire*. I was surprised by how many of them asked me to autograph their copies not in the front of the book, but on specific pages that had special meaning for them.

The most popular choice was the passage in Chapter 15 where I mentioned the strain that Betsy and I went through during the media assault that followed my firing: "She was extremely supportive," I wrote, "but there were moments when the strain got to us both. 'What have you done to *my* children?' she blurted out one night."

Although only a small part of *Under Fire* dealt with the problems we had worked through in our marriage and with our family's struggle to maintain a normal life, most of the people whom I met, or who wrote me about the book, focused on these topics. I was constantly reminded that there are a lot of troubled families in this country. If, as it appears, some readers have been able to benefit from my overcoming my reticence and disclosing some of our problems, then I'm glad that I paid attention to Jim Dobson, Gladys Carr, and Jim Buick—all of whom urged me to be candid about my personal life.

# III

As a Marine, I was blessed to spend most of my adult life in the company of brave men. I expected that this would no longer be true when I was assigned to the National Security Council staff, but I was wrong. It wasn't always easy to find brave individuals among the self-serving political types who inhabit Washington, but they did exist.

And perhaps because they were harder to find, those brave souls who were around tended to shine a little brighter. Some, like Howard Teicher, were among my colleagues at the NSC; others, who cannot all be named, were part of the CIA, the FBI, and the various other agencies engaged in our efforts to stem international terrorism. There were also some brave allies. The Nicaraguan resistance was full of them, from the small unit leaders who led the commando teams deep into Nicaragua, to the Cuban-American doctors who gave up lucrative practices in the United States to tend the wounded in camps along the border.

Some of the most courageous people I worked with were overseas: British officers assigned to take on the IRA, German GSG-9 officers contending with the Baider Meinhoff Gang and the Red Army Faction, Italian carabinieri facing off against the Red Brigades. I also had the privilege of working with good and fearless individuals in Spain, France, and Israel. There were brave men and women in Latin America whom I came to know and admire, including several in El Salvador who found themselves caught in the cross fire between the death squads of the right and the terrorists of the left. In Colombia and Costa Rica there were those like minister of public security, Ben Piza, who fought the narcoterrorists straight on.

But of all the individuals I worked with during my five and a half years at the NSC, nobody showed more courage than Terry Waite.

Terry, an emissary of the Church of England, was essential to achieving the release of three American hostages held in Beirut. Make no mistake: Benjamin Weir, Martin Jenco, and David Jacobsen were freed in large measure because of Terry's compassion, his Christian faith, and his extraordinary courage. But as we all know, Terry Waite paid a heavy price for his caring when he himself was taken hostage.

Today, Terry Waite is alive and well and free. His was a story I could not tell in the original edition of this book. While I certainly wanted to acknowledge his efforts, I didn't want to be the cause of any further mistreatment by his brutal captors in Beirut.

We met during the summer of 1985. I had gotten two calls, the first from one of Vice President Bush's military aides and the second from Ambassador Eugene Douglas at the State Department. Both callers asked me to meet with Waite, whom they described as "a British churchman working behind the scenes to achieve the release of the western hostages in Beirut."

Before agreeing to meet him, I had Terry Waite's name checked by both the FBI and the CIA. I already had a lot on my plate, and by now we had been approached about the hostages by practically every charlatan and imposter in the Western hemisphere.

But I quickly learned that Terry Waite was indeed a respected envoy of the Archbishop of Canterbury, and that he had been engaged in these kinds of missions before—in Iran, in Libya, and perhaps elsewhere. I also learned that he was not a favorite of the British Foreign Service.

Indeed, as a British government official put it in one of those marvelous English euphemisms, Terry Waite tended to raise "a bit too much dust." But even he had to admit that Waite was both courageous and effective. To me, his complaint sounded all too familiar—the typical jealousy of an official bureaucrat toward a person who was able to get things done when governments couldn't. Unfortunately for Terry, that made him even more appealing in my eyes.

Terry was a giant of a man in several respects—physically, energetically, spiritually, and certainly in his irrepressible good humor. Our first meeting was in New York, at the residence of the presiding bishop of the

American Episcopal Church. He was accompanied by the Reverend Samir Habiby, the American churchman who had first contacted me at the White House. Terry and Samir initially focused on the two American churchmen: Ben Weir, the Presbyterian missionary, and Father Martin Jenco. It quickly became apparent, however, that Terry was anxious to do what he could for all those being held.

Before long, Terry Waite became an essential part of our own hostage recovery effort, especially when we learned from intelligence sources that both the hostage takers in Beirut and their mentors in Tehran were searching for some kind of humanitarian or spiritual intermediary to whom they could release any hostages they freed. Later, I heard this same message from the Iranian intermediaries with whom I met in Europe, in Washington, and in Tehran.

In their terms, this wasn't hard to understand. The Hezbollah leadership in Lebanon had maintained all along that they were pursuing "holy" objectives in Beirut. They had even been known to pray before beating the hostages. From their perspective, the participation of a church official made it easier to explain the releases to their fundamentalist followers and associates in both Lebanon and Iran.

For more than a year, until I was fired late in 1986, Terry Waite and I stayed in touch. We met in New York, London, Washington, and even Beirut. We talked by phone and communicated through various intermediaries, including Reverend Habiby, whose extensive contacts in the Middle East and at the U.N. exceeded my own. Most importantly, Terry and I shared the same goal: the release of the hostages.

During one of his many trips to Beirut, Terry called me in the midst of a furious firefight that was raging on the street outside his hotel. "Hallo, William," he said, using my alias. "Things are a bit unsettled here at the moment." These words were followed immediately by the furious staccato of an automatic weapon being fired. From my end, it sounded like the machine gun was going off right next to Waite's head.

"Terry, are you all right?"

"Well, William, it seems that some chap needed to use the window of my hotel room to send a message to someone outside. I've asked him to stop, but he seems fairly intent at the moment."

"Are you safe?"

"Safe? I suppose so. I'd get under the bed except that's where my bodyguard is hiding."

Not long after my first meeting with Terry Waite, Ghorbanifar, the Iranian middleman working with the Israelis, was directed by the Iranians to find an acceptable humanitarian or spiritual figure to whom they could release Benjamin Weir, an American hostage. This would enable the Iranians to "dress up" the transaction they were about to enact—five hundred Israeli TOW missiles for one American clergyman.

I suggested to Bud McFarlane, my boss at the time, that Terry Waite might be the right person to satisfy this new demand. At McFarlane's direction, I told Waite that we believed a hostage release was imminent, and that our intelligence indicated it wouldn't happen without the involvement of a church figure. When I asked Terry if he would fly to Beirut to expedite the release, he agreed.

What I did *not* tell him was that we knew the expected release was related to an Israeli arms shipment. In our view at the time, this knowledge would have risked compromising the Israeli operation and placed Terry in far greater jeopardy. We all assumed that it was safer if Terry didn't know too much.

It is also possible, of course, that if we had told Terry the full story of the arrangements with the Iranians, he would have refused to help us. I honestly don't know the answer to that. After his release, he said that if he had known that the United States was exchanging arms for hostages, he wouldn't have participated. I can't blame him for saying that. That had been my original position, and I should have stuck to it.

But how much Terry Waite should have been told was not a decision made at my level. Early on in this whole endeavor, Bill Casey, Bud McFarlane, Admiral Poindexter, and the handful of others in the government aware of the Israeli transactions all agreed that Waite should be told as little as possible. After the United States became operationally involved in the shipments in late 1985, this policy remained in effect. Terry was simply told that we were "in contact with elements in Iran," and that we had additional intelligence that would confirm the timing of certain hostage releases.

Like many people, he may have assumed that our information was the result of ongoing meetings between the governments of Iran and the United States at the International Court of Justice in The Hague concerning Iran's financial claims from the days of the Shah.

Time after time, Terry would leave his home and family to meet with the hostage takers in Beirut. In early 1986 he was able to do something we had tried to accomplish in a dozen different ways but had failed at completely: establishing contact with the captors in Lebanon.

Many people have assumed that we never tried to communicate directly with the hostage takers. But we did. And though we used every possible intermediary in this effort, Waite was the only one who succeeded. Terry provided positive proof about the condition of the captives. In fact, the last pictures we received of William Buckley before he died in captivity were brought to us by Terry.

Of this I remain certain: Terry Waite was absolutely essential to the release of the three American hostages. Had we not had the services of *the* Terry Waite, we would have required the help of *a* Terry Waite.

After Admiral John Poindexter and I were fired in November 1986, and though we were no longer in contact, Terry continued to work for the release of the hostages in Beirut. I learned form news reports that two months later—January 1987—Terry had returned to Beirut. Within days, he himself was taken hostage. For me this was one of the worst moments in the entire ordeal. For Terry and his family, it was a catastrophe.

Prior to his release in November 1991, I had been asked countless times to reveal the details of our relationship. Out of concern for his safety, I had always demurred. From friends in government and old allies in the counterterrorism effort, I knew that Terry was thought to be alive, but was suffering terribly. Whenever another hostage was released, I would scan the news and the debriefing reports for some sign of Terry's condition.

In November 1991, I was about to leave for the European leg of my book tour when Terry Waite was freed as part of the hostage release mediated by the United Nations. By then I was well accustomed to negative treatment from the news media, but what happened next still took me by surprise.

No sooner was Terry Waite released than he was savaged by the press, both here and especially in the United Kingdom, for cooperating with the Americans. Television news and newspaper reports in both countries ran outrageous stories about him.

The worst of these said that Terry had been taken hostage because he was carrying or wearing some kind of electronic device when he was searched by the terrorists he was meeting with in Beirut. And, said the media, Oliver North had given him the device!

The fact is *I never gave Terry Waite any kind of electronic device or tracking equipment or beacon or any other such apparatus.* But that didn't matter to the press. They made up their minds and proceeded to portray this heroic man variously as an egomaniac, a dupe, a pawn, and a stooge of Oliver North and the U.S. government. The press described in vivid detail how the "device" I had allegedly given him made me personally responsible for his capture in 1987. Though I was on a nationwide book tour and available to the press every day, no reporter or editor bothered to ask me about a beeper before they ran stories about an electronic device. They were, of course, totally false.

I found the British press to be especially irresponsible. Not only did they fail to make any effort to confirm the accuracy of these claims about a beeper with me before running the stories, but they rushed into press while American hostages were still being held. To me, it was as if they were saying, "I've got mine; the heck with yours!"

While I was being interviewed on British TV, I wondered aloud why Terry was being portrayed as a prideful zealot when he should have been commended for his compassion and courage. And I offered this analogy: if a Marine throws himself on a live grenade in an effort to save his comrades, we accord him the highest honors our nation can bestow. But I suspect that the British press would describe such an act as "self-destructive."

When they asked whether I felt responsible for Terry's having been taken hostage, I said no—that the terrorists who took him were responsible. The terrorists in Beirut and their allies in Tehran certainly knew the true nature of Terry's role in the hostage releases. The revelations in November 1986 about our providing arms to the Iranians didn't come as news to those who had seized Buckley, Anderson, and finally Terry himself. Why they chose to seize him in January 1987 and hold him for nearly five years is known only to them.

They may have taken him as a face-saving gesture for their fundamentalist patrons and supporters, given all the wild stories flowing from Washington in the wake of November's firings. Or perhaps it was simply their loathing for all things Western, and Terry was just the next, most available target for their unremitting hatred. Considering all this, it is not surprising that they took him.

What *is* surprising to me are the attacks on Terry Waite in the Western media—particularly in the United Kingdom. Even if he had done all the things the media accused him of doing—which he didn't—he was trying everything within his power to save innocent lives. I find totally baffling the virtual absence of any anger in the media toward the people who captured Terry Waite and his fellow hostages. Where is their outrage at those who would deny good men their freedom simply because they are American, British, Irish, or German?

Even after the flurry of phony charges about Terry and me died down, the press continued to focus almost exclusively on how the last of the British and American hostages came to be freed. The stories went on at length, theorizing about the intrigues of U.N. Secretary General Perez de Cuellar and what kind of "deal" might have been struck to obtain their release.

In all of this speculation, the media elites missed a very important point. There are only three ways that hostages or kidnap victims get freed: they escape; they are rescued; or some kind of accommodation is made— ransom, relief from reprisal, or "a deal."

Rather than ruminating about what was done to bring about the releases, the press might better serve the public by reflecting on what is being done to bring to justice those who take hostages. Where are the calls for the capture of these terrorists who prey on our citizens? The investigative reporters who so willingly publish state secrets for the titillation of their readers and the admiration of our adversaries know well that the United States government has the means to bring these people to justice. We did it with the *Achille Lauro* hijackers. We did it with Fawaz Younis, the terrorist who was tried and convicted when I was on trial. Instead of bashing Terry Waite, why not call for the capture of those who held him so long in bondage?

Obviously, if I could turn back the clock, I would have done everything possible to discourage Terry from making any further visits to Beirut after November 1986. But I was out of contact by then. And, with the wisdom of hindsight, there are a lot of things I would have done differently.

None of us can turn back the clock and undo the past. The best we can hope to do is to learn from our mistakes and try not to repeat them. As an imperfect individual, I make mistakes every day. I didn't need a congressional committee to tell me that. I have four kids who are more than happy to remind me.

Many readers have responded to what I wrote about the faith that has sustained my family and me through a long and difficult ordeal. Rather than having my faith shaken or broken by what we have been through, it has been strengthened further by the outcome.

But I also hope that those who read *Under Fire* will understand that it is not *my* faith that matters. What really counts is *His* faithfulness to us. That's what reinforces my belief that we are not here simply to endure a desperately uneven contest, but to use the gifts we're given to change this world for the better. Our purpose is not to complain about the steepness of the climb, but to help each other on a way that is often difficult and sometimes even perilous. And in the end, all that we do should be done not to glorify ourselves, but to glorify Him. For only He is truly, Always Faithful: Semper Fidelis.

> O.L.N.
> Narnia
> March 6, 1992

# INDEX

531